ADVERTISING
TO THE
AMERICAN WOMAN
1900-1999

ADVERTISING
TO THE
AMERICAN WOMAN
1900–1999

Daniel Delis Hill

Ohio State University Press

Columbus

Library of Congress Cataloging-in-Publication Data
Hill, Daniel D.
    Advertising to the American woman 1900-1999 / Daniel D. Hill
        p. cm.
    Includes bibliographical references and index.
    ISBN 0-8142-0890-8 (alk. paper)
    1. Advertising—United States—History—20th century. 2. Women consumers—
United States. 3. Women in advertising—United States—History—20th century.
4. Social values—United States—History—20th century. I. Title
    HF5813.U6 H55 2002
    659.1′082′0973—dc21

                                                                2001052085

Jacket design by Jennifer Shoffey Carr
Text design by D. Hill
Type set in Times, Futura and Helvetica by D. Hill
Printed by Thomson-Shore, Inc.

9 8 7 6 5 4 3 2 1

CONTENTS

PREFACE

Following the Civil War, advances in industrial technology, new processes for manufacturing, and improved channels of distribution for raw materials and manufactured goods all contributed to the emergence of a second industrial revolution in America. As the variety and output of manufactured products rapidly increased, businesses began to seek ways of expanding their market share from local and regional niches to a national scale. Key to the success of this objective was the creation of a mass market of consumers, a broad base of customers who would be persuaded of a need or desire for the mass-produced goods pouring from mills and factories coast to coast. From this goal of a mass market evolved the kernels for marketing strategies that eventually included product research and development, creation of line extensions, brand management, competitive analysis, and sales promotion.

The first step in a marketing strategy was to identify and understand who the customers were and how to target them. Nineteenth-century manufacturers, distributors, and retailers (all overwhelmingly male) had only to look to their own homes for answers. Their mothers, wives, and daughters were unquestionably the consumers in their households, even if not necessarily the end users. A number of sources have suggested that as much as 85 percent of all manufactured consumer goods were purchased by women. The Curtis Publishing Company advised marketers in a 1915 ad that the American woman's purchasing power extended far beyond "groceries and gowns"; the wise marketer would know that: "Woman today is admittedly a powerful force in the purchase, not only of automobiles but also of tires, self-starters and other equipment, of the family insurance, of building materials, of men's clothing and underwear, and of many other products which used to be considered outside her sphere."[1] Several generations after the Curtis ad, a 1998 survey by Haggar Clothing Company indicated that "89 percent of all men's clothing purchased from department stores is chosen by women."[2] Hence, across the entire twentieth century, the target for a considerable majority of manufacturers of consumer products was the American woman.

This is not to say that men were disregarded by marketers as potential consumers or as significant influences in purchases made for the home, although that debate is an old one. For instance, in her 1929 book *Selling Mrs. Consumer,* Christine Frederick maintained that "The American male himself often testifies that he labors in order that his wife and children should enjoy luxury and comfort. He seems to enjoy himself most at earning, while content to leave the pleasure of spending to his women. . . . Such a condition puts buying power into women's hands on a tremendously broad scale,—so broad indeed that in a research made by Dr. H. L. Hollingworth of Columbia University, the only item that men bought entirely by themselves, without consultation with women, was their own collars! The purchase of not another article of apparel was free from the cooperative purchasing influence of women."[3] Still, those marketers with vested interests in targeting male consumers often had views contrary to the "hoary assertion" that American women made "85 percent of all consumer buying," as *Fortune* avowed in 1956. For example, "surveys for women's magazines suggest that women buy more than 60% of men's shirts and an even larger percentage of men's ties, robes, socks, and underwear. Men's magazine surveys, however, tell a somewhat different story."[4] No doubt the considerable advertising revenue that was lost by men's periodicals was a significant factor in the skew in their findings. Yet, the evidence would seem to indicate that mass marketers such as Procter & Gamble and General Foods did not recognize or attach much significance to the man's influence in home operations. Issues of *Fortune* and *Esquire* stretching back to their beginnings in the 1930s show a noticeable dearth of ads for cleaning and cooking products, kitchen appliances, and other consumer items for the running of a household. On the other hand, there are volumes of ads in women's magazines for men's clothing and underwear, men's grooming products, and men's recreation goods and services. Even business services such as insurance, personal finances, and travel were widely advertised in women's publications. In these categories of goods and services, "men dominate here, but much of their spending is in behalf of women," admitted *Fortune,* affirming what marketers had asserted all along.[5]

Once the machinery of mass production was rolling, manufacturers and retailers had to get the message out to the consumer, and that meant communication in the available mass media. Prior to the emergence of commercial radio in the 1920s and television in the 1940s, the options for marketers were the many forms of print: signs, flyers, direct mail, newspapers, and particularly magazines. In 1960, former advertising executive Helen Woodward published *The Lady Persuaders,* in which she examined the history and influence of women's magazines on the whole of American society. To Woodward, "women's magazines with their millions of readers played a major part" in the fact that by the end of the 1950s women controlled "seventy percent of the wealth of the country" and "ruled the roost" at home. She wrote: "To the uninitiated, a woman's magazine may seem merely a powdery bit of fluff. No notion could be more unreal or deceptive. That is just the style in which the magazines express themselves, for if the top layer seems fluffy, the underlying base is solid and powerful. These publications involve a giant business investment, and have an overwhelming influence on American life."[6]

Although the legacy of these magazines extends back to when the first issue of *Ladies' Magazine* was published in 1828, these periodicals began to be a significant vehicle of communication for marketers only in the 1880s and especially the 1890s. Magazines initially resisted the advertiser with what Richard Ohmann called their "aristocratic scruples," despite the temptation of huge revenues that were possible even in those early days of advertising. The turning point seemed to be the economic panic of 1893 when fiercely competitive publishers reacted to one another with a newly devised "formula of elegant simplicity": "identify a large audience that is not hereditarily affluent or elite, but that is getting on well enough, and that has cultural aspirations; give it what it wants; build a huge circulation; sell lots of advertising space at rates based on that circulation; sell the magazine at a price *below* the cost of production, and make your profits on ads."[7] Circulation numbers of popular magazines soared from 18 million in 1890 to 64 million in 1905, which translated into about four different monthly magazines in each household.[8] Such a reach to this enormous audience of consumers was highly beneficial to manufacturers and distributors in their efforts to get their marketing messages out and to create a mass market. Marketers put their messages where the customers were. For example, based on the Haggar menswear survey cited above, the company included advertising in *Elle* and *Cosmopolitan* as part of its marketing strategy. A 1997 ad for Hearst Magazines showed readership of its titles for men at 22 million, but readership of its titles for women and the home were well over four times that at 98 million.[9] By the end of the twentieth century, the "Seven Sisters" alone (*Better Homes & Gardens, Family Circle, Good Housekeeping, Ladies' Home Journal, McCall's, Redbook, Woman's Day*) reached almost 34 million consumers,[10] and these were but a few titles from a list of forty-eight hundred magazine titles.[11] "Readers will buy more stuff from a magazine they love to read," concluded an *Advertising Age* editor in 1998.[12]

Moreover, marketers knew only too well that their ad messages were not the sole force in creating and driving a mass market. From the macrocosms of urbanization and immigration, war and peace, legislative and judicial decisions, or political elections to the microcosms of home, family, or interpersonal relationships, manufacturers and distributors tried to predict and react to the innumerable variables at play in the American consumer market. Even at the end of the twentieth century, with all the sophisticated methods of measuring the consumer's response to advertising, there was doubt about its effectiveness. In a 1998 editorial, *Advertising Age* admitted: "most [marketers] do not know whether those advertising dollars are well spent—that is, if they actually increase sales and profit or help develop lasting brand equity."[13] There also were notable failures despite powerhouse brand names and huge advertising budgets. For instance, confectionery giant M&M/Mars shelved its energy bar Vo2Max even though the projected market potential for the energy bar industry was a tempting $250 million.[14] Similarly, Miller Brewing Company thought it had the right product, the right marketing, and the right advertising message for its Miller Lite beer, only to suffer a 2.6 percent decline in sales volume.[15] Probably the most telling disappointment was the highly visible and popular milk moustache ads that for years children had pinned up in their rooms and office workers stapled to bulletin boards; by the end of 1998 milk consumption had declined by 5 percent.[16]

Still, there were enough success stories and experiences for marketers to continue to have some degree of faith in advertising. Sometimes all the marketing elements came together perfectly and a business thrived as a result. It is beyond the scope of this book to evaluate the sales success of the ads featured here. The ads are representative of the kinds of goods and services that were marketed to the American woman consumer, and more important, they represent the marketing messages about those products and about the consumers of a given period of time.

An in-depth examination of advertising as an accurate reflection of social reality across the decades also is beyond the scope of this book. Certainly the manufacture and promotion of a great many products contributed to social change, and a number of those changes are noted in this study. For instance, prior to the mid-1920s, smoking for women was an absolute social taboo, even outlawed in some places; however, after only a few years of aggressive advertising by the tobacco industry, millions of women became hooked on cigarettes, and the social taboo became merely a bad habit. Some social realities were conspicuously absent in advertising, such as depictions of the poorer working classes and, prior to the 1970s, of ethnics who were not stereotyped. "People did not usually want ads to reflect themselves, their immediate social relationships, or their broader society exactly," wrote history professor Roland Marchand.[17] Instead, marketers tried to reflect in their ads what they thought were the aspirations of an ever increasing mass market of consumers. Advertisers had a greater vested interest in reflecting people's needs, desires, and anxieties than in depicting their actual circumstances and behavior. Similarly, throughout the twentieth century, the stereotypical middle-class, usually white, "Happy Homemaker" was never far from the ad man's concept of the target customer in the American mass market. This is not to say that the biases of marketers resulted in ads devoid of social realities. To the contrary, ads provide glimpses of an enormous array of past social conditions. For instance, images in ads of uniformed gas station attendants happily cleaning auto windshields reflected a common sight seen by all classes of society once upon a bygone time.

All of these representations of the American dream live today in surviving copies of retail catalogs, in preserved sales promotion materials, and in volumes and volumes of magazine ads. It is primarily the empirical evidence of ads from magazines that is represented in this book. With huge numbers of magazines having been published over the decades, substantial quantities have survived intact. For the most part, ads reproduced in this study have been taken from two categories of periodicals, those targeting "Mrs. Consumer" and those targeting the advertisers themselves. The greatest assortment of consumer ads were provided by mainstream women's magazines such as *Ladies' Home Journal, Good Housekeeping, McCall's,* and *Woman's Home Companion,* and mass-circulation titles such as *Life, Collier's, American,* and *Saturday Evening Post.* Many researchers today might be unfamiliar with some of the mainstream publications that were the most popular of their time. For instance, the *Munsey* had the highest mass circulation of all monthly magazines at the end of the nineteenth century,[18] and as such, the volume of its advertising pages was more extensive for that period than that of competing magazines such as *Cosmopolitan* or *Life,* whose titles remain household names today. As for ads that targeted marketers, most are from the better-known business and trade publications such as *Printers' Ink, Advertising Age, Adweek,* and *Fortune.*

The extensive availability of these resources as well as their manageable reproduction for the format and production of this book have been determining factors in their use here. Still, as most students and practitioners of marketing and advertising know, ad campaigns crossed the full range of mass media and were easily adapted from one format to the other. The marketing message remained the same; only the presentation may have varied. This is especially important in understanding the methodology of this study. The fact that magazine ads are the primary media used to support and illustrate the thesis is not to imply that other media were less significant. Depending upon the target consumer, of course, manufacturers and distributors may have concentrated their advertising efforts in media exclusive of magazines. Makers of preschool toys, for instance, would be far more likely to reach their end users with lively TV spots placed during cartoon shows than in any form of print, and purchasers (moms) would more likely respond to a direct mail discount coupon for those toys than to a product or image ad in a magazine. However, in the overall view of the history of the American mass market, magazine ads are an excellent documentation of what products were mass produced in a particular era, and especially how marketers communicated their messages about their products, brands, and company images.

The reader should consider one other point about the methodology of this book. For those ads that are included here, original sources are not cited in the chapter notes because, except in a few instances where details were specifically relevant, ads are reproduced in their entirety and are dated in the captions. Hence, where excerpts from the ad copy might be quoted in the text, both the date and the entire text of the ad are provided in the illustration. Where the content of ads is quoted but the ads are not completely reproduced, the sources are then noted. This methodology has been necessary because of the condition of most of the several hundred ads that were selected for this study. The great majority is from a private collection of about twenty thousand tearsheets in which, although the ads were dated, the original sources were not specified. It also should be noted that for collectors of advertising materials, ironically, sources of origin are not usually relevant. Collectors who seek ads from famous illustrators such as Norman Rockwell or Maxfield Parrish, or ads with specific themes such as Santas or trains, or ads by certain marketers such as Coca-Cola or Ivory seldom care in which periodicals the ads appeared. To economize storage space, collectors and dealers tend to dismantle magazines, retaining only the ads and noting the dates in the margins.

These ads serve as the foundation for this examination of what and how marketers advertised to the American woman. They provide a broad look at the evolution of the mass production of goods and the methods and techniques that have been used to get messages to the consumer about products, brands, and corporate images. They give us a glimpse of the life styles and aspirations of Americans in the twentieth century. In celebrity testimonial versions they show us the personalities whom society regarded as noteworthy. They are a tangible history of the American century and the American dream.

—Chapter 1

MARKETING

AND

MAGAZINES

The emergence of a mass consumer market • Market competition and product branding • The substitution battle and consumer protection • Expanding market share and target marketing • Creating a mass market through mass communication • Magazines as the best avenue to reach women consumers

In May 1893, the huge Columbian Exposition opened in Chicago to celebrate how far Americans had come in the four hundred years since Columbus set foot in the New World. Indeed, by the closing years of the nineteenth century Americans could look back with great pride at the nation they and their ancestors had forged from a wilderness. Between the end of Reconstruction and 1900, industrialization, urbanization, and immigration had caused cultural shifts unlike those of any generation before. Tremendous leaps in population and wealth had occurred. Except for a brief confrontation with Spain, the country had enjoyed the longest period of peace in its history. Transcontinental railroads had linked the Atlantic coast with the Pacific. The last continental frontiers had been settled, and the West had been won.

All of this had helped fuel a second industrial revolution. Dramatic changes in manufacturing technologies and methods of distribution had led to the emergence of an ever expanding mass market of consumers. By the end of the nineteenth century, more manufactured products were purchased and fewer things were made at home than just a generation earlier. (Figure 1-1.)

Throughout the last third of the nineteenth century, advances in factory technology had led to sophisticated

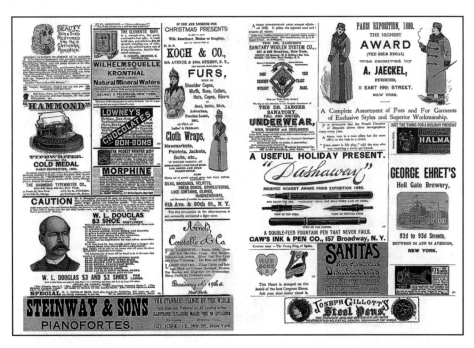

Figure 1-1. By the end of the nineteenth century, a huge American market of consumers was ardently courted in mass advertising such as these omnibus pages from an 1889 *Puck's Magazine*.

Figure 1-2. Congress enacted special legislation in 1912 to permit the post office to carry parcels. This greatly boosted catalog sales and widened the consumer market.

PEARLS IN THE MOUTH.

Beauty and Fragrance

Are Communicated to the Mouth by

SOZODONT,

which renders the teeth pearly white, the gums rosy, and the breath sweet. By those who have used it, it is regarded as an indispensable adjunct of the toilet. It thoroughly removes tartar from the teeth, without injuring the enamel.

SOLD BY DRUGGISTS.

CHERRY BLOSSOM

PERFUME TOILET POWDER & SOAP

NUN NICER

principles of flow production, which evolved into the twentieth-century concept of the assembly line. By 1900, massive batches of raw materials were being processed to manufacture every conceivable category of consumer goods for the home and family.

Manufacturers' distribution channels became broader with the expanded network of regional railroads and interstate road systems of the late nineteenth century. More goods could be moved to more parts of the country than ever before. The postal service became an affordable and effective means for moving mountains of merchandise from manufacturers and retailers straight to customers' doors coast to coast. (Figure 1-2.)

As manufacturers developed more efficient, lower cost methods of production, the need to sell higher volumes of products rapidly expanded. Marketing strategies evolved that were specifically designed to convert a population accustomed to homemade products and generic bulk merchandise into consumers of branded products. A significant part of this marketing strategy included introducing American consumers to products they did not even know they needed, such as toothpaste or perfumed soaps. (Figure 1-3.) Creating a mass market required mass communication for which advertising, in all its variations, proved to be the key.

It was not enough for manufacturers to get the consumer to buy more soap, boxed cereal, or ready-to-wear clothing. The challenge was to make sure that their brands of products were the customer's first choice. Much to the chagrin of many manufacturers, their advertising efforts could also help increase the competition's sales, since the result was often an increase in the total consumption of a commodity. In today's marketing terms, the need was product differentiation. After all, the benefits of using Crisco shortening, for example, might just as easily be applied to all commercial shortenings. In the 1910s, Procter & Gamble aggressively used advertising to define the competitive advantages of its newly launched Crisco shortening over those of Snowdrift and other brands. Ads emphasized that foods prepared with Crisco were "delicious and easy to digest" and "free from any fatty, grease-soaked taste."[1] This implied that other brands of shortening tasted greasy and

Figure 1-3. Consumers in the nineteenth century were introduced to many new products they did not even know they needed, such as toothpaste and perfumed soaps. Sozodont ad 1884, Cherry Blossom ad 1889.

caused problems with digestion. Such methods of advertising a product's differentiation became an integral part of the manufacturer's brand marketing strategy and the focus of thousands of advertising campaigns throughout the twentieth century.

Product Branding and the Substitution Battle

One major hurdle manufacturers of branded products faced was that of substitution by retailers. Early on, advertisers of brand-name products recognized that a customer might ask for a specific brand from a retailer, but if the product was not available, or if the merchant could make a higher profit margin with a product substitution, the branded product would never achieve market share. Battles lasted for decades between manufacturers striving to protect branded goods and retailers resentful of slim profit margins or other distribution restrictions. One defensive measure used by manufacturers was to advertise warnings against substitutions and to advise customers to ask for products by brand name. During the 1890s, for instance, Franco American Foods warned consumers to "lookout for frauds" and "beware of brands offered... 'just as good and cheaper than Franco American.'"[2] Ivory Soap issued "a word of warning" in its 1890s ads, noting that some white soaps were "represented to be 'just as good as' the Ivory [but] they are not." (Figure 1-4.)

Going one step further, many manufacturers insisted in their ad copy that the customer send back imitations substituted by grocers. (Figure 1-5.) "Unscrupulous grocers will tell you 'this is as good as' or 'the same as Pearline,'" but "IT'S FALSE," advised the copy in dozens of variations of Pearline Soap ads. "Send it back," the ads often concluded in boldface type. In such ads the consumer not only was warned against the dangers of substitution but also was urged not to be a victim of the retail bullies who practiced substitution. Take action and demand our product by name, the copy often suggested.

At the turn of the century, some manufacturers tried a second assault against substitution by advertising warnings aimed at the merchants. (Figure 1-6.) Such ads suggested that retailers risked the goodwill of their customers by substituting inferior products when specific brands had been requested. A Pillsbury ad from 1900 shows a grocer presenting a generic brand of flour to the customer. Presumably the grocer has sung the same old refrain: "This flour is just as good." Forewarned by advertising, the savvy woman shopper knows better and points to what she wants—the sack of Pillsbury flour. "Consumers are warned not to accept substitutions," the ad copy reads, but it was the grocers who were more emphatically warned by the header: "Losing a good customer." Similarly, that same year a Sapolio Soap ad poetically advised retailers that the customer knows the brand she wants, and "what she wants must go."

To combat the substitution by grocers of its cornflakes for cheaper bulk cereal, Kellogg's also hammered away at name and product recognition by prominently featuring its logo and illustrations of its distinctive cereal package in ads. The script logo was accompanied by captions such as "none genuine without this signature" or "the package of the genuine bears this

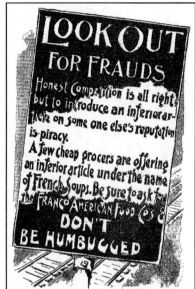

Figure 1-4. Consumers so frequently received inferior substitutions for branded products from retailers that many ad campaigns included warnings against this nefarious practice. Franco American ad 1897, Ivory Soap ad 1899.

1893

Lost his Position.

That really happened to a certain grocer's clerk, because he couldn't induce customers to take an inferior brand of washing powder in place of **Pearline**. The grocer said, "If you can't sell what I want you to sell, I don't want you." Now it doesn't take a very wise woman to decide whether this was an honest grocer. And a woman wise enough for that, would be likely to insist upon having nothing but **Pearline**. There is nothing "as good as" or "the same as" **Pearline**, the original —in fact, the only—washing-compound. If they send you something else, send it back.   JAMES PYLE, New York.

1897

"It's Cruel

for them not to give you **Pearline** for your washing. Your folks can't know much about it. My! They could save their money, and all your hard work besides. I'm thankful the lady I live with is just the other way. She knows what **Pearline** will do, and she wants it. She'd never let me lose my time trying to get things clean with soap—and she wouldn't stand it to have her clothes all worn out with rubbing, either."

That's the truth. The lack of **Pearline** comes just as hard on the mistress' clothes as it does on the laundress' back.

Send it Back Peddlers and some unscrupulous grocers will tell you "this is as good as" or "the same as Pearline." IT'S FALSE—Pearline is never peddled, and if your grocer sends you something in place of Pearline, be honest—*send it back.* 437   JAMES PYLE, New York.

Are They Dangerous

—the imitations of Pearline? How are you going to find out? A few washings with them won't show any damage. It's only after some months, when your clothes go to pieces suddenly, that the danger can be seen and proved. Are you willing to risk your own clothes in the experiment? It is better to be sure that you are safe, by using the original washing compound—**Pearline**. All the others are founded upon that. Will it pay to use these imitations? Figure up all that they may offer—prize packages, cheap prices, or whatever it may be—and put it against what you may lose.

Send it Back Peddlers and some unscrupulous grocers will tell you "this is as good as" or "the same as Pearline." IT'S FALSE—Pearline is never peddled, and if your grocer sends you something in place of Pearline, do the honest thing—*send it back.* —JAMES PYLE, New York.

"Substitution"

is often an effort to get rid of unsalable goods —things that have been forced on the dealer by schemes which promise excessive profit. Such washing powders are urged in place of **Pearline**.

When a woman gets a useless imitation, on the assurance that it's "the same as" or "as good as" Pearline, she's pretty likely afterward to do her trading somewhere else.

Don't argue the matter—use Pearline.

1897   1899

Figure 1-5. Advertising not only warned consumers against the dangers of product substitution by retailers but also advised them to send a strong message to these retailers by returning the inferior substitute.

signature." Nevertheless, the substitution problem persisted. As a result, in a 1908 ad the usual illustration of the smiling Kellogg's Corn Maid was replaced by that of a peeved woman who, it was implied, had just been given a substitution for Kellogg's cornflakes. (Figure 1-7.) Her response to this presumption by the grocer is to state firmly, "Excuse me—I know what I want, and I want what I asked for—Toasted Corn Flakes—Good day." The theme of losing a good customer was just as emphatic here as with the Pillsbury and Sapolio ads eight years earlier.

The significance of the consumer's demand for a branded product went beyond name recognition. In the years before the 1906 Pure Food and Drugs Act, and even for some time afterward, product safety was a vital issue with consumers. Horror stories of patent medicines being loaded with alcohol, cocaine, or opium abounded in medical circles. Manufactured foods such as flour were sometimes weighted with fillers such as chalk or sawdust.[3] Customers had a sense of helplessness when purchasing products manufactured by some distant, unknown business entity. Branded products offered some reassurance for quality and safety. If a grocer or druggist substituted a requested brand-name product with one that was unknown to the customer, the health and safety dangers might be very real.

When the Pure Food and Drugs Act was signed into law by Teddy Roosevelt in 1906, many manufacturers of branded products incorporated references to the new legislation into their ads. "Truth in advertising implies honesty in manufacture," a 1906 Colgate ad stated just above its logo. "Complies with all Pure Food Laws," declared a 1907 Jell-O ad. "Where

Figure 1-6. By the turn of the century, ads warned merchants that they ran the risk of losing customers by substituting inferior products when customers requested their brands. Pillsbury ad 1900, Sapolio ad 1900.

purity is paramount" became the logo tagline for Ralston Purina Mills. "Guaranteed under the Pure Food and Drugs Act," promised Coca-Cola in ads.[4]

However, the practice of substitution remained so prevalent that by 1913, *Ladies' World* ran ads in competing publications to promote a pending exposé on such "grocery sins." (Figure 1-8.) Among these offenses was product substitution. The illustration in the magazine's promotional ad shows a pitiful grocer, his head hung in shame, being guarded by armed allegories of outraged housewives. In the article, titled "Just as Good," Anna Reese Richardson wrote: "When a grocer discards the products of established, reliable firms and substitutes an entirely new line of factory, canned or bottled goods, he must have a reason, and it is your business to find out what that reason is. Even if the new goods are offered at a few cents less, it pays to investigate."[5]

Even well into the 1920s, product substitution remained a significant issue between manufacturers, consumers, and retailers. John Schlachter interviewed executives at several major manufacturers about product substitution for *Printers' Ink* in 1921. At Lyon & Sons, makers of dentrifice products, he was told: "While we do not feel that we have entirely solved the substitute menace, yet we believe that this condition is much improved, due, no doubt to the fact that during the past few years both dealer and consumer have found trade-marked goods were the most dependable. Therefore, our principle effort is directed through our advertising, in its various branches, in keeping our goods constantly before the public."[6]

This confidence that brand advertising had begun to effectively undermine product substitution and had enhanced market share for the national

Figure 1-7. Kellogg's replaced its usual depiction of the happy Corn Maid with one showing a peeved customer in a 1908 ad. The implication was that women shoppers should take their business elsewhere if merchants practiced substitution. Left ad 1907, right ad 1908.

This Is the Grocer of Cheat'em Town
Whose Affable Ways Won Great Renown

Until the housewives of Cheat'em Town discovered that
his affable ways covered a multitude of grocery sins. They
found that his bottles of flavoring extract were short in
quantity, that he always had something

"Just As Good"

as the thing they wanted. They found that his store was
overflowing with "sweat shop" foods, nameless food-orphans
with false claims to quality. His ketchups were made of
apples; his canned peaches were picked green; his "borax"
soap oozed lye.

The housewives of Cheat'em Town decided that he was
oozing lies all over, so they got after him as only determined
housewives can until *they got the food they wanted.*

Their story is told in vivid language by Mrs. Anna Steese
Richardson in THE LADIES' WORLD for NOVEMBER.
It touches on some monstrous conditions in our cities and
towns.

It will do you good to read it.

All News Stands

THE LADIES' WORLD

Ten Cents a Copy—One Dollar a Year

Figure 1-8. Product substitution by retailers persisted despite decades of advertising efforts to warn consumers. This dangerous practice was still so prevalent in 1913 that *Ladies' World* widely advertised a pending expose on the topic.

labels was bolstered by the rapid spread of chain stores. Originating with the first Piggly Wiggly stores in Memphis in 1916, more than twenty-one hundred self-serve grocery stores dotted the American landscape by 1929.[7] (Figure 1-9.) Despite enormous propaganda and legislative efforts by home-based businesses to keep the national chains out, the tide was overwhelming. "One reason why the chain store is crowding out the oldtime [retailer]," Schlachter noted, "is they give you what you ask for and do not attempt to sell you something of their own, in spite of the fact they do retail many articles under their private label."[8] Consumers and brand-product manufacturers welcomed the concept of the self-service grocery store.

The chain store phenomenon initially was confined to large urban areas and took decades to fully integrate a broad base of markets nationwide. Meanwhile, customers still bought soap and cornflakes, and merchants continued to substitute inferior products for brand labels. "The 'something just as good' fiend," Schlachter lamented, "often finds customers for such goods easy picking."[9] However, with ads like those by Pearline and Kellogg's warning against substitution, customers no longer relied exclusively on their local grocers for recommendations on the best soap or packaged breakfast cereal. Customers asked specifically for Pearline Soap or Kellogg's Corn Flakes. For manufacturers, the marketing strategy of brand advertising proved highly successful, and businesses grew steadily.

Another benefit for the manufacturers of branded products was an inherent defense against the many factions of progressive reformers. Even before the Civil War, groups had formed to demand consumer protection legislation against manufacturing and advertising abuses. The widely advertised guarantees of a branded product's quality implied that the manufacturer took responsibility for the product and the conditions under which it was produced. As a result of this perceived accountability, the brand stood for the customer's expectations of the product: with an Ivory Soap logo on the product, it must be "pure," or with Post's logo on the box, the product must be nutritious.

Federal statutes and regulatory agencies eventually were created to answer the demands of consumer advocacy groups. Throughout the twentieth century consumers witnessed the various agencies at work protecting the public against advertising fraud and unsafe products. Even into the 1990s, product recalls were common occurrences as manufacturers rushed to stem liability lawsuits and prevent actions against them by federal agencies. Phoenix chocolate-chip cookies, Schwan's ice cream, Keebler's graham crackers, and Coca-Cola's Diet Lemon Nestea were among the many food

Choose for yourself .. help yourself

Like many other of today's customs,
it is at once delightful and sensible.

A special plan of shopping that has
become a nation-wide vogue.

At last women are free to make
their own decisions when they buy
foods. There is no one to persuade, to
urge at the Piggly Wiggly Store. There
are no delays—no hurry.

Here women choose for themselves
—help themselves. A fascinating way

*A few years ago the first Piggly
Wiggly Store was opened. Today
there are over 2100 from coast
to coast. New this unique shopping plan is offered in over 600
cities and towns*

to cut costs and still serve more tempting, healthful meals.

On the open shelves, famous and
familiar packages await you, with
fresh, inviting fruits and vegetables.
And by each item hangs a big, square
price tag that spells convenience—the
celebrated swinging price tag of the
Piggly Wiggly Stores.

The choice foods of the world—
fresh and packaged—are spread out
for you to examine at Piggly Wiggly.

You take what you please from the
shelves—look it over, compare prices
—make your own decisions. Gain new
ideas for dishes and menus.

Best of all you save money week in
and week out at Piggly Wiggly. Consistently low prices are assured by our
special method of operation.

That is why 2,500,000 women come
daily to Piggly Wiggly. Try this plan
of shopping. Visit the Piggly Wiggly
Store in your neighborhood.

PIGGLY WIGGLY
STORES

*Unusual opportunity to own and operate a profitable
local business with the merchandising co-operation of a
national organization—motivates Piggly Wiggly fran-
chises. Available in cities where stores have not been
established. Open only to men who control sufficient
capital to finance a number of stores. Address Fran-
chise Department, 617 American Bldg., Cincinnati, Ohio*

In using advertisements see page 6

Figure 1-9. In 1916 Piggly Wiggly stores inaugurated the concept of self-serve shopping. Ad 1929.

Figure 1-10. Ads for labor-saving appliances emphasized the idea of leisure time for a broader range of socioeconomic classes of American women. Frantz Premiere ad 1915, Maytag ad 1927.

products recalled in the 1990s due to health hazard classifications by the Food and Drug Administration.[10]

Similarly, the Federal Trade Commission kept vigilance over advertising claims. Over nearly nine decades since its creation in 1914, the FTC has compiled an impressive list of cease and desist claims against advertisers. In the better-late-than-never category is Listerine Antiseptic, which for decades had been advertised as a preventative for colds. A 1970s court order compelled Warner Lambert to spend millions of dollars disclaiming that Listerine could not prevent or lessen the severity of a cold.[11]

Marketing Strategies and the Target Customer

Besides adapting to stringent regulations of product manufacturing and advertising, manufacturers increasingly faced the challenge of expanding their markets and targeting more customers. Beyond the consumer's basic needs for products such as Ivory Soap, Kellogg's Corn Flakes, and hundreds of similar consumables, a host of new products and services became available to the American consumer, especially in the years preceding the First World War. The mass production of labor-saving electrical appliances, phonograph players, automobiles, and other such high-end goods helped move the consumer society into a new phase—from merely purchasing manufactured goods for the daily needs of life to purchasing wants. Among the most wanted products of the time were those that eased the burdens of housework and made possible more leisure time. (Figure 1-10.) "The uncivilized make little progress because they have few desires," President Calvin Coolidge said at an advertising conference in 1926. "The inhabitants of our country are stimulated to new wants in all directions."[12]

In response to this progress of civilization, the business strategies of manufacturers, distributors, and retailers evolved into the complexity of marketing. As a business science—some would say art—marketing expanded beyond the simplicity of brand advertising. By the 1920s, full-scale marketing plans began to incorporate a broader reach of business processes, including consumer research and targeting, competitive analysis, expanded distribution channels, and modernized sales force planning. Research and development of new products to capitalize on brand equity began to generate specialization of products such as soaps that were made exclusively for skin care, laundry, dishes, or even solely for interior woodwork. For companies such as Campbell's, Post, and Nabisco, the manufacturing and distributing processes were already in place to produce new products that were similar

Figure 1-11. Brand equity made possible the use of a manufacturer's established name to effectively expand a product mix. Ad 1916.

Figure 1-12. Strathmore Paper Company published its version of an ideal ad designed with "luxury and daintiness" to appeal to women. Ad 1920.

to the established product mix. The step from chicken vegetable soup to beef vegetable soup or gingersnaps to lemon snaps did not require new manufacturing plants to be built or existing production equipment to be reengineered. Product ingredients were similar, and only packaging labels needed to be redesigned. Capital investment could be minimized, with the bulk of the budget for a new product launch reserved for advertising. (Figure 1-11.)

As sophisticated and diverse as marketing became, all of these methods and strategies sprang from one fundamental question: Who is our target customer? For the overwhelming majority of manufacturers, the conclusion was undeniable. Across the socioeconomic and geopolitical spectrum of America, advertisers trained their sights on women consumers.

In 1920, U.S. women were granted the right to vote with the ratification of the Nineteenth Amendment to the Constitution. That same year, Strathmore Paper Company published an ad in business periodicals headlined "Appealing to Women in Advertising." (Figure 1-12.) "Fifty percent of all advertising matter is intended to appeal to women," the opening sentence stated. That was a conservative estimate. A decade later, the J. Walter Thompson agency asserted that 85 percent of all advertised products were bought by women.[13] With the female population of the U.S. in 1930 estimated by the Census Bureau at 61 million, that was a considerable target market.[14]

Even though enfranchisement was a momentous leap in the changing social roles of women in American society, the significance of the event was negligible to advertisers. Not one article in any of the weekly issues of *Printers' Ink* in 1920 explored the impact of the Nineteenth Amendment on women as consumers. To the business community, women as a consumer group had not changed. For the 84 percent of women who were homemakers in 1920,[15] the demands of home and family were a daily concern; infrequent elections and politics could not compete with that.

For manufacturers and advertisers, it was still business as usual. To appeal to contemporary women, as the Strathmore ad had maintained, "luxury and daintiness" remained the typical guidelines. Even though the Strathmore ad mostly ran in business periodicals, the delicate line drawing, peach spot color, and serif typeface created an example of what the company thought advertisers should be doing to most effectively appeal to the woman of 1920. The words "cold and unfeminine" were pointedly used in the copy as a caution to businessmen who failed to understand their target customer.

The concept expressed in the Strathmore ad also reflects a fundamental change in advertising as an industry at this time. In earlier years, ads by agencies had relentlessly promoted the idea of advertising and its importance to the success of business. (Figure 1-13.) However, by the 1920s, self-promotional ads by agencies began to emphasize that they understood target marketing—and that the most important target for advertising was women.

The Ayer & Son agency published striking house ads along this line all

Figure 1-13. Early self-promotional ads by advertising agencies, such as this verbose example by Lord & Thomas, primarily emphasized the idea of advertising. Ad 1906.

through the 1920s. Copy still spoke generally of the benefits of advertising, but half the space of each ad clearly expressed in visual terms to whom that advertising should be directed. (Figure 1-14.) One ad, headlined "The Challenge," showed a happy woman shopper recognizing a product on display. Being familiar with the item or brand through advertising, she confidently says the magic words, "I'll take that, please." Other ads in the series presented different art styles depicting women consumers, which as a second benefit to the agency subliminally demonstrated to potential clients the sophistication and diversity of Ayer's art directors. In the ad titled "Building a Business," the illustration was a nostalgic look at serving women consumers fifty years earlier. "Good-will" and "fair dealing" may have been achieved by one-on-one contact with customers in olden days, the copy asserted, but today, "advertising creates goodwill." Branding was addressed in the ad titled "A Nation's Shopping List," which featured in the illustration the consumer of the future—a little girl with a shopping basket over her arm. Then there were the economic and social strata within the women's target market, which Ayer implied it well understood in the "Tradition of Excellence" ad. The single sentence in the copy that stood alone as a paragraph said it all: "And she went shopping."

The idea of target marketing to women even became a theme used in consumer ad campaigns during the 1920s. For the fiercely competitive grocery retailers A&P and Piggly Wiggly, numerous ads about targeting women customers ran in women's magazines for years. Rather than selling

Figure 1-14. By the 1920s house ads by advertising agencies such as Ayer & Son began to show an understanding of target marketing. Ads 1924–25.

a sale or presenting a product promotion, these ads focused on how the modern woman experienced grocery shopping. The advertising for both A&P and Piggly Wiggly not only had to position the businesses competitively against each other, but just as important, it had to convince women to change the way they shopped for groceries. Instead of making trips to the neighborhood butcher shops, bakeries, produce stands, and small grocers, women had to be sold on the idea of self-serve, one-stop shopping offered by the chain stores. Establishing a good reputation with customers took time and persistence, especially against home-based retailers, which often had a substantial history with their customers. "Woman's confidence in advertising bears a direct ratio to her response to it," wrote Christine Frederick in a 1920 *Printers' Ink* article. "If she has an 80% confidence, she buys 80%—if she has only a 20% confidence, she buys only 20%."[16]

The A&P "Women of America" series of ads was designed to position the grocery retailer as a trusted brand where women could shop with confidence. (Figure 1-15.) Women's concerns were superbly addressed in each of these ads. Besides promising economy of time and money, the copy presented the store in warm, friendly terms. Shopping at A&P was a "positive delight," and each store was as orderly and spic-and-span as their own homes, one of the ads assured women. Both visually and in text, the ads suggested that A&P understood the dreams and aspirations of most every American woman, whether she was a factory worker of modest means or the wife of an affluent business executive.

In a 1927 ad headline, A&P posed the question, "Who is this woman?" Drawn into the ad by the striking illustration of a stylish, confident-looking woman, readers were told that she is "one of America's most representative women" who thinks of food "in terms of quality and nourishment and

Figure 1-15. During the 1920s A&P ran a series of ads to position the chain store as a trusted brand to women.

1926

1927

1928

healthful variety." In this instance, though, the message of the ad was twofold: A&P catered to the grocery needs of middle-class women who attended "bridge-teas and party-suppers," as represented by the illustration of a woman wearing a fox stole and trendy cloche, as well as to the needs of those women who served the daily meals of the nation. "Table luxuries, both imported and domestic" were conveniently available at A&P, but it was the quality, value-priced "staples of every day" that would keep the multitudes of average customers coming back to shop week after week.

Another headline in an A&P ad asked, "Do women think differently today?" The subhead answered the question: "This changing habit proves they do." With the emphasis on "change," the modern woman reading this ad had but to look to her Victorian mother for a palpable measure of change. As A&P and its competitors recognized and emphasized in their advertising, one-stop shopping would broaden the scope of women as consumers. Centralized product diversity and brand availability, with timesaving convenience, were beyond the dreams of women just a decade earlier.

By the 1930s, the paean of advertisers was unquestionably that of woman and her preeminence as consumer. In 1930, the Charles Daniel Frey agency presented a quietly poetic ad about the woman consumer. (Figure 1-16.) With deft alliteration, the header acknowledged the power that the American woman held "in the hollow of her hand." The delicate line art vignette of a woman, the open-faced serif type, and the airy line spacing of the text disguised the blunt force of the message that "she is the spender of the nation." The copywriter had noted astutely that even when the advertising was for men's products, the target customers most likely were women. On the whole, women bought huge volumes of men's clothing, accessories, toiletries, and luxury goods for husbands, fathers, and sons. Whatever you have to sell, the Frey ad told manufacturers and retailers, aim your message at the American woman.

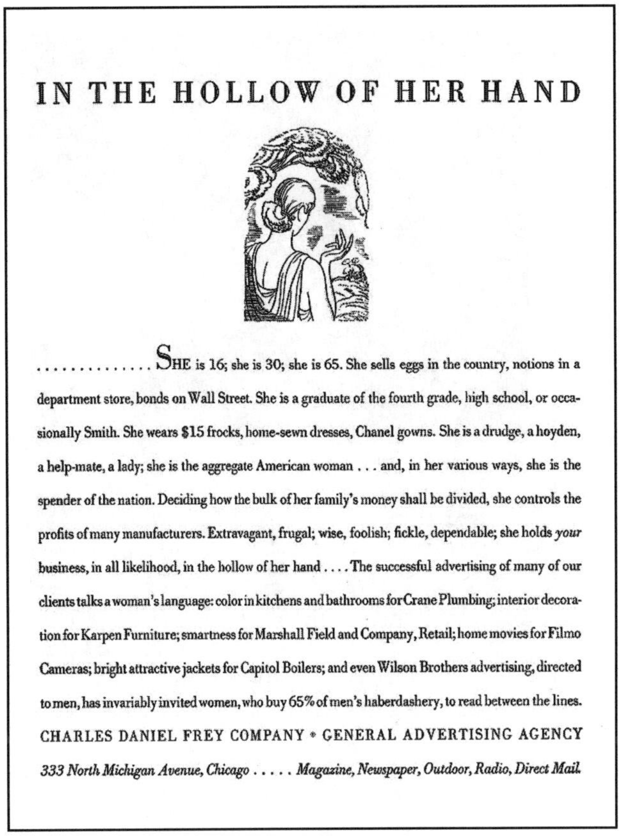

A year after the Frey ad was created, J. Walter Thompson advertised how its agency's marketing methods translated into ads that would most effectively target women customers. (Figure 1-17.) Simply put, the Thompson group started with the fundamentals by asking women what they thought and what they wanted. Such methods of demographic research paved the way for the focus group and intercept polling that would become so integral to planning marketing strategies in later decades. In the ad, the prosaic black-and-white photographs of the (male) "maker" and the (female) "user" are as stark as any sales graph in a corporate annual report. The header that stretches between the captions "Maker" and "User" subtly emphasized that the Thompson agency could seek out "the very heart of a problem" and bridge any gap.

Niche marketing became one way ad agencies claimed to bridge gaps to the consumer. For the Newell-Emmett agency, that niche was the beauty industry. In a 1932 house ad, it represented "Beauty" marching forth from a foil of small, unimposing houses to spend $4.5 billion on cosmetics and clothing. (Figure 1-18.) "To reach this market . . . is a matter of developing the right appeal," the ad stated. Newell-Emmett was telling the beauty and fashion industries that this market segment was its specialty: the agency

IN THE HOLLOW OF HER HAND

. . . . SHE is 16; she is 30; she is 65. She sells eggs in the country, notions in a department store, bonds on Wall Street. She is a graduate of the fourth grade, high school, or occasionally Smith. She wears $15 frocks, home-sewn dresses, Chanel gowns. She is a drudge, a hoyden, a help-mate, a lady; she is the aggregate American woman . . . and, in her various ways, she is the spender of the nation. Deciding how the bulk of her family's money shall be divided, she controls the profits of many manufacturers. Extravagant, frugal; wise, foolish; fickle, dependable; she holds *your* business, in all likelihood, in the hollow of her hand . . . . The successful advertising of many of our clients talks a woman's language: color in kitchens and bathrooms for Crane Plumbing; interior decoration for Karpen Furniture; smartness for Marshall Field and Company, Retail; home movies for Filmo Cameras; bright attractive jackets for Capitol Boilers; and even Wilson Brothers advertising, directed to men, has invariably invited women, who buy 65% of men's haberdashery, to read between the lines.

CHARLES DANIEL FREY COMPANY * GENERAL ADVERTISING AGENCY

333 North Michigan Avenue, Chicago . . . . . Magazine, Newspaper, Outdoor, Radio, Direct Mail.

Figure 1-16. "She is the spender of the nation," declared an ad for the Frey agency in 1930. Even if you are advertising men's products, you are still advertising to women, the copy reminded manufacturers and retailers.

Figure 1-17. As stark as a graph in an annual report, this pedantic duo of photographs, labeled "maker" and "user," spoke volumes even without the editorial copy. Ad 1931.

knew how to create ads that would "interest these women and girls." This kind of market segmentation would continue to narrow and focus until, by the 1990s, marketing agencies became highly specialized, concentrating exclusively on prioritized consumer groups such as African-American women, women executives, plus-size women, working moms, and women in sports, to name a few.[17]

A key aspect of targeting women consumers was how to reach them. At the dawn of the twentieth century, the options of mass media were already fairly extensive: magazines, newspapers, posters, billboards, flyers, catalogs, trade cards, direct mail, trolley placards, and product packaging. As the century progressed, mass electronic media entered the daily life of women and evolved from radio to television to global computer links through the Internet. Still, to many marketers, print remained the prevalent and most effective way to advertise to women. Reporting on a Beta Research study in 1997, an ad for the Magazine Publishers of America noted, "A new study says 20% more adults had shopped for a product after reading a magazine than seeing a TV commercial." Continuing to quote independent research, the ad stated, "A Foote, Cone and Belding Media Research Report demonstrates that the top 25 magazines deliver significantly more GRPs [gross rating points] than the top 25 prime time TV shows and do so at 50% less cost."[18]

Magazine Advertising

The relationship of advertising and magazines, and magazines and women readers, evolved fluidly during the last quarter of the nineteenth century. Magazine publishers had resisted including advertising in their periodicals despite the possibility of enhanced revenues and profits. "A publication seldom actively sought ads," advertising historian Frank Rowsome noted. "Publishers commonly believed that advertising was a marginal, not quite respectable business practice—a sign of commercial distress, something engaged in just as bankruptcy loomed."[19] Those publications that did condescend to print ads usually gathered them at the back of an issue. Those advertisers who bought only small space ads ran the risk of having them wedged into an omnibus page like a puzzle piece, as is shown in Figure 1-1. Too often, headers, price points, body copy, and illustrations were scattered across these ad sections and all blurred into a visually confusing mosaic.

By the end of the nineteenth century, advertising revenue emerged from being just a pleasant by-product of magazine publishing to become a vital economic necessity. As the volume of advertising increased, publishers discovered they could sell their magazines below cost and still make substantial profits. As advertising dollars began to impact the publications' bottom lines, so grew the influence of advertisers on the publications themselves. Eventually manufacturers, retailers, and ad agencies would directly influence

Figure 1-18. Agency house ads began to emphasize the need for niche marketing and advertising for specialized industries. Ad 1932.

the content of editorials, the choice of news features, and even magazine layouts. Campbell's Soups advertised so widely and consistently from the 1910s through the 1950s that it was always able to command premium positioning. Month after month, full-page Campbell's ads were placed on the first right-hand ad page following the editorial in dozens of publications such as *Ladies' Home Journal, Woman's Home Companion,* and *Good Housekeeping.*

Early on, advertisers had received tacit encouragement to make demands of publishers. By the 1930s, encouragement had given way to open invitation. For example, *McCall's* ran a series of double-paged ads in business publications showing situations such as a shoe salesman offering canned spaghetti to a customer or a maid offering cold cream to a woman at the dinner table. (Figure 1-19.) In these ads, *McCall's* promised manufacturers and retailers that their ads would be complemented by appropriate editorial content and placement. Accepting such offers from *McCall's* and other magazine editors, advertisers soon pushed their demands to the limits.

By the 1990s, major advertisers were able to submit insertion orders that specified not only where their ads must be placed in the magazine, but also what the publishers had to do with their own editorial content or even with other advertisers. In her book *Moving beyond Words,* Gloria Steinem revealed some of her behind-the-scenes experiences with advertisers while at the helm of *Ms.* magazine. She cited examples of advertisers' demands including the requirement by S. C. Johnson & Son (makers of Johnson's Wax) that its ads "should not be opposite extremely controversial features or material antithetical to the nature/copy of the advertised product." For Procter & Gamble, antithetical material included anything on "gun control, abortion, the occult, cults, or the disparaging of religion." Similarly, the American Tobacco Company ordered that its Misty cigarette ads be placed away from any "editorial relating to health, medicine, religion or death," and Lorillard's Newport cigarette ads had to be separated by a minimum of six pages from nicotine patch products.[20] In 1997 *Esquire* created a furor among

1931

1933

1934

Figure 1-20. Ads from women's publications touting descriptions and demographics of their female readers were placed in business periodicals to target executives of ad agencies and corporate marketing departments.

editors nationwide when it buckled under a demand from Chrysler, which had issued written warnings to magazine sales staffs against running its ads in any issues containing "offensive" or "provocative" material. Overreacting to the demand, *Esquire* killed a short story containing homoerotic scenes rather than lose the Chrysler ad, and subsequently came under a firestorm of widely publicized criticism. Among those commenting publicly on the controversy was Tina Brown, editor in chief of the *New Yorker,* who said in an interview at the time, "The criteria shouldn't be will the advertiser not like this, but is this appropriate for my reader."[21] Nevertheless, with accounting balance sheets in hand, many advertising sales managers continued to wield the greater power.

A further step taken by the publishers of periodicals to attract more advertising dollars was to define the women's market and its segmentations for advertisers. Typical was a 1920 full-page "tombstone" ad of all text published in *Printers' Ink* by the *Philadelphia Record.* "Women read the Record because it caters to their interests in so many ways—they trust it," the copy stated simply. "Women buy the bulk of merchandise sold today," the ad concluded; "the moral is clear."[22] Women's magazines likewise advertised in business publications such as *Fortune* to reach the decision-makers in advertising agencies and corporate marketing departments. (Figure 1-20.) If your target customer is "a woman lean and brown...alive from the flat soles of her calfskin shoes to the tips of her sunburned bobbed hair," advertise with us, a 1931 ad for *Better Homes and Gardens* declared. An ad of the time for the *Farmer's Wife* cited demographics about its rural readers, such as "she is the purchasing agent for 39.3% of the population" with "billions of dollars of necessary current buying to do." Similarly, in response to the highly publicized domesticity of the German hausfrau of the 1930s, *Woman's Home Companion* reached out to advertisers of women's leisure

Figure 1-21. The "shadow of the man" series of ads by *Redbook* suggested to manufacturers and distributors of men's products that women should be their target customers. Ads 1933.

and beauty products with its ads. "Mr. Hitler would not approve," stated the headline of a 1934 ad, "but he'd have a tough time restricting her to the kitchen and nursery."

During this same time, *Redbook* ran a particularly effective campaign that focused on targeting women consumers. In the ads, large shadows of a man's hand or profile loomed behind various versions of Mrs. Consumer. The "shadow of the man" theme reminded manufacturers and retailers of men's products and services that they too should advertise in magazines traditionally regarded as women's publications. (Figure 1-21.) Whereas the Frey ad shown in Figure 1-16 spoke of women in general as target consumers of men's products, *Redbook* went a step further by offering a direct way to reach these customers. In one ad, the photograph depicts a pensive woman in a grocery store. The copy reads: "When a woman buys shirts for her husband, she buys the kind he prefers. When she buys perfumes for herself, she is thinking of her husband's tastes. When she buys food for both of them, she averages her likes and his before she names a brand." In the "Mrs. Peebles" version, *Redbook* reiterated to marketing and advertising agency executives that women do "85% of the purchasing" of all goods—including a substantial bulk of products used by men. The last paragraph of each of these ads concluded with the statement, "Sell the family and you sell all."

By the mid-1950s, even the venerable *Saturday Evening Post* ran promotional ads in business and trade publications to appear women-oriented. (Figure 1-22.) Although regarded as a mass-market periodical with a skew toward male readers,[23] the *Post* advertised that it ranked "as one of the very top women's magazines,"[24] based on an Audit Bureau of Circulations report of newsstand sales in 1956. Ad layouts featured large photos of women shoppers and ran the slogan "America reads the Post" at the bottom of each page. In one example from the campaign, the bag of groceries the woman has bought dwarfs the man at the magazine rack. She has even taken time while shopping to buy a beverage and read the *Post* (for even more consumption persuasion from advertisers).

Figure 1-22. By the mid-1950s, even mass-market publications such as the *Saturday Evening Post* were assiduously pursuing the women's market advertiser. Ads 1955.

Women's magazines, however, did not have to be so subtle. (Figure 1-23.) Running at the same time as the *Post* campaign, ads in *Ladies' Home Journal* proudly advertised the magazine's status as the best conduit to women. The subhead in a 1955 campaign read, "Never underestimate the power of the No. 1 magazine for women." Similarly, ads in the 1950s for women's specialty magazines touted circulation statistics such as "4 million influential women read the Bazaar," and "2,300,000 women buy Better Living." These ads were the direct descendants of the first marketing segmentation ads run by magazines in the 1920s and 1930s.

Even a woman's age had become a significant segmenting factor for the fiercely competitive periodicals by the 1950s. "One magazine completely dominates the great under-20 market," *Seventeen* declared in a 1955 ad. Yet the illustration is not of a typical teenager at play or socializing with peers, but rather of an adult woman with a grocery cart full of merchandise. "It's

Figure 1-23. During the 1950s, ads by women's magazines promoted their effectiveness in reaching women consumers by citing demographic and circulation statistics. Ads 1954–1955.

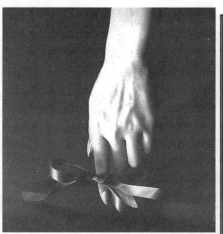

Figure 1-24. Despite the rejuvenation of the feminist movement in the 1960s, advertisers mostly continued to regard American women as they had their mothers and grandmothers: the "Happy Homemaker." Ads 1963–64.

easier to start a habit than to stop one," the ad header stated in bold type around the young woman's uplifted hand holding a canned food product. "Start her with your brand in Seventeen," concluded the subhead.

Less than a decade after these magazine brand-positioning ads ran, Betty Friedan shook American culture to its foundations with her best-selling book *The Feminine Mystique*. In a 1963 interview with the author, *Life* called Friedan the "angry battler for her sex." Her book indicted all who have preached that "a woman can only fulfill herself as a wife and a mother," the article explained.[25] However, as with other momentous social events in the history of American women—such as the 1920 Women's Voting Rights Act and the massive recruitment of women into the workplace during World War II—Friedan's book did not affect women as a consumer group.

A sampling of magazine promotional ads of the time shows that even though women's consciousness about themselves was being broadened, they continued to be the target customers for most manufacturers and distributors of consumer products. (Figure 1-24.) The theme *Seventeen* had started in the 1950s—"it's easier to start a habit than to stop one"—had become part of its logo floorline in ads a decade later. Copy in a 1963 *Family Circle* ad submitted that women read the magazine "not when they want to get away from it all, but when they're thinking about homemaking." The opening sentence in a 1963 *Redbook* ad told advertisers, "If you're looking for young women (best customers for almost everything), call Redbook."

Stereotyped depictions of women as apron-clad homemakers and devoted moms lingered in self-promotional ads for periodicals well past the reality of women's social evolution in the 1970s and 1980s. The demographics shifted considerably during these decades. Women began to defer marriage for education and career opportunities, and motherhood often was postponed or bypassed entirely. Gradually—some might even say reluctantly—magazine marketing ads began to represent women as the diverse and consumer savvy group they had become.

Kiplinger's. Financial Independence.

Figure 1-25. Ads for magazines depicted the American woman of the 1990s as independent and self-sufficient, but still very much the target consumer. Ad 1998.

In a number of magazine promotional ads targeting the American woman of the late twentieth century, her self-assurance was represented by the solitary female figure. (Figure 1-25.) Subject to the reader's interpretation, she might have just gotten away from it all—job, husband, children, home—for a few quiet minutes of self-reflection, or perhaps she is contemplating a commitment to herself as an independent woman whose limitless options included the traditional roles of spouse and mother. These ads suggested to marketers that even in a woman's moments of solitude, she is still a consumer, whether planning her next mutual fund investment or a Saturday shopping trip to the mall.

Conclusion: Reaching the Primary Target

Despite the trial-and-error development of American advertising in the nineteenth century, a great many manufacturing and merchant princes realized phenomenal successes as a result of investing in the practice. In the 1880s and 1890s especially, advertising helped to convert a population accustomed to homemade products into consumers of mass-produced goods. By the beginning of the twentieth century, the use of advertising emerged as a vital marketing strategy for businesses to test and launch new products, to establish brand names, to expand market share, and to combat competition.

Creating a mass market required mass communication, the kind readily available through the well-established distribution channels of newspapers and magazines. Although initially reluctant to engage in what was regarded as an unsavory by-product of the industry, publishers of periodicals began to yield to bottom-line realities by the 1890s. Magazines began to aggressively court advertisers and by the 1930s were providing manufacturers and retailers with promises of complementary editorial content and even special considerations of their magazine's layout and format. For advertisers, the opportunities to reach an even broader audience through the network of national magazines were quickly exploited to the fullest.

Early in the process of creating a mass market of consumers, manufacturers, distributors, and retailers recognized the importance of using their advertising to target women as a group. Ads were written, designed, and illustrated primarily to speak to women. In the years preceding World War I, marketing techniques for targeting women consumers became increasingly sophisticated and effective. Advertising agencies began to explore methods of market research that would provide manufacturers and retailers with more concise directions for product development and sales. By the 1920s marketers began to segment women consumers into niche markets.

Magazines capitalized on this new marketing strategy by positioning themselves as the best avenue to reach women consumers. Even though the barrage of advertising media eventually came to include the powerfully persuasive forces of radio, television, and the Internet, magazines continued to be the most enduring, prolific, and effective vehicle for advertisers to reach a mass market of women. With forty-eight hundred different magazine titles being published at the end of the twentieth century[26] and almost 50 million female readers being reached by just seven Hearst publications alone,[27] magazines continued to be as significant of a method to reach the American woman as they had been a century earlier. A 1997 ad for Magazine Publishers of America proudly presented the key findings of a current media research report: "We submit that when you measure magazines against TV on almost any basis—reach, cost, effectiveness, connecting with customer—magazines make a very, very powerful argument."[28] Advertisers agreed, and the number of ad pages in magazines continued to swell so that by 1998, double-digit gains over the previous year were posted by *Good Housekeeping* (16 percent), *Ladies' Home Journal* (21 percent), and *Family Circle* (29 percent).[29] The September 1998 fashion issues of *Vogue, Elle,* and *Harper's Bazaar* contained almost one thousand combined pages of niche advertising for the health, beauty, and fashion industries. The advertising tide for magazines had continued to surge, and marketers continued to reach their primary target, women, in partnership with the publications.

─Chapter 2

THE
ADVERTISING
BARRAGE

Communicating to the woman consumer in print: the immediacy of newspapers, the directness of direct mail, and the ubiquity of signs • Delivering the message on radio and television • Marketing to women in cyberspace

All through the twentieth century, advertising in mass-circulation magazines offered enormous opportunities to manufacturers, distributors, and retailers to reach women as a captive audience. Magazines were far more likely to be kept in the home than any other vehicle used for advertising. Recipes, fashion ideas, beauty tips, serial stories, medical reports, child-care recommendations, and similar topics of interest to women ensured a long life of the periodical in the consumer's hands. "Advertiser messages thus have exposure over the period of time during which repeat reading of individual issues occurs," advised media planner William Weilbacher.[1] Advertisers could expect their ads to be seen repeatedly and read thoroughly as readers revisited issues.

One key method magazines used to draw the attention of potential customers for their advertisers, as well as for the publications themselves, was the cover design. Depictions of happy children, fashionable women, celebrities, furry kittens, beautiful homes, colorful flowers, and delicious foods all captured the attention of women. Arranged around a magazine stand, drug store rack, or grocery store checkout line, these covers provided significant statements of image and brand positioning for the publications. Mastheads and logos became so well known that some magazines allowed cover designers and illustrators incredible artistic license. From the 1910s into the 1940s, the creative use of type design for the mastheads of *Vogue, McCall's,* and *Vanity Fair* became itself a hallmark of style for these publications.

Figure 2-1. The creative use of type for magazine mastheads such as those by *Vogue, Vanity Fair,* and *McCall's* was an integral part of each publication's image and brand positioning. *Vogue* covers 1920s–40s (details).

(Figure 2-1.) On the other hand, the size and placement of the masthead for the *Saturday Evening Post* was so consistent decade after decade that even when nearly obscured by an illustration, the masthead was instantly recognizable by its remaining portion. (Figure 2-2.)

Yet, magazines were but one vehicle for advertisers to reach their target customers. By the beginning of the twentieth century, manufacturers and retailers were afforded a huge variety of other methods to get their advertising messages before women consumers.

Newspaper, Direct Mail, and Collateral Print Media

One of the earliest forms of mass communication in print that was used by advertisers was the newspaper. (Figure 2-3.) Inventories of merchandise were fluid and finite, and sale events were of limited duration, so exploiting the flexibility of a newspaper's daily run proved ideal for grocery stores, department stores, specialty retailers, and service providers. From the start, newspaper advertising was primarily reactive. A merchant could respond quickly to inventory levels, weather, merchandise shipments, fashion changes, and other ephemeral impacts on business. For example, an early autumn cold snap might prompt a clothing merchant to have a preseason coat sale for which a newspaper ad could be produced and in customers' hands within twenty-four hours in most cases.

With the advent of the advertising supplement, retailers could pack even more time-sensitive promotional material into a newspaper. By the 1950s, Sunday editions of big-city newspapers could be 90 percent advertising material by bulk. Retail insertions around key holidays could include one hundred pages or more each and might vary in size from quarter tabloids to full broadsheet sectionals. This meant massive amounts of advertising linage went into American homes each week.

The primary problem with newspaper advertising, though, was circulation. City newspapers were local publications for local consumers. Few had national prominence, and those that did did not carry a wide readership of women. Even by the 1990s, newspapers with extensive lists of mail subscribers, such as the *New York Times* and the *Washington Post,* contained ads that were almost exclusively local.

The kind of reactive hard-sell advertising that newspapers made possible and the proactive image positioning that magazines provided could be combined effectively in one of the most successful methods of advertising to emerge from the nineteenth century: direct mail. The contents of direct mail pieces were usually time sensitive, but with less urgency than would be found in newspaper ads; a direct mail offer might be valid for several weeks or even

Figure 2-2. The banner for the *Saturday Evening Post* was so recognizable that cover illustrations could virtually obscure the name and yet it was still instantly recognized. February 25, 1933, issue.

Figure 2-3. The newspaper was one of the earliest forms of mass communication in print to be extensively used by advertisers. Full page of ads from the *Pennsylvania Packet,* July 11, 1782.

months. As with magazines, many direct mail pieces, particularly catalogs, remained in the home for an extended period of time and consumers could leisurely choose when to buy.

No other advertising vehicle could more personally target a mass group of customers than direct mail. As early as the 1840s, mail lists were available to advertisers from the subscription rolls of dozens of periodical titles. By the end of the twentieth century, computer databases of mail lists were so sophisticated that potential customers could be targeted by age, geography, profession, income, marital status, clothing size, and even favorite color. A whole industry of marketing and list management services became available to any business wishing to target specific groups of consumers with direct mail.

The postal service was an obliging partner with direct mailers from the start. The postal reform acts of 1845 had created a discounted rate for any printed matter that did not include written correspondence.[2] (Figure 2-4.) As a result, direct mail had become a widely used and powerful form of advertising by the end of the nineteenth century. Variations of the medium ranged from simple postcards and circulars to illustrated envelopes stuffed with multiple pieces of advertising to the mammoth catalogs produced annually by major retailers.

The first mass-market catalog company was started in 1872 by Aaron Montgomery Ward. (Figure 2-5.) Ward had two objectives: to reach a broader base of customers than localized retailers could, and to eliminate wholesale middlemen, which would allow him to sell goods at lower prices. The marketing concept was so successful that just a decade later the Montgomery Ward catalog listed nearly ten thousand items. In addition, at a time when advertising promises were often suspect, Ward's offered a money-back guarantee.

A number of catalog rivals to Ward's, such as Sears, Penney's, and Wanamaker's, also became well-established direct marketers by the end of the nineteenth century. Their core product catalogs, known popularly as "wish books," usually were produced annually. Smaller, more specialized supplements would be mailed throughout the year, which afforded retailers greater flexibility in marketing seasonal goods such as ready-to-wear or merchandise used in home maintenance, gardening, and yard care. (Figure 2-6.)

Besides magazines, newspapers, and direct mail, numerous other forms of advertising print materials made their way into the home. A 1928 ad for

1900

Figure 2-6. Even before catalogs were off the presses, direct marketers advertised for women to write in for copies of the latest editions.

1901

1910

1919

1917

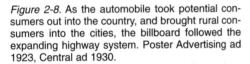

Figure 2-7. Flyers, booklets, folders, brochures, and other forms of print material were sent home with women shoppers or inserted into delivery parcels. Ad 1928.

Warren's Papers encouraged both advertisers and retailers to provide plenty of sales promotion materials to send home with women shoppers. All those flyers, booklets, folders, and brochures (printed on good paper, of course) would "keep alive your interest in her dream," the ad copy assured. (Figure 2-7.)

Despite the success of all these forms of advertising in reaching women in their homes, marketers looked for ways of getting their messages before consumers when they ventured outside their front doors. Certainly the oldest form of print advertising is the sign. In ancient times, stories of the gods were depicted on the walls of temples to educate the illiterate masses. State use of signs for propaganda and public relations in most ancient civilizations is evident still on the carved walls of many surviving public buildings. Commercial application of this effective method of communicating to the public was not far behind. In Pompeii, for example, many exterior business signs have survived, including representations of grapes that once directed travelers to a tavern, sheaves of wheat that advertised a bakery, and a row of hams designating a butcher shop.[3] Throughout the centuries, the sign has continued to be one of the most ubiquitous forms of mass communication to the public.

By the 1860s, municipalities began to regulate the use of public spaces for the posting of signs and advertisements. Community ordinances were passed to prevent midnight billposters from blanketing public buildings and parks with advertising materials. Once such legislation was enacted, not only did advertisers run the risk of having their expensive posters and signs removed, they also faced fines and criminal penalties for their illegally posted ads. To limit and better control the use of public spaces for signs and billposting, municipalities granted leases for these spaces to advertising jobbers—the precursor to ad agency media buyers. These advertising salesmen assumed the responsibility for controlling and maintaining the installation of advertisers'

Figure 2-8. As the automobile took potential consumers out into the country, and brought rural consumers into the cities, the billboard followed the expanding highway system. Poster Advertising ad 1923, Central ad 1930.

Figure 2-9. As railroads and roadways extended across the nation, outdoor advertising followed. Exposed boulders, promontories, fences, and barns were prime sites for advertising. Barn roof 1997.

posters, signs, and handbills in authorized areas—although the occasional urban construction site fence or rural oak tree remained fair game for free posting.

As an extension of billposting, freestanding billboards became a significant part of outdoor advertising. (Figure 2-8.) Soon after the Civil War, billboards were lining train routes across the country. Later, when automobiles began to take potential consumers into the countryside or bring rural consumers into the city, billboards began to follow roadways.

Advertising jobbers also contracted space on streetcars, inside and out. Initially, these spaces were sold for local use by local advertisers, but by the 1880s national marketers had discovered streetcars to be the source of yet another captive audience of consumers. Eventually, car cards made the transition to city bus racks and exterior panels. By the end of the 1990s, entire public transportation vehicles, including the windows, could be wrapped in giant ads made of vinyl sheets that appeared opaque from the outside but were transparent from within.

Another method of outdoor advertising that originated in the nineteenth century and continued into the twentieth was the painting of promotional messages directly onto exposed boulders, promontories, barns, fences, and even riverboats. Wherever a traffic pattern might provide an advertiser with an audience, the most visible sites would be sought for placements of ad messages. One enduring example is the painted barn-roof sign used by Rock City, a theme park in Chattanooga, Tennessee. (Figure 2-9.) Beginning in the 1930s, the roofs and sides of barns along highways in fifteen states were painted with simple variations of the slogan "See Rock City."[4] The company was still maintaining a number of barn roofs at the end of the century.

As a form of outdoor advertising, the front window display of a store achieved a dual purpose by promoting the featured merchandise and enticing the customer into the establishment. Department stores hired in-house trimmers to keep windows fresh and inviting to prospective customers passing by on the street. Manufacturers and distributors sent display designers into the field to train retailers to effectively exhibit their products. Many other marketers sent colorful window cards, three-dimensional die-cuts, and point-of-sale fixtures to stores with instructions on how best to arrange the displays. (Figure 2-10.)

The use of visual merchandising as a marketing tool became so highly developed that by the 1890s practitioners had their own periodical, *Show*

Figure 2-10. Manufacturers began to provide point-of-sale displays to merchants in the nineteenth century. Visual merchandising evolved into an integral part of marketing for both the manufacturer and the retailer. Johnson's Wax ad 1925, Coke ad 1955.

Window, which was founded and edited by Frank Baum before the success of his Wizard of Oz books. Eventually, almost every aspect of function, design, and esthetics was being scrutinized by visual planners to produce the most effective displays for capturing the attention of customers. In a 1934 article for *Printers' Ink,* merchandising expert Nathan Danziger wrote about the intricacies of successful displays. Using Coca-Cola as an example, he noted that the company's visual merchandisers "intimately understand the requirements of soda fountain display. Glass cases must be treated differently from marble or mahogany ones. They know what use may be made of doors, of high windows. They know the grocery retail store. They understand store layout."[5]

Even as visual merchandising evolved to achieve a superlative level of marketing sophistication, the objective never changed from its inception in ancient marketplaces. "Implicit in the gambit of window display is therefore a mandate for behavior," wrote designer Sara Schneider in 1995; "customers must undergo the kind of emotional change that makes them desire things and crave to buy them."[6]

The many varieties of advertising discussed thus far have been basically forms of print, whether a small postcard placed in the customer's hand by the post office or a huge billboard viewed from a train or automobile. Over the course of the twentieth century, variations occurred in presentation techniques, but the purpose of communicating ad messages to consumers remained constant. For instance, after electricity became more widely available and affordable, some billboards were made to flash with dazzling spectacles of neon lights or became kinetic with huge moving components. With advances in printing technology, magazines and catalogs became slick pieces of full-color art and photography printed on glossy stock and studded with eye-catching advertising inserts. In the 1990s, direct mail started arriving in homes on computer disk. Virtual storefronts on the Internet became extensions of the retailer's window displays. Despite the creative and technological innovations in print media, the advertising message still had to be viewed or read.

Broadcasting the Message on Radio

From the second quarter of the century on, a new medium presented an alternative to print advertising: broadcasting. First radio and later television faced the same dual economic fronts that magazines and newspapers had initially encountered. A mass market for the product itself—the radio set and the television set—had to be created. Then, after a sizeable listening or viewing audience had been built, the medium of broadcasting could be sold to the advertiser. As with many new consumer products, a wary public first had to be taught the benefits, and the need, of owning a radio or television set. "Is [radio] just another fad that will run its day and die out?" wondered an editorial writer for *Printers' Ink* in 1922. "Just one year ago who would have dreamed that the radio [set] would today be the subject of such widespread advertising!"[7]

However, commercial radio broadcasting in America emerged very slowly following World War I. Although wireless transmission had been invented by Guglielmo Marconi in 1901, its applications had been primarily for military or shipping communications station-to-station. In 1915, wireless technology advanced to the next phase by replacing the transmission of dots and dashes with that of voice, and radio was born.

The presentation of early radio programming was the domain of exclusive sponsors. Some radio stations even were owned by businesses that had a vested interest in selling radio sets or components, and their frequency call letters were acronyms of the company names. Examples included WGBS in New York, owned by Gimbel Brothers' Stores, and WGEC in Schenectady, owned by the General Electric Company.[8]

Surprisingly, even into the late 1920s, program sponsorship seemed to be the most acceptable approach to advertising on radio. The difference between the concept of broadcast advertising and print advertising at this time was a perception of intrusion into the home. Whereas a magazine or newspaper could be hidden from children or sensitive members of the family, and objectionable direct mail or other promotional materials could be whisked away to the rubbish bin, a medium as instantaneous as broadcasting did not permit any preview screening. Well into the 1920s, trade and business publications rejected radio as an advertising medium for just this reason. "The family circle is not a public place, and advertising has no business intruding there unless it is invited," one trade journal writer avowed.[9] Even after radio commercials became commonplace, public protests continued. In 1935, *Printers' Ink* cited results from a survey "to improve radio" that was published in the *Annals of the American Academy of Political and Social Science*. Of those surveyed, 92 percent wished to "exclude all programs advertising products such as laxatives, cures for skin diseases, and other bodily disorders unsuited for dinnertime conversation."[10]

In the same year as the academy's survey, the Women's National Radio Committee was formed "to serve as the link between the radio and organized womanhood." Among the committee's recommendations was the elimination of certain kinds of commercials altogether, such as those for laxatives. It also suggested a toning down of the "ballyhoo" and "high pressure salesmanship" used in commercials, and even recommended cutting out half the

1922   1922

1924

1926

Figure 2-11. Throughout much of the 1920s, a radio was an expensive luxury item. Such high-end goods became available to more consumers with the widely available installment credit plans.

commercials usually aired because "they are superfluous, as the program itself sells the product by creating goodwill."[11] Upon reading the committee's recommendation, one critic wrote, "It has a definite place in any civic plan, but it is questionable how much value it is to advertising."[12]

Besides resistance by many marketers on the grounds of intrusiveness, radio as a medium for advertising to a mass market was also discouraged by the limited audience. As with the first automobiles, radios in the early 1920s were toys of the affluent. A deluxe model with loudspeaker could cost more than two hundred dollars at a time when Ford paid workers a high-end wage of five dollars a day. Radio technology improved rapidly, though, and mass production eventually brought down the cost of sets. As the number of broadcasting stations proliferated, and programming hours and variety expanded, radio purchases skyrocketed. Mass consumption of home radios was additionally aided by retail credit programs. As with cars and other high-end goods, installment contracts allowed greater numbers of consumers with modest levels of income to buy now and pay later.

Because of the limited use of broadcasting as a viable advertising medium and the limited number of home-owned radios, women were not specifically depicted in ads as target radio listeners until the 1930s. Instead, women shown in radio ads of the early 1920s usually were listening participants with the family or party crowd. (Figure 2-11.) Even in a 1924 Atwater Kent ad showing a solitary woman, she is dressed in an evening frock and holds back draperies over a doorway that the viewer presumes leads to a room full of party guests or family who are listening to the broadcast.

Despite the widespread calls to keep radio programming genteel and limited in its use of advertising, the first steps toward spot commercials were taken and the results tested in the late 1920s. Early experiments with ad script formats led to the interwoven commercial, which combined advertising messages in a style that was compatible with the character of the program. For

instance, a musical variety show may have included the star singing a sponsor's jingle, or a talk show may have included a short discussion of the sponsor's products with the guests or members of the audience. Similarly, in a minidrama commercial the program's fictitious characters would discuss the sponsor's products as part of the continuing storyline.

In addition to interwoven ads and minidramas, crooners such as Rudy Vallee and Bing Crosby were scripted with introductions to sponsors' products on their programs. Those items then became associated with the stars in the minds of consumers, especially when the radio commercials were followed by endorsement ads in print. Such product endorsements by popular entertainers—or most any other celebrity—had precedents from the nineteenth century, such as when the famous stage actress Lillian Russell appeared in ads for Recamier cosmetics and the legendary Sarah Bernhardt in ads for Pear's Soap.[13] Later, Hollywood studios exploited this method of

Figure 2-12. Radio programs initially were produced in conjunction with sponsorships. Program stars and fictional characters became linked to sponsors' products in the listeners' minds. This connection was reinforced in sponsors' print ads that also listed program schedules and information. (Details of ads.)

Every Day
MILLIONS of WOMEN LISTEN
while one man talks

NATIONAL BROADCASTING COMPANY, Inc.
A RADIO CORPORATION OF AMERICA SUBSIDIARY · NEW YORK, CHICAGO, SAN FRANCISCO

Figure 2-13. In the 1930s, radio programming expanded into daytime hours with home shows and the first soap operas specifically produced for a female audience. Ad 1933.

publicity for their stars and films, so the format was comfortably recognized by the consumer. Besides, many of these ads afforded the public a glimpse at the faces that belonged to the familiar voices they listened to week after week. To take advantage of the double advertising opportunity of combining broadcasting and print, many advertisers also started including radio program information in their print ads. (Figure 2-12.)

As programming began to more specifically target a female audience, especially with the advent of the first soap operas in 1933, broadcasters began to focus on women as their marketing target as well. Figure 2-13 shows a typical promotional ad run by broadcasters in business periodicals of the 1930s. For the ad, NBC staged a photograph showing a Happy Homemaker listening to a radio program while doing housework. Although the message was obvious in the illustration, the point was reinforced with a header in caps declaring that "every day millions of women listen." Advertisers quickly got over any sensitivity to the intrusion factor.

In spite of the efforts of the Women's National Radio Committee to raise the cultural standards of radio programming and commercials, millions of women did indeed tune in daily to hear what the committee referred to as "the lowest common denominator . . . bootleg material for the person who is interested in racy stories."[14] These typical women listeners, as Roy Durstine wrote in a 1935 trade publication, received a daily dose of commercials that created "a glamourous land of make-believe in which forlorn maidens are told that they will win a husband by the use of a certain soap or face powder . . . in which the lures of beauty and success are held out to a public that does not accept them wholeheartedly but wants to try them anyway, just in case they might work. It fattens upon a certain state of mind comparable to the way in which most people approach a fortune teller or a reader of horoscopes. They don't quite believe it but aren't quite willing to disbelieve it."[15]

Advertisers certainly counted on this to be true.

Delivering the Message on Television

During the same time that radio as an industry was struggling with its technological growth and moral dilemmas about intrusive programming and advertising, the development of television was well under way. In the late 1920s, experimental television stations were established in most industrialized nations of the world, including the United States, Britain, Germany, France, and Japan. Just as with early radio, television technology evolved slowly, with the first sporadic attempts at programming in the U.S. occurring in the late 1930s. In July 1941, after much debate and committee analysis, the Federal Communications Commission officially set the common technical standards for the television industry and two networks were launched from the status of experimental to commercial television broadcasters: the National Broadcasting Company (NBC) and the Columbia Broadcasting Company (CBS).[16]

With only ten to fifteen hours of programming a week being aired in the months before the bombing of Pearl Harbor, there was no great consumer rush to purchase television sets. Also, as had been the case with early radio sets, cost was a significant factor. TV models exhibited at the New York World's Fair in 1940 were priced between $200 and $660.[17] A good radio

Figure 2-14. Before World War II, a television set could cost as much as a new car. Used as a prop in this 1940 ad for Fisher manufacturing, the television set conveyed a sense of modernity and luxury.

cost less than $20 by then. In addition, early television sets were radiation hazards, and images could only be projected vertically onto a tilted mirror, which then reflected them horizontally for the viewer. (Figure 2-14.)

The most serious impediment to the development of home entertainment television was World War II. In Britain, the British Broadcasting Corporation (BBC) abruptly shut down on September 1, 1939—the day Britain declared war on Nazi Germany—to prevent German pilots from using the broadcasts to gauge their bearings. When the U.S. entered the war, most broadcasting technicians and engineers went off to aid in the war effort, as they had in Britain, and electronics manufacturers converted their plants to wartime production. With no more televisions being produced after 1941, and as a result, no audience, American television virtually petered out for the duration.

Still, electronics manufacturers continued to keep alive the idea of television and its potential impact on a postwar America in their advertising. In a 1943 ad, General Electric promised to be at the forefront of television production after the war. (Figure 2-15.) The copy suggested that besides making the home "a window on the world," television would provide businessmen with a new opportunity for advertising. "Not only will you tell the public about your product, as you do now by radio, you will show the public the actual product, package and all."

As the war wound to its conclusion in 1945, electronic equipment manufacturers began to plan for television production again. A month after Germany's surrender, Belmont Radio ran ads in popular magazines declaring that it would be "out front" in television technology. (Figure 2-16.) Indeed, great strides were made in television research and development through the late 1940s, with RCA performing the first color television experiments in 1946.[18] Advancements included replacing the monstrous sizes of prewar sets with more compact console and table models. Screen sizes more than doubled from the miniature five- to nine-inch models to RCA's sixteen-inch version. Most significantly, the cost of a well-equipped TV set dropped to less than two hundred dollars. (Figure 2-17.)

Unlike early ads for radio sets, the ads produced by TV manufacturers specifically targeted women consumers from the start. In a 1940 Fisher Body ad, the illustration told the reader that the woman of taste and fashion would be a television viewer. In a 1943 General Electric ad, the little girl calls to her mother to come see the circus on TV—planting the seed for consumers to regard the TV as a surrogate babysitter. In a 1945 Belmont ad, an affluent woman is depicted as the viewer—wearing her gold wristwatch and high heels and gracefully sitting with her well-manicured hands clasped before her.

Just as gramophone manufacturers had done at the end of the nineteenth century, and radio manufacturers had done in the 1920s, television manufacturers recognized that women were the arbiters of culture in the home. They also knew that women held the persuasive powers of purchase for

Figure 2-15. The technological and production needs of World War II interrupted the progress of television as a mass medium. Nevertheless, electronics manufacturers periodically reminded consumers of the future of television. Ad 1943.

Figure 2-16. When World War II ended, electronics manufacturers used their war research to resume production of television sets. Teaser ads put the idea of home television entertainment back in front of the consumer. Ad 1945.

Figure 2-17. By the end of the 1940s, advances in television technology had increased screen sizes and reduced retail prices of TV sets. Ad 1949.

these high-end items. Ads for TV sets of the early 1950s carried through the image of their target customer from a decade before. These later ads still showed affluent households. Carefully coifed and fashionably dressed women posed with the product like showroom mannequins. Typical of these TV product ads was the superbly subtle example produced by Admiral in 1953. (Figure 2-18.) Not only is a large part of the ad space devoted to showing a beautiful, fashionable woman, but the lead copy block describes the cabinet's looks and styling. In the same vein, the images on the TV screens are women oriented: fashion, glamour, romance. The more pedantic aspects of the product—performance and value—are specified in copy blocks at the bottom of the page as a footnote in case the husband needs further persuasion.

By 1950, barely 9 percent of American households had a TV set; by the end of the 1990s, more than 98 percent of American households had at least one.[19] During the postwar years, two primary factors deterred any rush to purchase home television sets on a national scale. First was limited broadcast availability. In 1950, only 109 commercial television stations were scattered across thirty-three states.[20] Second was the quality of programming. In 1947, *Life* examined the status of the new medium with an article titled "Television, It Is a Commercial Reality but Not Yet an Art." Using the quality of television news and sportscasts as the benchmark of the industry's excellence, the critic wrote: "If all its programs were up to this high standard, then the promise of a wonderful invention would be realized. They are not. Between [news and sportscasts] and almost all other programs yawns a fearful gulf. Television . . . has cruelly disinterred some of the hoariest acts in vaudeville. It has concentrated on its screens some of the worst aspects of radio."[21]

The networks quickly began to heed the many calls for improvement in programming quality and encouraged creative experimentation and innovation from program producers. Critically acclaimed radio programs such as *Inner Sanctum, Dragnet,* and Jackie Gleason's *Life of Riley* made the transition to TV. *Kraft Television Theater* and *Philco-Goodyear Playhouse* presented outstanding original dramas. Early comedies such as *I Love Lucy* were so superbly performed that episodes were still being rerun at the end of the century. Historians would mark this period of broadcasting originality and creativity as the "golden age" of television.[22]

Daytime programming for women emerged only during the early 1950s after networks and local stations began to expand their broadcasting hours. The well-established formats of radio game shows, homemaker programs, and especially soap operas were easily adapted to television for daytime slots. (Figure 2-19.) The huge, female listening audiences that had avidly followed such radio programs during the 1930s and 1940s were comfortably receptive to the television versions.

All through the 1950s and 1960s, both daytime and prime-time TV programming helped perpetuate the image and role of the Happy Homemaker. Lead female characters in such popular programs as *The Donna Reed Show* and *The Adventures of Ozzie and Harriet* demonstrated weekly how the ideal American housewife should look and behave. This post–World War II generation of women existed "in a TV-shaped dreamscape of suburban patios and family dens," wrote Susan Faludi.[23] American women eagerly looked to

1953 1955 1957

Figure 2-18. Television manufacturers knew that women held the persuasive powers of purchase for big-ticket home items. Ads for television sets especially emphasized cabinet styling and entertainment for women.

this televised "public image to decide every detail of their lives," observed Betty Friedan at the time. These TV programs, with their archetypal female characters, were the "textbooks" for a generation of American women.[24]

In the same year that Betty Friedan blasted the myths of the American woman, ads for an ABC affiliate told advertisers that they had the best network programming with which to reach all those Donnas and Harriets. (Figure 2-20.) Far from the idealized beauty of Donna Reed or the fastidiousness of Harriet Nelson, the model in one ad depicting Friedan's "textbook" housewife wore house slippers, rolled jeans, and a pullover with the sleeves shoved up (but still clutched a house-cleaning implement). She had just relaxed into a chair for her 10 A.M. coffee break and was ready to hear the advertisers' pitches for whiter laundry and tastier meals.

As television programming for women increased, manufacturers and distributors began to move more advertising dollars into television broadcasting. (Figure 2-21.) In the 1954 *Printers' Ink Annual,* A. C. Nielson and the J. Walter Thompson Agency profiled the top 162 U.S. TV markets. Gross network billings for advertising were up from $12 million in 1949 to an astounding $180 million through 1952. The number of estimated "TV sets in use" between 9 A.M. and 3 P.M. was more than 5 million.[25]

Throughout the 1950s, the TV ad pitch to the American housewife was made primarily through sponsorship. (Figure 2-22.) Many program titles even incorporated sponsors' names such as the *Colgate Comedy Hour, Gillette Cavalcade of Sports, Philco TV Playhouse, U.S. Steel Hour,* and *Texaco Star Theater* (Milton Berle's variety show). Advertisers exercised nearly complete control of the programs they sponsored—approving everything from set designs to scripts. Examples of egregious abuse of the sponsor's authority abound in the annals of television history. For example, in 1953 Westinghouse had Kipling's *The Light That Failed* presented under the title *The Gathering Light* because a company division manufactured light bulbs. An even worse incident occurred two years later when the American Gas Association sponsored *Judgment at Nuremberg,* during which an audio engineer deleted the word "gas" every time it was spoken, even though viewers could still clearly read the actors' lips.[26]

The sponsors' power and control over program production remained absolute until the quiz show scandals of 1959. Congressional hearings and Justice Department investigations revealed the widespread practice of game show producers' providing answers to selected contestants. Viewers were outraged by the scandals and lost faith in the integrity of television. As a result, widely advertised products and well-established brand names were tarnished by association. Numerous programs were quickly canceled as networks and advertisers scrambled for damage control.

For the networks, this meant finally being able to wrest control of the programs from the sponsors and to put into place the magazine concept of selling advertising. That is, networks would sell ad time the way magazines sold ad space. Just as magazines maintained control of editorial—or so TV executives thought—so too could networks control the production of their programs. For the remainder of the twentieth century, this was the industry process.

However, advertisers maintained a powerful influence over the networks, even if they could no longer design the sets or strike words from scripts at will. A network could find itself unable to sell time for controversial programming, having instead to resort to public service announcements and self-promotional spots or discounted rates. During the 1997–98 season, ABC found itself facing controversies with three programs involving sex, religion, violence, and language. The police drama *NYPD Blue* had presented numerous episodes with nudity, violence, and strong language; the lead

Figure 2-19. Daytime television programming for women was easily adapted from well-established radio formats. Homemaker programs, game shows, talk shows, and soap operas have filled the daytime schedules of networks since the early 1950s.

1954

1955

1973

Figure 2-20. TV programs with their archetypal female consumer characters were the "textbooks" for a generation of American women, Betty Friedan wrote in her 1963 best-seller, *The Feminine Mystique.* Ad 1963.

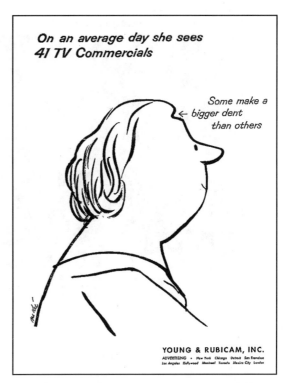

Figure 2-21. Between 1949 and 1952, gross TV network billings for advertising leapt from $12 million to $180 million. Ad 1954.

character in the sitcom *Ellen* was openly gay; and *Nothing Sacred* featured a priest who questioned church doctrine. Advertisers such as Isuzu Motors, Weight Watchers, Red Lobster, and Kmart pulled ads in a panic-stricken reaction to noises from conservative groups.[27]

Despite some steps backward, television often led society forward in presenting social trends and differing perspectives of modern women. A generation before *Ellen, The Mary Tyler Moore Show* had opened the door on a new type of American woman—a single, never-married career woman in her thirties with no inclinations toward a family. This new image of the American woman was much more of a reality than most people realized at the time. According to U.S. Census records, only 34 percent of the adult female population worked full time outside the home in 1960, but that number had climbed to 41 percent a decade later. The percentage of working women continued to increase dramatically during the last quarter of the century, rising to 57 percent by 1990.[28]

The career woman was "where the money is," said a 1997 CBS ad. (Figure 2-23.) The photograph showed a woman of confidence and obvious success; above her head was listed her annual salary: $85,000. On the facing page was shown, presumably, the target customer for cable TV and "fringe" networks—a disheveled teenager who earned $5.75 an hour. The succinct comparison was compelling to marketers.

Figure 2-22. Throughout the 1950s, television advertising was produced by sponsorships. After the quiz show scandals of 1959, networks were able to sell spots for whichever program they wished, much as magazines sold ad space. Ad 1953.

Figure 2-23. With 60 percent of American women in the work force by the end of the 1990s, advertisers targeted a different female consumer from that of a generation earlier. Ad 1997.

Targeting Women in Cyberspace

Another place for advertisers to reach the career woman of the 1990s was on the Internet. Devised during the cold war years of the 1960s as a defense against the possible interruption of communications in the event of a war, the Internet became a global network of computers, phone lines, and satellite links. Initially, it was the domain of "netheads"—mostly teenage boys exploring chat rooms and playing videogames. The percent of women online—that is, connected to the Internet by a service provider—was too negligible to interest many advertisers even into the late 1990s. An *Adweek* writer noted in 1997: "There isn't enough reach among the demographic groups major advertisers want. The lack of bandwidth and slow modem speeds at home greatly limit the animation capabilities of most online ads. Most Web sites have poor or negligible measurement systems in place to track users. Production headaches abound."[29]

Besides the slowness of modems and limited image capabilities of online ads, security also was an issue. Despite sophisticated programs for buying online by credit card, breaches of security were common. Horror stories about the theft of credit card numbers abounded in the press. In January 2000, an unknown hacker broke into the database of a popular online music store and seized three hundred thousand credit card numbers as part of a blackmail scheme. When the company refused to pay for the return of the credit files, twenty-five thousand card numbers were posted on the Web. Banks and credit card issuers had to scramble to cancel card numbers, contact cardholders, and issue new cards.[30]

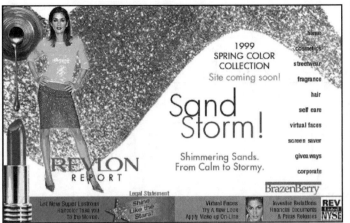 

Nevertheless, computer-literate career women did comprise a significant segment of the upper-income women's market in the 1990s, and Web site providers began to position themselves as the gateway to these consumers. (Figure 2-24.) "She's smart. Sexy. Successful. And spending money everywhere," the opening copy read in a Thrive Web site ad. For women on the Web, "we've captured their attention," a Home Arts Network ad promised advertisers in 1997; "shouldn't they see your ad message too?"[31] Candice Carpenter, chief executive officer of the women's-interest site iVillage, told *Advertising Age* in a 1997 interview, "Whoever captures [women's] online hearts and minds early on will have a significant advantage over time."[32]

Figure 2-24. High-income, computer-literate women comprised a significant segment of the women's market by the late 1990s. Web site providers created virtual storefronts for retailers and distributors to reach these women on their office or home computers. Web sites 1999.

Conclusion: Getting the Message Out

Marketers have continually poured billions of dollars into methods for communicating their sales messages to consumers. Magazines provided advertisers with opportunities for brand positioning and company enhancement, since back issues often were kept and revisited by readers. Newspapers created a sense of urgency with consumers and offered an immediacy perfectly suited to retail advertising. Direct mail evolved to include an array of ways to interest prospective customers—from response coupons, product samples, and bonus gifts to entire stores in the form of catalogs. Signs were everywhere and in every imaginable dimension and configuration, some even animated with flashing lights or moving components. Radio and television brought ad messages to life with a directness and intimacy that was unavoidable for consumers. In fact, advertisers exploited just about every conceivable method and vehicle possible to get their marketing messages to their target customers.

For the overwhelming majority of marketers, the target they sought to reach most was the American woman. From the product packaging stacked in her kitchen cupboards to the magazines and newspapers in her parlor, from outdoor billboards and posters to point-of-sale displays in stores, the American woman of 1900 was influenced every day by advertising. By the end of the century, her great-great-granddaughter was even more influenced by advertising, from the television in her bedroom to the radio in her car, from the direct mail pieces on her office desk to the Internet on her home computer.

—Chapter 3

HOME, HEARTH,
AND
HOUSEKEEPING

Marketing new ideas and new ways of homemaking • The evolution of consumerism and technology in the kitchen • Easing the labor of laundry and housework • Cooking, canned goods and processed foods • Consumption and housecleaning

American women of all classes historically have shared one particular common denominator: cooking. Prior to the second quarter of the nineteenth century when mass-produced cast iron and steel stoves were more available nationwide, cooking was a labor-intensive chore done on an open fire in a fireplace. Wood or coal had to be hauled into the house, and ashes removed daily. Worse was the limited variety of food that could be cooked by this method. Kettles of stews or soups were easy enough, but the art of banking fires over Dutch ovens or piles of bricks or stones for baking took considerable experience. Likewise, choosing the types of wood that burned hotter or longer and then arranging the fuels for consistent fires required great skill. Even when successful, though, early American cooking was regarded with disdain both at home and abroad. English novelist Frederick Marryat wrote in the early nineteenth century that there were "plenty of good things for the table in America; but 'God sends meat, and the devil sends cooks.'"[1]

Figure 3-1. Selling for as little as five dollars—freight paid—the freestanding cast iron stove provided greater control and versatility in cooking than did the open hearth. Majestic ad 1900, Magee ad 1901.

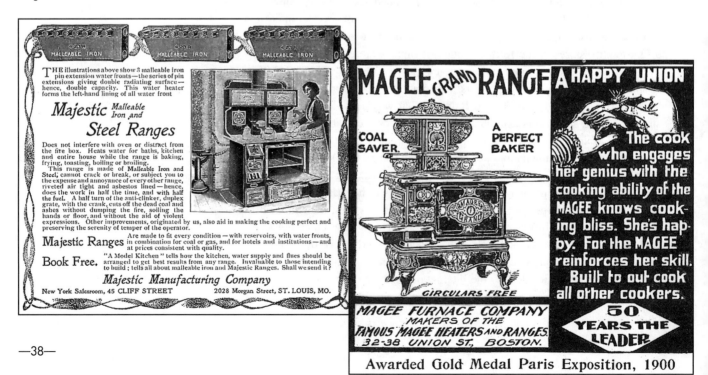

Echoing Marryat's assessment of American cuisine, Count de Volney wrote in 1804: "In the morning at breakfast they deluge their stomachs with a quart of hot water, impregnated with tea, or so slightly with coffee that it is more colored water; and they swallow, almost without chewing, hot bread, half baked, toast soaked in butter, cheese of the fattest kind, slices of salt or hung beef, ham, etc. . . . at dinner they have boiled pastes under the name of puddings, and their sauces, even for roast beef, are melted butter; their turnips and potatoes swim in hog's lard, butter, or fat; under the name of pie or pumpkin, their pastry is nothing but a greasy paste, never sufficiently baked."[2]

New Appliances in the Kitchen

The mass production of the freestanding cast iron stove in the 1830s made greater control and versatility in cooking possible. Still, the work was as laborious and time-consuming as on the open hearth, if not more so. "The stove . . . augured the death of one-pot cooking or, rather, of one-dish meals—and, in so doing, probably increased the amount of time women spent in preparing foodstuffs," wrote Ruth Cowan in *More Work for Mother*. "The diet of average Americans may well have been more varied during the nineteenth century, but in the process women's activities became less varied as their cooking chores became more complex."[3] Just as the colonial housewife had to know how to build and bank open-hearth fires for cooking, the nineteenth-century housewife had to know how to regulate the dampers of her stove and how to position cookware in and around the firebox to simmer, boil, and bake simultaneously.

In addition, the affordability and availability of mass-produced cast iron stoves made it possible for families even on remote farms and in poor city tenements to have reliable kitchen stoves. Many models sold for as little as five dollars, freight paid. (Figure 3-1.)

For all its benefits, the cast iron stove required constant maintenance. Untended fires cooled or went out. Coal or wood still had to be hauled in and ashes had to be hauled out. In addition, blacking had to be applied weekly to prevent rusting—an exceptional chore for those women who had chosen a stove model with all-over high relief or open fretwork ornamentation.

Another problem with cast iron stoves was inflexibility. During the summer, stoves were not usually kept burning. That meant either eating cold meals or suffering from the heat to build a fire. The solution came easily enough with oil- and gas-burning stoves. (Figure 3-2.) In a 1909 ad for the New Perfection Cook-Stove, the next great leap

Figure 3-2. The next great leap in cooking convenience was the on/off stove switch. Oil and gas ranges reduced the labor of cooking by eliminating the need to haul coal or wood, build and maintain fires, and remove ashes. Ad 1909.

Figure 3-3. Although electric ranges were widely advertised before World War I, the limited availability and high cost of electricity prior to the 1930s deterred sales. GE ad 1915, Florence ad 1923.

in cooking convenience is illustrated: the on/off switch, providing a cook-fire instantly, anytime. Ironically, the convenient, clean-burning gas/oil stove was not new to the twentieth century. It had been demonstrated at industrial expositions in the 1850s and advertised extensively throughout the last quarter of the nineteenth century. Yet, of fifteen pages listing cook-stoves in the massive Sears catalog of 1902, only eight models were for oil or gas; all others were wood- or coal-burning stoves. In his book on house-hold technology, Daniel Cohen cited two reasons for consumers' resistance to the gas/oil stove for so long. Wood and coal were much cheaper fuels than gas or oil; in addition, the manufacturers of oil/gas stoves did not understand the psychology of the human experience with food. "People who had grown up with food cooked with wood or coal fuel felt that gas-cooked food somehow 'tasted different,' or they worried obscurely that the food would not be properly cooked and would therefore be unhealthful."[4] Eventually, persistent advertising helped the message get through to the masses, and depending on where one lived, oil- or gas-burning ranges were the best choice available even long after the first electric ranges were made.

Although electric ranges were widely advertised as early as the 1910s, electricity was unavailable to huge sections of the country until the late 1930s when the New Deal Rural Electrification program was implemented. (Figure 3-3.) As Christine Frederick wrote in her 1913 book *The New Housekeeping:* "I am enthusiastic in favor of electric equipment, but from observation I have found it is, as yet, too expensive to supplant hand power in the operations of devices in the home. It is also true that while city dwellers have come to believe in the prevalence of the electric button, electricity is in use by only a fraction of our population."[5]

For decades, gas and oil range manufacturers continued to drive home the comparative cost issue in their advertising. Oil was "the most inexpensive fuel," a 1924 Florence oil range ad stated succinctly. A list of electric appliances sold by the New York Edison Company in 1925, with the cost of operation per hour, included:

vacuum cleaner. . . . . 1¢
washing machine . . . . 2¢
sewing machine . . . . 1/2¢
stove. . . . . 5¢
toaster. . . . . 3¢
waffle iron . . . . 5¢[6]

Added together, operating an electric home could be an expensive under-taking, so it was hardly surprising that many Americans were wary of electricity, despite the labor-saving advantages. In their Middletown study, Robert and Helen Lynd noted that though 99 percent of the homes in their survey were wired for electricity, two-thirds cooked with gas, and most of the rest used coal and other fuels, but only "a very few electricity."[7]

Stoves such as the Florence Oil Range also were meant to be beautiful pieces of furniture—styled with cabriole legs, painted in color enamels, and accented with the sparkle of contrast metal trims. But with all the open spaces beneath and around the burners, cleaning the stove remained a considerable task. In the 1930s, the redesigned New Perfection Range minimized the cleaning chore with a cabinet style that enclosed all the components of the stove. (Figure 3-4.) Airborne grease particles and drips or splatters from cooking could easily be cleaned off the smooth, flat surfaces of porcelain enamel. By the 1940s, this concept of the enclosed range became the production model for both gas and electric ranges. With minor design enhancements over the decades, the closed box style has remained the standard ever since.

The next technological advancement in the all-purpose cookfire came with the microwave oven. (Figure 3-5.) Speed was the benefit of this new type of electric cookfire. Although developed at the end of World War II, due to the cost and size of early models only about ten thousand microwaves were sold in the United States through the 1960s, mostly to restaurants and airlines.[8] By the 1970s, manufacturers had solved the size and cost problems of microwave ovens and began mass-marketing efforts. However, sales were not brisk due to a number of reasons: microwaves needed specialized cookware, consumers had to learn new methods of preparing food for microwaving, and numerous public safety warnings kept circulating. Amana chairman Alex Meyer recalled: "The housewife didn't understand it. It was too technical for her. She didn't understand that we were stirring these molecules 2,450 times per second. She didn't understand that the friction of the molecules was the source of the heat. There are no flames. There is no calrod heater . . . it was a little scary."[9]

Figure 3-4. The closed-cabinet style of later stoves minimized the chore of cleaning components, which on earlier models were exposed to airborne grease particles and splatters from cooking. New Perfection ad 1938, General Electric ad 1948.

If all this were not enough to deter sales, early ads for microwaves depicted a product that looked disturbingly like a computer. By the 1980s, though, people were comfortable enough with so much push-button technology in the home that ads could show the Happy Homemaker at ease using her new microwave. Instead of devoting so much ad space to techno-ese copy—as was necessary with earlier versions—advertisers focused on the product's benefits in everyday language. Additionally, the microwave especially suited the fast-paced life style of many American women of the 1970s and 1980s who used the microwave to quickly heat leftovers, frozen foods, soups, beverages, and snacks.

As electricity became more widely available after World War I, manufacturers of electric appliances found ways of broadening their product lines by making the home cookfire more specialized. Implements for cooking specific foods evolved from stone, ceramic, and cast iron gadgets for the fireplace or stove into customized appliances. Simple toasted bread no longer had to be prepared on a skewer by hand and tended every second to prevent scorching. Instead, a miraculous new electric contraption held the slice of bread near a heated coil to toast it any way desired. Indeed, by the late teens, the electrified cookfire could be contained in specialized devices to brew coffee, bake waffles, or grill a beefsteak, all without ever going near a stove. (Figure 3-6.) The eager consumption of such appliances, the Lynds observed in their Middletown study, led to an average increase of 25 percent in kilowatt hours of electricity used between 1920 and 1924.[10]

Not all food had to be cooked. From the earliest times, hunters and gatherers knew that certain fruits, vegetables, roots, and other assorted plants

Figure 3-6. By the end of World War I, manufacturers broadened their product lines with a wide variety of specialized kitchen appliances. Universal ad 1917, General Electric ad 1919.

1895

1914

1926

Figure 3-7. The kitchen icebox remained a common form of home refrigeration well into the 1940s.

were edible raw. They also knew that such foodstuffs went bad, and if consumed when spoiled could result in illness or death. Some food preservation was eventually made possible by salt packing, smoking, sun baking, or, in wintertime, storing in the cold.

Prior to the Industrial Revolution, controlled refrigeration was a luxury of the wealthy. Great homes such as Thomas Jefferson's Monticello had icehouses or ice cellars used to store huge slabs of ice harvested from rivers and lakes frozen in winter. During the second and third quarters of the nineteenth century industrial inventors began to experiment with mechanical refrigerating machines, and dozens of prototypes were patented. By the 1880s, industrial refrigerators were widely in use by breweries, meat packers, railroads, and transoceanic ships. At the same time, commercial icehouses used the huge refrigerating machines to mass produce ice year round. This made possible the affordable home icebox, which was to remain a common form of home refrigeration well into the 1940s. (Figure 3-7.)

Cold that keeps

For You—This Priceless Treasure Chest

Not once upon a time, but today, every day, women are transforming their refrigerators into household treasure chests with Kelvinator—"cold that keeps"—the twentieth century magic.

Kelvinator gives dry, abundant, unfailing cold. Treasures of health come from its constant protection of food at a scientifically determined temperature—the Zone of Kelvination . . . Treasures of enjoyment in its dainty, delicious frozen salads and desserts; of

convenience in its plentiful supply of ice; of comfort in its automatic certainty of operation.

For over twelve years Kelvinators have been in continuous and satisfactory use. Telephone or visit the Kelvinator Dealer; or write us for full information. Kelvinator, 14202 Plymouth Road, Detroit, Michigan, Division of Electric Refrigeration Corporation. Kelvinator of Canada, Ltd., 1131 Dundas Street, East, London, Ontario.

Kelvinator

Oldest Domestic Electric Refrigeration

1927

It keeps your food safe
—the temperature is well below 50° always!

For family health • for appealing menus • • • this is vital

In the General Electric Refrigerator the temperature is kept several degrees below fifty . . . always! Fifty degrees is accepted by scientists as the "danger point" in the preservation of food. When the temperature rises even a degree or two above that, bacteria multiply, foods become unsafe.

Perhaps you think your own refrigerator is always "cold enough." You cannot be sure unless you actually take your refrigerator's temperature under varying conditions. It is constant cold which is needed. When you own a General Electric Refrigerator, you need never worry about temperature.

Note these vital points of superiority

Countless superiorities give the General Electric Refrigerator its outstanding position . . . an hermetically sealed, dust-proof mechanism, mounted on top . . . an accessible temperature control . . . a new standard of quiet operation . . . no oiling . . . no troublesome machinery . . . simplified installation . . . no radio interference . . . an unqualified two-year service guarantee.

Mass production brings greater savings for the public. The new all-steel General Electric Refrigerators are now priced as low as $215 at the factory. A small amount down places a General Electric in your home . . . a perfect servant . . . then you come to own it.

Visit the nearest General Electric Dealer—see these new models—you'll agree that they offer the greatest values of all . . . and any comparison will surely confirm your judgment. Or if you prefer, you may obtain the whole story of refrigeration by writing Electric Refrigeration Department of General Electric Company, Hanna Building, Cleveland, Ohio, for Booklet D-7.

Not a dollar for repairs

More than a quarter of a million homes are enjoying the convenience, economy and health-guarding service of the General Electric Refrigerator. And not one of these owners has ever paid a dollar for repairs or service . . . that was our guarantee to them. It's a record in the industry.

GENERAL ELECTRIC
ALL-STEEL REFRIGERATOR

1929

Thousands Are Alive Today . . .

because in 1914 Man First harnessed Cold!

Enteritis, or "summer complaint," was once the most feared scourge of infant life.

Yet today, for every 100 babies that formerly succumbed, 87 are safe. A great factor in this victory is Kelvinator's invention of an electric refrigerator . . . which made scientific food preservation possible at home.

Now Comes *Today's Cold-making Marvel! The Silver Jubilee Kelvinators with Amazing Polarsphere*

When, twenty-five years ago, Kelvinator gave to America the first electric refrigerator, its makers were pardonably proud.

Today, Kelvinator celebrates another history-making event . . . the presentation of the Silver Jubilee Kelvinator—perfected product of a quarter-century.

If you would know how far ahead of its time it is . . . compare it with the "modern" refrigerator of just a few years ago!

It freezes in one-third the time, costs 50% less to run, and offers you 40% more refrigeration.

Thanks to the silent Polarsphere—a miracle mechanism sealed in a gleaming steel globe—today you get 72 big ice cubes for one penny at national average electric rates! Reserve power enough for five refrigerators . . .

The sensational Polarsphere . . . the most efficient of all refrigerating units. Sealed away forever from dust and air. Never needs oil. Uses only a thrifty trickle of electricity!

with cold-making capacity equal to more than half a ton of ice per week!

Look inside. You'll find the Silver Jubilee Kelvinator has more usable room . . . though new, flexible shelf design.

Twin lights inside give you shadowless brilliance. Two large vegetable crispers are glass-topped for see-at-a-glance convenience . . . and a Cold Chest with an ideal flavor for days.

Best of all, the Silver Jubilee Kelvinator is easy to have . . . you can own it for just a few cents a day. Be sure to see these new models at once!

Kelvinator, Division of Nash-Kelvinator Corporation, Detroit, Michigan.

Silver Jubilee **KELVINATOR**

SEE THESE OTHER SILVER JUBILEE HOME APPLIANCES

1939

Figure 3-8. During the 1920s and 1930s ads for electric refrigerators emphasized the benefits of health and food safety.

YOU'LL ALWAYS BE GLAD YOU BOUGHT A GENERAL ELECTRIC

The Truth About Today's Refrigerators!

No matter what reliable make of electric refrigerator you choose today, you'll get more value for your dollars than ever before.

★ For today's good electrical refrigerators are as fine an example of mechanical perfection as human ingenuity, skill, science and experience have produced. They're more than twice as efficient as the refrigerators of ten years ago, yet cost about one-half as much—so little that almost every family can afford the best in modern refrigeration.

★ Whatever make you choose, be sure to: (1) Get a refrigerator that's big enough for your family; too many of the early purchasers have wished for more storage space. (2) Get a refrigerator that's completely equipped—for the little conveniences become very, very important multiplied

over the years of use. (3) Get a refrigerator that's made by a reputable, experienced manufacturer, for actually it costs more to the mechanical life of many automobiles. (4) Ask your neighbors, shop carefully, and get all the facts, for you won't be buying a refrigerator again very soon if you choose wisely. (5) Remember that in refrigerators as in most other things, you get what you pay for—so the best model you can afford is your best investment.

★ Naturally we'd like to see you buy a General Electric, for we believe it's the finest machine ever built. Of course, we're prejudiced—but be sure you look at a G-E before you make up your mind.

★ Maybe we build the G-E Refrigerator so well, because we have had a lot of experience as the largest builder of electrical conveniences. We do

know that we offer, in this refrigerator, features tested by time and a mechanism that's just about tops in the engineering world.

★ G-E was first with an all-steel cabinet—first with the sealed mechanism—first with many other vital improvements. Its record for low cost, dependable service is unsurpassed. And according to correct surveys it is preferred by more people than any other refrigerator! We try hard to give people their money's worth and to keep our prices low. A General Electric is priced no higher than other good refrigerators—as little as $114.95* buys a big 6-cu.-ft. model. We believe G-E actually costs less than any other refrigerator over the years!

*Listed and more more, if not additional. Prices higher (other than in the West and South. For these reasons General Electric builds.

GENERAL ELECTRIC

1941

⅓ more food space...in General Electric's 1948 Space Maker Refrigerator!

Gives you ⅓ more refrigerated food storage in the same kitchen floor space!

If you had this new wonder-refrigerator in your kitchen today, you'd be as proud of owning it as we are of making it!

For we honestly consider the 1948 Space Maker the greatest refrigerator ever to bear that symbol of fine refrigerators—the General Electric trade-mark.

Dependability—proved 1,700,000 times over!

Above all else, G. E. offers you dependable performance, day-in, day-out, month after month, year after year. Reason: the sealed-in refrigerating system, pioneered by General Electric.

Notice how the new General Electric 8-cubic-foot Space Maker fits in the same floor space as the old-style 6-cubic-foot model—yet gives you one-third more refrigerated food-storage capacity!

Important advantages in the Space Maker!

• Butter Conditioner—keeps butter at right spreading temperature.
• Big Freezing Compartment—holds 24 packages of frozen food, plus 4 ice trays.
• Deep Drawers—6 inches deep. Will hold standing roasts and more than two-thirds bushel of fruits and vegetables under refrigeration.
• Bottle Storage Space—holds 12 quart-size milk bottles, also tall bottles.
• Sealed-in compressor mechanism—more compact, efficient, and economical than ever.

Let your General Electric retailer show you the 1948 Space Maker Refrigerators—three 8-cubic-foot models and two 10-cubic-foot models. General Electric Company, Bridgeport 2, Conn.

GE *Space Maker Refrigerators*

More than 1,700,000 Refrigerators in Service 10 Years or Longer

5-Year Protection Plan—Included in the price of every General Electric Refrigerator is a 5-year protection plan. This plan consists of a one-year warranty on the complete refrigerator, plus additional four-year protection on the sealed-in refrigerating system.

GENERAL ELECTRIC

1948

ONLY DUAL-TEMP GIVES YOU ALL 4 FEATURES!

No defrosting*

① Dual-Temp Home Freezer really quick-freezes at 15° below zero. Stores up to 70 lbs. of frozen food safely for months. A big freezer right in your refrigerator!

② Dual-Temp Moist Cold Compartment never requires defrosting! High humidity keeps food fresh and moist without covering dishes. More room for food!

③ Dual-Temp Hydramp retards mold . . . helps preserve food longer.

④ Dual-Temp Moistrol . . . the drip tray that automatically empties itself. Many more outstanding features . . . see Dual-Temp at your Admiral dealer, today.

ADMIRAL ELECTRIC RANGE America's most beautiful electric range with simplified automatic cooking. Just 3 controls to set . . . cooks while you're away! Large, flexible oven provides 17 different rack positions. Flex-O-Heat "no-slip" controls allow the exact amount of heat needed. See the Admiral today!

Admiral
DUAL-TEMP Refrigerators

Performance proved in over 200,000 kitchens!

1948

Figure 3-9. Advances in refrigeration technology and increased production during the 1940s and 1950s helped reduce the prices of refrigerators. Advertising focused more on quality-of-life benefits rather than food safety.

The technology for an electric compression motor small enough to outfit a domestic refrigerator was not developed until 1914. Even a decade later, the home electric refrigerator was still only in its developmental stages. Leaks were common; refrigerants were toxic or highly flammable; motors, compressors, or thermostats malfunctioned frequently; and the noise was considerable.[11] Only in the late 1920s did innovations begin to solve most of these problems, making refrigerators more efficient and affordable on a mass scale.

Electric refrigerator manufacturers then began to aggressively promote their products. In 1923, the industry's advertising expenditures totaled about forty-five thousand dollars and climbed rapidly to almost $20 million by 1931.[12] During this time, ads for electric refrigerators featured health and food safety at the top of their lists of benefits. (Figure 3-8.) A "priceless treasure chest" was how Kelvinator referred to its 1927 model. First on the checklist of the treasures was health—tacitly guaranteed by the refrigerator's "constant protection of food at a scientifically determined temperature." Likewise, the banner in a 1929 General Electric ad proclaimed that its refrigerator "keeps your food safe." Even at the end of the 1930s, refrigerator manufacturers continued to emphasize health and food safety issues in ads. The header in a 1939 Kelvinator ad declared that "thousands are alive today because in 1914 man first harnessed cold!" As a competitive advantage statement, Kelvinator advised holdout owners of iceboxes that the 1939 Silver Jubilee model had the "cold-making capacity equal to more than half a ton of ice per week." This is not so surprising an argument for advertisers to use, given that more than half of all American homes still used iceboxes in 1940, even though almost 80 percent of all homes had electricity.[13]

As refrigeration technology progressed through the 1940s and 1950s, food safety ceased to be the focus of refrigerator ads. By then the public had been well educated on this point by home economists and advertisers. Enhancement of the quality of life became the objective of later ads. (Figure 3-9.) Larger storage capacity meant greater economy when food shopping, not only in increasing the volume of food that could be purchased but in reducing the number of trips to market. An ad for the 1948 GE Space Maker model compared the storage capacities of a 6- and an 8-cubic-foot space by illustrating piles of food at the base of open refrigerators. Manufacturers also emphasized easy maintenance in their ads. Women welcomed the advent of the frost-free freezer, as announced in the 1948 Admiral ad. The drop in cost of refrigerators was a key selling point in later ads. General Electric noted in its ads of 1941 that current models of its refrigerators cost half as much as those of ten years earlier—"so little that almost every family can afford the best in modern refrigeration."

Doing the Laundry

After food preparation, housekeeping was the second most important concern for the American housewife. In 1911, home economist Laura Clarke Rockwood wrote for *Popular Science:* "Those who insist that a woman's place is at home by divine decree need only to study the life of primitive man to find out how very human are some of our domestic customs, for they will

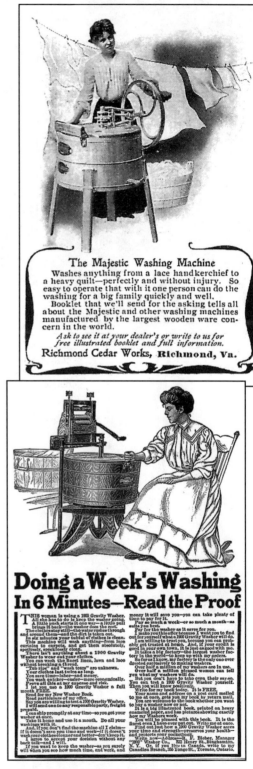

Figure 3-10. Despite advertising claims, early washing machines saved little time and not much labor, and they frequently damaged clothes. Majestic ad 1904, Gravity Washer ad 1907.

Figure 3-11. Electric clothes washers replaced the exhausting hand cranking of manual tub washers with automatic agitation. Ads for electric washers promised to "dispel the gloom of washday" and leave the housewife "entirely fresh" for most any activity that evening.

see this distinction, that while nature has specialized woman for child-bearing, it is society which has specialized her for housework."[14]

Since most women expected and accepted this "specialized" niche into which society had placed them, manufacturers rushed to their aid with a host of labor-saving devices to help them more easily and efficiently fulfill their role.

The most arduous household chore for women was laundry. For many, this was a two-day project every week, usually commencing with the washing on Monday, followed by ironing, folding, and mending on Tuesday. The housewife of the nineteenth century had to haul gallons of water from wells or pumps and maintain kettles of boiling water for the wash. Scrubbing, wringing, and carrying heavy, wet garments and linens to the clotheslines—and then retrieving the dried laundry—wearied and abused almost every muscle in her body. Her hands and arms were exposed to caustic lye-based detergents and scalding water for hours at a time. As Susan Strasser noted in *Never Done,* "From all available evidence—how-to-manuals, budget studies of poor people's households, diaries—it appears that women jettisoned laundry, their most hated task, whenever they had any discretionary money at all." Relief came "in the form of washerwomen, commercial laundries, and mechanical aids."[15]

The first of these mechanical aids—the home washing machine—was manufactured shortly after the Civil War. These early washers were little

Figure 3-12. Even though washers became more sophisticated with technological advances, washing clothes was still a dreaded chore. The promise of relief from washday drudgery continued to be emphasized in ads. Maytag ad 1946, Kelvinator ad 1954.

more than a washtub on a stand with a hand-cranked, flywheel-driven set of agitators. (Figure 3-10.) They often leaked, bolts rusted quickly, and worst of all, they frequently damaged clothes. These manual washers saved little time and not much labor, but until the first electric washing machines were manufactured in the teens, they were the best relief that technology had to offer women who did laundry at home.

The electric washing machine was the first truly effective aid in easing the burdens of doing the laundry. (Figure 3-11.) Easy fill and draining eliminated heavy lifting of water buckets, and automatic agitation replaced the hand cranking of manual tub washers. The Blue Bird Electric Clothes Washer "delights in dispelling the gloom of washday," avowed the copy in its 1919 ads. Where "once she would have taken to her bed" after washday, the Easy Washer owner of 1928 could do laundry in the morning and still be "entirely

Figure 3-13. With the proliferation of synthetic fabrics used in ready-to-wear clothing and home textiles, washing machines became multicycle, multispeed, multiagitator, and multitemperature to meet contemporary washing challenges. Whirlpool ad 1962, Hotpoint ad 1966.

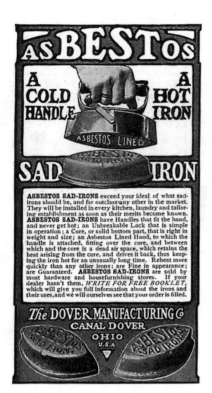

Figure 3-14. Ironing with a heavy, cast iron flatiron was a grueling chore requiring hours next to a hot stove to heat the irons. Ad 1902.

fresh, ready to dance, to play bridge, or to see a show that same evening," declared the ad copy. With the invention of an exclusive spin cycle, Whirldry promised housewives in a 1927 ad that "you can soak, wash, blue, rinse and dry a tubful of clothes without putting your hands in water."[16]

Even with advances in washing machine technology, laundry remained a hated chore. The promise of relief from washday burdens continued to be a successful focus of washing machine ads. "Look . . . no work!" beamed the housewife in Maytag's 1946 ad. "The great new Maytag is designed to set you free from washday drudgery," continued the copy. In 1954, a Kelvinator ad announced a "new way to end washday drudgery," this time including the automatic dryer as part of the solution. (Figure 3-12.)

By the 1960s, the proliferation of synthetic fabrics used in ready-to-wear clothing and home textiles presented new challenges and opportunities for manufacturers of automatic washers and dryers. (Figure 3-13.) "Because you wash all kinds of things," a Whirlpool ad reminded women in a 1962 ad. An assortment of those kinds of things was shown in the accompanying photo—a composite of six views of a typical housewife wearing everything from a cocktail dress to a blanket. Similarly, in 1966, Hotpoint offered "an infinite number of speeds" to wash all the varieties of man-made fabrics. "Every fabric in this room can be washed by this new Hotpoint," the ad header boasted. Beneath the photo of a woman caressing a fine-washable garment were listed the futuristic sounding fibers, including Fortrel, Dacron, Arnel, Orlon, Kodel, Chemstrand, and Celanese.

By the end of the twentieth century, the woes of washdays were further mitigated by multi-water-level, multicycle, multitemperature, multiagitator washers. As a result, the standards of cleanliness continued to rise to the point of an obsession with ring around the collar and whiter whites, problems that became the challenge of the detergent manufacturers discussed later in this chapter.

Part two of the laundry chores was ironing, which was usually done the day after washday. With the volumes of fabric used in garments, and the details of tiered ruffles, pleats, tucks, and flounces typical of women's clothing before the First World War, ironing was truly intensive labor. Before the availability of the electric iron, numerous variations of the cast iron flatiron were used for this arduous task. (Figure 3-14.) Most homes had several flatirons since they were cheap, durable, and easily available from most any dry goods store. Ironing was usually done in the kitchen so the flatirons could be continuously heated on the stove. A series of irons could be kept on the stove and rotated to expedite the process.

Although patented in 1882 and first sold in 1893, the electric iron did not become a mainstay appliance in most American homes until the 1920s. In 1913, General Electric ads offered "comfort on ironing day" with electric irons that were not only lighter than the cast iron versions, but that produced consistent, even heat—perfect "for the family ironing, or for little pressings in your boudoir or sewing room." (Figure 3-15.) Initially, though, the cost and limited availability of electricity deterred widespread sales of the electric

Figure 3-15. Ads for the early electronic irons assured consumers of "comfort on ironing day." Ad 1913.

iron. Even fifteen years after its first electric iron ads, General Electric was battling competition from the ubiquitous flatiron. GE ads still used the word "comfort" in the copy, but went further by suggesting that if women were continuing to iron next to the kitchen stove with heavy flatirons, they were sacrificing their health "for a few cents' worth of electricity." (Figure 3-16.)

Improvements in the electric iron led to greater reliability with the adjustable thermostat in the late 1920s, greater ease of use with the steam iron of the 1960s, and greater safety with the automatic shut-off in the 1980s. (Figure 3-17.) Still, despite all the high-tech conveniences that were available on models at the end of the century, ironing remained tedious work. Just as in 1900, a hotplate had to be pushed over laundered garments to press out wrinkles and set creases.

Easing the Labor of Other Chores

For a great part of the American population, the transition from the use of manual housekeeping devices to electric appliances was very slow. Among the numerous old-fashioned household furnishings and equipment that continued to be in widespread use up through World War II were the wood cook stove, the icebox, the washboard, and the cast iron flatiron. Truly, it was the accessibility of electricity that most aided women in easing the burdens of housework, especially since many electric appliances were so affordable. (Figure 3-18.) In observing the impact electricity had on the American housewife and her labors, Mark Sullivan wrote in 1927 that "an electric wire in a modern house excels a fairy-story." Beyond even the most hopeful fantasies of housewives just a generation earlier, Sullivan noted that:

> In any house, at the same hour, electricity might be producing heat in one room, cold in another, light in a third. To yet another it brought voices of friends from thousands of miles away. It heated water, it cooked, it froze ice in the refrigerator, it carried healing through ingenious pads that curved on aching backs; it swept, sewed, ironed—and it provided heat for the curling iron with which the housewife beautified herself for the evening's gaiety, a housewife who in the preceding generation would have accepted old age at forty and been too much preoccupied with the work, now done for her by electricity, to give much thought to adornment or gaiety.[17]

As we have seen thus far, even before the First World War women's magazines were jammed with ads for all sorts of electric household appliances. Sullivan observed that these labor-saving tools of housekeeping "did not retain the status of novel luxuries, but became familiar needs overnight."[18] "Should I have to part with them, I know I would miss them sadly," confessed home economist Clara Zillessen in a 1927 article written for the *Ladies' Home Journal*.[19]

Figure 3-16. One series of ads for electric irons suggested women who continued to use the cast iron flatirons were needlessly risking their health. Ad 1928.

Figure 3-17. Greater reliability for the electric iron came in the 1920s with the adjustable thermostat. Greater ease of use came with the steam iron of the 1960s, and greater safety came with the automatic shut-off in the 1980s. Ad 1965.

Figure 3-18. Advertising helped make electric appliances "familiar needs overnight," as one social historian wrote in 1925.

The dishwasher was another major household appliance that helped reduce a woman's workload. (Figure 3-19.) Although it was not as high on the housewife's wish list as a washing machine or refrigerator, any appliance that helped reduce a woman's workload was welcomed. "It makes dishwashing a pleasant task," stated the copy in a 1914 Whirlpool dishwasher ad. The pleasant part may have been that "hands never touch water" and drying dishes by hand could be eliminated, but early dishwashers still required a lot of work. Dishes had to be rinsed or scraped free of most food residue, tubs had to be manually filled and drained for wash and rinse cycles, and heavily encrusted cookware might require two or more machine washings. Eventually, though, technology addressed these problems, especially with the introduction of later electric models. The worst of the chore then became simply loading the dishwasher and putting away the dishes afterward.

Perhaps just as important as the laborsaving benefit of using a dishwasher was the promise of sanitized dishes. Whirlpool had included the word "sanitary" in the header of its 1914 ad. Almost forty years later, a 1953 ad for American Kitchens emphasized that the water could be hotter and detergents stronger than human hands could endure, and that "hot-air drying eliminates dish-towel germs." (Figure 3-20.)

Despite these bonus benefits, the dishwasher was primarily advertised as a labor saver. A long-running KitchenAid campaign during the 1950s and 1960s emphasized that women deserved a break from dishwashing and could find much better things to do with their time. Ads headlined "more time for living" showed housewives closing their KitchenAid dishwashers and heading off to enjoy leisure-time activities: an evening out with the husband, a scout gathering with junior, or a PTA meeting with fellow housewives.[20]

Cleaning floors, and especially rugs, also was backbreaking work for the Victorian housewife. Between the endless clouds of dust entering the house from unpaved streets and the residues of soot and ash deposited daily from fire grates and oil or gas lamps, staying ahead of dirt was a constant challenge. One of the most important aids in this household battle was the carpet

Figure 3-19. Early dishwashers, as with clothes washers, were still labor intensive despite the benefits touted in ads. Ad 1914.

Figure 3-20. Ads for automatic dishwashers noted that not only were women spared hours of labor—as well as "dishpan hands"—but dishwashers also provided health security since water could be hotter and detergents stronger than human hands could endure. American Kitchens ad 1953, General Electric ad 1961.

Figure 3-21. Invented in the 1870s, the carpet sweeper was a simple technological wonder that spared women the backbreaking labor of hauling rugs outside to be beaten. Goshen ad 1892, Bissell ad 1921.

sweeper. (Figure 3-21.) This marvel of ingenuity was created in the 1870s by the husband and wife team of Melville and Anna Bissell, who initially hand-made the sweepers in their home. Two brushes mounted on the axles of the wheels swept dirt into a compartment as the sweeper was pushed over a rug or floor. Through extensive advertising, the sweeper became so popular that numerous other manufacturers produced variations, including a private-label model for the *Ladies' Home Journal* catalogs of the 1890s. The carpet sweeper, a 1902 Bissell ad stated, "has done more to lighten woman's work than any invention that has been produced during the past quarter century."[21] More than 125 years since its creation, the carpet sweeper has remained virtually unchanged and is still widely used.

Despite the ease of use, affordability, and effectiveness of the little carpet sweeper, the implement had limited cleaning capabilities. In 1908, Hoover addressed these limitations with the introduction of the electric suction sweeper, the appliance that would revolutionize housecleaning. (Figure 3-22.) According to a 1963 Hoover ad, the company's founder had said at the time, "It'll sell itself if we can get the ladies to try it." Almost as soon as production of the appliance was under way, Hoover mobilized a sales force to take his vacuum cleaner straight to consumers for home demonstrations. In fact, this aspect of marketing vacuum cleaners was so highly effective in generating sales that fifty years later the offer of a home demonstration was still frequently advertised.[22] Some brands of vacuum cleaners, such as Electrolux, continued to be available only by home demonstration.

As a result of this successful combination of advertising and well-trained teams in the field, sales of the electric vacuum cleaner ran well ahead of most other electric appliances, except the iron, all through the teens and twenties. Frantz Premier boasted in a 1914 ad that eighty-five thousand housewives already had been given "freedom from sweeping and dusting" with the purchase of its brand of electric cleaner. Three years later ads for the same company announced that three hundred thousand women now owned one of its cleaners.[23] A special testimonial to the efficacy of the marketing and advertising strategies of vacuum cleaner manufacturers came during the implementation of the Rural Electrification Administration in the late 1930s. Much to the chagrin of home economists at the time, one 1939 survey showed that 40 percent of the recipients of new electricity hook-ups in Ohio had purchased vacuum cleaners rather than much needed water systems.[24]

Vacuum cleaners were not inexpensive. The 1914 Frantz Premier cost $32.50 with attachments. By the 1920s, installment plans had become the most popular way for manufacturers of high-end goods to sustain mass production and for retailers to broaden their base of customers. Makers of vacuum cleaners enthusiastically promoted their own installment programs by popping the down-payment price in their ad banners. "Yes, madame, $6.25 is all you need to obtain a Hoover complete with household cleaning equipment," read the header of a 1924 ad. Only in the last line of the copy was the

1920

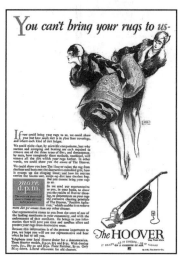

1929

1963

1937

1946   1967

Figure 3-22. From its earliest versions, the electric vacuum was a hit with the American housewife. Hundreds of thousands were sold during the teens despite their considerable cost.

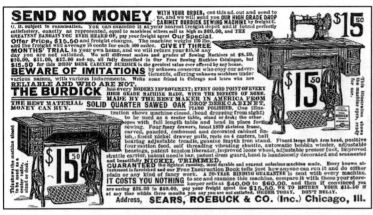

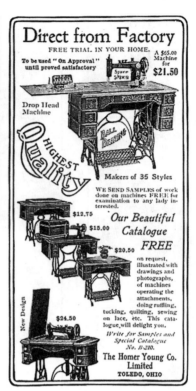

Figure 3-23. The sewing machine was proclaimed the "Queen of inventions" by *Godey's* in 1860. The labor and time saved in sewing garments by machine versus by hand were dramatic. A man's shirt that took more than ten hours to sew by hand took only a little over an hour by machine. Sears ad 1900, Homer Young ad 1902.

Figure 3-24. The electric motor for the sewing machine spared women the tiring task of pumping a foot treadle. Ad 1917.

whole story revealed: "The few remaining payments are so small they'll be no burden at all."[25] Although this kind of deceptive advertising eventually led to the 1938 passage of the Wheeler-Lee Amendment, which prohibited the dissemination of false or misleading advertising,[26] the marketing strategy sold a lot of vacuum cleaners.

The Queen of Inventions

As previously mentioned, cooking was a common denominator shared by women of all classes. Similarly, sewing was a skill that crossed all classes. For most women of the nineteenth century sewing was necessary to produce clothing, bedding, table linens, curtains, and most anything else made of textiles; for others, it was a pastime that yielded decorative cushions and needlepoint wall hangings.

The labor of sewing by hand was one of woman's earliest domestic chores eased by mechanized means. The home sewing machine was introduced in the 1850s and widely sold in the decades after the Civil War. (Figure 3-23.) In 1860, *Godey's Lady's Book* welcomed the sewing machine as "the Queen of inventions."[27] A table of comparisons published in its study of labor and time saved showed that a man's shirt would take one hour and sixteen minutes to complete by machine, but ten hours and thirty-one minutes by hand.[28] In addition, unlike her ancestors of a century earlier, the housewife of the late nineteenth century no longer had to do the spinning and weaving of textiles, thanks to the mass production of inexpensive fabrics by the numerous textile mills of the New England and southern states. That, coupled with Ebenezer Butterick's introduction of paper garment patterns in the 1860s, encouraged women to more often embellish or alter their existing wardrobes, or to try to keep up with fashion trends by sewing new outfits as they appeared in the magazines.

Prior to the introduction of the electric motor for sewing machines in the early teens, the most common model required pumping a foot treadle to operate. When Westinghouse advertised its new electric motor for the sewing machine in 1917, it emphasized the health benefits more than the versatility or economy of home sewing. (Figure 3-24.) The ad copy promised: "No treadle to work up and down till one's legs are stiff and one's back aches. No more fatiguing toil to make the doctor say 'You'll have to stop running a sewing-machine'… it means relief from the tax on health and strength they have been paying for running a machine."

Even before the invention of the electric sewing machine, sewing as a necessity for production of clothing and home furnishing textiles was impacted on two fronts during the last quarter of the nineteenth century. First was the rapid development of the ready-made industries, and second was the mass distribution of this merchandise by retailers such as Montgomery Ward and Sears Roebuck. Sewing, then, became relegated to a lesser role in the housewife's scheme of home chores. Certainly some women continued sewing as a source of home economy, a point especially advertised by sewing machine manufacturers during the Depression. Others continued to enjoy sewing as a home craft—a creative hobby that produced tangible evidence of their domestic skills. (Figure 3-25.)

Figure 3-25. During the Depression home economy was a key focus of sewing machine ads. By the second half of the century sewing machine advertising emphasized fashion and domestic crafts for the homemaker.

1921

1946

1952

Figure 3-26. To most Americans, the hallmark of a successful homemaker was her ability to cook. American society inculcated girls with this gender-role socialization at an early age, and food product manufacturers stereotyped the idea in ads.

Food Preparation and Consumerism

Food preparation has been foremost among the categories of housework for women throughout the centuries. Skill at cooking was one of the measurable benchmarks of a prospective bride, since fertility commonly was not tested prior to marriage, and beauty was in the eyes of the beholder. (Figure 3-26.) From an early age girls were inculcated with this message of successful homemaking. Royal Baking Powder used the age-old cliche "the way to a man's heart" in its 1921 ad, where a plain, preteen girl is shown triumphing over a beautiful rival for the attentions of a boy when she proudly presents her homemade cake. In 1952, a Procter & Gamble ad showed a startled groom embracing his bride next to a huge header asking, "Can she cook?" In answer, P&G assured the new husband (and bride) that Crisco always "pleased wives because it made cakes and pies that kept Papa coming home for dinner." Campbell's soup ads also periodically told women not to worry if they could not cook. A 1946 version advised young brides that he'll think he "courted an angel and married a cook [when they] include one of his favorite soups."

Feeding the family was one household responsibility that women would even rise from their sickbeds to perform. Before 1900, preparing meals was a major undertaking. Few manufactured food products were purchased to relieve the housewife's cooking chores. Instead, women made trips to the market virtually every day for fresh food. That could mean live fowl to be killed, plucked, and dressed, or fish to be gutted and scaled. Green coffee had to be roasted and ground before brewing, bulk sugar cut and pounded, spices chopped and ground, flour sifted, nuts shelled, raisins seeded, fruits peeled and pitted, and dozens of other tasks performed before cooking could even begin.

Figure 3-27. Canned foods helped reduce food preparation time and efforts for the housewife. Seasonal fruits and vegetables were available year round, and prepared foods eliminated the need for cooking altogether. National Canners ad 1920, Continental Can ad 1934.

However, by the beginning of the twentieth century, process food manufacturers had begun to create a diverse product line of precooked and packaged foods that would eliminate some steps in a meal preparation. Chief among these prepared foods were canned goods. (Figure 3-27.) Hermetically sealed food containers had been in use since the Napoleonic Wars. By the start of the Civil War, more efficient processes for cutting and soldering cans and for reducing cooking time had lowered the cost of canned foods. Most canned foods, though, were used largely by the military until the 1890s, when companies like Franco American, Heinz, and Campbell's began to promote their own labels and expand product lines for mass consumption.

Canned foods had become a basic commodity in most American homes by 1900. With safety and cost issues less of a concern for the consumer, especially after the enactment of the 1906 Pure Food and Drugs Act, advertisers concentrated on the value of canned foods to the housewife. (Figure 3-28.) "Why run to your grocer every time when you want a good meal in a hurry?" a 1909 Van Camp's ad asked. "You should have a dozen cans on the shelf." Writing for the *Ladies' Home Journal* in 1916, Christine Frederick agreed with this idea. "It is quite easy to estimate how many cans of this or that product will be used in a week, month or season, then to make up an order and purchase by the case, or at least by the dozen," she wrote.[29] The cost savings of buying in large quantities could be about 15 percent, but the time savings was the real value.

By the same token, prepared baked goods were as widely distributed in the early 1900s as were canned foods. Although 75 percent of American

Figure 3-28. Ads for processed foods advised women that a pantry well-stocked with canned goods provided flexibility and variety in menu planning year round, as well as eliminating the need for frequent trips to the market. Ad 1909.

Figure 3-29. Images such as the National Biscuit boy in his rain slicker and the cookie clown with his open umbrella visually reinforced in ads the promise of safe, protected food packaging. Uneeda ad 1901, ZuZu ad 1910.

housewives baked their own bread about twice a week,[30] packaged cakes, cookies, and crackers became standard stock items in most kitchens. Manufacturers of packaged goods resolved consumers' concerns about shelf life, freshness, insect infestations, and sanitation of products usually sold by bulk. The typical sack of bulk crackers or cookies scooped out of insanitary barrels at the local grocer's was replaced by sealed packages and cartons of standardized products.

In 1898, the National Biscuit Company introduced its In-er-seal carton, an airtight package lined with wax paper. During the next few decades, this safety packaging was widely advertised with the image of a boy clad in raingear or a clown with an open umbrella. (Figure 3-29.) Such visual icons as the slicker boy and the cookie clown instantly conveyed to consumers that the In-er-seal packaging guaranteed protection from moisture and external contaminants.

In conjunction with food safety messages, National Biscuit ads also promoted the convenience and variety of its packaged foods. "Many a wise homekeeper finds that it is far easier, and far better, to stock the pantry shelf with a few varieties of National Biscuit Company products than to stand and bake for hours, with all the attendant uncertainties of baking day," said one 1922 ad. (Figure 3-30.) Susan Strasser cites the importance of this kind of widely distributed advertising campaign as "product education." National Biscuit "was promoting not simply its own products but the product category: packaged crackers and cookies."[31] Ads that generated product education to a mass market benefited the competition as well, so the third purpose of National Biscuit's saturation of advertising was brand awareness. All three messages—food safety, product education, and branding—helped catapult the company into the preeminent position it would retain for more than a century.

As self-serve grocery stores expanded across the country in the 1920s, lines of packaged products that fit the new way of food shopping likewise expanded. In a 1928 ad by Hostess Cakes, the question of serving guests store-bought packaged cakes was addressed. (Figure 3-31.) Written in an editorial format, with the byline of a fictitious Alice Adams Proctor, the copy

Figure 3-30. The National Biscuit Company suggested in ads that the "wise homekeeper" did not waste time baking when she could stock up on quality baked goods from its kitchens. Ad 1922.

Figure 3-31. Ads for Hostess Cakes were presented in an editorial format featuring the fictitious Alice Adams Proctor, who extolled the social acceptability of serving guests store-bought baked goods. Ad 1928.

assured readers that with Hostess Cakes so easily available at their nearby grocery store, "baking cake at home is utter folly." Hostess, like the National Biscuit Company and other packaged food manufacturers, persistently used such advertising for product education during the early decades of the century. Part of this process was designed to help consumers overcome the stigma that the homemaker who relied on packaged or canned foods "was held in open scorn by her neighbors as lacking in culinary skill, or perhaps shirking her duty," as a writer for *Good Housekeeping* later recalled.[32]

For the housewife of the twentieth century, use of packaged and canned foods helped reduce the time and labor in grocery shopping and in cooking meals. Yet, although women liked the convenience of these products and relished the freedom from so much time in the kitchen, most women still wanted to preserve some creativity and craft satisfaction with their cooking. Food manufacturers found a product niche between processed foods and cooking from scratch: the mix. The more than thirty steps and several hours needed for baking as outlined in a 1913 Gold Medal Flour ad was reduced to simply adding milk to a mix by the 1950s. (Figure 3-32.) In the end, both

Figure 3-32. Food manufacturers found a product niche between processed foods and cooking from scratch: the mix. Gold Medal ad 1913, Pillsbury ad 1955.

Figure 3-33. Decade after decade, Jell-O assured homemakers how quick and easy desserts could be made with its mixes. Left ad 1911, right ad 1959.

methods achieved the same result—home-baked foods fresh from the oven.

Jell-O, too, had long advertised that its flavored gelatin mixes were so easy any-one could successfully—and quickly—produce a perfect dish every time. (Figure 3-33.) "She may spoil everything else, but she will make a fine dessert of Jell-O," the copy said in a 1911 ad, "for she cannot go wrong there." Almost half a century later, the same message was directed in an ad to brides: "because friend-in-deed Jell-O can't burn, can't fall and can't fail to delight the light of your life."

Eventually entire meals were boxed for convenient yet fresh-from-the-kitchen cooking. (Figure 3-34.) Chef Boy-Ar-Dee introduced a line of complete dinners in the 1960s that allowed women to feel that they had prepared a "homemade" meal. "In 15 minutes you can prepare a spaghetti dinner that would take an Italian chef 4 hours," the ad copy declared. Instead of having to peel toma-toes to make a sauce, roll and cook meatballs, prepare pasta dough, and grate cheese, the cook found everything premeasured in an assortment of contain-ers boxed together. Other complete meal packages developed by food man-ufacturers included Chinese and Mexican dinners, as well as dozens of one-pan dishes to which the cook simply added a favorite meat or fish.

Figure 3-34. For the homemaker who wanted con-venience and yet wished to maintain some craft sat-isfaction with her cooking, entire meals were pre-measured and packaged ready to cook. Ad 1965.

Figure 3-35. By the 1950s the use of frozen foods was part of virtually every American housewife's meal preparation—from truly fresh-tasting fruits and vegetables to the complete TV dinner. Philco ad 1956, Banquet ad 1963.

The ultimate in cooking convenience, frozen foods, was developed commercially in the 1930s by Birds Eye. Consumers could now enjoy the year-round availability of truly fresh-tasting fruits and vegetables, which accounted for more than half of all commercial frozen food production prior to 1960.[33] Prepared foods for the freezer had been tested throughout the 1940s and culminated in the "TV dinner" of the early 1950s. (Figure 3-35.) With the frozen dinner, women surrendered all control of meal preparation. The manufacturer determined the menu and portions of each dish, seasoned and applied butter or sauces, and even eliminated the need for dishwashing by arranging the meal on a disposable tray.

By the 1970s, convenience food manufacturers were able to have it both ways. For women too busy to cook or disinterested in culinary arts, the variety of microwave, boil-in-a-bag, frozen, canned, or packaged meals was enormous. For women who enjoyed cooking, manufacturers began to advertise the added value of their convenience foods. The cook could create the main dish from scratch but add frozen side dishes, microwave a frozen entrée but bake fresh bread from dough in a can, or combine convenience foods to create an original dish of her own.

Housecleaning Consumables

Cooking may have been the most important daily chore a woman could do for her family, but cleaning was by far the most time consuming. The need to wash, scrub, scour, mop, dust, and polish everything in the home week after week generated a whole industry of consumables to aid women in this domestic pursuit. Innumerable soaps, detergents, cleansers, waxes, polishes, and specialized household chemicals were created to lessen the intensity of their many cleaning labors. Ironically, the addition of all these specialized products to the household cleaning routine created more tasks. For instance, specialized products for cleaning wood, glass, porcelain, metal, and fabrics all required individual steps and different equipment for use. Studies from the 1950s showed that "women actually spent more time on household chores than had their mothers ... logging a 99.6-hour workweek."[34] A similar study cited by Betty Friedan indicated that American society—and marketers—wanted women "to have their cake and eat it too ... save time, have more comfort, avoid dirt and disorder, have mechanized supervision, yet not want to give up the personal achievement and pride in a well-run household."[35]

The industry that by the middle of the twentieth century would fill entire aisles of grocery stores with cleaning products started out simply enough. An ordinary bar of all-purpose soap was what most women of 1900 used to wash just about everything from laundry and dishes to their children. Commercial soap production had originated in the mid-nineteenth century as a by-product of other industries such as meatpacking and cottonseed oil processing. Several brand-name, all-purpose soaps were already in wide distribution by 1900, including Ivory, Sapolio, and Gold Dust. In fact, at the time Ivory was created in 1878, the Cincinnati soap firm that was to become Procter & Gamble already had twenty-four other varieties of soap on the market.[36]

Figure 3-36. Manufacturers of all-purpose bar soaps advertised the versatility of their products as well as the quick and easy results. Ivory ad 1906, P & G ad 1916.

To wash clothing the bars of soap had to be chipped into the washtubs, or else a solution of soap dissolved in boiling water was used. (Figure 3-36.) Some manufacturers produced soap powders, but before the granulated process was developed these powders often solidified into chunks that were more difficult to dissolve than chips from bars. The promise of the product, though, as spelled out in early soap ads, was quick and easy results. That clothes came clean with most any soap was understood. What drove the competitive advantage of branded soaps was the claim of how much quicker and easier one cleaned than the other. One such ad in 1916 told women they could save their energy for more pleasant things than washing clothes because P & G soap "does not merely help you wash; it, by itself actually washes; . . . it does your part too."

Bar soap used for laundry and household cleaning was gradually replaced by more specialized cleaning products. In 1906 Lux introduced boxed soap chips, and in 1918 Rinso created the first clump-free granulated soap powder.[37] Other manufacturers quickly followed suit with forms of their own. (Figure 3-37.) By the end of World War II, the arduous chore of washing the entire laundry by hand had been mostly replaced by the washing machine, whether in the home, apartment laundry facility, or coin-operated laundromat. The inconvenience of hand-chipping bar soap into an automatic washer and the annoyance of gummy residues sometimes left by boxed soap chips made granulated detergents quickly become the most popular choice of consumers. Detergent manufacturers even developed cooperative promotional programs with washing machine manufacturers to provide a sample box of their brand with new washer models. (Figure 3-38.) In turn, detergent manufacturers used this as an endorsement in their ads, and machine manufacturers got co-op advertising plus a bonus customer incentive.

The bottom line for marketing these products was, by the 1950s, product differentiation. If soap powders were basically all the same, consumers might wonder, then how did one detergent clean better than its competition? Tide ads claimed to work in the "hardest water," Surf contained "ultraviolet whitener," and Dash was "concentrated fury." (Figure 3-39.) Though most of these vague claims were distinctions without a difference, they effectively played on what Daniel Cohen

1922

1931

1935

Figure 3-37. Boxed laundry soap chips were first produced in 1906, and granulated detergents followed in 1918.

Figure 3-38. Laundry detergent manufacturers developed co-op programs with washing machine makers to provide sample boxes of their brands with new washer models. Dash ad 1956, Tide ad 1966.

refers to as the American "cult of cleanliness" created by advertising in which "housewives are mortified by . . . clothes that are 'dingy' and shirts with 'ring around the collar'."[38] There, in the ads of issue after issue of magazines, and daily in TV commercials, were the answers to a housewife's laundry dilemmas.

Before the segmentation of general-purpose soaps into specialized soaps such as laundry detergents, most manufacturers promoted the versatility of their brands. A 1906 series of Ivory ads illustrated a single use in each, including washing hands, hair, infants, dishes, clothes, and even ostrich feathers.[39] Clearly the more things the housewife could use bar soap to wash, and the more often she washed them, the more soap she needed to buy.

Figure 3-39. By the end of World War II, machine washing had mostly replaced hand-washing, and granulated detergents had surpassed chips and bar soaps for laundry use. Brand product differentiation on packages and in ads for detergents centered on degrees of cleaning effectiveness rather than convenience of use.

1949

1957

1967

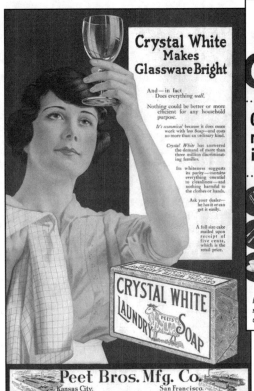

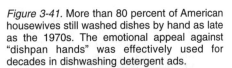

Figure 3-40. Soap manufacturers reformulated existing detergents to address the problems of spots and streaks left on dishes by automatic dishwashers. "Sparkling" and "spotless" were the key words used in ads and TV commercials. Peet Bros. ad 1917, Cascade ad 1955.

Dishwashing was a perfect example where soap manufacturers could get frequent use of their product. Unlike laundry, which was a weekly chore, dishwashing was done daily. During the first decades of the twentieth century, most all household soap makers advertised their brand for dishwashing about as often as for laundry. The label on Crystal White read "laundry soap," but an ad promoted its use for washing dishes or "any household purpose." (Figure 3-40.) The actual effectiveness of soaps for dishwashing did

Figure 3-41. More than 80 percent of American housewives still washed dishes by hand as late as the 1970s. The emotional appeal against "dishpan hands" was effectively used for decades in dishwashing detergent ads.

1917

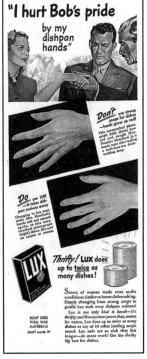

1944

1967

not become an issue until automatic dishwashers became more widely used. Old-fashioned hand washing and hand drying would assure "glassware bright" results regardless of the soap used; not so with automatic dishwashers, which could leave dishes spotted and streaked or worse, still encrusted with food. Manufacturers such as Procter & Gamble and Lever Brothers were already positioned for this market segmentation and reformulated existing soap mixtures to address the particular problems of the automatic dishwasher. "Spotless" and "sparkling" were the key sell words for package designs and ad copy.

Even at the conclusion of the great wave of suburbanite consumerism in the 1950s and 1960s, only 19 percent of American homes owned automatic dishwashers in 1970.[40] That meant a lot of housewives were still washing dishes by hand. Advertisers had targeted these women early with the promise to protect them from the dreaded "dishpan hands" syndrome. (Figure 3-41.) In 1917, an Ivory ad listed three reasons to use its soap for dishwashing, including assurances that it "cannot redden or roughen the skin" and will leave "hands soft, smooth and white." This emotional appeal recurred in dishwashing soap ads decade after decade. It was the focus of a 1944 Lux ad in which a housewife embarrasses her husband with her dishpan hands at a social function, and it became the basis for the blindfold tests comparing the hands of mothers and daughters in TV and print ads for Ivory Liquid in the 1960s.

In addition to laundry and dishwashing detergents, numerous other specialized household cleaning products were developed to aid the housewife in her daily chores. By 1940, 70 percent of all American homes had indoor

Figure 3-42. Scouring cleansers were introduced in the 1860s for the more difficult cleaning chores of the kitchen and bathroom. Manufacturers distanced their products from the many rough, homemade formulas of the time by promising in their ads that their cleansers were safe to most all surfaces.

1902

1917

1938

1982

Figure 3-43. The exceptional promise made in ads for toilet bowl cleaners was that the products would do the work for you. Sani-Flush ad 1917, Vanish ad 1967.

Figure 3-44. Even the cleanest homes could still be dens of infection, warned ads from disinfectant manufacturers such as Lysol.

plumbing (94 percent in urban areas).[41] As tubs, showers, sinks, and toilets became permanent fixtures in the home, the housewife faced new cleaning problems. Water stains, mildew, soap residue, mineral buildup, and rust all left their marks on porcelain, tile, ceramic, and steel surfaces. Cleaning these stains was no job for a mild bar soap. Instead, manufacturers such as Sapolio and Bon Ami introduced scouring powders as early as the 1860s. (Figure 3-42.) Comprised of powdered soap and pulverized mineral abrasives such as calcite and feldspar, these commercial cleansers were aggressively marketed for the difficult cleaning chores in the kitchen and bathroom. Yet, consumers initially resisted these commercial cleansers for two reasons. First, many housewives used homemade abrasives such as potash and even ground sand, or inexpensive scouring bricks made of dried clay, all of which were highly effective in removing stains.[42] Second, the homemade scouring cleansers frequently damaged the surfaces they cleaned, so consumers presumed commercially made cleansers were equally harmful. However, with logo taglines like Bon Ami's "hasn't scratched yet," consumer confidence in manufactured scouring cleansers eventually grew, and so did market share.

One of the best promises a cleaning product could make was to do all the work for you. This is what toilet bowl cleaners claimed from the time they were introduced in the 1890s. (Figure 3-43.) "Cleans without fuss or mess," read the label of early Sani-Flush containers. These cleaners contained

1935

1942

1976

chemicals that reacted with water and fizzed away stains and rings. "No hands in the bowl," Vanish assured housewives in its ads.

Despite daily scrubbing and scouring, a clean house may not be enough, suggested some chemical manufacturers. (Figure 3-44.) Some of the most melodramatic ads created in the 1930s and 1940s were for Lysol Disinfectant. In a 1935 ad, a nefarious "criminal" was shown lurking in the shadows just outside the window of an ideal, clean home. The sensational-ized copy told readers that the "criminal at large" was infection, which caused "more illness, more unhappiness, more deaths than all the gangsters of the world put together." During World War II the ad copy and imagery were updated from the gangster metaphor to that of wartime concerns. Even if put in a gas mask, the copy and illustration warned in a 1942 ad, children may not be safe against infectious disease. Terms like "enemies," "invaders," and "home defense" made the copy relevant to the national cri-sis of the time. Decades later, with all the advances in medicine, education, and home-care technology, women were still being told in ads that "even the cleanest homes need Lysol," if only to eliminate household odors. "House-atosis" became the latest social stigma marketers invented for housewives in the 1960s. The word was derived from "halitosis," the term for bad breath, which itself was a word invented by a mouthwash advertiser of the 1920s.

From the dawn of civilization, homes had been plagued with all manners of dust, dirt, soot, and ashes deposited throughout interiors from open doors, open fireplaces, and open-flame lamps. Protecting floors, woodwork, and furnishings through preventative maintenance had been emphasized in ads by manufacturers of polishes and waxes since the mid-nineteenth century. (Figure 3-45.) By 1900, the housewife had a good selection of products from which to choose for protecting her interior woods from any permanent dam-age all this dust and grime might have caused. O-Cedar not only manufac-tured a polish that protected floors and furniture, it also produced dusting pads and mops that according to its ads reduced "cleaning, dusting, and pol-ishing to almost nothing." Johnson's Wax went one step further to encourage women to wax their wood and linoleum floors more often; the company began renting electric floor polishers in the 1920s. As home interiors changed from the Victorian era to the modern era, wood home furnishings and floors were replaced by those made of metals, glass, plastics, vinyl, and other syn-thetic materials or surfaces. The need for protective polishing and waxing became obsolete in many homes, and dusting was easily done with antistat-ic sprays and ammonia-based cleaners.

Conclusion: All the Better to Cook, Clean, and Care for the Home

"The fact that women say they 'hate housework,'" wrote Laura Clarke Rockwood in 1911, "does not lessen their responsibility for doing it well."[43] In each succeeding generation throughout the twentieth century, women who faced the daily drudgery and labor of housework saw their lot improve over that of their mothers and grandmothers. By the 1920s, the burdens of housekeeping already had been dramatically altered by the mass marketing of an extraordinary array of electric home appliances, processed and pack-aged foods, and specialized household cleaning products. A deluge of mass-media advertising inspired and cajoled women toward improved, easier

Figure 3-45. Besides polishes and waxes, manu-facturers created line extensions to include imple-ments for applying their products. To urge home-makers to use even more of its products, Johnson's Wax rented electric floor polishers for those who could not afford to buy them. O-Cedar ad 1913, Johnson's Wax ad 1931.

ways to clean, cook, and care for their homes and families. As their era and society permitted, these millions of women consumers responded to the advertising from home product manufacturers, distributors, and retailers and bought mass quantities of soaps and canned soups, electric irons, washers, dryers, and fryers, all in the quest for safer, cleaner, and more comfortable homes. From the start of the century, women's social structures had begun to rapidly evolve and extend beyond traditional boundaries as marketers led consumers to new ideas and new ways of homemaking. For instance, while the social stigma of using processed foods instead of cooking from scratch was gradually alleviated by persistent advertising, the social stigmas of dishpan hands, spotted glassware, or house-atosis were newly created by advertising.

Another dichotomy in this evolutionary process of housekeeping was one of quality versus quantity. Unquestionably, manufactured household goods helped ease the burdens of labor-intensive and time-consuming housework and improved the resulting quality of the housewife's cooking or cleaning efforts. The electric washing machine and iron were milestones in work reduction for women. Canned goods and processed foods helped eliminate steps in cooking as well as in food shopping. Specialized cleaning products answered the challenges of relentless stains, dirt, and grime. Yet, with the continuous segmentation of housekeeping products into specialized variations different and additional types of housework emerged. Each appliance may have lessened the labor of a respective chore, but as the appliances accumulated added tasks of care and maintenance came with them. Cleaning carpets and rugs with a vacuum cleaner, for example, was less intense work than using a broom. However, vacuum cleaners had to have dust bags changed or emptied and washed, sweeper brushes unclogged, attachment tools cleaned, and worn hoses, belts, and cords replaced.

In her 1963 book *The Feminine Mystique,* Betty Friedan examined this phenomenon of marketing and "housewifery." In her observations of a fifteen-year study by Ernest Dichter of the Institute for Motivational Research, Friedan wrote that the moral of the study was explicit: "Since the Balanced Homemaker represents the market with the greatest future potential, it would be to the advantage of the appliance manufacturer to make more and more women aware of the desirability of belonging to this group. Educate them through advertising that it is possible to have outside interests and become alert to wider intellectual influences . . . . The art of good homemaking should be the goal of every normal woman."[44]

To this end—"the art of good homemaking"—the advertising messages of household product marketers throughout the twentieth century were designed to reaffirm women's roles as housewives, while at the same time to lead them into new, ever expanding arenas of consumerism. What Friedan and later social critics might deem as a stereotyping of the American woman was for advertisers a realistic reflection of her role in society. To marketers, the housewife of 1999 wanted better ways to cook, clean, and care for her home, just as her great-grandmother had in 1900.

—Chapter 4

THE AMERICAN
BRIDE AND
MOTHER

The image of the bride as an advertising hook
• Niche marketing to the bride • Mass marketing to American mothers • Promoting products
for a child's health, safety, and well-being

In October 1996, members of the United States Congress felt compelled to define in legal terms what a "wife" was in the Defense of Marriage Act. Social, judicial, and legislative forces throughout the last quarter of the twentieth century had, many Americans thought, undermined the traditional role of a married woman as helpmate and partner to her husband. In the prologue to the 1983 edition of *The Feminine Mystique,* Betty Friedan summed up the kinds of changes that had taken place just since the 1960s:

> Firewoman, chairpersons, housespouses, the gender gap, Ms., pal-
> imony, take-out food, woman priests, woman rabbis, woman
> prime ministers out-machoing male dictators in miniwars,
> women's studies, women's history, double burden, dressing for
> success, more women now going to college than men, assertive-
> ness training, male consciousness raising, role strain, role rever-
> sal, networking, sexism, displaced homemakers, equal pay for
> work of comparable value, marriage contracts, child custody for
> men, first babies at forty, the two-paycheck family, the single-
> parent family, Victor-Victoria, Tootsie. Who could have predicted
> some of these?[1]

For many Americans, all this was too much, too fast. The traditional role of wife and mother needed to be shored up, legitimized in the face of a perceived onslaught against those institutions. Conservative groups in the 1980s had taken advantage of the political climate generated by the Reagan administration to defeat the Equal Rights Amendment, to push for state laws restricting abortion, and to limit perceived feminist legislation. To writers such as Susan Faludi, a backlash against the backward-looking "New Right Reaganites" was then set in motion for the 1990s. Despite the "frightening misinformation on spinster booms, birth dearths, and deadly daycare," Faludi wrote, "women continued to postpone their wedding dates, limit their family size, and combine work with having children."[2] As she and other feminists acknowledged, the question became not so much if to become a wife and mother, but rather what kind of each or either. The smorgasbord of possibilities was enormous, and women had never had such a vast assortment of choices: the "supermom" who chose to maintain a career as well as a marriage and children; the "soccer mom" who, like her suburbanite grandmother

After the wedding comes the home-making, when the young wife has often her first experience with those problems that make the weal or woe of the new home. As cleanliness takes a high place in the qualities that bring comfort and welfare, soap must be had. There is one soap that is always satisfactory because always pure. She may try others said to be just as good, but perfect comfort will come only with Ivory Soap—it is the standard.

Figure 4-1. Whatever the product, advertisers knew that the image of a bride in her wedding regalia was eye-catching for most women. Ad 1900.

Figure 4-2. Images of happy brides were popular particularly with makers of health and beauty aids. Ad 1924.

of the 1950s, chose to stay home and nurture her children full time; or any one of many gradations in-between. "The fundamental question is no longer, Who is the man you want to live with for the rest of your life?" concluded Karen Lehrman in *The Lipstick Proviso* in 1997; "it is, who is the woman you want to be for the rest of your life?"[3]

Herein lay the great dilemma for marketers of the 1990s. If women were constantly redefining themselves, how could they be targeted effectively? Was the modern American woman, with all her subtle complexities, less definable than had been her antecedents during the other eras of major social change for women in the 1920s and 1970s? In those earlier periods, advertisers (overwhelmingly male) could, with confidence, simply ignore social changes. Surveys, focus groups, and studies of social behavior conducted during these eras proved that the target customer was still the housewife-mother. In the Middletown study by the Lynds in 1925, the conclusion in the chapter about marriage was that the qualifications of a good wife were "not only to 'make a good home' for her husband and children, but to set them in a secure social position."[4] Similarly, in the one-hundredth-anniversary issue of *McCall's* in 1976, a survey of women readers showed that 87 percent were "satisfied" with their lives, and that they credited their satisfaction to motherhood (71 percent), marriage (67 percent), and their homes (66 percent).[5] The gamble, then, for advertisers in the 1990s could be certain enough. The results of polls and surveys aside, advertisers had had more than a century of experience with the condition and conditioning of American women. They continued to feel certain that generation after generation, the majority of women had been basically conservative on most all socioeconomic fronts, and that this prevailing posture would continue with the majority of those women who were poised to become wives and mothers as the twentieth century concluded.

A hundred years earlier, though, advertisers did not have to gamble at all with their definition of the ideal woman consumer; to them, her place in American society was unequivocally clear. They felt confident that they thoroughly understood women, women's roles, and women's needs. After all, it was advertisers who had helped create the modern woman of 1900. The dichotomy for advertisers and these women who stood on the threshold of a new century was that for all the promises of a modern new age, women were nonetheless products of Victorianism, inexorably steeped in an unchallenged, stagnant traditionalism. From the constraints of their tightly laced corsets to the narrow confines of their kitchens and nurseries, most women understood and accepted how society had pigeonholed them. "Idle ornament or hard-working mother of ten, the lady on the horsehair sofa led a short, sheltered life in a man's world where woman's place was certain," historian Oliver Jensen wrote of turn-of-the-century women.[6] For advertisers, therefore, she was predictable and malleable within her clearly defined and regulated boundaries.

Marketing the Image of the Bride

To fulfill of her role, a woman first had to become a wife. Throughout the whole of the twentieth century, the bride remained a constant in advertising. Like images of children and animals, the picture of a bride in her wedding regalia was especially eye-catching for most women. (Figure 4-1.) For the woman who had already traversed the route to the altar, there was the comparison of her gown and ceremony with that depicted in the photograph or artist's rendering; for the woman yet to be married, the images provided hope, fantasy, and guidance for what was socially acceptable and expected in this rite of passage.

Guidance to the altar, particularly, was an integral part of marketing beauty, health, and personal hygiene products. If one were to believe these ads, the fact that many women had a wedding day in the first place was due in large part to the use of this brand of skin soap or that brand of mouthwash. Such "parables of advertising," as historian Roland Marchand called them, "promised readers no insurmountable limitations and offered a reality easily within the reach of the heart's desires."[7] From a marketer's perspective, what greater heart's desire was there for most women than marriage?

Colgate used an "actual" occurrence from a wedding as the subject of a 1924 toothpaste ad. "The joyful strains from Mendelssohn," the copy began, "and the happy pair turned to accept well wishes from their friends," only to hear a guest exclaim to the bride, "Oh! What wonderful teeth." (Figure 4-2.) Would this be the most enchanting anecdote a bride should hope to remember from her special day, one might wonder. To the female reader of 1924, the commercial message of the toothpaste would be less significant than the visual image of the bride's headdress, the cut of the gown's bodice, and the composition of the floral bouquet. Colgate knew that the image of this bride and the "actual incident at a recent society wedding" would linger in women's minds.

Similarly, in a 1925 ad for Pompeian cosmetics, the "reward of beauty" headline, coupled with the portrait of a beautiful bride, was an effective albeit not very subtle message to single women. The first two paragraphs of the copy reinforced the romanticized wedding moment before segueing into "Mme. Jeanette's secret of how to . . . " (achieve your own reward of securing a husband). (Figure 4-3.)

"A man's love for a woman" might culminate in a grand wedding ceremony, a Mum deodorant ad of 1925 suggested, but to attract a husband in the first place, "a woman's personal daintiness must be safeguarded against the distressing odor of perspiration." A bridesmaid in the foreground of the ad ponders this advice with one finger to her lips, revealing a ringless left hand. (Figure 4-4.)

Manufacturers of personal hygiene products such as Mum deodorant knew that such subjects as body odor were not topics of polite conversation. Even friends will not tell you, many personal hygiene ads warned. "Such deficiencies of advice gave advertisers the opportunity to dispense the needed counsel in conjunction with their product," wrote Marchand.[8] Taking heed of an advertiser's counsel could help change the status of a ringless left hand, implied these ads with their wedding themes and images.

Figure 4-3. The cosmetic industry especially promoted the promise that "the reward of beauty" was a bridal veil and wedding bouquet. Ad 1925.

Figure 4-4. Even beauty may not be enough to get a man to propose marriage if a woman ignores her "feminine daintiness," warned advertisers of personal hygiene products. Ad 1925.

Figure 4-5. For personal subjects as sensitive as bad breath, advertisers felt at liberty to counsel the public with warnings and advice. Left ad 1931, right ad 1956.

Another shortcoming advertisers felt at liberty to discuss with readers was bad breath. For Listerine, advice was interwoven in a wide assortment of melodramatic parables in ads that spanned generations. Despite the sentimental picture of the happy bride and groom in a 1931 ad, the copy implied that a serious threat to their marriage might loom on the horizon. (Figure 4-5.) The use of negative words and phrases such as "till breath do us part," "grounds for separation," "extreme cruelty," and "unhappiness with her husband" were specifically chosen to inflame paranoia in both brides and grooms, as well as readers hoping to become one or the other. This same

Figure 4-6. Ads for beauty soaps frequently used images of real-life brides and their "testimonials" about the featured brands.

1934

1949

1951

1957

1971

1942

Figure 4-7. Whatever type of marriage ceremony the bride might expect, the one common denominator was the wedding ring. Spanning the entire century, ads for jewelers especially targeted brides.

wedding day melodrama was played out in a 1956 ad from Listerine in which the "poor girl" cannot figure out why she is "often a bridesmaid . . . never a bride." The footnote at the bottom of the page explains all and is punctuated with a bottle of the product small enough to simulate an exclamation point.

Pictures of real-life brides were especially popular in ads for beauty soaps. (Figure 4-6.) "Brides . . . because they made themselves lovelier than other girls," a Lux Toilet Soap ad of the 1930s asserted; "proof positive that the girl with a radiantly lovely complexion always wins in the game of hearts." Likewise, the Woodbury soap ads of the 1940s and Camay soap ads of the 1950s presented depictions of real brides with romanticized vignettes of their newlywed lives. Like looking at wedding pictures that were passed around in women's social circles, these ads were irresistible to female readers. Once drawn into the ad, the cause and effect message—that is, that by using the advertised soap these women became brides—was not lost on the consumer.

The most obvious use of a bride in advertising was to promote those products made specifically for the wedding day. At the top of the list was the wedding ring. Whether the ceremony was to be large or small, religious or civilian, formal or individualized, the common denominator for all weddings was the ring. Spanning the century, ads for jewelers especially focused on the bride as their primary target. (Figure 4-7.) How and where the finger ring was first used in conjunction with marriage is still debated among historians.

Figure 4-8. Jewelry advertisers helped create a bride's expectations of a high-quality diamond ring by which her friends would take the measure of her husband. Ad 1927.

Some scholars have maintained that the wedding ring was first used about five thousand years ago by the Egyptians of the Third Dynasty, for whom it symbolized the circle of eternity for which marriage was binding. Other authorities maintain that the ring grew out of the use of fetters that were placed upon the necks, ankles, and wrists of captive women in ancient times and symbolized "man's absolute authority over the bride."[9] Whatever the origins of the wedding ring, for most women of the twentieth century it was a status symbol beyond the gold content or size of the diamond; it was proof they had achieved their singular goal in life—to be married.

The design, illustrations, and copy used in ads from wedding ring manufacturers and retailers demonstrated their particular understanding and exploitation of women's traditional thoughts and feelings about weddings and marriage. With product names like Keepsake and ad slogans like DeBeers's "a diamond is forever," the psychological emphasis to women readers was on "keep" and "forever." The romantic images of the happy bridal couple or other trappings of a wedding were easily complemented with the expected maudlin sentiments in the ad copy. "I want all things that women have always dreamed of," a bride seems to be saying on behalf of all brides in a 1971 DeBeers ad; half the space features a photo close-up of a wedding cake topped by the traditional bride and groom figurines beneath a symbolic bell.

Even when describing wedding rings as consumer commodities, copywriters carefully chose words that echoed the theme of the wedding event. The 1942 Keepsake engagement sets may have been "the choice of lasting pride and satisfaction," but any bride-to-be reading the copy would have hoped the same of her marriage. Palladium rings "faithfully" reflected "true" colors in their diamonds, the copy avowed in a 1957 ad, just as the bride would want "true" love and a "faithful" husband.

Many jewelry manufacturers and retailers cleverly targeted both the bride and the groom with their ads. One of a series sponsored by a jewelers association in the 1920s was directed specifically to the groom with the title "The symbol of her pride in you." (Figure 4-8.) Not only is the groom told that his choice of rings will be "the standard by which her friends will find your measure," but the bride is told that her expectations of "enduring happiness" would begin here, with her man's choice of rings. More than half a century later, this bride's granddaughter would read the same message—as would her fiancé—in a long-running DeBeers campaign of the 1980s and 1990s. One 1983 version advised grooms that "a really nice diamond" costs about "2 months' salary." After all, it is a "question of priorities," concluded the copy, "and what's more important than the woman you love?"[10] Although the texts of both of these ads, written generations apart, specifically targeted men, the illustrations were aimed at women to be sure they too read the copy.

In addition to jewelers, ready-to-wear and fashion accessory makers, stationers, and caterers, another business that had a special interest in product merchandising for weddings was the flower industry. (Figure 4-9.)

Figure 4-9. Weddings and anniversaries provided opportunities for florists, candy manufacturers, and greeting card distributors to establish brand loyalties with consumers. Ad 1947.

Figure 4-10. A marriage created a new entity with "visions of the many, many purchases" yet to be made, as this Warren's Papers ad noted in 1926.

Representations of brides in ads such as those produced by the Florist Telegraph Delivery served a dual purpose, as the copy suggested in a 1947 version. From the bridal bouquet to every "succeeding anniversary," a wife should expect flowers to "tell her that you remembered . . . that you love her." Like ads for wedding rings, this was another example of how both men and women were targeted with messages that were designed to set a wife's expectations and inspire a husband's obligations. The end result was a product loyalty that served not only florists and jewelers, but also the candy, gift, and greeting card industries as well.

The tradition of giving gifts to the bridal couple is an ancient one practiced in societies all around the world. (Figure 4-10.) For most young couples of the twentieth century about to set up housekeeping and start a family, the list of needs was lengthy. A 1926 ad for Warren's Papers showed a bridegroom surveying the display of gifts and seeing "visions of many, many purchases he never thought he would have to make." This groom, united with his bride, "becomes at once a new sort of customer," the ad copy advised manufacturers and retailers, which meant that "two pairs of eyes will look with new interest at shop-windows, at booklets, and at catalogs." However, even before the newlywed becomes this "new sort of customer," family and friends of the couple were expected to shower them with gifts for setting up housekeeping. "Every peal of a wedding bell is the beginning of a response to somebody's advertising," the Warren's ad stated. For manufacturers of products that were appropriate to give as wedding gifts, that meant another opportunity to

Figure 4-11. Manufacturers of flatware, cutlery, china, cookware, and other such household necessities sought to capture the attention of affianced women with depictions of fashionable brides in ads.

1916

1921

1926

1948

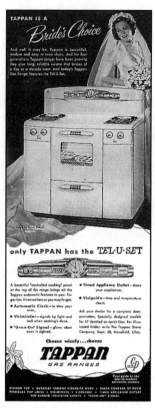

Figure 4-12. For manufacturers of home appliances, the newlywed wife was an ideal target for their marketing efforts. General Electric ad 1938, Tappan ad 1948.

depict a bride in ads and draw the attention of women consumers. For brides, these ads provided ideas for their wish lists.

Silver manufacturers particularly capitalized on the wedding as the key event for marketing their products. (Figure 4-11.) The new bride would need flatware and cutlery from the very start of her new life. "In the best American homes the service of Alvin Silver begins on the wedding day," said the copy in a 1916 ad. For ads in the 1920s by Wallace and Holmes & Edwards, the bride is shown removed from the wedding ceremony and is represented in an adoration of the product—in both cases, a teaspoon bearing the design of a current flatware pattern. The pattern illustrated in a 1921 Wallace ad was "ideally suitable as a wedding gift," suggested the copy. "For the day of all days, the gift of all gifts is exquisite silverplate," recommended a Holmes & Edwards ad in 1926. In fact, throughout the twentieth century the gift of silverware continued to be as much of a wedding tradition as the bouquet and veil, due in part to the assiduous marketing efforts of silver manufacturers.

As the Warren's Paper's ad shown in Figure 4-10 advised manufacturers, a "wedding day is a birthday of new needs." Setting up housekeeping was an expensive undertaking, and the majority of newlywed couples needed most everything, from silverware to home appliances. The image of the bride, still in her wedding gown but anxious to begin her life as a homemaker, was the perfect visual hook for brand positioning of refrigerators, stoves, washing machines, and other household appliances to newlyweds. (Figure 4-12.) Even if the young couple could not afford such major purchases, or their families could not afford to give such expensive items as wedding gifts, the ads placed the products' brand names before the bride

1929

1935

1963

Figure 4-13. The image of the bride was effective in targeting women consumers even if the products advertised were unrelated to weddings.

who would presumably purchase them at some point in her domestic life. "And they lived thriftily ever after," the opening paragraph promised in a 1938 General Electric refrigerator ad. "Reliable service that brides of a day or decade want," a 1948 Tappan range ad touted.

The image of a bride in many ads did not necessarily relate directly to the product or service being promoted. (Figure 4-13.) Comparing the "important decision" of choosing a floor varnish to that of choosing a spouse was a stretch for Berry Brothers in a 1929 ad. Invoking part of the wedding vows in the copy, the varnish manufacturer warned that to use an ordinary varnish would be to finish one's floors "for richer, for poorer—for better, for worse." Still, for brand positioning, the beautiful painting by the famous illustrator Andrew Loomis was compelling to women readers. Similarly, throughout the century, brides were depicted in ads as diverse as those for auto parts and wristwatches, whose marketing message had little or no relationship to a wedding. Advertisers knew that few women could resist being drawn into these ads for closer examination of the models' gowns, or to read the copy beneath headers declaring "happily ever after" or "get 'em to the church on time."

Marketing the Image of Mother and Child

Across the greater part of the twentieth century, no images—not those of brides, fashionable women, celebrities, or furry animals—were more powerful or prolific in advertising than those of children.

"The great object of the conjugal union is the transmission of life," wrote physician George Napheys in his *Physical Life of Woman* in 1870.[11] Despite

Man's debt to WOMAN

One of the finest traditions of the human race is the sacrifice women make to bear children. Since time began, they have gladly risked health, beauty, life itself, if necessary—and seldom counted the cost. Medical science will never hold a surer claim to immortality than the record of its painstaking efforts to lighten the shadows of child-birth.

Today, motherhood is easier and far safer. And this is due not only to the modern hospital and the great strides made in obstetrics, but also to the spread of beneficial knowledge into the home, to a wider understanding of such things as diet, exercise and simple everyday care.

Since 1858 the House of Squibb has led in producing simple, trustworthy products for the medicine cabinet, many of which contribute to the comfort and welfare of the expectant mother. Into the making of these products goes exactly the same high skill as is devoted to preparing the important vaccines and anti-toxins for which the Squibb Laboratories are so well known. And we count it a tribute indeed that numberless physicians instinctively specify the name Squibb when they prescribe milk of magnesia, liquid petrolatum or any of the familiar products used in the home.

Whether to meet an emergency or to fill the needs of everyday life, the Squibb label is a pledge of purity and safety . . . the guarantee of an extra value which Squibb Products have always contained: The Priceless Ingredient, the Honor and Integrity of the Maker.

E. R. SQUIBB & SONS

Squibb's Home Necessities

Many Squibb Products are helpful during pregnancy and valuable in the care of the baby. A few are described below. Your physician will advise you concerning them.

SQUIBB'S LIQUID PETROLATUM (Pure Mineral Oil)—an effective internal lubricant for preventing constipation . . . odorless, tasteless—non-habit-forming, non-fattening. Safe for expectant mothers and for even the youngest baby.

SQUIBB'S MILK OF MAGNESIA—a safe, effective antacid and gentle laxative—free from any suggestion of earthy taste. Valuable in combating hyper-acidity during pregnancy. As a mouth-wash, good for the teeth and gums.

SQUIBB'S COD-LIVER OIL—a pure, refined product uniformly rich in Vitamins A and D. Widely used by the expectant mother to build reserve strength and also to promote the formation of sound bones and teeth by the baby.

SQUIBB'S VITAVOSE—a wheat flour sugar for milk

modification, exceptionally rich in Vitamin B and assimilable iron salts. Promotes growth and stimulates the appetite.

SQUIBB'S DENTAL CREAM—made with 50% Squibb's Milk of Magnesia—neutralizes acids, protects as it cleans. Guards The Danger Line. Combats "gingival tooth decay," a form of tooth decay particularly associated with pregnancy.

SQUIBB'S NURSERY POWDER—an unusually fine, impalpable powder, prepared from the best Italian talc. Pure and non-irritating. Fragrant and soothing.

SQUIBB'S OLIVE OIL—a pure oil pressed from the finest-quality hand-picked olives. Use will prefer its crystal-clearness. Used by many mothers for massaging the baby.

SQUIBB'S BICARBONATE OF SODA—refined to an unusual degree of purity, hence more palatable and efficacious. Often recommended by physicians for an upset condition of the stomach.

SQUIBB'S CASTOR OIL—special Squibb processes of refining and manufacture make it tasteless, and it stays that way.

AT ALL RELIABLE DRUG STORES FEATURING SERVICE AND QUALITY PRODUCTS

New York . . . E. R. Squibb & Sons of Canada, Limited, Toronto
Manufacturing Chemists to the Medical Profession since 1858

Figure 4-14. The sentiment of motherhood provided universal appeal as a theme in advertising. Ad 1930.

the other significant political, economic, and social objectives of marriage throughout the centuries, the fundamental basis of wedlock, and of woman's reason to exist, the Victorians maintained, was childbearing.

To question this premise was unthinkable for women prior to the twentieth century. Even then, any woman who would want to remain childless was regarded as being abnormal. "I don't want to be a mother," wrote Margery Lawrence in an article for *Cosmopolitan* in 1929. "Because—quite honestly—I don't want to! And I bluntly declare, moreover, that there is nothing whatever wrong with me, mentally, morally, or physically, in not wanting a child."[12] Even in the Roaring Twenties, such an opinion was a scandalous anomaly, the kind intended more to sell magazines than to reflect any kind of significant social change. In fact, when *Cosmopolitan* ran an ad promoting the Lawrence article in other Hearst publications, the editors of *Good Housekeeping* included a disclaimer: "Good Housekeeping families will challenge that statement. ['I don't want to be a mother.'] Yet being fair-minded, they will want to hear Margery Lawrence state the views of a type of woman increasingly common today—the kind who may be called the frankly non-maternal."[13]

In actuality, the trend of couples remaining childless by design was not "increasingly common." In the Middletown study, the Lynds cited a 1925 newspaper editorial that more likely expressed the prevailing sentiment of the time. Readers were told that "married persons who deliberately refuse to take the responsibility of children are reasonable targets for popular opprobrium."[14] One can well imagine the kinds of letters that flooded in to Margery Lawrence and the editors of both *Cosmopolitan* and *Good Housekeeping.*

One of the many typical marketing tributes to the sentiment of motherhood was presented in a 1930 ad from Squibb pharmaceutics headlined "Man's debt to woman." (Figure 4-14.) The scenario depicts the mother soon after giving birth as she lies in her recovery bed and is attended by her husband. The illustration is composed almost like a religious painting with warm colors bathed in a glowing light from above. Next to the mother's head, the ad copy opens with an explanation of the headline: "One of the finest traditions of the human race is the sacrifice women make to bear children." Certainly, no Middletown woman consumer could resist reading every word of this ad.

The social and political status of the post–World War II American mother has been the topic of much scholarship and debate. "Once the image makers in the magazines, on radio, and on television had guided girls toward their wedding days and their tidy houses in the suburbs," wrote Annegret Ogden in *The Great American Housewife,* "the experts in the universities

began to convey information and advice that would make American women
the most informed and sophisticated mothers in the world."[15] The many studies and textbooks on Sigmund Freud's theories of child development and
social Darwinism may have influenced trends for child care, but to marketers of consumer goods, such trends impacted advertising strategies very
little. Mass-media surveys such as those in the one hundredth anniversary
issues of *McCall's* in 1976, *Ladies' Home Journal* in 1984, and *Good
Housekeeping* in 1985 provided a better finger on the pulse of the American
woman's consumerism than esoteric research by experts in academia, government agencies, and private foundations. In fact, the influence could run
the other way, with social changes affecting the conclusions of the experts.
For instance, as the percent of working mothers increased during the 1970s,
Benjamin Spock significantly altered his 1976 edition of *Baby and Child
Care* by moving his discussion of the working mother out of the section on
"special problems";[16] society's attitude had changed, and as a result, had
changed the attitude of the expert.

Still, throughout the twentieth century, a predominant segment of
American women wanted to have children and all that that encompassed.
For advertisers, empirical evidence and research data reaffirmed this decade
after decade and made target marketing fairly easy and predictable. In her
1990 book on advertising and identity, Carol Moog noted:

> About the second month of a baby's life, when seemingly end-
> less feedings, diaperings, and pacings have cranked the new par-
> ents' frazzle level to an electric high...the baby smiles. It isn't
> just one of those random smiles that occasionally tag along with
> a sneeze or burp—she smiles *back* at her parents.
>
> Ingenuous design. There's a powerful psychological function
> in that wonderful, irresistible smile. It's nature's lock on sur-
> vival. And it works because it's part of our psychobiological
> makeup to be suckers for kids.
>
> So it's no accident that children in advertising are notorious-
> ly superb attention-grabbers. That's one of their biggest job
> assignments in life, and it's our job to respond.[17]

Most ads that employed images of children targeted mothers and their
parenting needs: providing food and clothing, caring for and nurturing their
children, ensuring and safeguarding their children's health. Moreover, a
great many other ads depicted these "notoriously superb attention-grabbers"
to sell everything from auto tires to camera film.

The foremost concern of mothers was feeding their children and therefore, assuring the good health of their children. Nutrition and diet were much
studied and written about in the nineteenth century. Women's magazines
were filled with advice columns such as "Mother's Corner" in the *Ladies'
Home Journal,* which focused on proper foods and menus for children. In
the American consumer society that emerged during the second half of the
nineteenth century, a wide assortment of products were manufactured to aid
the mother in providing nutrition for her children. Photographs and illustrations of robust, chubby infants in ads assured mothers that much could be
done for the health of their children, and commercial products were readily
available to help. (Figure 4-15.) The nation's high rate of infant mortality
and its links to disease and nutrition were topics frequently used in the

Figure 4-15. Commercially prepared infant formulas were introduced in the 1870s. Although these easy-to-use mixtures saved the mother hours of preparing homemade recipes, the nutritional benefits were the primary focus of sales promotions. Ads 1900–1901.

accompanying ad copy for these products. For example, a Nestlé ad from 1895 featuring a mother and baby cites a U.S. Department of Agriculture report about impure milk, noting that "20, 30 and even 50 per cent of certain herds that supply New York City with milk are affected with tuberculosis; and other able veterinarians have testified to the same condition of affairs in other parts of the country."[18] As a result of such alarming reports, pasteurized canned milk and powdered milk products became more widely distributed and advertised.

Since cow's milk alone was not sufficient for the complete nutritional needs of infants, Victorian child-care books contained complicated recipes for baby formulas to augment diets of cow's milk. Just one feeding could take more than half an hour to prepare. One recipe from the 1860s provided step-by-step cooking instructions after combining the ingredients: "This mixture is then heated upon a slow fire, being constantly stirred until it begins to get thick. At this period, the vessel is removed from the fire, and the mixture is stirred for five minutes, is again heated, and again removed when it gets thick, and lastly it is heated till it boils."[19]

It is hardly surprising that commercially prepared formulas, which needed only to be spooned into warm milk, were an instant success when introduced in the late 1870s. These formulated milk additives, made of such ingredients as powdered grains and eggs, were promoted as the means to assuring a baby's chances of survival. "Give the baby Mellin's Food if you wish your infant to be well nourished, healthy, bright, and active, and to grow up happy, robust, and vigorous," the ad for one formula promised in 1893.[20]

In addition to these advertised claims, manufacturers of processed baby foods often produced child-care guides containing recipes and suggestions for feeding children. Mothers at the turn of the century were invited to write for a free sample of the product and a copy of booklets such as Allenbury's *Infant Feeding and Management,* Nestlé's *Infant Hygiene,* and Eskay's *How to Care for the Baby.*[21] Since these helpful guides often were written by physicians, women came to trust the brand-name products for which the

1936

1951

1957

Figure 4-16. With the baby boom following the First World War, manufacturers of processed foods for infants expanded product lines to offer greater variety. Thereafter, few mothers would bother with the tedious and time-consuming preparation of homemade strained foods and formulas for their infants.

publications were produced. "By offering both the product and the comforting advice," wrote historian Harvey Green, "the corporation began to take the place of the doctor or family."[22]

This comforting advice was also the core of much of the ad copy for processed baby foods throughout the twentieth century. Mothers would scour the sell messages in these ads for suggestions, warnings, and recommendations on better child care and parenting. (Figure 4-16.) Two contrasting images made the dual message in a 1936 Heinz ad clear. The captivating rendering of a happy baby bespoke good food, while the black-and-white photo of a harried mother struggling to prepare her own strained baby foods reinforced the convenience of processed foods. Why bother, the copy asked, when you can have "peace of mind" with Heinz's ten varieties, which in addition to being convenient to mothers and tasty to babies "are accepted by the American Medical Association's Committee on Foods." Such "peace of mind" was similarly offered in a 1951 ad to mothers who chose one of the varieties of Pablum, especially since the brand truly was "prescribed by doctors." During the 1950s and 1960s, Gerber ads were formatted as advice columns titled "Bringing Up Baby." The ads featured "hints collected by Mrs. Dan Gerber, mother of 5," including suggestions for child training and safety as well as the expected advice on nutrition.

Nutrition was but one aspect of a child's welfare for which manufacturers and advertisers provided solutions and advice to mothers. During the baby boom following the First World War, a myriad of specialized health-care

1925

1933

Figure 4-17. Ads by soap manufacturers advised mothers that special attention to a baby's skin care was important to the child's health.

1947

products burst onto the American consumer market. Mothers especially were targets of the ads for children's skin-care and first aid products, cold remedies, and over-the-counter medications. After all, greater quantities of these products were likely to be used for children; their immune systems were more vulnerable to viruses than those of adults; they were subject to far more cuts, scrapes, and bruises; and their tender skin needed more protection from the elements. The remedy instructions and advice offered in ads and on packaging for health and first aid products were much welcomed by mothers. Even into the 1930s, visits to doctors, and especially hospitals, were for life-threatening emergencies only. As the Lynds observed in their Middletown study during the 1920s, this was particularly true given the persistence of a "strong pioneer individualism," which regarded issues of health as a family's "private matter."[23] The "Doctor Mom" theme used in ads by A. H. Robins in the 1990s was very much a reality for most mothers through the first half of the century.

The American consumer society did not leap to buy everything manufacturers created for children, even when the products were marketed under the umbrella of health care. For example, specialized products for protecting a child's skin were not readily accepted initially. Instead, manufacturers had to overcome the firmly entrenched Victorian "culture of the skin," as books on child care popularly called the notion. Experts of the time insisted that a child's skin needed to be kept absolutely clean and completely covered as the best method to "ward off disease." Even the use of soap for bathing the child, including brands "of the best kind," could lead to "various eruptions" if the mother was not careful, warned Dr. Napheys in his 1870 book. "If due attention were paid to the condition of the skin in early life," he wrote, "many of the most common ailments of childhood would be averted."[24]

Manufacturers thus had to counter this guarded child-care tradition with their own advice on cleanliness and health through their advertising. To redirect women's thinking on baby's skin-care needs, nineteenth-century soap manufacturers began to depict playful, happy, healthy babies and children in their ads. Ad copy likewise began to emphasize the importance of using the right soap to best secure a child's health. In an Ivory ad from 1892, the copy recommended that "to achieve the full measure of strength, health and stature, boys should be encouraged early in life to frequent bathing, especially after perspiring and cooling, so that the skin pores may be promptly opened and healthful reaction take place."[25] In addition to aggressive advertising, another successful method of marketing soaps to mothers was the creation of brands specifically formulated for children, such as Kirk's Juvenile Toilet Soap, introduced in the 1890s.

By the first decade of the twentieth century, soap manufacturers had their ad messages finely tuned and well focused. (Figure 4-17.) The irresistible images of babies and children were the hooks, and endorsements from "doctors" in the copy created a sense of credibility. "Mothers know it protects," proclaimed the header in a two-page Lifebuoy ad in 1925, but the advice in the copy is signed by "the Health Doctor." A doctor is quoted in a 1933 Palmolive ad as saying "olive oil in soap is best," and a 1947 Ivory ad claimed that "more doctors advise Ivory Soap for babies' tender skin than all other brands put together."

The success of soap manufacturers, with their advertised advocacy of cleanliness and health for children, opened the door for marketers of related skin-care products. By 1900, manufactured baby powders, oils, lotions, and shampoos were standard nursery items. (Figure 4-18.) In a way, manufacturers of these products actually perpetuated the nineteenth-century "culture of the skin" idea. Although the Victorian mother may have been reluctant to powder and anoint her child as these products recommended in their ads, she would have easily recognized the language used in the ad copy. "Do you know that your baby's health depends partly on the skin?" asked the opening sentence in a 1922 Johnson & Johnson ad. "Because it speedily banishes itching, chafing and tormenting irritations, Johnson's Baby Powder relieves the nervous fidgeting so harmful to health," continued the copy, followed by a list of "reasons why physicians prefer Johnson's." Similarly, a 1922 Bauer & Black ad for baby talc offered the advice of "what 112 doctors told us." Written in a format mothers would have recognized from books and articles on child care, the ad copy presented scientific causes for skin rashes and infection, while recommending a comforting remedy: B&B Baby Talc.

Figure 4-18. Child skin care advertising by soap manufacturers paved the way for marketers of related products such as baby powders, lotions, and oils. Ads 1922.

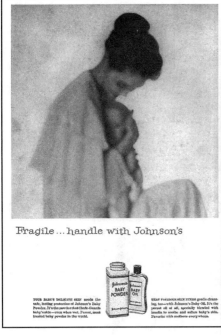

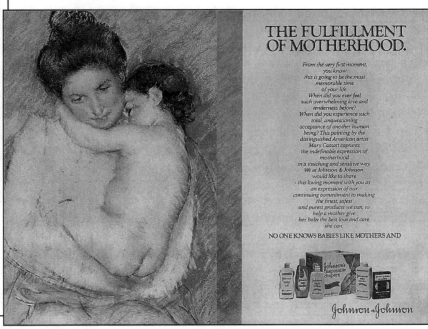

Figure 4-19. Images of a mother and her baby used in advertising were often intentionally reminiscent of familiar Madonna and Child artworks. Left ad 1957, right ad 1980.

Both of these ads were typically illustrated with a mother holding her baby, intentionally reminiscent of familiar Madonna and Child artworks. Even the linear rendering and costuming of the figures in the illustration of the B&B ad seems to be derived from fifteenth- century Italian painters like Botticelli. Decade after decade, these images of a mother and child were featured in innumerable ads and never failed to achieve an impact of sentiment that was irresistible to most women. (Figure 4-19.)

Protecting the child's sensitive skin extended to products far removed from the pharmaceutical industries that produced baby powders, oils, and

Figure 4-20. The health and care of a baby's skin also became a marketing segmentation of tissue and toilet paper manufacturers. Left ad 1926, right ad 1950.

FOUR QUESTIONS TO ASK
before you treat a child's cold

It's dangerous to *experiment* with children's colds. A cold, improperly treated, may lead to mastoid trouble, flu, pneumonia. Take no chances, Mother. Before you use any cold remedy, ask yourself these questions:

1 Is it dependable? Vicks VapoRub has been *proved* dependable—by mothers in 70 nations.

2 Is it safe? Vicks VapoRub is absolutely safe. It is used *externally*. With VapoRub, you avoid the risks of constant internal dosing

which so often upsets delicate digestions.

3 Is it suitable for children? Being applied externally, VapoRub can be used freely—and as often as needed—even on the youngest child.

4 Is it prompt? Just rubbed on at bedtime, VapoRub goes right to work to relieve the cold . . . brings medication *direct* to the seat of trouble. By morning, almost always, the worst of the cold is over.

Vicks ★
VapoRub

BEST FOR
CHILDREN'S COLDS

VapoRub's famous poultice-vapor action works all night long. Through the skin it "draws out" tightness and soreness. At the same time, its soothing medicated vapors are inhaled *direct* to irritated air-passages, bring soothing comfort and relief! . . Your druggist has Vicks VapoRub—in the original amber or new *stainless* white.

for Stopped-Up Nostrils..
..use MENTHOLATUM

Aids *Freer Breathing*
Restores COMFORT

When your child has a cold nothing must be allowed to rob him of the one thing he needs more than ever—plenty of sleep. If a stopped-up nose due to a cold makes it hard for him to breathe, put cool-

ing, soothing Mentholatum in both nostrils. Mentholatum will help to clear the nasal passages, thereby promoting easier breathing. And it is perfectly harmless to the delicate tissues of the nose.

MENTHOLATUM

Figure 4-21. Few images in advertising were more heart-rending to women than that of a sick child. Manufacturers of over-the-counter pharmaceuticals challenged the mother's preparedness in these ads. Vicks VapoRub ad 1934, Mentholatum ad 1935.

lotions. For instance, manufacturers of facial tissue and toilet paper also targeted mothers of babies and young children. (Figure 4-20.) Prior to the mass production of such disposable paper commodities in the late nineteenth century, mothers had been advised by child-care authorities to clean their babies between diaper changes with soft flannel cloth. Reusing washcloths meant having to do even more laundry, and more frequently than just on Mondays. For many women, the convenience of paper products more than offset the expense.

Convenience, however, was not the focus of advertising for paper products. The headline "Mother's Responsibility" next to the illustration of a giant roll of toilet paper in a 1926 ScotTissue ad was an unmistakable message. "She cannot afford to have anything that does not protect and promote the health and comfort of her children," explained the supporting copy. The marketing strategy for ScotTissue was not only product education, but also competitive differentiation. "Harsh, non-absorbent" tissues could "harm or irritate" the sensitive skin of children, these ads warned, but ScotTissue "is safe for children." The Victorian culture of the skin had found new meaning in the twentieth century. "His skin is so sensitive even the tiniest harshness might irritate it," said the copy in ScotTissue ads of the 1950s, continuing the theme from decades earlier.

An even more compelling image to mothers than that of a happy child is the depiction of a sick child. (Figure 4-21.) Such ads are "aimed at the soft underbellies of doting parents," wrote Carol Moog. As intended, she noted, these ads "make parents reevaluate, uneasily, their medical preparedness."[26] For the pharmaceutical manufacturers that mass produced remedies for the common cold or flu, ads featuring sick children were meant to induce parents to stock their home medicine cabinets in anticipation of the inevitable contagions.

Figure 4-22. As with the makers of cold remedies, first aid manufacturers emphasized in their ads the need for medical preparedness. Double-Sure ad 1916, Band-Aid ad 1963.

Ironically, by extension, the ads for these products also benefited the patent medicine industry well into the twentieth century. A decade after the first Middletown study, the Lynds observed in the 1930s that "In such a world, where sickness and money are so closely related and the institutional world encourages self-help, it is not surprising that patent medicines flourish today as in 1925."[27] Even as late as the 1950s, readers could flip through the back pages of many legitimate periodicals to find dozens of small-space ads for medicines and health treatments of dubious efficacy. In 1958, *Redbook* was still warning mothers against "quack medicine" and the perils of misleading, though "honest," words in medicine ads and packaging.[28]

Certainly, the use of misleading, "honest" words was evident in the battle of ads between Tylenol and Bayer in the 1970s. Tylenol claimed to be "safer than aspirin" because "aspirin causes very serious side effects in infants and children," including upset stomach and "dangerous aspirin build-up in their systems." In response, a contemporary ad from Bayer blasted its competition with the boldface headline, "No, Mother, Tylenol is not found safer than aspirin!" Quoting from a finding by the Food and Drug Administration, the Bayer ads warned mothers against the possibility of "liver damage" from acetaminophen, the active ingredient in Tylenol.[29] Despite the confusion sometimes created by such advertising adversaries, a significant part of the success of the over-the-counter drug industry was due to advertising that targeted mothers.

Many of these ads did contain beneficial medical and health information. For instance, ads sometimes taught mothers how to recognize the symptoms of childhood's more common ailments, as well as suggesting methods of relief or cure. Also, text in food and drug ads many times provided advice on the significance of certain vitamins and minerals in preventing or combating illness. This "educational advertising," as Christine Frederick noted in her 1929 book *Selling Mrs. Consumer,* helped a mother learn "to be a very competent home health guardian."[30]

Another distressing image effectively used by advertisers was that of the injured child. (Figure 4-22.) Mothers might be able to

Figure 4-23. Mothers regarded with keen interest the advice, recommendations, and warnings in ads about children's health and safety. Ad 1930.

1916

1926

1947

Figure 4-24. The various related businesses in the auto industry often included the theme of child safety in their ads. Images and headlines such as these examples most likely sent many a mother to her husband or auto center to question the condition of her car's tires or shocks.

1956

1971

guard against a child's health problems caused by inadequate nutrition and sanitation, but minor injuries from frequent accidents were unpredictable and unavoidable with children. The theme of advertising for first aid products was similar to that for cold remedies: be prepared. Before the creation of the Band-Aid in the 1920s, advertisers suggested that a well-stocked first aid kit should include several varieties of dressings, as well as antiseptic ointments and topical treatments. "These things must be kept on hand if you hope to cope with an emergency," the copy advised in a 1916 Double-Sure ad. The image of the injured child, familiar to all mothers, was always presented in a non-life-threatening scenario in these kinds of ads. The reader could instantly identify with the mother depicted in the ad without connecting negative feelings to the product that a more graphic image might generate.

The health and welfare of children also included the parents' protection through prevention. In the American consumer society that advertising helped create, mothers were besieged with ads that cajoled and manipulated them into making purchases for the benefit of their children. Such advertising illustrated or tacitly implied the dangers of ignoring the protection a product could provide for a child's safety and health. In the preceding chapter we examined how advertisers promoted the use of household disinfectants to the homemaker. It was her responsibility to protect her family with

FIRE! WITH A SCREAM I SNATCHED LITTLE RUTH

We scarcely had time to move, the fire spread so fast. But Pyrene was quicker than gasoline fire. It stopped the blaze before any damage was done.

"John," said I, as we drove on, "wasn't it thoughtful of you to get those Pyrenes for our car and home?"

"If I hadn't and you or Ruth had been hurt in that fire," he replied, "I could never look you in the face again."

$10 buys Pyrene and bracket. Pyrene makes your car perfectly safe against the danger of quick spreading gasoline fire. It keeps women and children from being trapped in burning homes, too.

Pyrene Manufacturing Company, New York City
Fire Extinguishers, Hose, Engines, all fire appliances

Pyrene
KILLS FIRE
SAVES LIFE

Figure 4-25. Mothers were besieged with ads that cajoled and manipulated them into making purchases of products for the protection of their children. Pyrene ad 1917.

a germ-free environment, these ads insisted. Similarly, Flit insect spray melodramatically advertised in 1930 that it was "the mother who stands between her children and disease." (Figure 4-23.) Quoting from a U.S. Public Health Service report, the ad challenged mothers to "be on your guard" against typhoid fever spread by the common housefly.

In fact, judging from the two Middletown studies, contagious diseases such as diphtheria, cholera, smallpox, and typhoid fever indeed were serious threats to children well into the twentieth century. Despite the efforts of public service programs of the 1920s to prevent epidemics through education, organizations such as the Social Service Bureau, the American Red Cross, and the Visiting Nurses Association made little headway against local business interests and state government bureaucracies.[31] In the 1935 study of Middletown in transition, the Lynds concluded that regarding "the problem of public and private health ... Middletown stands today substantially where it stood in 1925."[32] As a result of these unyielding social attitudes and conditions, marketers knew that mothers paid attention to the advice, recommendations, and warnings in ads featuring information on child care.

Child-safety issues also served the marketing efforts of the auto industry. Ads for cars and related products used this emotional appeal early in the century and throughout each succeeding decade. (Figure 4-24.) The carnage that could result from a serious auto accident would never be appropriate for advertisers to illustrate. Although a few tire ads of the teens and twenties depicted auto accidents where children were shown lying unconscious in the street, blood and gore were never in evidence. Such negative emotional attachments to a product would be counterproductive. Instead, the depiction of a happy child in a mother's embrace could say it all. "Confidence," was the header in a 1916 Baker ad; "the mother finds comfort in knowing that the safety and pleasure of her little ones are enhanced because of this driving simplicity," continued the text. The copy that accompanied a 1926 Firestone ad, which was headlined "why women buy tires," probably sent thousands of mothers to their husbands asking about the brand of tires on their cars. Safety and peace of mind were at the top of the list of benefits in a 1947 Body by Fisher ad—ahead of the usual style theme that had been the hallmark of the company's marketing for decades. "Do it for their protection," a 1956 Dunlop ad told suburbanite housewives who chauffeured their children about. The attention-grabbing photo of a child with a "loaded" gun used in a 1971 ad for Columbus shock absorbers underscored the safety issue of worn shocks and prompted many mothers to question the condition of the shocks on their cars.

Besides selling new cars, tires, or shock absorbers, these emotional appeal ads also served to ensure future sales through brand positioning. Advertisers were building women's trust in a product's label so that whether they made the purchase or influenced the purchase, the brand would be foremost in their minds as a product that provided safety for their children.

Mothers also responded to terrifying ads about the dangers of fire. (Figure 4-25.) In a 1917 Pyrene ad, the dialog in the copy assured readers that the child and mother featured in the illustration escaped the fire they were shown fleeing, thanks to a Pyrene extinguisher. By the end of the century, smoke detectors were the products most aggressively advertised for a family's protection against fires. Insurance policies required them in homes and

Figure 4-26. For some subjects that parents may have found difficult to discuss with their children, such as the facts of life, ads sometimes provided help with scripts in the copy. Kotex ad 1928, Modess ad 1971.

apartments, as did many city ordinances. News stories about fires involving fatalities emphasized when smoke detectors were absent or, worse, simply lacked functioning batteries.

Teaching children to survive in life extended beyond just the physiological needs. The social preparedness and psychological well-being of a child were considerable concerns to all parents. Generation after generation, child-care experts addressed social and psychological subjects in the advice columns of women's magazines and in countless books on parenting. The dilemmas parents faced in securing proper social and psychological preparedness for their children provided yet another avenue for marketers to exploit emotional appeal in their advertising. The parental obligation to educate children extended far beyond the classroom and the three Rs. "Sometimes the man grows up to reap the results of untidy habits," a 1928 ad for a soap maker's association warned mothers; above the copy was an unsettling illustration of a disheveled homeless man on a park bench.[33] "Don't mother him to death, mother," scolded the copy in a 1943 Wilson Sports Equipment ad; instead, "urge him to enter our rugged American sports at school or college or on our playfields or sandlots wherever they are available. Nothing you can do will demonstrate your love for him as much as this."[34] Such were the typical kinds of self-serving advice from marketers that mothers could read in the editorials and ads of most any periodical throughout the century.

Most ads, though, were more reassuring than the soap or sports equipment examples. For instance, the sensitive issues of how to prepare a daughter for puberty were addressed candidly in ads by manufacturers of feminine hygiene products. (Figure 4-26.) "However carefully she may guard and advise, no mother can protect her daughter . . . at certain times," said a 1928 ad for Kotex. In case parents were not sure how to discuss the topic of a

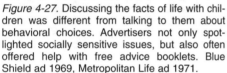

Figure 4-27. Discussing the facts of life with children was different from talking to them about behavioral choices. Advertisers not only spotlighted socially sensitive issues, but also often offered help with free advice booklets. Blue Shield ad 1969, Metropolitan Life ad 1971.

girl's first menstruation, Kotex provided a working script in the ad copy. Even decades later, despite advanced methods of public education and the influences of mass media on their children, parents were urged by marketers to do their part. "When you tell your daughter the facts of life, how many facts can you tell her about sanitary napkins?" asked a Modess ad in 1971. For those mothers who did not themselves know all the details, the Modess ad spelled out the benefits of their product, and even offered further help in a free booklet. "So she'll always be safe," the Modess ad concluded.

Talking to children about the facts of life was different from talking to them about behavioral choices, especially in the aftermath of the social upheavals of the 1960s. Advertisers with vested interests in the welfare of children, such as insurance companies, graphically captured the parent's attention in ads with timely topics such as substance abuse. (Figure 4-27.) "If you don't talk to your kid about drugs, this man will," a 1969 ad from Blue Shield warned by showing a nefarious-looking character lurking in a neighborhood. "A junkie's parents shouldn't be the last to know," stated a Metropolitan Life ad from 1971. "You could talk to your kid about drugs," continued the copy, "but your kids would know more than you do." Both ads concluded with the offer of a booklet on how to approach the subject of drug abuse with children.

Conclusion: Marketing Images and Messages for Brides and Mothers

For American brides and mothers, advertising was a constant source of information and guidance in their lives. Whether a woman was planning a wedding, setting up housekeeping, or facing the daily challenges of raising healthy, happy children, a wealth of consumer products awaited her every step of the way. From the pages of magazines and other print material to the airwaves of radio and television, brides and mothers received advice, suggestions, recommendations, directions, and warnings, all in the form of neatly packaged ads.

Throughout the twentieth century, advertisers of women's health and beauty aids used images of brides and weddings to convey a cause and effect message. The use of our soap or deodorant, these ads implied, will cause you to be more appealing and as a result will help you achieve the desired effect, a marriage proposal. Manufacturers of products that were relevant to the wedding ceremony and to the homemaking needs of the newly married woman used images of brides to specifically target those consumers. From wedding rings to bridal bouquets, from silverware to kitchen appliances, marketers were obliging with product and brand recommendations in their ads to the American bride.

Following the conventions of marriage and homemaking, most women undertook the delights and dilemmas of motherhood. Advertisers especially sought to target and influence this enormous segment of consumers. Baby pictures permeated women's periodicals by the thousands year in and year out. In 1924, a *Printers' Ink* columnist noted that marketers were increasingly "inventing legitimate reasons for the child appeal, because of its known power to attract, and its unvarying popularity with the greatest number of people." The writer explained that "The childless are inordinately fond of children. Old people have that grandmother and grandfather hunger for the chubby arms of Youth, which is at once inherent and instinctive. You are sure of this audience. A mother sees in every picture of a pretty child, her own child. Yes, this is, indeed, the universal appeal."[35]

Ads that featured these attention-grabbing images persuaded mothers to think specifically of brands and categories of products that provided special benefits for their children: gentler soaps, softer toilet paper, more reliable and effective medications. Women perused ad copy for child-care advice. Marketers successfully linked children's health and safety issues to products as diverse as processed feeding formulas and automobile tires. With the aid of scripts in ad copy, parents were even urged to discuss the facts of life with their children, from the physiological, such as puberty, to the social and psychological, such as substance abuse.

Across the twentieth century the American woman received countless advertising messages suggesting that at her nearest druggist or grocery store, via mail order or from the telephone directory, she could find the solutions to most all her needs as wife and mother.

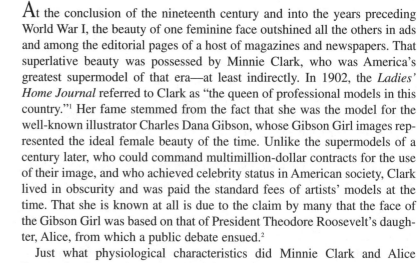

—Chapter 5

THE QUEST
FOR BEAUTY
AND HEALTH

The changing ideals of feminine beauty • The emergence of the cosmetic industry • Marketing beauty treatments and makeup regimens • The evolution of hair-care products • Specialized products for skin care—from soaps to suntan lotions • Removing unwanted hair • Promises of health • Dental care and oral hygiene • Personal hygiene and social cause and effect • The obsession with being thin • Mass marketing diet products • Fragrance and femininity

At the conclusion of the nineteenth century and into the years preceding World War I, the beauty of one feminine face outshined all the others in ads and among the editorial pages of a host of magazines and newspapers. That superlative beauty was possessed by Minnie Clark, who was America's greatest supermodel of that era—at least indirectly. In 1902, the *Ladies' Home Journal* referred to Clark as "the queen of professional models in this country."[1] Her fame stemmed from the fact that she was the model for the well-known illustrator Charles Dana Gibson, whose Gibson Girl images represented the ideal female beauty of the time. Unlike the supermodels of a century later, who could command multimillion-dollar contracts for the use of their image, and who achieved celebrity status in American society, Clark lived in obscurity and was paid the standard fees of artists' models at the time. That she is known at all is due to the claim by many that the face of the Gibson Girl was based on that of President Theodore Roosevelt's daughter, Alice, from which a public debate ensued.[2]

Just what physiological characteristics did Minnie Clark and Alice Roosevelt possess that epitomized female beauty at the beginning of the twentieth century? (Figure 5-1.) Representations of the two women present striking similarities of features: heavy-lidded eyes accented with thick lashes; fine, high eyebrows; pronounced cheekbones and firm jawlines; and full lips over perfect teeth. In glancing back at the images of these women from the perspective of a century, one is struck by the fact that their idealized beauty has remained a constant standard decade after decade. The quest for such ideals of feminine beauty, which Minnie Clark and Alice Roosevelt possessed naturally, would create a $2.5 billion cosmetic industry in the United States by the 1990s.[3] Ironically, makers of cosmetics did not succeed

Figure 5-1. The Gibson Girl exemplified the ideal beauty of women in early-twentieth-century America.

in expanding the women's consumer market as rapidly, nor as broadly, as had manufacturers of food, beverage, and household products. (Figure 5-2.) For the Victorian woman, applying a touch of face powder to preserve the virginal purity of an unblemished complexion was about as far as she dared go with makeup. The use of lip and cheek rouges was almost as scandalous as smoking cigarettes. The "painted lady" stigma was very real for women in American society. "The tinting of face and lips is considered admissible only for those upon the stage," advised an 1890s women's magazine.[4] It would take a cataclysmic event—World War I—combined with the influence of a multibillion-dollar industry—the movies—to bring down the walls of those social mores.

Writing for the *Ladies' Home Journal* in 1929, Mary Roberts Rinehart examined the roots of change during and immediately following World War I that had led to the "chaotic decade" of the 1920s. After two years of "comparative freedom of action," she explained, "the whole people were mentally below normal." Further, she wrote: "Nor was this true [solely] of the men and women whose lives had been radically altered by the war. It was true of the entire American people. The excitement had buoyed them, stimulated them; under it many of them had given money and effort, had sacrificed themselves cheerfully. But in return they had been given a vast, incredibly dramatic interest. With the sudden withdrawal of that interest they suffered from a sense of defeat and anticlimax. Daily lives became dull and humdrum once more."[5] When this mass feeling of lethargic "anticlimax" was coupled with a postwar economic recession and the passage of the Eighteenth Amendment prohibiting the sale of alcohol, the stage was set for dramatic social change.

With the dawn of the 1920s, the economy began to recover and then to roar. An era of exuberance began to unfold for the nation, and a new American woman stepped into the spotlight at center stage. Enter the "flapper."

Hollywood's contribution to the creation of this new woman was to obligingly nudge her into the 1920s with the promise of "all the excitement you lack in your daily life," as one film promotion put it.[6] She witnessed the fictional lives of glamorous and beautiful women in the flickering lights of movie houses all across the country. These glittering stars of the screen demonstrated how the modern woman could and should behave. A new morality was presented to a mass audience daily with each feature film, and a great many women eagerly embraced the new ideas and possibilities they witnessed there. If they could not in reality be caressed by the Great Lover, Rudolph Valentino, as Vilma Banky was in *The Sheik,* at least they could look like her, or like the "It" Girl, Clara Bow, or Greta Garbo, or Gloria Swanson—with the help of cosmetics. "The slick surface of the celluloid image exuded an aura of female sexuality that shocked social housekeepers and purity crusaders," noted historian Mary Ryan, "but it conformed nicely to the ambitions of the producers of consumer goods and their advertising agents, legitimizing as it did impulses for personal gratification, be they material or sexual."[7]

Marketing Beauty

At the start of the century, the cosmetic industry, including fragrances, generated nationwide sales barely totaling $7 million, but by 1921 cosmetic and fragrance sales had mushroomed to $52 million.[8] In fact, prior to 1920, only

A Lovely Face

Is often disfigured and its charm dispelled by a rough, muddy, lifeless complexion, while many otherwise plain faces are made lovely by a clear, pure skin.

LABLACHE
Face Powder

Brings beauty to every face — makes every complexion perfect. Removes all blemishes and roughness; freshens, heals, soothes the skin, making it clear, soft and smooth. It preserves a fine complexion—restores a faded one. Invisible on application. Delightful to use.

Beware of cheap substitutes

Flesh, White, Pink and Cream Tints. Price, 50c per box. Of all druggists, or by mail.

BEN. LEVY & CO.
French Perfumers
125 Kingston St., Boston, Mass., U.S.A.

Sold by ROBERTS & CO., 5 Rue de la Paix, Paris; 76 New Bond Street, London. KINGSFORD & CO., 54 Piccadilly, W., London. H. H. SWANN, 12 Rue de Castiglione, Paris. GEO. BAUMANN, 40 Pragerstrasse, Dresden.

Figure 5-2. The stigma of the "painted lady" was very real for Victorian women. Makeup for respectable ladies in the early 1900s extended solely to the use of a bit of facial powder. Ad 1900.

Figure 5-3. Of the nine items promoted in a 1902 Colgate ad as necessary for a "properly equipped" woman's boudoir vanity, none is a makeup product.

two cosmetic manufacturers in the country had sufficient sales even to pay federal income tax. By 1928, more than eighteen thousand cosmetic enterprises paid taxes.[9]

One reason for the leap in cosmetic sales during the post–World War I years was the expansion of product lines. In 1902, an ad for Colgate's toilet articles listed nine items the company deemed necessary for the "properly equipped" woman's boudoir vanity, none of which was a makeup item. (Figure 5-3.) The only cosmetic product, a facial powder, was listed elsewhere in the copy. Even well into the teens, the product mix of most American cosmetic manufacturers continued to be limited to facial powders and toiletry items. (Figure 5-4.)

However, by the early 1920s, a properly equipped woman's vanity might contain more than a dozen makeup and skin-care items, such as those shown in Vivaudou ads. (Figure 5-5.) Scarlet and carmine lipsticks, shades of foundations, and colored powders were introduced by the score. Even the simple cold cream had proliferated into Vivaudou's specialized skin-care treatments, including one that "bleaches and whitens the skin," one for "exposure to extremes of weather," a third that "helps build the tissues," and still another "to tighten sagging muscles and close enlarged pores."

Another important factor in the rapid growth of cosmetic sales in the 1920s was the equally rapid expansion of chain stores across America. Five-and-dime department stores such as F. W. Woolworth and W. T. Grant opened in cities and towns by the hundreds during this decade. As cosmetics researcher Maggie Angeloglou wrote, the stores "made cosmetics a certainty for many girls who were apprehensive about them; products and prices could be inspected, and a cheerful anonymity made these stores more alluring."[10]

Figure 5-4. Even by the start of World War I, cosmetic manufacturers limited their makeup product lines solely to facial powders and toiletries. Palmolive ad 1915, Jonteel ad 1917.

Figure 5-5. The influence of Hollywood on the social acceptability of makeup is evident in cosmetic ads of the 1920s. The glamorous women depicted in many of these ads were a sharp contrast to the demure beauties of a decade earlier. Left ad 1923, right ad 1924.

Especially notable was the change in the depiction of beautiful women in ads of the early 1920s. The shy and demure women of the Palmolive and Jonteel ads shown in Figure 5-4 had been replaced by confident, sexually charged women whose imagery closely reflected that of Hollywood's glamorous screen stars. Ads such as those for Vivaudou avowed that its bottles, jars, and boxes contained the "beauty secrets" that would make a woman "irresistible," perhaps even to one's self, as might be deduced from the illustration of a woman kissing her reflection in a mirror. "To be socially acceptable, to be attractive, to win a husband, to keep a husband, women had to look sexy, free and available," wrote historian Carol Hymowitz of the new woman of the 1920s.[11] Marketers not only recognized this phenomenal change, but emphasized it in their advertising.

From this expansion of products came the promotion of the beauty regimen by cosmetic manufacturers. (Figure 5-6.) This was to become a part of the life of most every American woman throughout the rest of the century. In 1928, the copy in an Armand ad opened with an acknowledgment of "this era of woman's freedom and activity," but concluded with a guide for a daily beauty treatment that, ironically, probably required a half hour each day to complete. Included in this beautifying package of products was a cold cream to cleanse the skin before makeup application, a skin tone foundation, lip and cheek rouges, and the finishing touch of an eau de cologne. A decade later, Dorothy Gray Cosmetics had expanded that beauty regimen to include a second facial powder—an "opaque" finish to a "transparent" layer—plus the addition of eyeshadow, eyeliner, and mascara. From there through the end of the century, manufacturers were relentless in producing new items for the makeup regimen, and in marketing cosmetic beauty.

Here again, Hollywood contributed to the success of the mass marketing of cosmetics. By the late thirties, color film was in wider use for moviemaking, and women all over America could see up close how Max Factor and

1928

1936

1945

AVON CALLING WITH 199 COSMETICS

1960

Figure 5-6. As demand for makeup products rapidly increased in the 1920s, manufacturers began to promote the beauty regimen. Brand line extensions even included specialized skin-care products and fragrances.

other professional makeup artists used color for accentuating beauty. As Maggie Angeloglou noted: "Previously, the outline of make-up had been seen and viewers had known how to dress their hair in floppy bangs, and the correct shape of a cupid's bow mouth, they knew how to pluck their eyebrows, and all these imitations of celluloid reality needed no more than home aids, such as curlers, tweezers, and a contorted face, but with the success of color films many women throughout the world saw with dismay that the shape of cosmetics was not enough without the exact shades of red which were necessary to emulate Deanna Durbin's or Joan Crawford's lips."[12]

The marketing approach was relatively simple for cosmetic manufacturers. The physiological details that had made the Gibson Girl beautiful were not unique to her. As was mentioned earlier, Gibson's drawings of women emphasized heavy-lidded eyes accented with thick lashes beneath fine, high eyebrows. The viewer was supposed to believe these features were natural and unadorned. Hollywood, on the other hand, made no such pretenses and candidly presented their stars on screen wearing every possible makeup advantage. Silent film actresses carried over from the stage the art of makeup to enhance and define their features against the harsh lights of a studio set. This included eyeliner and mascara to enlarge the eyes and shadow to give them depth and proportion. Following the lead from Hollywood, cosmetic manufacturers were quick to begin offering various makeup products for the eyes. (Figure 5-7.) "How much more your eyes can say," a 1925 Maybelline ad proclaimed; "expressive and ready tattlers of your thoughts." Cosmetics went from simply defining the eyes in the 1920s to creating "eyes of fashion" in the 1930s with "fashion right" eyeshadows in color. Most women would from then on include eye makeup in their beauty treatment.

1925   1939   1950

Figure 5-7. Beginning in the 1920s, makers of mascara, eyeliner, and eyeshadow found an eager market of women who wished to have eyes as striking as those of film actresses.

1969

Similarly, lip rouge once again became a makeup standard for all women. (Figure 5-8.) Whereas the egalitarian revolutions of France and America of the eighteenth century had ended the six-thousand-year run of lip tinting as an accepted beauty enhancement, images of Hollywood screen queens, with their glossy, dark mouths, brought it back with a vengeance. In 1915, Maurice Levy moved lip rouge from a jar or palette to a lipstick with his invention of the metal tube dispenser. Instead of lip rouge being a vanity-table item, it now was portable and became an indispensable component of the contents of most women's handbags. In her 1929 study *Selling Mrs. Consumer,* Christine Frederick wrote, "We may hear old-fashioned people decry the use of lipstick by high school girls, but they are simply witnessing the extension of use of harmless cosmetics into every corner of our country and down to the earliest years of girlish adolescence." She warned readers that now "American women desire to be beautiful from the first years of their social consciousness."[13] This was good news to cosmetic manufacturers, and a point they emphasized in their ads. "Now run the lipstick over your lips—carefully, lightly, delicately," instructed a Tangee ad from 1925; "your lips curve in a smile that changes you from a pretty Cinderella into an exquisite Princess!"

The final stage of the makeup treatment was the manicure. (Figure 5-9.) Originating in ancient times both in Egypt and China, well-manicured and colored fingernails denoted social status. Only the upper classes could afford the luxury of possessing hands unmarred by physical labor. This was the concept that manufacturers of manicure products conveyed in their ads prior to the 1920s. A Cutex ad from 1917 depicted the kit for a home manicure that would provide women with "shapely, well-kept nails that make any hand lovely." The Nail White bleached the underside of the nails and the polish was little more than a transparent pinkish wax.

1925

1946

1954

1967

Figure 5-8. From wealthy socialites to shopgirls and housewives, the types of women portrayed in movies almost always had tinted, beautifully defined lips. In the 1920s, cosmetic makers responded to consumer demand with the convenient lip rouge in a stick form.

Then, on the bright screens of their local movie houses, all classes of women across America saw portrayals of grande dames and socialites as well as everyday shopgirls, secretaries, and housewives with immaculately shaped and color enameled nails. At first, manufacturers hesitatingly produced translucent liquid polishes in subtle pinks, not far removed from the natural look of wax polishes used a decade earlier. In 1925, Cutex introduced its "brilliant" pink nail polish for the woman who "gaily flaunts her rose-tipped fingers in the face of a stodgy world." Then, around 1930, a palette of opaque red shades ranging from burgundy to bright ruby and cardinal were produced with widely popular appeal. From there, colors became frosted in the 1950s and glittery or metallic in the 1960s. Nail shapes evolved from the oval tips of the 1920s to the squared, flat edges of the 1990s. By the late 1980s, nail salons became as trendy as nightclubs, with women maintaining weekly appointments for the indulgence of a professional manicure and polish. As the century concluded, popular nail colors included shades of blue and green and younger women applied painted patterns, decals, and rhinestones.

Part of the effectiveness of cosmetic marketing was in the expectations of beauty instilled in women as they viewed and read the ads. The beauty treatment and makeup regimens outlined in cosmetic ads paralleled the guides and recipes in so many other familiar consumer product ads. "Trust me," these kinds of ads would say, in effect, and you will have your heart's desire: cleaner laundry, tastier casseroles, healthier children, or a more beautiful and desirable you. Despite protests and arguments from feminists, especially in the 1980s and 1990s, the cosmetic industry continued to succeed in its burgeoning businesses decade after decade. Susan Faludi complained in her

1917

1925

1937

Figure 5-9. The natural look of fingernail waxes was replaced in the 1920s with glossy sheen created by translucent liquid enamels. By the 1930s opaque nail polishes included palettes of red shades.

book *Backlash* that "the formula that the industry has counted on for many years—aggravating women's low self-esteem and high anxiety about a 'feminine' appearance—has always served them well."[14] Other women writers such as Nancy Friday found power in women's beauty. "My own vote for courage," Friday wrote in 1996, "goes to the risk taker who flaunts the rules of morality and dares to wear paint."[15] Cosmetic manufacturers happily obliged year after year with new types of products, new colorations of existing lines, and tens of thousands of column inches in advertising. By the beginning of the 1990s, magazine ad revenues from cosmetics and fragrances skyrocketed to more than $650 million, while household cleaning products yielded only about one-tenth that amount.[16] The marketing strategies of the beauty makers worked superbly.

The beauty makers were not restricted to products for the face and hands alone. The Victorian sentiment that "beauty is shorn of her strength when shorn of her hair," as one hair tonic ad declared in 1898, was prevalent up to

Figure 5-10. The sentiment of a woman's hair as her "crowning glory" persisted well into the twentieth century. Ads for hair tonics and restorers would promise not only to produce long, silky tresses, but also to eliminate gray hair and even prevent baldness. Pinaud's ad 1903, Rexall ad 1908.

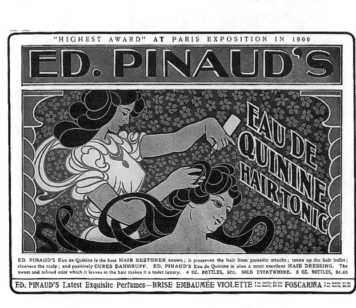

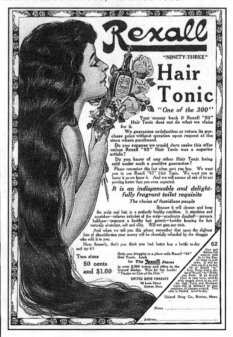

Figure 5-11. For safety as well as convenience, many women working in factories during World War I cut their hair short for the first time. Hollywood helped make the trend of short hair fashionable and more widely accepted. Ad 1920.

World War I.[17] With biblical references, the American woman of the nineteenth century regarded her hair as her "crowning glory." The Gibson Girl swept it up on top of her head in luxuriant twists and knots held in place with decorative combs. For those women who were unable to grow the long, silky tresses so prized by society, hair-care manufacturers created restorers and tonics. (Figure 5-10.) The promises in Pinaud's art nouveau ad from 1903 included restoring hair, preventing parasites, and curing dandruff. A few years later, ads for Rexall's Ninety-three Hair Tonic guaranteed all this, plus the prevention of baldness, or your money back.

By the second decade of the century, three occurrences changed society's attitude toward long hair for women. First, during World War I women were called upon to fill in for men in the workplace. Besides the time involved in caring for long hair, safety concerns in factories made it acceptable for women to cut their hair. Second, the glamour queens of Hollywood made short hair look fashionable and modern. (Figure 5-11.) Women wanted to imitate their favorite stars, and the short bob was an affordable way to do so. Third, a "wave of feminism" exerted its influence, as Lillian Eichler noted in 1924: "Perhaps bobbing the hair is a reaction from the long ages of enforced adherence to the fashion of long hair. Perhaps woman is expressing freedom by extending to herself the privilege which man created for his own comfort and convenience—the privilege of cutting the hair. It is significant that men, as a whole, are opposed to the bob. They declare, as the Bible did more than 2000 years ago, that 'If a woman have long hair, it is a glory to her.' Is woman, in defiance, attempting to prove that short hair can be a glory too?"[18]

Long or short, hair had to be kept clean. Throughout the last decades of the nineteenth century, tar soaps especially were advertised as being ideal for shampooing hair. (Figure 5-12.) Made from distilled pine tars that were used

Figure 5-12. Beauty soaps were used for washing hair in the years before liquid shampoos were manufactured. Packer's ad 1900, Fairbanks ad 1902.

1918

1927

1949

Figure 5-13. Specialized liquid, paste, and cream shampoos were first introduced in the early teens. By the 1940s, manufacturers had segmented products into formulas for different hair types. In the 1970s, hair-care regimens began to include conditioners as a second product line to complement shampoos.

1953

in glycerines and antiseptics, tar soaps were extensively used for washing hair in the years before liquid shampoos were manufactured.

By the start of World War I, numerous varieties of liquid, cream, and paste shampoos were introduced. (Figure 5-13.) Just as packaged food manufacturers first had to sell the idea of their products, shampoo makers had to carve out a market niche from the multipurpose tar soaps. The "harsh effect" of ordinary bar soaps cannot give your hair the "real life, lustre, natural wave and color" you want, suggested a 1918 Watkins shampoo ad, nor would "ordinary, old time methods" of shampooing work for the "simplicity of the bob," a Watkins ad of a decade later stated. In the 1940s Breck took product segmentation one step further with separate shampoo formulas for "three quite different hair conditions." Lotion shampoos containing conditioning ingredients such as lanolin became popular in the 1950s and were the precursors of the two-step shampoo and conditioner rinse of the 1970s.

The step between cleaning the hair and styling the hair, for many women, was coloring the hair. (Figure 5-14.) In 1891, an ad for Imperial Hair Regenerator stated, "No lady who thoroughly appreciates good appearance would ever dream of appearing in society with streaky or gray hair. They are both unbecoming, and when a perfect preparation can be obtained for overcoming these difficulties there is no reasonable justification for their continuance."[19] In a typical hair treatment ad of the early 1900s, the copy for Ayre's Hair Vigor boldly declared that it "always restores color to gray hair, always." The message in all such ads was clear: no woman should have gray hair, and these products provided a way to stem that most visible sign of

1900

1926

1992

Figure 5-14. The message to women in most hair color product ads was "you look years younger" when you eliminate gray hair.

aging. With the emphasis on youthful exuberance permeating all of society in the 1920s, women were so keen on preserving their youthful looks that they were willing to endure hours of the awful smells from sulfur compounds prevalent in the new kinds of hair-coloring mixtures for home use. When the copy in ads such as that by Wyeth's Sage and Sulphur promised "and you appear years younger," the odoriferous struggle was worth the effort. Even at the end of the century, manufacturers could appeal to a large segment of the market with ad headlines like Clairol's "gray hair lies" in 1992. "Keep your hair young-looking and vibrant. (Like the rest of you!)," the copy concluded, echoing marketing predecessors of a hundred years earlier.

"Is graying ever not premature to its victims?" wondered Susan Brownmiller in her 1984 book *Femininity.* "I thought, and still think, that artificial color is a shameful concession to all the wrong values," she continued. "But it wasn't pleasant to bear living witness day after day in all sorts of social encounters to the sorry fact that gray hair does not look youthful, dazzling, feminine, with-it."[20] For writer Bernice Kanner, being "with-it" translated as being "in the loop"; in her 1997 article for *More,* she asked women readers in the title, "Do You Lie about Your Age?" She concluded that she and many others did in more ways than just a verbal fib: "In the loop is where most women want to be. That's why so many of us are not going gently into that good night. More women are Nice 'n Easying out the gray, surgically smoothing the wrinkles, contact lensing away their bifocals and spandexing off their middle-age spread."[21]

Nevertheless, even with intensive advertising, only about 7 percent of American women dyed their hair by midcentury. "The modern hair-coloring revolution came not through a safer product, or through a one-step, easy-to-use formulation," wrote historian Charles Panati, "but through clever, image-changing advertising."[22] Specifically, it was the long-running Clairol

Figure 5-15. The legendary "Does she . . . or doesn't she?" ad campaign launched by Clairol in the 1950s was so successful that sales of hair-coloring products were boosted for the whole industry. Ad 1957.

campaigns of the 1950s and 1960s that asked, "Does she . . . or doesn't she?" that helped eliminate the stigma for women who were trying "only to hide the few gray strands." With a wink, the subhead in these ads replied, "Only her hairdresser knows for sure." (Figure 5-15.) By the 1960s, hair-color manufacturers began to advocate in their ads that hiding the gray need not be the only purpose for coloring one's hair. (Figure 5-16.) Changing the color of one's hair as a fashion or personality statement became a new marketing tactic. Women were encouraged to be daring with a wide assortment of hair-coloring possibilities, from the trend of frosting, which was simply highlighting strands of hair, to a complete change of color. "You can be sand. Or fawn. Or pearl. You can be mist. Or sunlight. Or moonlight," wooed the copy in a 1976 Clairol ad. As the century came to a close, hair-color marketers could be content with their persistent advertising efforts when the industry topped $1 billion. One report in 1998 estimated that 30 percent of women colored their hair.[23]

Despite the overwhelming volume of ads cajoling women into making every effort to remain young-looking, many women chose instead to look their age. Hair-color manufacturers created products specifically for these women. (Figure 5-17.) Don't just be "plain gray," Clairol ads said in 1966, be "radiant silver" in seven different shades. In 1979, the politically incorrect catchphrase "free, white, and 21" became Clairol's headline "free, gray and 51" for its Silk & Silver hair color. "I like the way I look," declared the laughing model. "And you know what? I wouldn't be 29 again for the world."

For many social critics these kinds of ads were little more than slick gimmicks that pandered to women's "disdain for oldness," as Betty Friedan

Figure 5-16. To sell even more product, manufacturers began to advocate hair coloring as a means of personal expression. Left ad 1971, right ad 1975.

Figure 5-17. Hair-coloring makers even targeted women who chose to have gray hair with the promise to transform them from "plain gray" to "radiant silver." Left ad 1966, right ad 1979.

wrote in her 1993 book *The Fountain of Age.* "Instead of celebrating new realities of age, the sell is eternal, attractive youth." In most of these ads, the gray hair is shown on the heads of vibrant and vivacious models, not on sedate grandmotherly types. For Friedan, cosmetics and hair-coloring manufacturers had a vested interest in perpetuating this "age mystique." Her criticism about American society and attitudes toward aging was that "Obsessed with stopping age, passing as young, we do not seek new functions in the years of life now open to us beyond the sexual, child-rearing, powerseeking female and male roles of our youth. Seeing age as decline from youth, we make age itself the problem." [24] Whether persuading the stereotypical grandmother types such as First Lady Barbara Bush to choose a shade of gray for their hair, or persuading women such as First Ladies Nancy Reagan and Hillary Clinton to defy aging with hair coloring, it remained a win-win situation for the makers of beauty and hair-color products.

One other aspect of beauty, which is actually more closely related to fashion, is hair styling. Images of the tentacular marcel used in beauty parlors of

Figure 5-18. Images of the marcel used in beauty parlors of the 1920s and 1930s were so startling that they were used as visual gimmicks in totally unrelated ads. Coca-Cola ad 1935, Listerine ad 1936.

Figure 5-19. Introduced in the 1920s, early home permanent kits were smelly and complicated to use despite their economy. By the 1950s, one-step formulas had made the process easy and convenient. Halgar ad 1948, Bliss ad 1957.

the 1920s and 1930s to create hair permanents were so startling that they even were used as visual gimmicks in ads totally unrelated to hairstyling. (Figure 5-18.) For centuries women had subjected themselves to ordeals of heated combs and curling irons to change the natural condition of their hair to keep pace with the ever changing fashion of the time. "Probably the most active as well as effective human hunger underlying fashion," observed marketing professor Paul Nystrom in 1928, "is the desire for self-assertion, the desire to be different."[25] Where the mother of the flapper had been the Gibson Girl with her mounds of natural, unadorned hair, the daughter bobbed and permed hers into all sorts of short, wavy variations. Then, after witnessing their mothers and grandmothers return from beauty parlors with newly coifed and lacquered curls throughout the 1940s and 1950s, young women of the 1960s ironed their hair flat to have straight, flowing tresses. In turn, their daughters became the "big hair" debutantes at proms in the 1980s.

Through it all, manufacturers of hair-care products stayed attuned to the shifting winds of fashion and sought ways of expanding their market share. For women who could not afford or did not have the time for the beauty parlor, a mass market was created for the home permanent kit as early as the 1920s. (Figure 5-19.) Initially cumbersome, and best used with assistance, these kits involved numerous steps with vile-smelling chemicals that could take hours to complete. By the 1950s, manufacturers were making it easier with the all-in-one tube formulas for "the permanent that needs no help at all, not even from hair sprays," as the Bliss Home Permanent ads claimed.

Additionally, appliance manufacturers entered the beauty business just after the turn of the century with electric hairstyling devices. Although the electric curling iron preceded the hair dryer by almost two decades, the latter would eventually become the best-selling electric hair appliance. (Figure 5-20.) Some early vacuum cleaner ads actually recommended the use of the exhaust blower as a method for women to dry their hair. From this, electric appliance manufacturers incorporated the fractional horsepower motor with the hot-air exhaust blower of a vacuum cleaner to create the hand-held hairdryer in the 1920s. In her article on electric appliances written for the *Ladies' Home Journal* in 1927, Clara Zillessen recommended the electric

Figure 5-20. Sales of electric hair dryers soared in the 1960s as men began to grow their hair long. Home hair-styling kits eventually included multispeed blow dryers with numerous attachments. Left ad 1962, right ad 1973.

curling iron and blow dryer as cost-effective measures for "keeping short hair well groomed."[26] After decades of steady market growth, sales of blow dryers took off in the late 1960s when greater numbers of men started growing their hair long. From the basic blow dryer and curling iron, manufacturers of small electrics expanded their product mix to include ever more specialized items. In the 1970s hairstyling kits included multispeed dryers with different sizes of combs, brushes, and other styling attachments.

Skin-Deep Beauty

As a consumer market, American women eagerly responded from the start to the advertising of hair, makeup, and other beauty products. Segmentations of age, ethnicity, economic status, and other demographic factors allowed manufacturers to establish niches for their products and target specific groups of women with substantial marketing efforts. However, a more universal concern for women as a whole was the issue of health. Beauty through health was an underlying theme in many cosmetic ads: the promise of healthy skin, healthy hair, healthy nails. This was especially true when it came to skin-care products, particularly beauty soaps.

As has been mentioned in previous chapters, soap manufacturers aggressively advertised during the second half of the nineteenth century to build a consumer market and create brand-name recognition for their products. Advertisers had to persuade Americans that bathing was important to one's health beyond merely removing visible dirt from the hands and face. In 1870, Philadelphia physician George Napheys wrote in *The Physical Life of Woman* that "the whole surface of the body [should] be washed several times a week."[27] Such infrequent ablutions, though, would not use much soap, so soap makers included in their marketing campaigns versions of ads designed to persuade people to bathe daily. "But everyone who takes good care; All other kinds refusing; To get pure Ivory, grows more fair; With every day of using," concluded one of the many poems used in Ivory ads of the 1890s.

More succinct was the long running campaign for Pear's Soap that presented all sorts of intriguing scenarios, each with the caption, "Good morning,
have you used Pear's Soap?"[28] Such perseverance paid off, as Christine
Frederick noted in her 1929 Mrs. Consumer study: "Underlying all
American conceptions of good cosmetics and personal beauty lies her
emphasis upon cleanliness. Where a bath is a rarity on the Continent, a bath
is the possession and almost daily habit of the humblest women in America.
The American woman . . . believes in Cleanliness First. She does not use cosmetics to hide dirt or disguise odor. She is the world's greatest user of antiseptics, soaps, and other purely cleansing preparations, and, therefore, when
it comes to the matter of beauty preparations, she values them all from the
standpoint of still greater cleanliness."[29]

Victorian women had to be persuaded that not only should they bathe
daily, but also use specialized skin soaps in order to enhance and preserve
beauty. For soap manufacturers, these product line extensions required little
more than modifying existing formulas. By adding glycerines, distilled plant
"tars," and fragrances, beauty bars could be sold for two to five times the
price of all-purpose white soaps. For the manufacturer, production equipment and channels of distribution were already in place, so most of the marketing dollars could be applied to advertising.

In toilet soap ads of the late nineteenth century, hundreds of images of
beautiful young women were coupled with text that emphasized beauty. By
the first decade of the twentieth century, these tried-and-true ad formulas
were firmly in place and easily recognized by women readers. (Figure 5-21.)
"The best soap to make the skin most beautiful," suggested the 1900 ad for
Buchan's Toilet Soap; "makes the skin soft and velvety," a 1902 Fairbank's
ad assured women; "leaves the skin like a baby's cheek," promised
Woodbury's ads in 1904; "you will gain, or retain, a natural beauty no balms
or powders can imitate," insisted Hand Sapolio ad copy in 1906; and in
1909, a Pears' ad offered a "doctor's point of view" for the "most perfect
beautifying agent known." The promise of beautiful, healthy skin from the
use of a beauty soap never lost its appeal to women consumers throughout
the entire twentieth century and was a constant theme in beauty soap ads
year after year.

The most significant selling point in ads for beauty soaps, implied or stated, was the preservation of a youthful complexion. As discussed above,
beauty-product makers helped instill in women a fear of aging. A second category of women's skin-care products whose advertising and packaging
emphasized the promise of youthful looks was the beauty cream. Popular
ingredients in many of these topical creams included natural ingredients for
skin care known to women since ancient times. Aloe, lanolin, and oils from
plants such as olives and almonds have been used in homemade skin-care
mixtures for thousands of years. A formulated cold cream was first created
in the second century A.D. by the Greek physician Galen, and the recipe was
included in his book *Medical Methods.* Made of a wax base, olive oils, and
essence of rosebuds, Galen's cream was used for everything from a treatment for gladiators' wounds to a moisturizer for women of the Roman imperial family.[30] By the twentieth century, synthetic ingredients with the same
properties as natural ones ensured a longer shelf life and, hence, a wider distribution for skin-care products.

Well before the use of cosmetics became an acceptable method of dis-
guising the visible signs of aging, beauty cream manufacturers offered their
products as a first line of defense. (Figure 5-22.) The foremost message in
ads for these products stressed a woman's need, even obligation, to preserve

1900

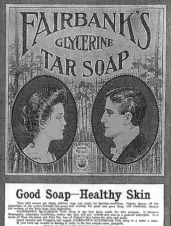

1902

1904

1909

1916

1917

1920

1928

1931

1932

1935

1942

1947

1950

1952

1957

the appearance of youth. "A woman is as old as she looks," insisted the headline in a 1905 Pompeian cream ad. If the reader was already past her youth in years, the implied promise in this and similar ads was a restoration to the bloom of the young woman featured in the photograph, but if the reader was still young, the message was a warning that she should begin using a beauty cream now to preserve her youthful looks. In a 1910 ad from Bel Bon cream, that recommendation was stated in the opening copy: "To have a good complexion at forty, begin its care at twenty." Using the word "girl" instead of "woman" in its copy, an ad for Creme de Meridor in 1918 assured young women that with the regular use of its products, they could avoid "the tiny wrinkles about the eyes, the tell-tale folds that presage a double chin." In 1936 an ad for Ingram's cream went one step further in persuading women to fight the appearance of aging. The product's namesake, Francis Ingram, is quoted in the copy as saying that the "recipe for holding a husband" must include preventing "a skin that has lost its freshness, its youngness." Given the uncertain mood of so many women in the Depression era, such a grim assessment probably had them pondering their personal lives as well as their reflections in the vanity mirror. A generation later, this beauty cream defense against the signs of aging even became specialized for particular parts of the face. A series of Tussy Eye Cream ads in the 1950s and 1960s focused on the elimination of crow's feet by showing illustrations of fashionable women doing battle with cartoon crows. Indeed, the bottom-line promise in all beauty cream ads was primarily the same, and was summed up perfectly in the floorline of a 1997 L'Oreal ad: "Reduces the signs of aging."[31]

By the end of the 1990s, keeping the secret of one's age became more of a challenge for a significant segment of the consumer market. With the baby boomers crossing into their midfifties, raising the median age of the entire population with them, manufacturers began to specifically target this age group with new products. A 1998 Procter & Gamble marketing study indicated that more than 78 million Americans were in the over-fifty crowd, and that that group "should grow by 50% by the year 2010."[32] Oil of Olay's ProVital sub-brand was created to target this fifty-plus age category. (Figure 5-23.) Said an Oil of Olay marketing executive in 1998, "Many women fifty

1963

Figure 5-21. The consistent formula for beauty soap ads, decade after decade, paired images of attractive young women with copy that emphasized youthful beauty.

1905

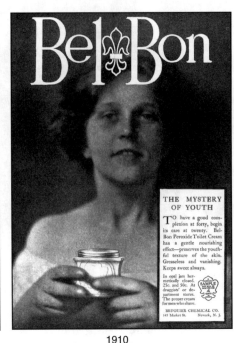

1910

1918

1936

Figure 5-22. Preserving the appearance of youth was the primary benefit promoted in ads for beauty creams.

and older told us that as they age, they feel more confident, wiser and freer than ever before. These women are redefining beauty."[33] Also in 1998, Rembrandt introduced Age Defying toothpaste with double-page magazine ads headlined: "Do your teeth make you look 10 years older?"[34] Both Oil of Olay and Rembrandt had selected age-appropriate models to feature in these ads, with crow's feet and laugh lines left intact.

A logical product line extension for beauty cream manufacturers was hand lotion. (Figure 5-24.) Makers of vanishing cream—so called because it "vanished" into the skin without leaving any residue—strengthened their formulas with ingredients that worked more effectively on damaged skin. Themes, advice, and warnings in hand cream ads could be as varied as the conditions that might affect the appearance of a woman's hands. In a 1931 Hinds ad, chapped hands caused by a "wintry blast" was the reason for the young woman's embarrassment. In a 1943 Pacquins ad, a woman's patriotic duty required her to make bullets in a factory, resulting in hands that looked like they belonged to "an old witch." In a 1953 Jergens ad, washing twenty-two thousand dishes a year stripped away the "natural oils and youthful softness" of Mrs. Mehle's hands. A 1969 Vedra ad emphasized the threat to women's hands from the use of caustic household cleaners.

Ironically, one of the biggest boosts to the sale of hand creams and lotions came indirectly from the ads for laundry and dishwashing soaps that focused attention on the "dishpan hands" syndrome. Both categories of products often used similar imagery of women examining their hands with a look of distress on their faces. (Compare with Figure 3-41.) A first glance might be deceiving as to which product was being advertised. Whereas soap ads promised to prevent rough, red hands, hand lotions promised after-the-fact aid and relief.

Just as there were two avenues for advertisers to use in approaching women about their hair care—health (tonics, soaps, shampoos, astringents)

Figure 5-23. As the baby boomers moved into middle age in the 1990s, manufacturers targeted this segment of consumers with health and beauty products formulated for their age categories. Ad 1998.

and style (hair coloring, permanents, cuts, spray lacquers)—so, too, were skin-care products presented from these same two vantages. The health of the skin involved beauty soaps and the topical application of creams and lotions, while the styling of the skin occurred with powders and, from the 1920s on, makeup. One other method of styling the skin first gained popularity in the late 1920s: the suntan. A 1929 Pond's ad explained the sudden fashion phenomenon: "It's smart to be sun-tanned! The fad began out of the clear blue sky. A Parisian élégante was told to bathe in the summer sun till she was brown as an Arab. Along with radiant health she achieved an irresistible new beauty which forthwith became the fashion."[35]

Besides the influence of the Parisian fashion set, the fad of sunbathing in America was boosted by the vacation boom of the 1920s. The improved interstate highway system and mass production of automobiles made holidays to the oceans and lakes more popular and affordable for many Americans. Also, the rapid development of Florida as a year-round vacation destination in the 1920s contributed to the increasing popularity of sunbathing.

Initially, beauty cream manufacturers promoted existing products for use during and after sunbathing. (Figure 5-25.) By the 1930s, though, specialized suntan oils and lotions were developed to screen out ultraviolet rays and prevent burning. Skol's formulas even included tannic acids to intensify the tanning process. In the 1940s, suntan products began to include moisturizing emollients such as aloe, chamomile, and cocoa butter. When the first massive waves of baby boomers reached their teens in the 1960s, Hollywood beach movies and surfer rock-and-roll music helped sales of suntan products soar as the young flocked to seashores and poolsides. (Figure 5-26.) Still, sunbathing often resulted in damaged skin from windburn, sunburn, and swimming pool chemicals, and the sale of beauty creams and lotions continued to benefit.

By the 1970s, reports on the dangers of sunbathing began to reach the mass media. Dermatologists were seeing the damaged skin of sunbathers from the 1930s and 1940s who had spent countless hours exposed to the sun each summer. These cautions from the medical community provided another opportunity for beauty cream makers to expand their product lines by reformulating sun lotions to become stronger sunscreens and even sunblocks.

1931

1943

1953

Figure 5-24. Themes, advice, and warnings in hand cream ads were as varied as the conditions that might affect the appearance of a woman's hands.

1969

(Figure 5-27.) "Premature aging of the skin is just one of the not-so-beautiful effects of the sun," warned the copy in a 1981 Johnson & Johnson ad. An alarming split-frame photo showed what a woman might look like in her middle age after too much sun in her youth. "If large numbers of women become convinced that the leathery, wrinkled look of a sea captain, or skin cancer, may be in store for them rather than a permanent extension of a sunny vacation, we may see a reemergence of the alabaster lady who eschews the noonday sun," predicted Susan Brownmiller in 1984.[36]

However, American women continued to want that golden glow of a vacation suntan. "It's easy to heed skin cancer warnings in late May, but come beach season, even smart women admit to sneaking 'a little sun,'" noted Joanne Chen in a 1997 report for *Glamour*.[37] In response to consumers' desire to sunbathe and their concerns for skin health, the makers of suntan products changed advertising strategies. "Be sun smart naturally!" urged the headline in a 1997 ad for Hawaiian Tropic. Invoking "medical science" as its guide, the body copy explained that Hawaiian Tropic tanning lotion provided "moisturizing sun protection" while you sunbathed.[38] Clearly, women were no longer willing to smear tannic acid-based lotions over their bodies to intensify the skin's reaction to the sun, but neither were they completely willing to forgo a summertime tan.

The dichotomy of women's desire to get a suntan without the dangers of too much exposure to the sun also became a challenge to the cosmetics industry. By the end of the 1990s, *Harper's Bazaar* editor Melanie Ward observed that "sun protection is now a full-time job (unless you stay inside indefinitely.) But companies have fixed it so it isn't a chore, adding sunscreens to just about everything."[39] The list of moisturizers, foundations, lipsticks, and blushes with protective sunscreens became extensive. Additionally, for the look of a suntan without sun exposure, cosmetic companies reinvented the

Figure 5-25. The sunbathing fad in America began in the 1920s. Initially, beauty cream manufacturers promoted existing skin-care product lines for use during and after sunbathing. Ad 1929.

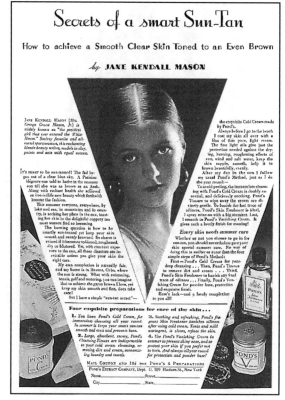

skin-tint, which had been around since the 1960s. Manufacturers such as Estee Lauder, Chanel, and Lancôme produced self-tanners that colored the skin real shades of brown, instead of the orangey, uneven results that had been common with earlier formulas. Magazines began to provide product recommendations and how-to suggestions for using self-tanners. "Women are very sensitive to the dangers of sun exposure, but they still want dark color," said a Lancome marketing executive in 1997.[40]

One final aspect of the pursuit of beauty that women of the twentieth century confronted was hair removal. Although Victorian women may have believed that an abundance of hair piled onto the head was a crowning glory, all other body hair was thought to be superfluous and unsightly. Numerous products for hair removal were advertised all through the last quarter of the nineteenth century, perpetuating the ideal beauty of skin as smooth and hairless as a marble statue. (Figure 5-28.) As women's clothing began to reveal more and more skin in the early twentieth century, first with sleeveless eveningwear and, by the 1920s, with briefer styles of swimwear, women were already conditioned to think of body hair as repugnant and unfeminine. (Figure 5-29.) "Can you stand the scrutinizing glance of your admirers at the beach? Can you wear sheer frocks which expose your arms, underarms, back and limbs?" asked a 1923 ad for Zip hair removal cream. Similarly, in a 1929 Del-a-tone ad, the "moments that matter" included: "When you slip your beach coat from your shoulders and your bathing suit seems all too brief. . . . When you tee off in front of a watchful gallery and the sunlight glances on your stockingless legs. . . . When the dashboard light of your favorite roadster shines full on your sheer chiffon hose . . . when you raise your arms to pin back a stray lock and your dress is sleeveless."

Figure 5-26. Skin-care products were reformulated in the 1930s to include sunscreens and tanning ingredients. Moisturizing emollients such as aloe, chamomile, and cocoa butter were added to suntan lotions in the 1940s. Skol ad 1944, Coppertone ad 1965.

Figure 5-27. Despite warnings from dermatologists in the 1970s, women continued to want the golden glow of a suntan. Beauty cream makers expanded their product lines by reformulating lotions to become stronger sunscreens and even sunblocks. Ad 1981.

In this instance, too, Hollywood contributed to the American woman's perception of ideal beauty. When the queens of the movie screen wore sleeveless gowns, their underarms were hair free; when they danced across the floor and skirts twirled up, their legs were smooth and shimmering from the hairless, clean lines of sheer silk hosiery.

Razor blade companies also were quick to recognize the significance of women as consumers. (Figure 5-30.) In 1915, Gillette presented women with a Milady Decolleté razor "by request." To wear the new styles of sleeveless gowns or dresses with their "semi-transparent yokes and sleeves," the ad copy advised, "the underarm must be as smooth as the face." In 1931, Schick introduced the electric dry shaver. The ads promised that besides being nick-free, shaving with an electric Schick "does not promote the growth of hair, does not coarsen it, does not darken the skin nor injure the delicate skin tissue." Even by the end of the century, when Remington was offering wet/dry shavers—complete with built-in bikini-line trimmers—cuts, nicks, and skin irritation continued to be part of the price to be paid for shaving away body hair.

This uniquely American obsession with a hairless body became a point of contention to some degree for feminists during the 1970s and 1980s. Susan Brownmiller wrote in her 1984 book *Femininity:* "Americans frequently have been accused of a Puritan attitude toward sex. If the removal of body hair is an indication of an unnatural fastidious, overly refined and repressed sexuality, then Americans deserve their reputation."[41]

Urged by advertising, the American woman's abhorrence of body hair persisted through the century and continued to inspire the creation of a host of hair-removal products, as well as advice guides for their use in magazines. A 1997 *Glamour* article on "painless hair removal" suggested "your best bets" were a nick-free shave, electrolysis with a topical anesthetic, washable waxing gels, cold-wax strips, depilatories with soothing emollients, and body-sugaring pastes.[42] Meanwhile, technology had even developed a "laser-based process" for Spa Thira that was advertised as being so effective, it guaranteed "freedom from unwanted hair from Memorial Day to Labor Day."[43]

Figure 5-28. Nineteenth-century ads for depilatories instilled in women the notion that except for the hair on their heads, all body hair was superfluous and should be removed. Ads 1897.

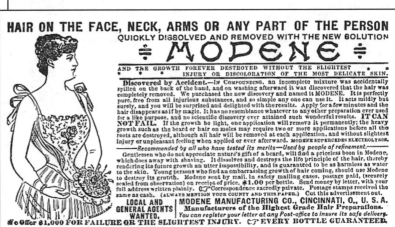

Figure 5-29. By the 1920s women had already been subjected by advertisers to decades of conditioning to think of body hair as repugnant and unfeminine. Zip ad 1923, Del-a-tone ad 1929.

1915

1937

1996

Figure 5-30. Shaving product manufacturers began to target women as consumers in the 1910s. Decade after decade American women were repeatedly told in advertising that body hair should be removed.

Figure 5-31. Before the passage of the Pure Food and Drugs Act in 1906, patent medicine ads promised women cures for just about everything from "nervous prostrations" to cancer. Some remedies contained as much as 40 percent alcohol or even narcotics such as opium or morphine, while others were little more than sugar and starch pills. Ads from *Godey's* 1888.

The Promise of Health

As aggressively as beauty and skin-care manufacturers marketed their products to women consumers throughout the twentieth century, the pharmaceutical industry marketed just as intensely with its own promises of beauty and health from the inside out. Unfortunately for women, medical science was still very much in the dark ages through most of the nineteenth century and, judging from the Lynds' Middletown studies, even well into the twentieth. From the perspective of more than a century, women of the 1990s might be amused to read the prevailing scientific analyses of women's health conditions as published in medical texts of the Victorian era. "Hysterics" was regarded as an actual "disease of the nerves." One doctor reportedly cured a group of hysterical girls in a female seminary by heating iron instruments before their eyes and telling them that "the first one who had a fit should be cauterized down the spine." The medical text concluded, "They all recovered immediately." Other female "nervous disorders" included "Green Sickness," a form of depression caused by iron-deficient anemia, and most "insidious" of all, "secret bad habits," i.e., masturbation. For the latter, the result was "bodily weakness, loss of memory, low spirits, distressing nervousness, a capricious appetite, dislike of company and of study, and finally, paralysis, imbecility, or insanity."[44]

With such diagnoses and recommendations promulgated in official medical texts, it is hardly surprising that women would believe the claims of patent medicine ads. (Figure 5-31.) Claims and promises of cures were sometimes all encompassing. Pond's Extract was advertised in the 1880s to be "invaluable" for everything from postnasal drip and toothache to

Figure 5-32. A circa 1900 ad for Ayer's Pills assured women relief from "that terrible headache," along with all the other symptoms of premenstrual syndrome. The diagnosis in the ad, however, was believed to be a "wrong liver."

diphtheria. Similarly, Buffalo Lithia Water remedied all from "nervous dyspepsia" to rheumatism; Lydia E. Pinkham's Compound cured conditions ranging from "spinal weakness" to "nervous prostration"; and Hostetter's Stomach Bitters relieved the symptoms of everything from "liver complaint" to "kidney troubles." Before the passage of the Pure Food and Drugs Act in 1906, women's health was often at great risk from these dubious tonics and pills, which were distributed at most local drugstores and widely advertised in popular magazines and newspapers. Some patent medicines contained as much as 40 percent alcohol or narcotics as strong as morphine, while others were little more than starch and sugar pills.[45]

The real problem was with accurately diagnosing women's ailments in the first place. Serious diseases aside, merely determining the various effects the menstrual cycle had on a woman was cause for confusion among doctors and provided perfect opportunities for patent medicine vendors. (Figure 5-32.) "*That* terrible headache,"—along with depression, sleeplessness, dizziness, and upset stomach—was caused by "wrong livers," advised a 1900 ad for Ayer's Pills. In her book *The Mismeasure of Woman,* Carol Tavris examined the history of the diagnosis of premenstrual syndrome. The term stemmed from an article written by a gynecologist on "premenstrual tension" in the 1930s. From there, limited research through the 1950s continued to perpetuate the belief that this condition had a debilitating effect on a woman's capacity to function normally. In 1964, Katarina Dalton published her findings in the book *The Premenstrual Syndrome,* and the term "PMS" entered the American vernacular. Much more study was done on the subject in the 1970s than in all the previous decades put together. However, much to Tavris's dismay, in 1987 the American Psychiatric Association included PMS as an official disorder in its reference manual. On the one hand, she believed, it "validates women"—that is, it provided a "medical and social reality to the experiences that were previously ignored, trivialized, or misunderstood." But, she feared, it also stigmatizes women. Her conclusion was that "The public and scientific fascination with PMS and allied 'normal disorders' of the female reproductive system is, in turn, part of a larger medical zeitgeist, reflected in the continuing effort to reduce all human problems and emotions to the correct gene, neurotransmitter, hormone or disease."[46]

Soon after the first research on PMS was published, pharmaceutical companies began to market specialized pain relievers that were formulated for the symptoms of that condition. (Figure 5-33.) In the 1930s, Midol was introduced to relieve the "distress" of monthly "functional periodic pain," as one ad at the time stated. As often as not, doctors simply recommended basic pain relievers for the effects of PMS. In a 1963 ad for Bufferin, the ad copy noted that "doctors have been unable to discover exactly what causes depressing menstrual pain," but nevertheless, women should "be prepared for next month." In 1986, an ad for Premesyn PMS (later marketed as Premsyn PMS) told women that "premenstrual tension is not in your head. It's in your body." For millions of women—and their families—this was a reassuring message, especially with the promise of relief from an over-the-counter medication. In addition to relief of the physical effects of PMS,

1938

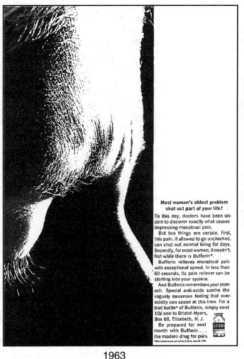

1963

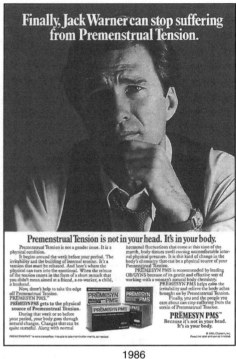

1986

Figure 5-33. Soon after the first studies on premenstrual syndrome were made in the 1930s, the pharmaceutical industry began to produce specially formulated pain relievers for women's monthly symptoms.

Figure 5-34. With sales eroding due to the decrease of home baking and the enactment of Prohibition in the 1920s, Fleischmann's successfully repositioned its yeast cakes as a natural laxative product. Ad 1922.

products such as Dimensyn also offered help for "the emotional side of menstrual discomfort," such as "irritability and nervous tension."[47] All such marketing messages assured women that the symptoms of PMS were regarded as serious health concerns for which an entire industry had emerged to provide comfort and relief.

Advertisers also linked women's emotional health to other physical ailments, including irregularity and constipation. One of the legendary testimonials to the power of advertising is the successful marketing of Fleischmann's Yeast as a laxative in the 1920s and 1930s. (Figure 5-34.) Between the decrease of home baking and Prohibition, yeast sales had plummeted after 1920. Executives of the company began to examine possible medicinal uses and ran a prize contest for the product's health propensities. Responses poured in, and an ad campaign was born. In one of the earliest ads, from 1922, an exhausted woman is shown collapsed in an armchair with hat still in hand from an outing. "Nervous, 'run down,' irritable—even in our twenties and thirties," read the caption beneath the illustration. "Regular daily elimination" is lacking, which "two or three cakes" of yeast each day would remedy. By the 1930s, ads for Fleischmann's Yeast included sagacious advice from doctors to any woman who was a "wreck," physically or emotionally. The copy in one 1934 ad advised these women that "if you're irritable, it is probably because poisons (due to constipation) are attacking your nerves." The solution was "three cakes of Fleischmann's Yeast every day . . . for at least 30 days" to restore health and "good spirits."[48]

Another significant category of women's health-related products included those that were designed and marketed for hygiene. Oral hygiene, especially, was the objective of advertising for toothbrush, toothpaste, and mouthwash manufacturers all through the twentieth century. Oral hygiene certainly was not an invention of American marketers. The people of many ancient civilizations are known to have been conscientious practitioners of dental care. One utensil they are known to have used to clean their teeth was the chew stick—a twig frayed on one end and rubbed over the teeth. Other materials used to clean the teeth included natural sponges, coarse linen, and even stiff quills. The first versions of the toothbrush were created by the Chinese in the fifteenth century. Bristles from Siberian hogs were embedded into wooden or bone handles to make these early toothbrushes. Once the toothbrush was introduced to the West, Europeans found hog's bristles too irritating to the gums and opted for softer brushes made from horsehair, badger fur, and even cut felt. However, after the studies of bacteriologist Louis Pasteur became more widely understood, dentists recommended the return to the hog's-bristle brush. The stiff bristle brushes dried faster than animal-hair brushes, thus discouraging bacterial growth. In 1938, nylon bristles were introduced under the name of "Exton brand bristling."[49] (Figure 5-35.) Within a few years fast-drying synthetic bristles had completely replaced the use of natural hog's bristles in the manufacture of toothbrushes.

Ads for toothbrushes were designed not only for building brand recognition, they also educated a mass market on the necessity of products most people did not know they needed. Well into the first decades of the twentieth century Americans were reluctant consumers of dental care products or services. In the twenty-three pages devoted to health in the Lynds' 1925 Middletown study, dental care was not even examined; in the 1935 revisit, the discussion of dental care focused on the impact of the Depression on dentists, rather than prevailing public attitudes toward oral hygiene.[50]

The complement to the toothbrush for successful oral hygiene was toothpaste. The use of an abrasive to polish the teeth had its origins about four thousand years ago in Egypt. Ancient records from there show that a powdered pumice was mixed with a pungent wine vinegar to rub over the teeth with a chew stick. Beginning in the mid-nineteenth century, the manufacture of tooth powders and paste quickly followed the mass production of toothbrushes. Ads, such as the one for Sozodont tooth powder from 1884 shown in Figure 1-3, emphasized the importance of oral hygiene to beauty. "Beauty and fragrance are communicated to the mouth," Victorian ladies were told in the headline of the ad, while the health messages about removing tartar and preserving tooth enamel were buried in the last sentence.

Although health and beauty were promoted in dental-care ads as the dual benefits of an oral hygiene regimen, emphasis was most frequently on women's beauty. (Figure 5-36.) In a 1928 Squibb's Dental Cream ad, a three-column copy block discusses dental care and health, but to capture

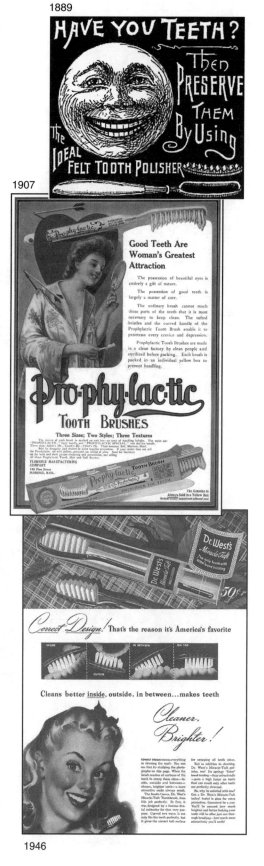

Figure 5-35. Before the introduction of nylon bristle toothbrushes in 1938, hog's bristles, horsehair, badger's fur, and even cut felt had been used to make toothbrushes.

Figure 5-36. Although both health and beauty were promoted in toothpaste ads, emphasis was most frequently on women's beauty. Squibb's ad 1928, Pepsodent ad 1933.

women's attention the header asked, "Is there an age when women must cease to look young?" The illustration of a smiling young woman has a "danger line" drawn across the gum line of her perfect teeth. Just as with the first oral hygiene ads of fifty years earlier, the public was still being educated by marketers. In a more dramatic lesson, Pepsodent illustrated the result of neglected dental care. "Gone!" exclaimed the header above a close-up of a dislodged tooth clamped in a dentist's pliers. The subhead explained the consequences of neglected oral hygiene in terms of beauty rather than health: "Another lovely woman pays the penalty of film."

This beauty-first approach worked so well that the ad formula continued to be updated decade after decade. (Figure 5-37.) "After I removed the 7 stains from my teeth, the telephone started ringing again," a smiling young woman tells a friend on the phone in a 1934 Colgate toothpaste ad; "I'd found a new beauty," she declared. In a 1953 ad, Chlorodent advised women to guard against "morning mouth" as they send their husbands off to work. "The attractive women he meets during the day don't have it," cautioned the caption beneath the photo of a woman preparing her spider's web. As had been done seventy years earlier in the Sozodont ad, the health message in the Chlorodent ad trailed last in the two columns of copy. The beauty hook was the more compelling, marketers continued to believe.

By the end of the twentieth century, personal dental care had expanded far beyond toothbrushes and toothpaste. Advertisers urged women to preserve their beauty—and dental health—with a wide variety of consumer products ranging from basic dental floss to electric water-irrigation devices.

Figure 5-37. Another common theme in toothpaste ads was the peril of social rejection from bad breath. Colgate ad 1934, Chlorodent ad, 1953.

1928

1939

1947

Figure 5-38. Mouthwash ads often presented scenes of social faux pas and melodrama that served as advice columns to the masses.

1950

However, even with the possession of "pearls in the mouth," a woman's beauty was not enough to ensure social success if an overriding case of halitosis was present. "Don't fool yourself," stated the headline of a 1928 Listerine ad. "Since halitosis never announces itself to the victim, you simply cannot know when you have it." Throughout the twentieth century, ads for mouthwashes presented scenes of social faux pas and melodramas with the same moral: It is easy to be offensive, and inexcusable given the preventative remedy of our product. These kinds of ads also served as advice columns to the masses. Historian Roland Marchand wrote: "People would resent being told about such failings by someone they knew personally. But they gladly tolerated 'intimate little scoldings' from advertisers. The very anonymity of advertisements made them perfect vehicles for such necessary, but hard to come by, advice."[51]

The consequences for one's personal hygiene "failings" could be grave—rejection in all its most devastating forms. (Figure 5-38.) Headlines in mouthwash ads for Listerine and Lavoris could be as sensational and, as a result, as captivating as story banners in *True Story* or *True Romance:*

"Why had he changed so in his attentions?" 1924
"Spring!...for everyone but her." 1929
"She bags the [wedding] bouquets but never a beau." 1930
"Must you be shamed or frightened into using a mouthwash?" 1930
"Even your best friend won't tell you." 1937
"Look Buttercup, your trouble is right under your nose." 1947
"Goodbye Jim . . . we could have had a wonderful life together." 1948[52]

Figure 5-39. Before commercial deodorants, a woman's recourse against perspiration stains and odors was the washable dress shield. Ad 1897.

Another personal hygiene "failing" that could lead to disastrous social consequences was perspiration odor. Although deodorant creams were introduced in the 1880s, advertising for the products was limited in the mass media since the subject was considered too indelicate. Instead, most women were content to bath regularly and protect themselves and their clothing with underarm dress shields. (Figure 5-39.) Even well after World War I, Odorono ads that ran in the *Ladies' Home Journal* so offended readers that in one instance two hundred subscribers canceled their subscriptions.[53] Nevertheless, the ads were highly successful and deodorant sales mushroomed. Manufacturers then became as aggressive with their advertising as any mass marketers of consumer products. (Figure 5-40.)

The problems of cream deodorants containing gritty particles or drying out in the jar were solved in the 1940s when squeezable plastic bottles made possible a "spray-on" powder deodorant. In the mid-1950s deodorant application was made even more convenient with the launch of liquid roll-on and aerosol spray antiperspirants.

Once the subject of perspiration stains and odor had been broached in advertising, manufacturers of antiperspirants and deodorants followed the cues from other hygiene product marketers with their own advertising melodramas. (Figure 5-41.) In a 1926 Odorono ad, the "ugly half-moon of stain under her arms" meant a woman "just doesn't belong" in polite society. Shown isolated in the foreground, an attractive young woman is clearly the topic of conversation between the two men in the background. Similarly, a 1934 Mum ad depicted "this beautiful woman whom men avoid; whom other women do not envy," all because she had "underarm perspiration odor." Decade after decade in these kinds of ads, the loss of romance, of marriage proposals, and even of a husband's affection was chalked up to "B.O." Other scenarios that might produce nervous tension perspiration, such as a visit from the mother-in-law or a boardroom presentation, were shown in ads with the obvious remedy being the protection of the featured brand of antiperspirant.

Probably the most controversial and difficult subject ever to confront advertisers was feminine hygiene. Manufacturers of disinfectant douches did not dare to advertise the effectiveness of their products until the more socially permissive 1920s. (Figure 5-42.) Even then, noted Marchand, "Not daring to use the phrase 'birth control,' they employed circumlocutions"; the advertised claims that these products " 'kill germs' were meant to be read as 'kill sperm.' "[54] In the 1933 Lysol ad that presented a case study by gynecologist Helga Bast, feminine hygiene was skewed to be "marriage hygiene." The "fear of a profound physical crisis," such as the "feminine irregularity" of a missed period, can be remedied with the use of Lysol, "because it is certain." The free booklet provided by Lysol could not have been clearer in its title: *Marriage Hygiene—The Important Part It Plays in the Ideal Marriage.*"[55]

Another part of feminine hygiene that first entered the American mass-market vernacular in the 1920s was the sanitary pad. Created in 1921 by the Cellucotton Company, the Kotex napkin became an instant success. (Figure 5-43.) From the start, emphasis in ads for Kotex was on "comfort and security." Headlines of ads in the 1920s reiterated this message in ways women knew instantly: "You live every day—meet every day—unhandicapped";

Figure 5-40. Body odor was considered an indelicate subject for ads even well after World War I. One Odorono ad in the *Ladies' Home Journal* reportedly so offended readers that two hundred subscribers canceled their subscriptions. Ad 1918.

1926

1934

1939

1948

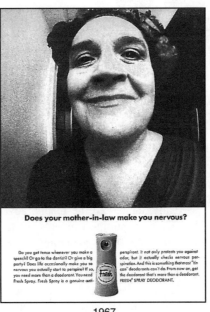

1967

1978

"Frocks sheer and enticing as you will, under the most trying of hygienic handicaps"; "Active women of today are free from the handicap of yesterday's hygienic worries"; and "Hygienic freedom such as women never knew before."[56] Competitors of Kotex, such as Modess and Tampax, captured market share with much the same approach to their advertising as had the Cellucotton Company. The modern American woman was much too busy to spend "five whole years" of her life, as a 1938 Modess ad estimated, indisposed due to her monthly period.[57] Instead, she was shown in many of these ads dancing, swimming, biking, canoeing, and engaged in all sorts of activities outside the home. (Figure 5-44.) "Accent on freedom" was the headline of a 1944 Modess ad. "So much a part of your active life," declared the copy in a 1958 Tampax ad. A product was even named New Freedom by Kotex in the 1970s.

Figure 5-41. Antiperspirant advertisers often dramatized the consequences of offensive body odor in scenarios of everyday occurrences.

Figure 5-42. Manufacturers of household disinfectants dared not advertise the use of their products as a douche until well into the 1920s. Even then, ad copy had to be subtle and vague. Left ad 1929, right ad 1933.

In the American woman's quest for beauty and health, advertising helped pave paths for her by building and changing many societal attitudes. Persistent marketing helped dispel the stigmas associated with the use of makeup and hair coloring, and candid discussions of personal hygiene in advertising helped raise the nation's health consciousness. Yet, by the last quarter of the century, advertising was increasingly criticized for its role in the most controversial aspect of a woman's quest for beauty and health: her weight.

During the 1980s and 1990s, much was written on the subject of health problems related to women's dieting and eating disorders. Feminists, especially, lambasted the media, advertisers, Hollywood, and American social values for putting women's health in jeopardy by equating ideal beauty with thin. "Yes, fat is a feminist issue," wrote Karen Lehrman in *The Lipstick Proviso* in 1997. "And why do women strive for a body that would undermine not only normal reproductive health, but also their social lives? Probably because that's the body they find in advertisements and the fashion magazines."[58] Indeed, despite feminist's protests, articles on dieting continued to be big sellers for magazines. In the spring of 1998, for example, virtually every women's magazine contained articles on dieting and weight control. A sampling of the titles included:

Figure 5-43. Introduced in 1921, the sanitary napkin was such a success that the manufacturer changed its corporate name from Cellucotton to that of the product, Kotex. Ad 1922.

"Lose 10 lbs. by Summer" (*McCall's*)
"Lose 5 Pounds—This Week" (*Redbook*)
"Drop 10 Pounds by Summer" (*Family Circle*)
"Think Your Way Thin" (*Woman's Day*)
"All You Can Eat" (*Elle*)
"The Fat of the Land" (*Vogue*)
"The Diet of the Century" (*Ladies' Home Journal*)
"Cosmo Diet" (*Cosmopolitan*)
"The Very Scary New Diet Drugs" (*Mademoiselle*)
"Do Diets Work?" (*Marie Claire*)[59]

1944

1958

1972

This obsession with being or getting thin had a dark side. The collective consciousness of Americans was first jolted into an awareness of eating disorders in 1983 when pop singer Karen Carpenter died from conditions related to anorexia nervosa. Similarly, in a public confession in 1992, Britain's Princess Diana admitted she had struggled for years with the eating disorder bulimia. Despite this increased public awareness, the threat of health risks could not overcome the desire by so many women to possess the ideal feminine beauty as represented in advertising and the mass media. Writing for *Vogue* in 1997, researcher Timothy Walsh suggested, "It is highly likely that our current cultural expectations, which lead us all to pursue thinness, play an important role in the development of anorexia nervosa."[60] For every article such as Elizabeth Berg's "In Praise of the Imperfect Body" for *Good Housekeeping* in 1997, there were dozens in praise of the thin body. "So you're not thin," wrote Berg, "but maybe your body is wisely doing what's best for you—even if that means adding where you'd like to subtract."[61] Still, just as the widely publicized health consequences of sunbathing were ignored, so too were the potential risks of weight control methods.

Subtracting was the name of the game for manufacturers of diet programs and foods. Certainly, the health risks for obesity were significant, and with a doctor's guidance weight reduction was a health necessity for obese women. Ads from public health organizations, weight loss clinics, and insurance companies reiterated the health issues and reinforced the social undesirability of being overweight. (Figure 5-45.) For the majority of women, though, as Timothy Walsh observed, the response was cultural. It was not enough merely to lose enough weight to be out of danger of heart disease or other such illnesses related to obesity; women wanted to be fashionably thin.

Even in the nineteenth century, considering the representations of beauty as depicted in paintings of nudes by Renoir, Degas, and Manet, one would think feminine voluptuousness would have been desirable. A glance at fashion magazines and ads of the time would prove different. In the commercial arenas of marketing and advertising, Victorian beauty was defined as thin. The ideals that equated beauty with thinness continued to be perpetuated in the twentieth century through mass media. The representations of beauty as depicted in paintings and photography of nudes by modern artists were far

Figure 5-44. The message of activity and freedom was prevalent in most all sanitary napkin ads. By 1972 Kotex had named the product "New Freedom."

Figure 5-45. Ads for insurance companies perpetuated the stigma of being overweight with unflattering illustrations and dire health messages in the ad copy. Ad 1938.

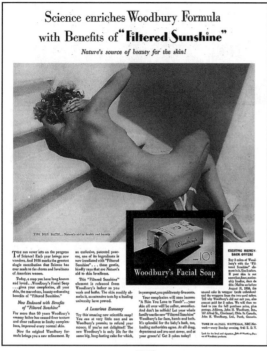

1936   1937   1951

1967   1973

Figure 5-46. The commercial ideals that equated beauty with thinness originated in the nineteenth century and was perpetuated throughout the twentieth in mass media.

removed from the ideals of Renoir, Degas, and Manet. No rolls or bulges around the midriff, no dimpled buttocks, no ponderous breasts were in evidence when advertisers depicted the ideal female form in its barest essence. (Figure 5-46.) When photos of slender nudes were coupled with the fashion plates of thin women in ads and the editorial sections of periodicals, these images became visual realities for women—references to how they thought they should look.

Unhappily for many women, though, when they looked into their boudoir mirrors they did not see a reflection that resembled those fashion plates in magazines. The desire of so many women to achieve an ideal fashion model figure led to the early and extensive marketing of products and programs for weight loss. (Figure 5-47.) Before the passage of the Pure Food and Drugs Act in 1906, such remedies might have been anything from distilled vegetable "tonics" to salt pills. The copy in the ads was filled with inflated promises but was vague about the product. Nevertheless, the significance of these ads is in the overall message they sent to women. "Fat" was an ugly word, and no woman wanted to be thought of as ugly. As the twentieth century progressed, diet products such as Ayds "low calorie candy" and processed foods from Sego, Slender, and Metrical provided safe appetite suppressants that allowed women to skip meals and curb hunger pangs. (Figure 5-48.)

During the youth movement of the 1960s, which was dually influenced by the Kennedys in the White House and the first massive wave of baby

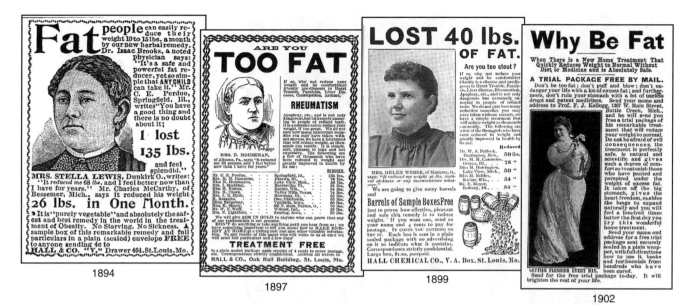

1894

1897

1899

1902

boomers reaching their teens, the sales of processed diet foods surged. (Figure 5-49.) American women wanted to look young, and that meant being slender. Margarines were mixed with a high content of water to reduce the calorie count to half that of the regular blends. Water also was added to processed meats to give them a lower fat content by weight. Artificial sweeteners replaced sugar in soft drinks and beverages. Bakeries produced breads without shortening and sliced loaves thinner to be able to list lower calorie counts per slice on package labels. Taste was compromised, but women on reduced-calorie diets did not suffer the psychological feelings of deprivation they had endured with pills or meal-in-a-can drinks. As a result, the diet food industry expanded steadily into the 1970s and 1980s. By the 1990s, marketers were designing food packaging, labels, and cartons with a universal

Figure 5-47. Before the passage of the Pure Food and Drugs Act in 1906, diet products could have contained most anything from vegetable "tonics" to salt pills.

Figure 5-48. Appetite suppressants became widely popular after World War II, encouraging women to skip meals without suffering hunger pangs.

1953

1963

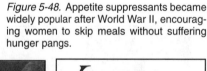

1973

Figure 5-49. During the youth-oriented 1960s, varieties of processed diet foods expanded dramatically as women tried to preserve the appearance of youthful slenderness. Ads 1967.

green color that consumers came to recognize as representing low-calorie foods with low-fat or no-fat ingredients. As a result, the vastly expanded varieties of diet foods were no longer confined to a special section of the grocery store, but could be found in most every food product category, aisle after aisle. In 1996, recommendations for a seven-day diet in *Good Housekeeping* listed a menu with column after column of processed foods that were labeled fat-free or low-fat, sugar-free or reduced-sugar, skim or part-skim, unsweetened, or light.[62]

Makers of regular processed foods also cashed in on the diet obsessions of American women. (Figure 5-50.) Food products that were naturally low

1939

1952

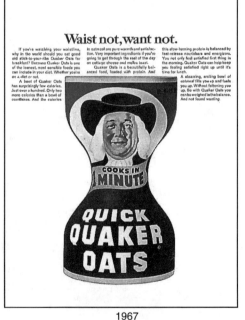

1967

Figure 5-50. Manufacturers of processed foods that were low in calories advertised their products as alternatives to less tasty diet products.

in fat or calories were advertised as alternatives to less tasty diet foods, pills, and formulas. Manufacturers of juices, cereals, soft drinks, salad dressings, gelatin desserts, soups, and crackers positioned their products with a marketing strategy designed to carve a lasting niche in the diet arena. They successfully banked on women never surrendering their battles with weight control.

So powerful was the American woman's obsession with being thin that from the 1920s into the 1950s, cigarette manufacturers advertised smoking as a way to control overeating. (Figure 5-51.) "For a treat instead of a treatment, treat yourself to Old Golds," suggested Lorillard ads in the 1940s and 1950s. One series from 1929 by Lucky Strike depicted attractive, slender young women and men with corpulent shadows in the background. "Avoid that shadow," declared the copy in these ads; "when tempted to do yourself too well, if you will reach for a Lucky instead, you will thus avoid overindulgence, maintaining a trim figure."[63] The magic selling words in the copy emphasized "trim."

The Finishing Touch: Fragrance

One final feminine touch has been a part of the beauty regimen of women all over the world since the early days of civilization: fragrance. Oils, alcohols, and extractions from sweet-smelling flowers, fruits, and nuts have been commercially produced for more than six thousand years. Cleopatra is known to have had different scents to apply to different parts of her body, ranging from subtle rose oils to more piquant lotions of cinnamon and citrus. By the end of the first millennium A.D., the Crusaders had introduced to Europe new types of perfume made from animal musk oils. Produced in Africa, Arabia, and even as far east as Russia, these potent scents were unusual mixtures of animal secretions and exotic regional flora. Ambergris from whales, castoreum from beavers, civet from civet cats, and musk from the Moschus deer were blended with rare plant essences to create the costly luxuries. The fixative and sexually stimulating properties of these animal secretions are still the basis of many modern-day perfume formulas.

Despite the availability of musk-based perfumes at the start of the century, American women much preferred the softly scented violet waters. (Figure 5-52.) More closely resembling alcohol-based colognes than perfumes, these inexpensive fragrances were common items in the boudoirs of American women. Ads for these floral scents often claimed a romanticized French connection. In a 1901 ad for Delettrez perfumes, the poetic hymn to the "modest violets" of "the Valley of the Var in sunny France" implied that only the unique flowers from this region were used

Figure 5-51. From the 1920s into the 1950s, tobacco companies suggested in ads that women should smoke cigarettes as a way to control their weight. Ad 1948.

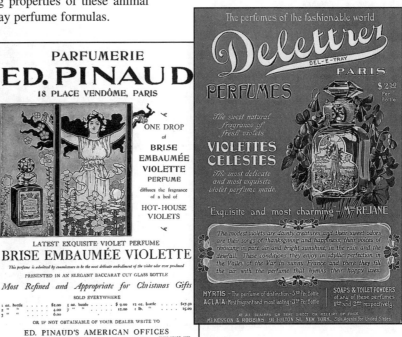

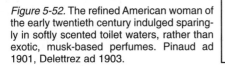

Figure 5-52. The refined American woman of the early twentieth century indulged sparingly in softly scented toilet waters, rather than exotic, musk-based perfumes. Pinaud ad 1901, Delettrez ad 1903.

Figure 5-53. Following the First World War, cosmetics and perfume makers began to present women with romantic fantasy and sensuality in the art and copy of their ads. Left ad 1918, right ad 1924.

to make the perfume. In actuality, to best assure a year-round supply of flowers for mass production, a considerable number of perfume manufacturers grew their blossoms in vast hothouses in America. Many of the most popular fragrances purchased by American women did, indeed, originate in France, such as Chanel's No. 5, whereas some French perfumes such as those created by François Coty were manufactured in the United States.[64] Even Yardley's English Lavender was made in America, although its ads in

1930

1942

1957

Figure 5-54. The ad formula of evocative images and minimal copy for promoting fragrances was translated into innumerable variations throughout the century.

Figure 5-55. Responding to patriotic fervor during World War II, American fragrance manufacturers launched new products with labels in English rather than the usual French names. Arden ad 1942, Leigh ad 1945.

the 1940s and 1950s ran disclaimers to remind its traditional customers that the scent was "from the original English formulae, combining imported and domestic ingredients."[65]

Copy in early ads for perfume was product specific. Despite the contemporary art nouveau illustrations and design elements, these ads were informational and would have served just as well in any ordinary mail-order catalog. By the end of the First World War, though, perfume manufacturers began to borrow advertising ideas from the French. (Figure 5-53.) The art deco illustrations by Fred Packer for Mavis perfume during the late teens and twenties instantly evoked feelings of fantasy and sensuality in women. Copy was reduced to a minimum in all these ads, with no product descriptions or price points, although the bottle is featured with other Vivaudou products. The trend of evocative ad designs and copywriting was quickly adapted by most all other American fragrance manufacturers. The results of this new image for a basically static product—floral scents—helped boost sales across the industry from $17 million in 1914 to $60 million in 1919.[66] With such a palpable success, it is hardly surprising that this minimalist, emotional-laden ad formula would be modified into innumerable variations throughout the rest of the century. (Figure 5-54.)

By the Second World War, some perfume manufacturers abandoned French affectations in favor of product labels and promotions all in English. (Figure 5-55.) Elizabeth Arden used her own name on her fragrance and beauty product lines and listed her New York address prominently beneath her logo in ads of the 1940s. Leigh Perfumes may have featured its best-selling Risque fragrance in its 1940s ads, but the other scent labels listed included Poetic Dream and Heartbeat. To emphasize the non-French labels, the Leigh ad floorlines stated, "Presenting the American era in fine perfume at an American price."

Although the French spell had been broken for American perfume makers, the romance and sensuality of the French mystique remained a significant component of their marketing. When Estee Lauder sought a name for a new line of beauty products in 1968, she returned from a trip to Paris with the French word "clinique" in mind. "The French sound would give our products panache!" she recalled saying.[67] Yet, her fragrance labels included the very non-French names Beautiful, Pleasures, and Knowing. Coty continued to introduce new fragrances, including labels in English such as Smitty and Nuance, while simultaneously launching Le Sport, all in the 1970s. While widely advertised fragrances by Yves St. Laurent, Christian Dior, Pierre Cardin, and Hubert de Givenchy kept the French language spoken at retail fragrance counters all through the 1970s and 1980s, domestic makers continued the American approach with names such as Revlon's Charlie and Scoundrel. Some American fragrance manufacturers eschewed Parisian pretenses altogether and introduced their new perfumes with labels solely in English, such as Calvin Klein's Escape, Obsession, and Contradiction. By the 1990s, even the famous European perfumeries acknowledged that American women were less enamored of unpronounceable foreign words on fragrance labels and launched scents with names in English: Dune by Dior, Envy by Gucci, Allure by Chanel, and The Dreamer by Versace, to name a few.

1959

1973

1997

Figure 5-56. That women continued to love wearing fragrances decade after decade is evidenced by the longevity of many popular brands.

Of course, there was much more to the production and marketing of perfumes than the mystique of a word or phrase on a label. In her 1991 book *Backlash,* Susan Faludi wrote of how women had been targeted by the fragrance industry since the 1970s. From their clumsy overtures to the "brash, independent, and sexually assertive" woman of the 1970s to their condescending representations of the "demure, alabaster brides" of the Reagan-Bush years, fragrance manufacturers failed to understand the American woman at all, Faludi decided. As perfume prices climbed to $165 an ounce for mass-produced scents, sales slumped industrywide. Citing a $20 million loss for upscale concentrated perfumes between 1980 and 1985, Faludi concluded that "none of these marketing strategies paid off." She further contended that had companies simply consulted their "own research" about women customers, they might not have suffered such dramatic losses in quarterly earnings as Avon's 57 percent drop in 1988.[68]

Still, through all the trial-and-error launchings and withdrawals of new scents by manufacturers, the American woman continued to respond to fragrance advertising. "If you think that perfume makes you smell good, then wear it," wrote feminist Susan Brownmiller; "it merely extends the prescription of sweetness to the olfactory senses, where pretense is easier than in matters of character and disposition, at least on first impression."[69] Clearly, decades of women have agreed with Brownmiller, as evidenced by the half-century longevity of brands such as Coty's Emeraude, Dana's Tabu, and the most famous of all, Chanel's No. 5. (Figure 5-56.)

Conclusion: Mass Production and the Promise of Beauty and Health

By the dawn of the twentieth century, advertising had been a part of the American woman's life for decades. Among the most prolific marketing messages she had received in ever increasing abundance were those that featured mass-produced products that promised beauty and health.

Initially, the advertising efforts of the beauty industry were merely reflections of society's values, and were designed to promote sales and brand recognition of existing products. Product lines were largely limited to practical toiletry items and the occasional facial powder. Advertising for these products cautiously steered clear of promoting any suggestion of a painted lady. Instead, it took the external forces of a national crisis during World War I, combined with the abrupt and instantaneous influences of Hollywood, to begin to change society's view of beauty, and how to acquire it. The Victorian lady's massive mounds of hair were cropped into bobs or page-boy cuts; faces were openly tinted with lip rouges, cheek blushes, mascaras, and eyeshadows. In response to the demands of consumers for new kinds of cosmetic products, manufacturers wasted little time in creating or extending product lines. In advertising, images of the alabaster lady disappeared forever and were supplanted by representations of the glamor queens of the movies. Aided also by the expansion of the five-and-dime chain stores across America, mass marketers of beauty products successfully reached a rapidly growing base of eager consumers.

Unlike with the beauty industry, a mass market of products created to enhance a woman's health had burgeoned from the start with the aid of advertising. Patent medicine businesses had flourished all through the nineteenth century with widely advertised promises of treatments and cures for all sorts of ailments. As manufacturing and advertising became more responsible for products and claims, due in part to government oversight and regulation, women began to benefit from the availability and affordability of many health products. Many ad messages conveyed valuable health information to consumers, such as the need for proper dental care or personal hygiene. New mass-produced products were created for a woman's unique health concerns, such as disposable sanitary napkins and medications formulated for premenstrual syndrome. Some health products were also marketed as beauty products, such as low-fat processed foods and skin-care treatments.

In examining the launch of a new fragrance in an article for *Harper's Bazaar,* James Servin posed two pertinent questions about the beauty and health industries, and women's attitudes, at the end of the 1990s: "Mirror, mirror, are we happy yet?" and "Can happiness be bottled?"[70] Ironically, these questions were best answered by a different article in the same issue that provided a first look at "the 'it' list" of "what's next" for women in the twenty-first century. On page after page were commentary and photos of lipsticks, blushes, foundations, nail polishes, beauty soaps, skin-care treatments, hair-care products, and fragrances.[71] One thing that was made clear from both these articles was that whatever avenues the American woman would explore in her quest for beauty and health in the twenty-first century, they would be heavily populated with directions from advertising. The promises contained in bottles, jars, tubes, and boxes of beauty and health care products would not be much different from those advertised to her great-great-grandmother at the close of the nineteenth century.

Chapter 6

FASHION
FORWARD

The emergence of the American ready-to-wear industry • Fashion trends through World War I • The rise and fall of hemlines in the 1920s and 1930s • Styles of the Second World War • Dior's "New Look" • The youth-oriented 1960s and 1970s • American style since 1980 • The evolution of women's unmentionables and swimwear • The art of fashion advertising

The American fashion industry of the twentieth century became a hybrid that combined two nineteenth-century European industries: French couture design and English mass production of ready-to-wear clothing. English clothing manufacturers had initially concentrated their efforts in producing uniform categories of garments that did not change in style, whereas French couturiers created seasonal models from which handmade copies could be tailored and sold to a wider market than had been possible with private dressmakers. These two divergent avenues merged and evolved into a unique commercial process in America. "Modistes"—agents for American ready-to-wear manufacturers and retailers—would visit the French couture houses at the beginning of the biennial fashion seasons and buy, or as many French designers complained, steal, the current trends. Models of garments could then be quickly constructed and modified for mass production and distribution to the American market.

As the nineteenth century concluded, the biennial fashion season had become biannual, and American manufacturers kept pace by constantly upgrading technology and methods of production. The principles of flow production were already in place for most ready-to-wear makers, and distribution channels continued to grow with the advent of wider parcel delivery services such as Rural Free Delivery, introduced by the postal service in 1896.

On the front lines of communicating the current trends to women all across America were the periodicals that contained fashion sections. Women's magazines, especially, eagerly awaited the reports from the Parisian fashion houses. In December 1888, *Godey's* apologized to readers for not yet publishing fashion plates of coming new trends because the modistes had returned late from Paris and current styles "could not be obtained earlier in the season."[1] By the 1890s, styles were changing so rapidly that numerous periodicals devoted solely to fashion and style were

Figure 6-1. The "new figure" for women of 1900 was defined by the s-bend corset, which shifted the spine and pelvis back while dropping the bustline. Ad 1900.

Figure 6-2. Prior to 1910 the straight-line front of bodices and blouses was emphasized by the contorting s-bend corset. Ad 1902.

launched. First published in 1892, for example, *Vogue* was a weekly magazine that, as one subscription ad stated, provided pictures that were "strictly accurate in every detail of the prevailing mode in dress."[2] The astounding proliferation of periodicals in the late nineteenth century kept American women fully informed about current fashions and the idea of fashion. As an 1898 *Vogue* ad affirmed: "Vogue answers questions and has the best chosen fashions with good workable descriptions. Such knowledge is very difficult for women to get who are not in society, who live away from large cities, and who do not have access to the best shops and dressmaking establishments."[3] Such fashion "knowledge," as presented in the pages of *Vogue, McCall's, Ladies' Home Journal, Harper's Bazaar,* and so many others, was disseminated to women across the country, from the residents of New York mansions to those dwelling in farmsteads on the prairie.

Close behind the fashion news of periodicals were fashion ads with their own announcements of styles and trends. Although couture reports had been features of women's periodicals throughout the nineteenth century, the first illustrated fashion ads for specific ready-made women's apparel were first published in the 1870s.[4] Within a generation, American women were receiving far more information on fashion from advertising than from magazine and newspaper editorials. Between the increasing volume of ad linage in periodicals and the endless flood of fashion catalogs, direct mail, and other print materials, women consumers were kept thoroughly informed of every nuance of American ready-to-wear fashions.

Fashion Trends through World War I

The first noticeable fashion movement of the early 1900s was the change in the female silhouette created by the "s-bend" corset. (Figure 6-1.) Instead of the erect hourglass shape of the 1890s, the bustline now dropped as the corset shifted the spine and pelvis back, and garment waistlines were pushed forward into an unnatural angle. In response to this new silhouette, French designers such as the notable Isador Paquin created the straight-line front for dresses and blouses. (Figure 6-2.) With the bosom shifted downward by the s-bend corset, vertical detailing such as plackets and pintucks were emphasized by a straighter line than with previous styles. Another difference was the sleeve. The voluminous leg-o'-mutton sleeves, so popular a few years earlier, were reversed into a bishop's sleeve with the fullness at the wrist instead of at the shoulder. Skirts remained full and long.

At the end of the first decade, American fashions had evolved some aspects independent of French influence. From the looser and shorter bicycle suits of the 1890s evolved the ankle-length walking skirt, which allowed active women freedom from the s-line corset and floor-length hemlines. The trend traveled to England first and then to Paris, where the straight-line bodice was married with the shorter skirt to create the "hobble" in 1908. Although the new hobble dresses and skirts were popularized by the famous designer Paul Poiret, Americans initially resisted them. Styles shown in the

Figure 6-3. Even a couple of years after French couturiers had abandoned the s-bend silhouette, American women continued to prefer the look. Ad 1910.

1910 "Paris Fashion Number" of the *Ladies' Home Journal* depicted the American interpretations still with the s-line silhouette. Within a few seasons, however, the narrowly tapered contours of skirts became the mode nationwide. (Figure 6-3.)

Part of the resistance to the new French styles at this time was due to the concerted efforts by U.S. manufacturers of apparel and textiles to promote American fashions for American women. Numerous periodical publishers supported the notion in editorials, especially *Ladies' Home Journal* editor Edward Bok. In an article titled "Can America Originate Its Own Fashions?" that ran in the 1909 "Autumn Fashion Number," writer Anna Westermann argued that despite how glamorous and artistic American women may think Parisian fashions are, "they are not for us." She criticized American clothing makers, retailers, and consumers for lazily accepting the rule of dress from Paris. "So positive has become both the need and desire in the evolution of an American style of dress," she concluded, "that we shall not only be co-equal with Paris, but perhaps excel it in cleverness and originality."[5] Nothing significant ever came of this flurry of campaigning, and ironically, the efforts faded just as World War I started. As Paul Nystrom noted, "Thus, at the very time when it might have attained its greatest importance, due to the isolation of France from the rest of the world by war, the movement itself had been deemed hopeless by American producers and distributors."[6]

By the second decade of the century, American women more readily accepted the trends as soon as they arrived from Paris. (Figure 6-4.) The bell-shaped skirts with yards of fabric dragging the floor had narrowed dramatically, and the hemline had cautiously risen about four inches to reveal the shoes. Because of the narrow skirts, multiple layers of petticoats had been reduced to only one or two. These two fashion trends helped cause a crisis in American textile manufacturing as ready-to-wear and intimate-apparel manufacturers cut orders for fabrics even as they increased output of units. Another significant change in fashions in the early teens was the adaptation of the directoire waistline that placed the line of the waist up under the bustline. This new silhouette helped eliminate the configuring s-line corset in favor of a more comfortable erect version. (Figure 6-5.)

In August 1914, the First World War began in Europe. The impact on the French couture business, and by extension the American ready-to-wear industry, was dramatic. Many couturiers, such as Poiret, left their salons to join the military. Others converted their businesses into factories

Figure 6-4. The tapered contours of the hobble skirt, launched by Parisian designers in 1908, were not popularized in American ready-to-wear until the early teens. National Cloak ad 1913, Bellas Hess ad 1914.

Figure 6-5. By the early teens, the s-bend corset had been replaced by more vertical, slenderizing versions. Ad 1913.

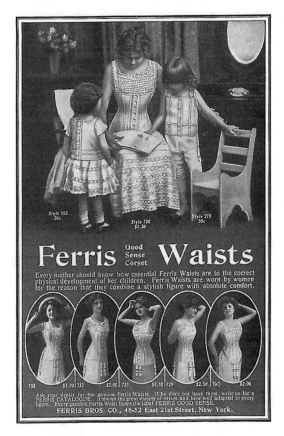

for the war effort. Some designers failed to anticipate the fabric and raw materials shortages and had to limit the number of styles in their model lines. In addition, everyone suffered from the restrictions on travel and shipping. As a result, French fashion production was reduced by half.

For those couturiers, mostly women, who were able to remain in business, the designs reflected the zeitgeist of war. (Figure 6-6.) Tight-fitting slim skirts were replaced by a fuller silhouette. By 1916, hemlines had risen to about eight to ten inches above the floor. Simplified designs and military embellishments such as metal buttons and epaulets replaced the excessive ornamentation of lace and beads that Poiret and others lavished on designs of a few years earlier. Fabrications and colors of garments became much more subdued. The elimination of extensive eveningwear collections reflected the somber mood of these years. In 1917 the French government even banned the wearing of jewels and evening dress to the Opéra, the Odéon, and the Comédie Française for the duration. With the world at war, both the French and Americans regarded conspicuous lavishness as unpatriotic.

This somber mood also was carried over into fashion advertising. An ad in 1918 from the H. Black Company addressed a "war-time message to the leaders of fashion." (Figure 6-7.) These fashion leaders were not the modistes, magazine editors, ready-to-wear manufacturers or retailers, but the "patriotic women" of America, who were urged to make "conservation charming" by preventing "the waste of adulterated fabrics and careless tailoring." The illustration in the ad depicted the new "cloth-saving silhouette" but warned that the available designs were "not in too great a variety."

Additionally, women's trousers made their debut with limited social acceptability during the war years. (Figure 6-8.) Yet, as fashion historian Georgina Howell noted, "the trousers and overalls of the women munitions workers and tram conductors, the uniforms of the nurses and postwomen were not considered part of fashion and scarcely surfaced to the pages of

Figure 6-6. In the years before the United States entered the First World War, American fashions followed Paris's lead toward fuller, looser silhouettes, which were more practical for the busy, war-preoccupied woman of the time. Standard ad 1916, Bonwit Teller ad 1917.

A WAR-TIME MESSAGE
to the
LEADERS OF FASHION

FASHION, usually concerned only with the graces and charms of costuming, now lends its hand to the stern business of war.

Labor, wool, silk, even cotton must be carefully conserved in the styles of this season.

America turns naturally to the leadership of the woman in each community who can achieve this most effectively, most artistically in her war-time wardrobe.

By example she makes conservation charming—and practical for patriotic women. In this way her choice is ultimately the choice of many.

You, who lead in fashions, already know the wanted authentic models. In the Wooltex Coats and Suits for Fall we show what you consider essential—the slender cloth-saving silhouette—designs that are smart, different, but not in too great a variety—fabrics that are as serviceable as they are beautiful. Each model is a happy style solution of conservation.

Perhaps not every woman can fol-low your lead in Wooltex Coats and Suits. We can make under war con-ditions only enough for eight women in every thousand.

What we have to offer, the choice styles and fabrics, can establish through your influence the keynote of fashions for Fall—save the waste of promiscuous styling—save the waste of adulterated fabrics and careless tai-loring.

Time is short. Good garments are scarcer every day. The important thing is to buy carefully and buy now.

In smart shops from Coast to Coast Wooltex Coats and Suits are ready. For good style, for conserva-tion—you will find no better guide than the well-known Wooltex Label.

The **H Black Co**
MAKERS OF WOOLTEX COATS AND
SUITS FOR YOUNG WOMEN
NEW YORK   CLEVELAND

Wardrobe–patriotism has fascination indeed when one may choose among a dozen or more Wooltex creations as youthful, as wearable, as this suit in rich Broadcloth. Hudson Seal trims the collar and pomls. Twilight, Medura, Bion, Taupe, Liberty Red are the wanted colors. Lined with Peau de Cygne, No. 5080. Moderately priced in your city. Ask your store or write to us for a copy of "The Tailored Woman," a fascinating magazine of fashions.

Vogue."[7] Nevertheless, these were not merely menswear donned by women for a temporary emergency. As a 1918 Finck ad explained, its women's over-alls were "essentially feminine" because they were "designed by women who know how to put style even into a work-garment." The groundwork had been laid for American women to appreciate the comfort and convenience provided by trousers as a fashion statement.

The Highs of the Twenties and Lows of the Thirties

From the end of World War I through the early 1920s, the couture houses of Paris released a confusion of styles, and American manufacturers were equally confused as to how to present them to their customers. The three ads shown in figure 6-9 show dress styles that represent everything from the revival of the directoire waistline to the redesign of the slim-line chemise. The postwar designers just could not seem to connect with women. The only common denominator was the shorter hemlines, which Anne Hollander described as "the new stripped format of female looks, which included a new look of immodesty."[8] Such an abrupt, broadly based change of style could not last, designers thought. Paris design houses repeatedly advised women that the trend of short skirts would reverse, and fashion editorials widely quoted couturiers on this point. However, as Paul Nystrom wrote, "instead of skirts growing longer as the Paris dressmakers had predicted as early as the spring of 1922 and continued persistently throughout the entire year 1922, skirts actually became shorter and shorter during all of 1923, 1924, 1925, 1926, and paused only when they reached to tops of the knees in the early part of 1927."[9]

These early years of the 1920s were difficult for the Parisian designers on several other fronts as well. European economies were in ruin. Shortages of fuels, fabrics, dyes, and labor severely impacted the fashion industries of France, Italy, and England. The postwar recession of 1921–22 caused finan-cial crises for many clothing and related business-es. Cheap imports of cotton and silk from Egypt, India, and the Far East devastated the textile indus-tries of France and England.

Across the Atlantic, the American fashion indus-try at last began to get on its feet. In 1918 more than fifty manufacturers leased land on Seventh Avenue in New York; in 1921 buildings 498 and 500 were completed and formed the core of what eventually became known throughout the world as "Fashion Avenue."[10] With inexpensive textiles

Miss America Says:—

"They Wear Like a Pig's Nose"
UNION MADE

Finck's "Detroit-Special" Women's Overalls

Necessary because women work-ers must adopt an efficient work-garment to produce effective results.

Modest because they are made along lines that are essentially fem-inine, having been designed by women who know how to put style even into a work-garment.

Comfortable because they are cut full and permit the free use of the body.

Safe because there are no loose ends or cumbersome skirts to become danger-points.

Efficient because the wearer can do better work with clothing suited to the purpose.

Quality and *Workmanship* main-tain the same high standard that has made

FINCK'S "DETROIT-SPECIAL" OVERALLS
that "Wear Like a Pig's Nose"—famous the world over

The sensible solution of a war-time need that will become a peace-time necessity.

W. M. FINCK & COMPANY
1101 Gratiot Ave.   Detroit, Michigan
Branches: St. Louis Dallas San Francisco Seattle Livingston, Mont.

Prompt Delivery: *But write us today, as these garments are in country-wide demand*

They Serve

Now that we have won the war, the girl in overalls who has helped keep her country's industries in oper-ation during war stress will merit fully her place of honor alongside the boy in blue or khaki.

Robbins & Myers Motors, because so simple to operate, clean, quiet and safe, have helped tremendously to make factory work attrac-tive to the woman worker. And R&M reliability and convenience of operation, together with woman's nat-ural adaptability, have enabled factories to change to women workers without a halt in production.

In addition to the service they are performing for the woman worker in the fac-tory, R&M Motors are also helping the thousands who have to do the home work. By operating the washing machine, electric sweeper and other household devices, they are freeing the woman at home from the need of household help.

Leading manufacturers of such machines have adopted R&M Motors to insure an absolute reliability of opera-tion of their product.

Power users seeking to better production; labor-sav-ing device makers anxious to insure a better operating performance of their prod-uct; electrical dealers desir-ous of increasing sales—all find their motor ideals in R&M Motors which range from 1-40 to 30 horsepower.

The Robbins & Myers Company, Springfield, Ohio
For Twenty-two Years Makers of Quality Fans and Motors
Branches in All Principal Cities

Robbins & Myers Motors

1920   1921   1922

Figure 6-9. Following World War I, French couturiers presented a confusing array of fashion styles, including revival silhouettes such as the narrow chemise and historical detailing such as the directoire waistline.

readily available, especially from southern states, and an abundance of garment factories stretching across the northeastern tier of states, the ready-to-wear business soared.

In addition, the American woman had emerged from the war years as a different being. She had gone to work, earned her own money, and with that had experienced true independence. In 1920, the Nineteenth Amendment was passed granting her the right to vote and, hence, further independence. Margaret Sanger and Marie Stopes had shown her methods of birth control, freeing her from child-rearing responsibilities, if not wanted. As a writer for the *New Republic* said of this New Woman in 1925: "Women have highly resolved that they are just as good as men, and intend to be treated so. They don't mean to have any more unwanted children. They don't intend to be debarred from a profession or occupation which they choose to enter. They clearly mean (even though not all of them yet realize it) that in the great game of sexual religion they shall no longer be forced to play the role, simulated or real, of helpless quarry."[11]

Instead of a revival of past fashion elements, the new look for women in the 1920s became that of a straight-line, boxy silhouette. "The ideal," wrote Jane Mulvagh, "was the physique of a young boy: straight, hipless, bustless, waistless."[12] (Figure 6-10.) To achieve this look, designers dropped the waists of dresses to hit at the hips and extended blouses, sweaters, and jackets in a straight-line tunic cut.

Among the designers who failed to heed the call of the modern, postwar woman was Paul Poiret, who continued to adorn women in fashions that were largely ornamental. The results were bankruptcy by the end of the 1920s and the permanent closing of his design house.

One Parisian designer who understood and worked the new trend was Jean Patou. As Paul Nystrom noted of the designer in 1928, "Patou has made his success by producing straight-line, youthful, boyish garments."[13] In fact, Patou especially targeted the American woman with his designs. Besides

1925

1927

1928

Figure 6-10. The straight-line, boxy silhouette dominated the look of women's fashions through the 1920s. As one fashion historian noted, the ideal woman's figure was that of "a young boy: straight, hipless, bustless, waistless."

being noted for his creations for many of Hollywood's glamour queens, he even imported American fashion models to work in his Paris showroom.

Of equal influence on fashions for the American woman in the 1920s was the "Chanel look." Gabrielle "Coco" Chanel especially created styles that were successful in American adaptations. Her special contribution to fashion of this decade was in turning sportswear into everyday clothes. She made jersey chic in simple little dresses that were unlike anything women had worn before. Her knit pullovers and pleated skirts were perfect for the new working woman who had decided to keep her job after the war had ended.

Just when the fashion industry was rolling on track again after the interruption of the First World War, another global crisis occurred, beginning with the New York stock market crash in October 1929. As a result of this economic disaster, U.S. banks and businesses failed; mortgages were foreclosed, displacing thousands; unemployment rose to more than 8 million; breadlines formed throughout the country; and labor riots left hundreds wounded or dead.

The American economic crash affected international markets almost immediately. For the French couture industry, exports dropped by 70 percent between 1929 and 1935. Losses were reported to be 2 billion francs, and clients defaulted on credit lines.[14] "Had fashion been the luxury many think it is, instead of a kind of barometer, the slump might have killed the couture," observed Georgina Howell.[15] Retailers and ready-to-wear manufacturers bought fewer models from designers to copy and even then sometimes combined resources to purchase one style to produce different variations among them.

The fashion barometer read strongly on the conservative side for the fall/winter season of 1930. As so often is the case at times of crisis, people turned to the security of the familiar past. The "lean and delicate shape of the Adonis-woman," as French historian Gilles Lipovetsky called the flapper, was replaced instead with a softer, more curvaceous ideal.[16] The waist returned, bringing with it a renewed emphasis on the bust and hips. Even though the leg disappeared beneath hemlines that dropped to within inches of the ankles, fabrications were softer and more fluid, which defined the thighs and curves of the calves. Colors and textile patterns were more subdued. (Figure 6-11.)

The exception to the subdued trends came from the Italian designer Elsa Schiaparelli, who became Chanel's chief rival in the 1930s. Hers was a brightly colored, theatrical response to gloomy times, with influences from an artistic circle that included Salvador Dali. In contrast, Lipovetsky noted, "Chanel inaugurated the 'poor' style, introduced the Apache sweater to the Ritz, lent elegance to the housemaid's shirt collar and sleeves, exploited the workman's scarf, and dressed queens in mechanic's overalls."[17]

Ironically, prior to the 1930s, Hollywood was not a trendsetter in the world of fashion, nor did it try to be. When Cecil De Mille ordered costumes from Paris for Gloria Swanson's movie roles, he specifically wanted exaggerations, not current trends of couture.[18] As Jane Mulvagh observed, "to greet an outfit with 'Whew! Pretty Hollywood,' had been an insult" during the 1920s.[19] By the 1930s, though, film actresses began to insist on fashion standards. Jean Harlow made popular the white satin evening gown designed by Adrian for *Dinner at Eight*. Katharine Hepburn and Marlene Dietrich wore tapered trousers and oversized jackets with such penetrating femininity that the look was widely copied. Also, movies such as *Belle of the Nineties* with Mae West and *The Merry Widow* with Jeanette MacDonald further augmented the revival of period costume elements in the mid-1930s.

Austerity Fashions of World War II

In September 1939, France and England declared war on Germany after the Nazi invasion of Poland. The doors to the world market were once again shut on the couture houses of Paris. Even so, they remained functioning enterprises, but only for local consumption. This time around, American

Figure 6-11. During the Depression the boyish shape of the flapper was replaced by a softer, more curvaceous ideal. In fashions the waist returned, bringing with it a renewed emphasis on the bust and hips. Simon Company ad 1931, Fashion Firsts ad 1937.

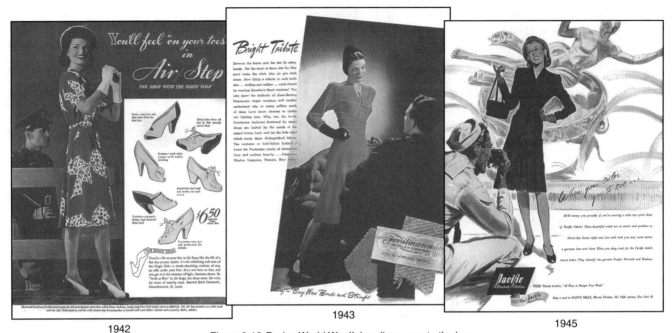

1942

1943

1945

Figure 6-12. During World War II, hemlines rose to the knee again, saving millions of yards of fabric for the war effort.

ready-to-wear manufacturers were much less dismayed by the loss of couture design imports than they had been during previous embargoes. To the contrary, they began to promote their own designers, such as Hattie Carnegie, Pauline Trigére, and Charles James. In a sense of nationalistic pride, American designers sought inspiration from every corner of the U.S. instead of looking to Europe for innovation. The 1940 fall fashion section of the *Ladies' Home Journal* opened with: "America claims its own! This year, as never before, all eyes turn to New York for fashion guidance. We of the Journal cover the collections as we would in Paris—with eagerness, and a sense of news emerging!"[20]

Although skirt lengths were basically unchanged in 1940 from the previous several seasons, by the time the U.S. was fully in the war two years later, hemlines had risen to just under the knees. In 1943, the War Production Board issued the L-85 regulation that restricted garment silhouettes and fabric use. Double-breasted jackets, fully pleated skirts, cuffs on trousers, and dozens of other fashion style elements were prohibited. This trend continued through 1945 and saved millions of yards of fabric for the war effort. (Figure 6-12.) Fashion designers selected fabrics made of all cotton, wool blends, or synthetics such as rayon. Pure wool was needed for uniforms, military coats, and blankets. Silk and nylon were primarily reserved for parachutes. Garment ornamentation was reduced, and colors were more somber than they had been in previous seasons. Just as it had been during the First World War, public sentiment regarded ostentation of any kind as unpatriotic at a time when conservation and self-discipline were critical.

During the war years of 1942 to 1945, more American women entered the workforce than ever before. History repeated itself from the days of World War I on a grander scale, as women cut their hair and donned pants to work in factories more safely. This time, though, women's slacks continued forward through the succeeding decades as a fashion item rather than merely utilitarian clothing. (Figure 6-13.)

Figure 6-13. As they had during the First World War, women in the early 1940s cut their hair and stepped into pants to work in factories more safely. After World War II ended, women's trousers became widely accepted fashion items. Ensenada ad 1942, Aralac ad 1945.

The "New Look"

After the war ended, the U.S. government lifted wartime austerity restrictions and couture fashions once again began crossing the Atlantic from Paris. Of all the designer names on the labels of the new styles, one was conspicuous by its absence. Coco Chanel had collaborated with the Germans during their occupation of Paris, so she retired to Switzerland, where she would stay until 1954. Into the vacuum caused by her departure was drawn an unlikely heir to her throne—the shy and reserved Christian Dior.

By the spring of 1946, *McCall's* fashion editor Marian Corey advised women that skirt lengths would be longer, "but not much longer. An inch or so"; but just eighteen months later, the "New Look" from Dior would have Corey writing that "suits and coats stand at 12 inches from the sidewalks; day dresses at 12 and 13; cocktail frocks may go down to 10."[21] This New Look completely swept through the fashion industry like nothing before. Emanating from Dior's debut collection in 1947, women were presented with longer skirts, detailed hats, gloves, high-heeled pumps, lots of jewelry, and an exaggerated silhouette created by the reemergence of the corset. (Figure 6-14.) Everything was important from head to toe: hats and jewelry accented the face, long skirts framed the ankles, gloves and bracelets defined the hands. Accessory and fabric manufacturers were ecstatic as their businesses boomed.

Figure 6-14. The "New Look" from Christian Dior's debut collection of 1947 swept the fashion industry. Hemlines were significantly longer, and the reemergence of the contorting corset created a narrow-waisted, wide-hipped silhouette. Head-to-toe accessories included hats, gloves, high heels, jewelry, and even parasols. Ads 1948.

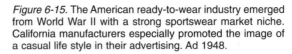

Figure 6-15. The American ready-to-wear industry emerged from World War II with a strong sportswear market niche. California manufacturers especially promoted the image of a casual life style in their advertising. Ad 1948.

The reintroduction of the corset that emphasized the bust and cinched the waist to broaden the hips was a particularly significant break from Chanel's influence. As Jane Mulvagh noted: "The New Look coincided with a return to the traditional lifestyle of marriage and motherhood for many women who had worked during the war. The narrow-waisted, wide-hipped silhouette acclaimed fertility, in contrast to the androgyny of twenties clothes. Many working women retired to their homes and contributed to the 'Baby Boom' of the late forties."[22]

Although this New Look silhouette would continue in couture fashions for the next fifteen years, American designers and ready-to-wear manufacturers created a spectrum of variations. One aspect of the fashion industry that had emerged from the war years as uniquely American was the California sportswear look. (Figure 6-15.) Manufacturers such as Koret and Cole were based in California and promoted that image of casual life style. Logos in ads even included the phrase "of California" to emphasize that fact.

American fashions throughout the 1950s continued to be dominated by the Paris couturiers and their enthusiasm for the New Look. (Figure 6-16.) However, running parallel with that was the influence of fresh perspectives at the hands of two new designers in couture, Cristobal Balenciaga and Hubert de Givenchy, whose work especially suited American women of the decade. The artifice of the Dior look—with all its trappings of accessories, corsets, and fussy details—was eased by the more casual innovations of Balenciaga and Givenchy. Rather than defying the body with constricted, contorted design elements, these two master craftsmen enhanced the feminine form with clothing that echoed movement and gesture. For active

Figure 6-16. The New Look, with its corseted artifice and trappings of accessories, remained the favored fashion style through the 1950s. Nelly Don ad 1950, Wool Council ad 1955.

1950

1955

Figure 6-17. Running parallel with the Parisian influence of the New Look in American ready-to-wear were more casual variations such as the simple shirtdress in all its many versions. Cranston ad 1955, Shelton Stroller ad 1957.

American women, their designs translated well into the many variations of the popular shirtdress. (Figure 6-17.) Even when versions leaned toward the Dior look—cinched waists, hats, gloves, and handbags all inclusive—the simple shirtdress afforded American women freedom of movement and a look of ease.

Givenchy's first collection in 1952 consisted of mix-and-match blouses, skirts, and pants as a deliberate contrast to the formality of Dior, Jeanne Lanvin, and Pierre Balmain. The American ready-to-wear market could not get enough of Givenchy's impeccable cotton separates, and expanded on the idea with everything from menswear shirts by Judy Bond to the ubiquitous bow blouse. (Figure 6-18.)

During the 1950s, changes in fashion were also the result of changes in society. Children of the Depression were now the youth of America, and the first baby boomers crossed into their early teens. There were television and rock and roll, space exploration and the threat of nuclear annihilation, McCarthyism and *Brown v. Board of Education,* and so much more for the young to question and challenge. Fads for the young outpaced the fashion industry with a turnover unequalled since the 1920s. Jeans (with saddle oxfords) violated many school dress codes in the early 1950s, but became mainstay items of every teenager's wardrobe by the end of the decade. (Figure 6-19.) As with earlier generations, teenagers used clothes to defy tradition and separate themselves from their parents. Circle skirts, ballet

1952

1954

1955

Figure 6-18. Some Parisian couturiers of the 1950s, especially Balenciaga and Givenchy, influenced American fashions with their collections of casual wardrobe separates.

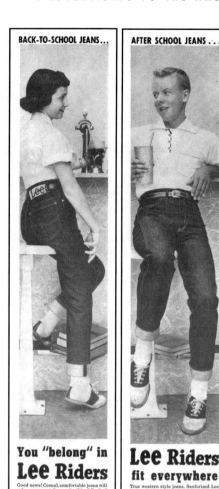

Figure 6-19. Jeans were regarded as inappropriate for school attire in the early 1950s, but became mainstay items of every teenager's wardrobe by the end of the decade. Lee ads 1954, Wrangler ad 1957.

pumps, baggy jumpers with sandals, cowboy drag, and beatnik leather all served as passwords into countercultures and social sets that most adults did not recognize or understand. The stage was set for the revolutions of the 1960s.

The Revolutionary Sixties and Cynical Seventies

A popular line of the late 1990s went, "If you remember the sixties, you weren't there." There were multiple meanings in that statement. First, it denied those who grew up in the cynical seventies any claim to the more politically and socially active era that preceded theirs. Second, the great majority of the Americans who were teenagers or adults in the sixties did not really experience the revolutionary aspects of that decade except vicariously through television or pop music. Third, for the "Woodstock Generation," the implication could be that they had been in a drug-induced stupor most of the time and as a result missed all the significant changes that had occurred.

Significant changes did indeed occur in fashions of the early 1960s, but not in America. The 1962 magazine spreads shown in Figure 6-20 reveal how very little American fashions had changed since the early 1950s. Except for the absence of corseted, cinched waists, most of these outfits easily could have appeared in a 1952 fashion catalog. In an ironic twist, the youth-oriented American woman should have been even more brave and daring in her fashion choices, given that the U.S. had a dynamic, young First Family in the White House. All America scrutinized every detail of the Jacqueline Kennedy's fashion style, from the 1960 presidential campaign to the 1963 funeral of her assassinated husband. For the First Lady, though, fashion was tastefully subdued. Her famous little pillbox hat was still part of the tradition begun with Dior's New Look fifteen years earlier. Despite her penchant for the French, though, Kennedy championed American designers such as Oleg Cassini and Roy Halston. In *Common Threads,* Lee Hall wrote, "Whether

wearing leisure clothing on the beach, or decked out in elegant formal garb, the Kennedys' use of clothing emphasized their handsomeness, energy and glamour."[23] Nevertheless, the First Family did not influence a change in American fashion of the 1960s—nor did Paris. That change came from Britain.

London designer Mary Quant, credited by many for popularizing the miniskirt, began a boutique in 1957 that catered to young women who were looking for clothes designed to reflect their contemporary attitudes. Individualism was a key component in Quant's success. "There was less interest in waiting for clothes to arrive from Paris collections, to be reverently recorded on the glossy pages of the magazine than in participating in fashion being invented on the spot," wrote Jane Mulvagh.[24]

In 1962 the thigh-high miniskirt officially arrived in fashion circles when it was featured in *British Vogue*. The following year, J. C. Penney signed a licensing agreement with Mary Quant to offer English mod styles to American girls. As designer Betsey Johnson recalled, Penney's executives feared their customers were too conservative to accept the mini as it was worn in England, so they lowered the hem by eight inches.[25] In fact, through the mid-1960s hemlines for most American women stayed just at, or even below, knee level—where skirt lengths had been twenty years earlier during World War II. (Figure 6-21.)

Even though significant changes had already begun in the American family structure and society as a whole in the 1950s, the great social movements and moments that were to so vividly characterize the midcentury were launched with the assassination of President John F. Kennedy in November 1963. From that point on, the nation suffered trauma after trauma: the escalation of the

Figure 6-20. American ready-to-wear fashions had changed very little in the early 1960s from the designs and silhouettes of the 1950s, despite the advent of the mod look in Europe. Ads 1962.

Figure 6-21. Even by the midsixties, skirt hemlines in America had crept up only to just below the knee, while thigh-high miniskirts had been popular in London and Paris for years. Ad 1965.

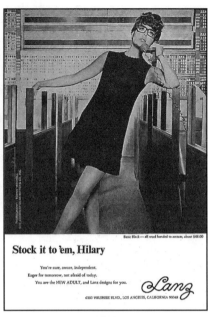

1968   1969   1969

Figure 6-22. By the time the miniskirt became popular in America, European couturiers had already begun to design longer hemlines.

Vietnam War, the sometimes violent antiwar backlash, racial conflict in the South, ghetto riots in the North, the assassinations of Robert Kennedy and Martin Luther King in 1968. The sixties produced hippies, the Summer of Love, *Laugh-In,* flower power, rock festivals, the Beatles' *Yellow Submarine, Midnight Cowboy,* President Richard Nixon, the moonwalk, the Age of Aquarius. More than 42 million Americans witnessed the changes and felt their influence each night through their television sets.[26]

Such social drama significantly affected American fashions during the second half of the 1960s. Hemlines moved up to the point of creating micro-minis, although these were to be found in trendy boutiques and not in mainstream fashion advertising. (See the 1967 Andy Warhol-inspired mini in the Dash detergent ad in Figure 3-39.) By the time American ready-to-wear manufacturers finally heeded the demand from women for the higher hemlines, it was almost too late. (Figure 6-22.)

In 1967, the blockbuster movie *Bonnie and Clyde* generated a renewed interest in the styles of the 1930s. Couture houses responded in 1968 by offering women the mid-shin midi and the ankle-length maxi. (Figure 6-23.) Both styles were rejected on both sides of the Atlantic except in their more practical application for outerwear. Designers then launched into a bewildering array of styles more confused and confusing than those created at the ends of the two

Figure 6-23. After several years when the hemline climbed to that of the micromini, couturiers in London and Paris introduced contrast to the short styles with the midi and maxi in 1968. Ads 1968.

world wars. Laura Ashley tapped into a nostalgic mood with her Victorian English cotton dresses and blouses, while Jean Muir and Sonia Rykiel focused on cleanly tailored knitwear. On the same runways with art deco- or art nouveau-inspired garments such as smoking jackets and Nijinsky shirts would be peasant or gypsy styles reflecting the pattern and textile mixing that was representative of the counterculture. The junk shop and military surplus looks brought the bell-bottom pant into universal popularity in American ready-to-wear by 1969. (Figure 6-24.)

As the antifashion styles at the end of the sixties made their transition into the looks of the "uncertain seventies," American fashion design became a "repertoire," according to Georgina Howell. She wrote in 1976: "If clothes are modes of expression, fashion is a vocabulary. Done right, fashion is the expression of women who are free, happy and doing what they want to be doing. One woman lives dozens of different lives—one at home, another at work, another out in the evening, another in the country, and at least two more for fun."[27]

During the early seventies, the repertoire evolved into an American chic aimed at the increasingly wealthy market of working women. Designers led by Roy Halston, Bill Blass, Calvin Klein, and Geoffrey Beene presented classic, well-tailored separates in combination with newly styled sweaters and knitwear. (Figure 6-25.) This new generation of designers understood that the American woman wanted easy, comfortable, coordinated clothing that could be added to a core wardrobe season after season. The emerging change in women's attitudes toward themselves and toward fashion was noted in the 1973 fall fashion edition of *Vogue*: "Today's clothes reflect today's mood, answers today's needs, not yesterday's. The whole swing of the times is to simplify—to unclutter—unencumber. Not simply because Vogue Magazine tells you so; the way you live tells you so."[28]

The unencumbered, uncluttered look evolved as a result of designers abandoning the architectural shapes and heavy fabrics of the midsixties for light materials that contoured the body. "In other words, fabric is what ultimately makes the difference," advised *Vogue* in 1975.[29] Linen, suede, cashmere,

Figure 6-24. The counterculture style of junk shop and military surplus looks brought the bell-bottom pant into mainstream American ready-to-wear. Ad 1969.

Figure 6-25. American designers responded to the confusion of styles of the early 1970s by creating well-tailored separates, especially knitwear aimed at the emerging market of working women. Neiman-Marcus ad 1972, Robinson's ad 1973.

Figure 6-26. Women's pants legs in the early 1970s became very wide, with flares reaching extreme circumferences. Cuddlecoat ad 1972, Lilli Ann ad 1973.

tweed, and flannel, plus new synthetics such as Du Pont's Qiana, served the designers well in their pursuit to please the modern American woman.

As for silhouettes, hemlines dropped to varying lengths. In 1972 Halston's ankle-length T-shirt dresses were worn on the same streets as Valentino's or Muir's halter dresses with their hemlines at the knee. Pant legs became very wide, with flares reaching such extreme circumferences that they were popularly called "elephant bells." (Figure 6-26.) The convenient and comfortable women's pantsuit began to be more prevalent in

Figure 6-27. Despite fashion alternatives such as "punk chic" or the Japanese-inspired "big look" of the late 1970s, American women continued to be satisfied with easy "shapes and textures." Ready-to-wear fashions of the time emphasized fabric, color, and texture. Ads 1977.

Figure 6-28. During the late 1970s extravagance in fashion reemerged in eveningwear designed for discos. Palais Royal ad 1978, Halston ad 1979.

offices; sweater dressing, with its innumerable variations of short- and long-sleeved cardigans, pullovers, tunics, skirts, and dresses, provided for year-round, seasonless looks. Fashion ads presented all these looks with no uniform emphasis beyond a subdued color coordination or the fluidity and textures of fabrications. (Figure 6-27.) "Although it is now customary to think of the 1970s as an age of freedom from the domination of fashion designers and the fashion business," wrote Anne Hollander in 1978, "the tyranny of fashion itself has in fact never been stronger than in this period of visual pluralism." The rejection of social conventions in dress, she maintained, was "now supposed to be the case that people may dress with a lack of regard not only for . . . Seventh Avenue but also for the guardians of convention, suitability, and propriety in dress according to age, sex, or occasion." Although it sounded like Hollander was making a case for "anything goes" in the 1970s, she concluded that "it is still never possible to 'wear anything.'"[30]

American women proved this to be true during the second half of the 1970s when designers such as Zandra Rhodes offered "punk chic." This sudden "violence" in style, as fashion editor Prudence Glynn wrote, reflected "a certain dullness of silhouette in fashion, . . . an ennui with established leadership in all sorts of fields."[31] Tattered hemlines, ragged cuffs, safety-pin jewelry, and other such homemade looks never took hold in mainstream American fashions except possibly as a peripheral variation in denim lines. Similarly the "big look" inspired by Japanese designers, whose styles were based on loose native garments, failed to spark the interest of American women. Many women had joined in the fitness boom and did not want to conceal the figures they had worked so hard to achieve. Instead, women continued to buy, and be satisfied with, free and easy "shapes and textures," as the subhead read in a 1977 J. C. Penney ad.

Where extravagance in fashion emerged during the 1970s was in evening-wear designs inspired by the disco craze. (Figure 6-28.) The 1977 movie

It was a cowboy who told us how to make jeans. We mean a *real* cowboy, with snake hips and long Texas legs and plenty of pride in his looks. Dickies were designed for *him*, but you know something? That design sits snugger on a cowgirl's hips and bottom than a lot of jeans that cost three times the price— *and* they're 100% cotton Sanforset. We think the Dickies horseshoe will be around long after some of these fancy pants are on their last legs. Williamson Dickie Apparel Mfg. Co., Fort Worth, Texas.

Figure 6-29. Without a designer label on the patch pocket of their jeans, many disco patrons were refused admission. Ad 1980.

Saturday Night Fever defined this cultural phenomenon with cynical characters who were keenly preoccupied with their youth, looks, and wardrobes. Was the movie an example of art imitating life or vice versa? Night spots and dance clubs began to admit only those who were appropriately dressed for the scene, which, along with anything that glittered and sparkled, included skintight designer-label jeans for both women and men. (Figure 6-29.) Disco fever had been fueled by a huge segment of consumers: the baby boomers, most of whom were in their twenties at the time. In response to the demand, the American fashion industry cranked out the costumes for their nighttime play.

American Fashion Style since 1980

Following the U.S. presidential election of 1980, the fashion industry took its cue from the West Coast couple who took up residence in the White House. Not only were Ronald Reagan and his second wife, Nancy, from California, they were genuine Hollywood. The Reagan "court" included many of the country's best-known glitterati, and after the modest simplicity of Jimmy and Rosalyn Carter, the fashion industry anticipated a return to flair and ostentation. Calvin Klein recalled that everyone on Seventh Avenue expected "that glamour would be back and we'd be doing glam evening dresses to show it off ... because the Reagans are Californian and California is pretty showy."[32]

In actuality, two trends in American fashion coursed through the first years of the decade simultaneously. Luxurious exhibitionism returned to fashion, inspired by a style-conscious First Lady who enjoyed showcasing fashions with her size 8 figure, coupled with the costume tableaus in prime-time television soaps such as *Dallas* and *Dynasty*. (Figure 6-30.) Designers such as Maryll Lanvin, Jean-Louis Scherrer, and Paul-Louis Orrier led the way with formal, luxurious, and abundantly decorated creations. "Unabashed extravagance, whether manifested in wearing a couture-calibre ball gown to shoot pool or in piling on dollar strands of pearls à la Madonna, suited the moment," summarized fashion historian Caroline Milbank.[33]

In contrast to the voluptuous styles of the Reagan circle and the Dynastyites was the strong current of conservatism in mainstream fashion at the same time. Despite the perceived glamour of Ronald and Nancy, American fashions responded more emphatically to the palpable ultraconservatism of the Reagan administration: the simplicity of Giorgio Armani's dresses, the clean lines of former architect Gianfranco Ferre's suit separates, the inexpensive materials of Beene Bag coordinates from Geoffrey Beene, the painterly colors of Perry Ellis's sportswear, and the nostalgia of clothing

Figure 6-30. Influenced by the Hollywood couple in the White House and the costume tableaus of prime-time TV soaps, luxurious exhibitionism returned to fashion in the 1980s. Ad 1984.

Figure 6-31. Despite the perceived glamour of the Reagans, most American fashions largely reflected the ultraconservatism of the administration and its chilling effect on society. Koret ad 1984, Leslie Faye ad 1985.

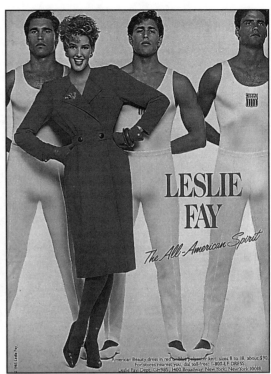

stylist Ralph Lauren. Advertising by American ready-to-wear makers followed the lead of the homegrown designers with minimalist ad layouts and static photo compositions. (Figure 6-31.)

Even by the late 1980s, *Vogue* was hard-pressed to gush over anything new for the fall collections. In 1987, one editor explained, "our view of the season is slanted a particular way . . . that the best of what's new has to fit different criteria today"; the "starting point" for this new criteria was "with clothes that are minimal, low-key, almost uniform in their simplicity."[34] In other words, no significant fashion changes had occurred since the decade began (except the addition of shorter skirt lengths to the variety of hemlines already in play). The following year saw more of the same. Among the designers interviewed by *Vogue*, Romeo Gigli stated, "I do not go in for dramatic revolutions in style. I tend to reinvent around an old theme." Echoing this thought, designer Azzedine Alaia said, "My collection never really changes."[35]

Following the conclusion of Reagan's second term in 1988, George Bush was elected president. Since he had been Reagan's vice president and closely linked with the conservatism of that administration, historians often refer to the two as one entity: the Reagan-Bush years. First Lady Barbara Bush was a large-size grandmother who often made fun of her sensible shoes and lack of designer labels in her wardrobe. Hence, the fashion industry had no political or social drama to inspire and generate any significant changes as the 1990s dawned.

As at the end of the Depression, when styles and silhouettes were unchanged but color provided fashion newness, so too emerged fashions in the nineties. "Color is the new luxury item," said designer Isaac Mizrahi in 1990 with an eye to French designer Christian Lacroix's "powerful brights."[36] Jewel tones and startling combinations of fuchsias, reds, and oranges were applied to the same styles of women's dresses, suits, and separates that had been produced during the preceding several years. In trying to figure out the "Paris dictates" of 1991, *Vogue* writer Suzy Menkes assured women that "short and tight is definitely out."[37] The following year, *Vogue*

continued to emphasize "the big question, skirt length." From the one hundred couture shows of Paris, New York, Milan, and London, *Vogue* editors determined in 1992 that "Length was going to change; every significant designer showed long skirts. It was never an issue. When skirt length changes, other things have to change as well."[38]

In actuality, things did not change. By 1994, *Vogue* had surrendered predicting where the hemline would be. "More evidence of fashion's new democracy," wrote *Vogue* editor William Norwich, "is the fact that women are free to wear their skirts whatever length they like."[39] Despite all the earlier predictions, the short skirt silhouette continued strong through the entire decade. (Figure 6-32.)

As the decade drew to a close, *Vogue* conceded that "Fashion has long ceased to be one thing, one mood, one idea. These days it's the mix that matters. Man-tailored coats over sexy slip dresses, masculine suits, beaded eveningwear—take your pick."[40]

Women did just that, opting for dresses and skirts with hemlines at lengths all up and down the leg, or menswear power suits and classic sportswear suit separates, or coordinates in synthetic and natural fabrications, and everything monochromatic or brightly colored or color coordinated, or in pattern mixing or color blocking; all of it buttoned, tied, snapped, zipped, hooked, Velcroed, or elasticized into place. Each of these styles—as a total look or in a mix with other styles—was widely advertised by ready-to-wear makers and retailers in their attempts to carve out or maintain their market niche. Fashion magazines became so jammed with ads that fall issues would top seven hundred pages by the 1990s. *Vogue* noted in 1992 that such mega-issues "some readers love because they get so much for their money—and some love to hate, because they can't find the fashion or the features for the ads."[41] Yet, the symbiotic relationship between the American fashion industry and advertising has created the greatest clothing consumer market in the world.

The Bare Essentials: Lingerie and Swimwear

Up to this point, little has been said about two other significant categories that should be included in any survey of women's fashion advertising: intimate apparel and swimwear. Both combined became $5.8 billion industries by the end of the twentieth century[42] and, despite much controversy in early decades, relied as much on advertising for their success as any other fashion category.

Although women's undergarments have a history as ancient as clothing itself, the contorting corset first appeared only in the 1400s. Throughout the succeeding centuries, the appearance of women's figures was reshaped as fashion dictated, from tubular girdlesteads to rigid stomachers to hip-widening contraptions such as farthingales. By the mid-nineteenth century, women's groups began to advocate dress reform, particularly the elimination of the corset. Doctors especially supported this notion. In 1870, George Napheys wrote in his *Physical Life of Woman* that due to the disfiguring corset, "so many women are forced to neglect their duties to their ownselves that so many thousands walk the streets of our great cities, living martyrs." Further, he complained: "We refer to the foolish and injurious pressure which is exerted on the lower part of the chest and the abdomen by tight corset, belts, and bands to support the under clothing: in other words, *tight lacing*. Why is it, by what strange freak of fashion and blindness to artistic rules, women of the present day think that a deformed and ill-proportioned waist is a requisite of beauty, we do not know."[43]

Various answers to Napheys's confusion have been proposed over the years. Some social theorists maintained that the restricting corset was an invention of men to keep women subdued and in the home. Another suggestion was that the hourglass figure suggested sexuality and implied fertility by emphasizing the illusion of broader hips and larger bosoms created by the exaggerated "wasp waist." Others have argued that the corset provided visible evidence of class separation, since tightly laced women were unable to do much physical labor.[44]

Whatever the reasons women of the nineteenth century chose to wear corsets, the garments continued to be a significant part of fashion and as such, a business that manufacturers and retailers unhesitatingly promoted. By the 1890s such unmentionables were mentioned often in ads throughout the entire spectrum of mass media. The issue in these early corset ads was not one of consumer education—women already wanted the items—but rather of product differentiation. Manufacturers' advertising efforts were aimed at positioning their designs as superior to those of the competition. Better corsets were made of silk or silk blends sewn over cotton that had been steam-molded into shape and reinforced with whaleboning, whereas cheaper versions were made with lesser grades of cotton or even buckram, and were structured with less durable celluloid or iron wiring that rusted when washed. Shown in figure 6-33 is a column of corset ads from an 1895 *Ladies' Home Journal*. Top-of-the-line Coronet offered styles made of brocaded sateen in colors for three dollars, plus a free guide on "how to choose them so as to fit." Competitors' corsets shown here and listed elsewhere in the same issue were mostly in the one-dollar price range, with children's and young miss sizes at twenty-five to fifty cents.[45]

Even as the twentieth century began, women refused to surrender their corsets. The difference from a decade earlier was the introduction of the new s-bend design, which dropped the bustline and pushed the hips back, creating a straight-line front for blouses and bodices. (Figure 6-34.) A Royal Worcester ad of 1909 lists corsets with better grades of whaleboning priced up to twenty dollars, a substantial sum in those days.

In the early teens, Paris fashions became more tapered and slender in silhouette. The distorted "modish figure" illustrated in a 1913 Madame Lyra ad was a typical example of how women wanted to look for the prevailing fashion trends. (Figure 6-35.) The ad copy assured women that the Madame Lyra corset would provide "the chic low bust, the sweeping length from waist to knees, the straight hip and altogether willowy figure of youth."

Corsets made during the war years and up to the early 1920s lost much of their bulk as fashions became more revealing through shorter hemlines,

Figure 6-33. Unmentionables were mentioned often in advertising to the American woman. Since corsets defined the fashion silhouette for decades, women's periodicals were filled with ads promoting the newest styles. Ads 1895.

1901

1902

1909

Figure 6-34. The s-bend corset made its debut at the turn of the century and made possible the straight-line front for blouses and dress bodices.

The Modish Figure

¶ Would you have the modish figure, that is, the chic low bust, the sweeping length from waist to knees, the straight hip and altogether willowy figure of youth, I would say, wear just the right model of **Madame Lyra Corsets** for your individual figure, and all this is yours. I can prove my statements. After studying the fashions abroad during the height of the season, I have reflected in the late models of **Madame Lyra Corsets** every exacting demand of the Parisian vogue. **Madame Lyra Corsets** will corset you (no matter what the type of your figure, for there is a model for every figure) according to these perfect demands.

¶ For **Madame Lyra Corsets** I refer you to merchants throughout the country handling exclusive corsets. Ask for **Madame Lyra Corsets**. You will be fully repaid for insisting upon having them.

Model 6008
(Like cut)
For slender and medium figures, giving the graceful lines of youth. Low bust, extreme length below waist. Boned the full length of the corset in back. No boning over hip bone, allowing perfect comfort but not at all taking away from the straight hip effect. The long cloth extension below the front clasp is hooked the entire length and ease in sitting is afforded by the insertion of four graduated sections of elastic. Material, very fine quality coutil, white, silk embroidery and heavy satin trimming. Three pairs heavy webbing hose supporters.
Sizes 18-30
$10.00

Made in Many Modish Models
$3.50 to $25.00

Send for Style Plates No Charge

¶ If, however, you cannot procure Madame Lyra Corsets thru a local merchant, I will send you, direct, whatever Madame Lyra model you wish upon receipt of the retail price, post or express prepaid. When ordering, state size corset you wear, whether you wish low or medium bust, long or extra long hip, and whether your figure is slender, medium or stout. ¶ For further information, write me personally, care Lyra Corset Makers, Lyra Building, Detroit, Michigan.
Very cordially,
Madame Lyra

short sleeves for daywear, and the elimination of multiple petticoats. The 1916 Gossard ad shows how sophisticated corset designing had become. (Figure 6-36.) On the far right of the ad is illustrated the "ideal average figure," which reveals the continuing preference for the dropped bustline and narrow, boyish hips. This silhouette would continue into the 1920s, when the flapper would discard the corset altogether. "The corset is as dead as the dodo's grandfather," wrote Bruce Bliven about the wardrobe of the flapper in 1925. He described "Flapper Jane's" everyday clothes: "These were estimated the other day by some statistician to weigh two pounds. Probably a libel; I doubt they come within half a pound of such bulk. If you'd like to know exactly, it is: one dress, one step-in [one-piece underwear], two stockings, two shoes."[46]

It is important to note that the flapper was universally thought to be about nineteen years old. For the other millions of fashion-conscious American women, the boxy, boyish look of styles in vogue during the 1920s could not be achieved without the contrivance of corsets. (Figure 6-37.) "Youth is beauty—youth is style," declared the header of an ad for P. N. Practical Front corsets in 1925. "The imperious gesture of Fashion's Finger commands the youthful outline," continued the theme in a similar ad.[47] In a 1926 version the copy promised that the design of the advertiser's corsets "restrains the bust and gracefully moulds the figure." Modern corsets now compressed rather than supported—exactly what was called for to simulate the thin, teenage figure of Flapper Jane. "Is the modern mania for strapping the body flat with brassieres, girdles and other harness robbing women of

Figure 6-35. In the years just before World War I, fashions became more tapered and slender in silhouette. The s-bend corset was replaced by a style that created a "willowy figure of youth," as this 1913 ad recommended.

Figure 6-36. During the war years and into the early 1920s, women's fashions became more revealing, with shorter hemlines and the elimination of multiple petticoats. As a result, corsets became lighter in weight and less bulky, but continued to contort the figure into an unnatural silhouette. Ad 1916.

their vitality and capacity for motherhood?" asked a 1925 editorial in *Physical Culture*; "well, I suppose it's the price that's required, for being strictly in the fashion!" bemoaned the columnist.[48]

Following the start of the Depression, hemlines dropped considerably and fashions once again emphasized the curvaceous silhouette. The use of lightweight and knit fabrics for the new designs meant that corsets could not have the bulk or structure of previous styles. Advances in textile weaving and the use of synthetic and elasticized fabrics helped make corsets of the 1930s lighter and stronger. (Figure 6-38.) Stays, cords, and bone or metal support inserts were replaced by engineered structure and stitching. The more abbreviated girdle was then made possible and gained popularity, especially as bras became better engineered and more comfortable. By the end of the decade, the zipper had eliminated the need to squeeze into the corset or girdle and lace-up stays.

Between the mid-1930s and the end of the 1960s girdles underwent changes more in engineering and fabrication than in the silhouette. (Figure 6-39.) Throughout all these decades, the purpose of the garment was figure control, not figure alteration, as had been a function of corsets.

By the 1970s, mass-media advertising of the girdle waned precipitously. Department stores relegated the garments to the back of intimate-apparel departments for the shopping comfort of the older female customers who still preferred them. A number of factors contributed to this abandonment of configuring corsetry. The youth-oriented culture of the 1960s had led many women to diet and exercise to preserve their appearance of youth. As the 1970s progressed, the body-conscious boom swept up even more women who wanted to show off the results of their disciplined dieting and exercise regimens. In response to this "running away from the grey pox," as Georgina Howell called it,[49] the fashion industry also provided new styles with trim cuts and soft fabrications to accentuate the youthful twenty-, thirty-, and even forty-something figure. Additionally, pantyhose and panties were made of ever stronger weaves and synthetic textiles or had built-in panels that provided some degree of support and control. In examining a 1975 Du Pont study on "What Happened to the Girdle," Elizabeth Ewing deduced from the research that "Wearing a girdle was until recent years 'almost a legal requirement.' Everyone did. Now, given the choice by casual dress and tights [pantyhose], by 'go natural' life styles and relaxed social standards, women *en masse* decided no."[50]

Besides corsets, other categories of women's intimate apparel that evolved during the first decades of the twentieth century included the brassiere, the panty, and sheer stockings. Millions of column inches of ad space likewise have been devoted to promoting these products.

Although versions of the "bust bodice" were available to women in the 1880s, the first actual patented brassiere was invented by Mary Phelps Jacob in 1914. (Figure 6-40.) It was a minimal-support

Figure 6-37. To simulate the boyish figure of the flapper, corsets in the 1920s compressed rather than shaped and supported the figure. Ad 1925.

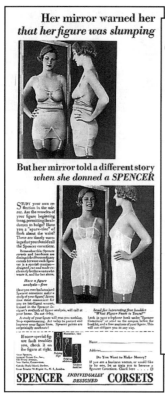

Figure 6-38. Reengineered designs for corsets of the 1930s replaced bone and metal supports with elasticized fabrics and new methods of garment construction. Spencer ad 1934, Talon ad 1939.

Figure 6-39. From the 1930s through the 1960s, girdles were an integral part of most women's wardrobes. After 1970, women largely abandoned girdles for control-top panties and pantyhose.

garment that was light, flexible, and easy to put on or remove. Early manufactured versions resembled more a camisole than the articulated cup styles of later years. Elasticized fabrics were first incorporated into the new brassiere designs in the 1920s, and in 1935 Warner's developed the alphabet cup sizes that would become the industry standard. In response to the image of bra-burning feminists in 1971, *Good Housekeeping* polled readers about the "rejection of bras." Ninety-one percent of the respondents voted to keep their bras.[51] "Most women still prefer to wear bras," wrote Elaine Benson twenty-five years later in *Unmentionables;* "witness the recent brouhaha

1948

1957

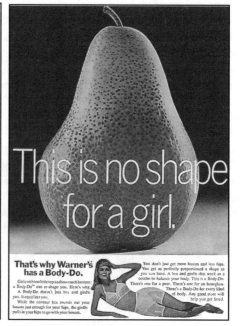

1967

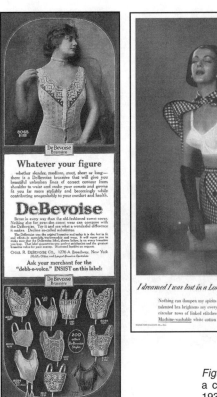

1916

1957

1966

Figure 6-40. The brassiere, first patented in 1914, evolved from a camisole-type garment into an articulated cup design in the 1930s and into a cleavage enhancer at the end of the century.

over the Wonderbra and the Super-Uplift, push-up bras said to impart the same cleavage that breast implants offer."[52] By the end of the 1990s, bras were offered in hundreds of designs, colors, and fabrics.

The metamorphosis of the panty from Victorian drawers and union suits occurred as women's fashions began to expose more and more skin. (Figure 6-41.) The sleeveless long johns the model wears in the 1919 Munsingwear

Figure 6-41. The metamorphosis of the panty from the Victorian "union suit" (so-called because a top and bottom were united into a single garment) occurred as women's fashions began to expose more and more skin.

1919

1928

1939

1918

1946

1955

Figure 6-42. As skirt lengths became shorter during the second decade of the twentieth century, silk hosiery was widely advertised as a vital fashion accessory. Nylons were introduced in 1940, followed by seamless styles in the mid-1950s and pantyhose in the 1960s.

ad had changed very little from their original design of four decades earlier. As dress hemlines receded to the knees in the 1920s, the short, one-piece "step-in" was designed to be well away from view. Also, following the trend of the two-piece swimsuit, women's underwear of the 1920s included the more daring tap pants worn with a long camisole, corset, or brassiere. Silk and rayon were the most popular fabrics used for these little underthings, although the more pedestrian cotton versions were also widely sold. From the 1930s on, the separate pieces of panty and bra were the most preferred styles, even though variations of the one-piece continued to be made even into the 1990s.

Hosiery also has an ancient history, with origins dating back to the woolen socks created by the north European tribes of the Roman Empire. Over the centuries versions of the circular-woven knee-high socks combined with the Roman military legging to evolve into the one-piece woolen tights of the late Middle Ages. The first known records of women wearing silk stockings are from the Elizabethan era, when William Lee invented a loom for machine-knitted stockings. Silk, though, was a luxury item even during the mass-production decades of the early twentieth century. A toe-to-waist pantyhose of all silk would have been an unthinkable extravagance. Instead, women wore individual stockings attached to a corset or garter belt. (Figure 6-42.) During the 1920s, a popular trend with flappers was to roll the thigh-high stockings down over garters to just above the knees into which make-up, flasks, perfume vials, or cash could be stuffed.

On May 15, 1940, Du Pont launched one of the biggest promotions in the history of consumerism when it introduced nylon hosiery. Selected retailers were sent a limited supply of hosiery made of the new "indestructible" yarn and were required to wait until the official "Nylon Day" to sell the product. As soon as doors were opened that day in May, a nationwide hysteria ensued that resulted in near riots at a number of stores. The next steps in the evolution of women's hosiery included the development of seamless stockings in the mid-1950s, followed by the creation of fashion tights for the miniskirt in the early 1960s that would ultimately lead to the mass marketing of panty-hose.

Related to intimate apparel, both in fashion styling and social evolution, is swimwear. Not until the middle of the nineteenth century did women's bathing suits originate as a distinct form of attire. Even then, the costume primarily followed the design of street dress. A high-necked, fitted bodice was worn with a full, knee-length skirt over voluminous bloomers, heavy black stockings, and flat canvas shoes. Wet, the outfit was a terrible weight burden, and drownings were common for the unwary. Wading or shallow bathing at the shoreline was the extent for which these suits were best designed.

The distinction between "bathing" suit and "swimming" suit would become more significant to marketers in the first two decades of the twentieth century. The costumes shown in a 1909 Ivory ad are still called bathing suits in the copy and are not far removed from the Victorian designs worn decades earlier. The skirts had become lighter, the bloomers less full and much shorter, and bodices were daringly sleeveless with decollete necklines. (Figure 6-43.)

In 1915, Danish immigrant Carl Jantzen developed a machine that produced lightweight elasticized knits. Although the knits originally were intended for use in sweaters, a friend who was a rower asked Jantzen to produce some athletic sportswear with the new rib-knits. The skintight stretch suits were soon worn by every member of the rowing team. In 1920, the company introduced swimsuit versions. Jantzen's Knitting Mills then began advertising its new styles of swimwear with the slogan, "The suit that changed bathing to swimming."[53]

Knitting mills all over the country quickly developed similar knit fabrications, and the silhouette of swimwear for women changed dramatically. (Figure 6-44.) The copy in a 1922 Bradley knitwear ad focused on the company's solution to the "foes" of a knit swimsuit—sun and saltwater—while the copy in a Spalding ad of a few years later promised that its suits would make the wearer "look like a swimmer." The rapid evolution of the style differences is readily apparent, too, with the new dropped neckline, the deep

Figure 6-43. Bathing suits at the beginning of the century were cumbersome, multipieced costumes that made swimming difficult at best. Ad 1909.

Figure 6-44. The lightweight knitted suit changed "bathing" to "swimming" in the 1920s. Bradley ad 1922, Spalding ad 1927.

1947

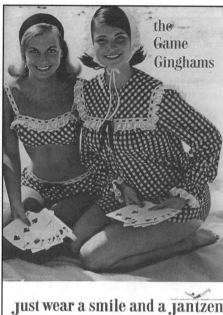

1965

Figure 6-45. When the bikini was introduced in Paris in 1946, American swimwear makers compromised cautiously on the design by producing a halter and midriff-bottom variation. By the 1960s the bikini was more accepted by young women, and by the 1990s the style had evolved into the thong.

1997

armholes, and the one-piece construction of the 1927 styles. The stockings and shoes still worn in the early twenties were soon discarded for the maximum exposure of skin. At the time of the Bradley ad, wearing a one-piece swimsuit on a public beach could get a woman arrested for indecency.[54] By the 1930s, the tubular menswear styling of women's swimsuits was supplanted by designs that contoured and emphasized the female figure. In 1935, the topless brief for men was introduced from France. Also that year, the first two-piece swimsuits that bared the midriff on women were launched.

The next great leap in swimwear design did not come until after the conclusion of the Second World War. Paris designer Louis Réard was about to launch a daring new swimsuit design and wished to generate as much publicity as possible. The bikini—named for one of the nuclear test site islands then in the news—made its debut on the runways of 1946 and generated more debate and condemnation than the bomb tests had. Ironically the concept of the two-piece bikini design had been around for decades and was a familiar feature of costumes in the Ziegfeld Follies and Busby Berkeley movies. For American manufacturers, though, the issue was moot; for many years their most daring response to the French bikini was the two-piece bandeau and midriff bottom that had been introduced in the midthirties. (Figure 6-45.) Cleavage was acceptable but the navel had to be covered. Gradually the bikini began to make its appearance on American beaches and at poolsides through the 1950s. When the youth-inspired beach scene became so popular in movies and pop music of the 1960s, young women—and those who wished to think young—readily donned the new, more revealing versions of the bikini. By the end of the 1990s, the narrow French-cut bottoms, and even miniscule thongs, were common, and many beaches even had areas where topless sunbathing for women was permitted.

It should be noted that makers of shoes, handbags, hats, jewelry, eyewear, scarves, belts, and other accessories advertised as extensively as did ready-to-wear and intimate apparel manufacturers. However, even the most cursory examination of accessory ads could fill another chapter and exceed the practical scope of this study. Entire books have been devoted solely to the history of hats or of shoes, for example. Suffice it to say that these products—as well as daywear (slips and petticoats), sleepwear, and numerous other classifications of garments—received their share of ad space wherever the American woman might have directed her gaze.

The Art of Fashion Advertising

One other aspect of fashion advertising that is worthy of mention is that of presentation. In looking at the dozens of ads included in this chapter, each reader probably would have an opinion on the old controversy of photography versus artwork. Among the issues in the debate is that of image as opposed to product merchandising. Did an illustration represent the garment in the ad well enough to produce sales? Ad agency chairman Martin Landey said of fashion advertising in 1997: "Although fashion must appeal to the emotions, and a strategy and an idea can seem to be cerebral, the execution of a strategy can be just as emotional as a fashion ad. The end result, however, is that the consumer will take away something more lasting when the advertising is based on an idea, not just a picture of the product."[55]

In product marketing of the 1990s, this debate of illustration versus photography similarly manifested itself in branding versus sales. "Branding," wrote Tom Peters for *Advertising Age* in 1998, "means nothing more (and nothing less!) than creating a distinct personality . . . and telling the world about it."[56] So, too, had been the argument of fashion illustrators who tried to convey the essence of a look or a style in their artwork without being restricted to literal depictions of garments. Many of the most famous fashion illustrators were able to achieve both objectives and miraculously please everyone in the process. The editors of *Harper's Bazar* (changed to *Harper's Bazaar* in 1929) were so proud of their illustrators that they ran a series of ads in 1922 crediting them by name. (Figure 6-46.)

The significance of the artist's style went not only to selling merchandise but also to establishing the image differentiation of the merchants. Jim

Figure 6-46. Fashion illustrators could achieve more than just a literal depiction of garments; they could convey the essence of a fashion look or style. Ads 1922.

Figure 6-47. The distinctive style of a fashion illustrator could establish a distinct and recognizable visual differentiation for a manufacturer or retailer. Ads 1918.

Howard's spectacular drawings for Bonwit Teller ads of the 1970s never failed to catch the eye every time they were featured in the *New York Times*. So, too, were Andre Dupré's fluid sketches for B. Altman, Antonio Lopez's exotic renderings for Bloomingdale's, and George Stravino's polished drawings for Bergdorf Goodman. Many retailers assiduously cultivated a specific look in their advertising to set themselves apart from the competition. One Florida store saw this confirmed when, in the early 1980s, a fashion ad ran in a large city newspaper without the company's logo; the piece of type had simply fallen off the paste-up in the newspaper's composing department. The customers so easily recognized the illustrator's distinctive style that they still knew where to go for the items depicted in the ad.

Over the decades, all these famous artists, along with thousands of anonymous in-house art staffs, inherited this legacy of image differentiation from the efforts of their predecessors at the start of the century. In examining the three fashion ads from 1918 shown in Figure 6-47, one is struck by the superlative quality of each illustration as well as the distinction of each artist's style. These are not mere representations of merchandise; they are statements about the fashion designers, retailers, and manufacturers who commissioned these artists to provide a powerful identity over that of their competition.

In writing of the midcentury's most prolific and famous fashion illustrator, *Vogue* noted that the fashion art of Eric (Carl Erickson) was "even more true than photography, for by selectivity and discrimination he lays bare the essential."[57] (Figure 6-48.) In the 1940

Figure 6-48. Vogue once said that the illustrations by Eric (Carl Erickson) were "even more true than photography" because he made fashion "move and live." Ad 1940.

Figure 6-49. By the end of the last quarter of the twentieth century fashion illustration had become a dying art.

Forstmann Woolens ad, that essence is readily apparent with the insertion of five photo vignettes across the top of the ad. By comparison, the photographs appear as representational portraits of the clothing rather than a statement of fashion, even with the dominance of the flamboyant hat in each frame. Eric's rendering of the same outfit, on the other hand, "makes fashion move and live," as *Vogue* once said of his work.[58]

The many great names in the field of American fashion illustration are too numerous to review here. By and large, much of their work was regarded as a disposable commercial product, time sensitive and readily discarded as the next volume piled into the prepress production departments of magazines and newspapers. Alas, one may sigh, by the end of the twentieth century fashion illustration had become a lost art. (Figure 6-49.) In more than four thousand combined pages of the 1997 and 1998 September fashion editions of *Vogue, Elle, Cosmopolitan,* and *Vanity Fair,* only two fashion ads and three shoe ads were illustrated primarily with artwork; all others were illustrated with photography. As Herwig Zahm of Mondi commented in *The Art of Creating Fashion,* "Fashion is an artistic refinement of historical moments, a commentary of the time, it even gives a time period impulses."[59] For most of the twentieth century, the fashion illustrator captured, interpreted, accentuated, and preserved those moments for future generations to admire and appreciate, even as the fashions themselves faded from style.

Conclusion: The Mass Production and Mass Marketing of Fashion

From the start of the twentieth century, the American fashion industry emerged as a mass-marketing enterprise. Unlike the French, British, and Italian couture houses with their uniqueness of product and select customer base, American fashion makers sought a broadly based market of consumers. Mass production was the aim of ready-to-wear manufacturers, and mass distribution was the goal of clothing retailers and catalogers.

The consumer demand for fashion was generated by two sources of mass communication, fashion journalism and fashion advertising, neither of which, ironically, was often synchronized with the other. The fashion reports of mass media, especially those in women's magazines and later from movies and television, were usually ahead of American public taste. The hobble skirt of the teens, the bikini swimsuit of the forties, and the miniskirt of the sixties were all significant fashion trends that were initially resisted, then embraced, by the American consumer. The result was that fashion journalism might have extolled the newest styles and trends, but fashion advertising continued to reflect the deferred interests of American women consumers.

Nevertheless, fashion did move forward, and advertising played a critical role in its progress. In succeeding decades since the first ready-to-wear ads appeared in the 1870s, American women received increasingly more information about fashion from advertising than from mass-media journalism. Whereas early issues of *Vogue,* for example, were about 65 percent editorial and 35 percent advertising, the ratio continued to tilt toward the marketer so that by midcentury issues were packed with as much as 70 percent advertising.[60] In addition, fashion retailers flooded women consumers with catalogs, newspaper supplements, direct mail, and other print material by the ton.

Not every marketing effort succeeded, as most any contemporary ready-to-wear manufacturer or consumer could testify. Predicting which fashion trends would spark the interest of consumers was a high-stakes gamble with enormous consequences for winners and losers. Despite the best advertising strategies, the colors, styles, or fabrics that were promoted as being "in" for the season often ended up on the retailers' clearance racks.

All in all, though, the mass marketing to the American woman of the idea of ephemeral fashion succeeded in creating a multi-billion-dollar fashion industry—an industry that never lost faith in the efficacy of advertising.

─Chapter 7

ACHIEVING
INDEPENDENCE

The dawn of American feminism • Mobility and independence—the bicycle and automobile • The progress of women's education • Images of women's sports and female athletes • Working women

Many historians point to the 1848 conference of women held in rural western New York state as the catalyst for the feminist movement in America. Elizabeth Cady Stanton and Lucretia Mott organized the meeting, which would produce the Seneca Falls Declaration of Sentiments—a declaration of independence for women. The issues discussed at the conference were straightforward enough: equal citizenship and equal political rights for women. Within those umbrella issues was a broad range of demands, including opportunities in education and employment, marital and property rights, dress reform, and voluntary motherhood. Yet, as the succeeding decades of the nineteenth century passed, these early feminists faced ever increasing hostilities on many fronts. In her book *Backlash,* Susan Faludi described this social resistance as the first in a series of backlashes against the progress of

Figure 7-1. With the introduction of the "safety" bicycle in 1889, average American women enjoyed their first taste of independence. Excursions took women out of cities and away from farms, their restrictive clothing was modified for bicycling, and they gained self-confidence operating the mechanical devices.

1891

1895

1896

the American women's movement, citing the relentless criticism of religious leaders, educators, medical experts, and government officials as the principle obstacle.[1]

A survey of women's periodicals in the last decades of the nineteenth century and the pre–World War I years would support Faludi's contention. Not only were women preached at by editors and writers, but advertisers contributed equally toward skewing women's perceptions of themselves as primarily wives, homemakers, and mothers. Indeed, the American woman's independence would not begin to evolve from the efforts of feminist advocacy groups, or the federal courts, or governmental legislation, but rather through social change inaugurated by technology in transportation.

On the Road to Independence

In 1889 the "safety" bicycle was introduced to replace the earlier "boneshaker" models. Featuring uniform wheels with inflatable rubber tires, a chain drive, and padded seat, the new bicycle models had greater appeal to a broader mass market, including, for the first time, women. Manufacturers wasted no time in targeting women consumers with advertising. (Figure 7-1.) Besides the fun and recreation of bicycling, as featured in the illustrations of many of these ads, the issue of women's health was also promoted. One 1891 Columbia ad recommended that "the judicious use of a bicycle by a lady will work wonders in the improvement of her health."[2]

The benefits of health and recreation aside, with the bicycle craze American women also began to experience independence in several ways. The clothing reform that feminists of a generation earlier could not inspire women to consider finally began to evolve from necessity for the active woman of the 1890s. Skirts were shortened into the "rainy daisy" versions for bicycling and walking exercises. By the middle of the decade, almost forty years after Amelia Bloomer first donned her oriental tunic and trousers, the divided skirt and breeches were publicly worn by the more daring and independent-minded women. (Figure 7-2.) By extension, the active woman also ventured onto hiking trails and into canoes wearing the practical divided skirts and breeches. In addition, less restricting corsets were specifically designed to provide a feminine shape without compressing the lungs to the exclusion of deep breathing.

Mobility was another way in which the bicycle afforded women their first steps toward independence. The Victorian woman who rarely strayed beyond the confines of the home except for treks to market and church now explored horizons far and wide. Afternoon bicycle excursions into the country could provide young women and their beaus time and distance from

Figure 7-2. Although feminists had been advocating women's dress reform for decades, it was the popularity of the bicycle that led women to unlace corsets and don divided skirts or breeches. Ad 1896.

Figure 7-3. Automakers targeted women in their advertising early on. They knew that women influenced all major purchases for the family and would be especially receptive to the mobility and freedom offered by the car. Columbia ad 1904, Oldsmobile ad 1905.

the supervision of parents. For married women, enjoying some leisure time out of the kitchen on a weekend bicycle outing broke the patterns of Victorian domesticity.

Finally, women experienced independence through operation of the bicycle. Maneuvering a mechanical device hurtling along on twin wheels contributed significantly toward helping women discover that their self-confidence could extend beyond the stove and nursery. This same self-confidence with the mobility and mechanisms of bicycling laid the groundwork for one of the most significant contributions to women's independence in the pre–World War I years: the automobile.

At the same time the bicycle was enjoying immense popularity, American inventors were experimenting with their first versions of the "horseless carriage." Charles Duryea of Chicopee, Massachusetts, successfully tested his model in 1893, and Elwood Haynes of Kokomo, Indiana, first demonstrated his automobile the following year. By 1895, about three hundred hand-built autos were on various roads in America; ten years later, with mass production devised by manufacturers such as Ford, Packard, and Pierce, almost seventy-eight thousand autos had been sold.[3] Even with mass production and intense competition, until the 1910s the automobile was largely a product for the affluent. "Runabouts" were priced in the $650 to $750 range, while luxury touring cars could cost as much as $11,000.[4]

Carmakers knew well the influence that women had on major purchasing decisions at home. As keen marketers, they also were aware of how successfully women had proven their independence with the bicycle, and that women would be even more receptive to the idea of the freedom and mobility offered by a car. (Figure 7-3.)

Almost from the beginning, auto manufacturers aimed a sizeable portion of their advertising at women. A 1905 Oldsmobile ad assured women that its car "has endeared itself to the feminine heart. Its ease of control and free-dom from getting out of order make every woman its friend." The woman behind the wheel depicted in the ad appears confident and comfortable in her operation of the vehicle, and just as significant, she is out on her own, mak-ing decisions about her time and her destinations. Moreover, a view of the house and gardens in the background tells us this is not just "every woman," despite the assurances of the ad copy. Before financial installment plans became common in the 1920s, this car had to be paid for in cash, a princely sum even for the bargain end models. Well into the teens, the independent woman behind the wheel was of the upper social strata—if not wealthy, then certainly upper middle class. (Figure 7-4.)

Cars for the proletariat would not be available until after World War I when Henry Ford would mass produce the Model T to be sold for under four hundred dollars. Even then, as Ford was to painfully learn, women cus-tomers did not buy cars, or influence their purchase, on price alone. Between 1914 and 1925, Ford produced only cars painted black. In trying to appeal to women's sense of style, Ford ads could lamely offer just one selling point about the "upholstery in soft shades of brown."[5] When the company finally, and reluctantly, began offering other colors, Henry Ford reportedly remarked to newspapermen that "we are no longer in the automobile, but the millinery business." In her 1929 book *Selling Mrs. Consumer,* Christine Frederick's response to Ford's retort was: "This was Henry's grudging way of paying a tribute to Mrs. Consumer, who was, I think, chiefly responsible for the rise of Chrysler and General Motors at the expense of Ford's Model T. Chrysler and General Motors supplied color and feminine luxury and

1916

1916

1917

Figure 7-4. Until the mass production of the Ford Model T in the 1920s, and the availability of installment financing, the auto was primarily a luxury item for the affluent.

| 1921 | 1924 | 1927 |

Figure 7-5. Manufacturers tailored car designs to suit women's needs and assiduously advertised them throughout the 1920s.

comfort until Mrs. Consumer disdained to step into a Ford Model T. Even the mighty Ford was brought to his knees by Mrs. Consumer's power, for everybody but Ford realized that cars are bought nowadays to fit woman's and family needs."[6]

Not only did Chrysler, General Motors, and other carmakers recognize the importance of tailoring their products to women, they assiduously promoted these efforts in their advertising throughout the 1920s. (Figure 7-5.) In 1921, Overland advertised its sedan as a "woman's car" in a cheery dialogue between two friends; unlike men who were "either all right or all wrong, but seldom one or the other for long at a time," said one woman in the ad, the performance reliability of her Overland was "consistent" as a woman. Similarly, Chevrolet ads of the twenties emphasized reliability and the ease with which the cars could be driven and parked, while the illustrations of fashionable women created a visual sense of modernity.

The importance of color in marketing and consumerism became a significant issue for manufacturers of just about everything in the 1920s, including cars. (Figure 7-6.) In examining the influence of color on women's purchases in 1929, a columnist for the *Ladies' Home Journal* concluded: "And that is why our car manufacturers have gone into the kitchen for inspiration. There they have been dazzled by the burst of colors in pots and pans, refrigerators, gas stoves and linoleum with which Madam has made her workshop cheerful."[7] This idea of color coordination and ensemble selling was certainly nothing new to women consumers. For decades, the fashion and home furnishings industries had successfully employed the color strategy to generate multiple sales and to establish a built-in obsolescence over time. As consumerism rose to new heights in the 1920s, manufacturers of cameras,

Figure 7-6. The importance of color as a marketing strategy expanded into most all arenas of consumer product manufacturing during the 1920s. Ad 1927.

Figure 7-7. Despite the disparaging clichés about women drivers, statistics at the end of the 1920s proved that men were involved in 94 percent of all auto accidents, as noted in a 1930 Texaco ad.

Figure 7-8. New car sales declined during the Depression, yet people drove as much as ever. Automotive service and product ads targeted women as caretakers of the family car. Ad 1934.

Figure 7-9. General Motors introduced show-room price charts in 1940 to explain auto costs to women customers.

silverware, and even furnaces were joined by carmakers in producing palettes of color choices for women consumers. It was all part of what Roland Marchand called "the consumer's quest for personalization of modern life."[8] Women increasingly were making their own decisions and exercising their influence with confidence in those decisions in the home, workplace, voting booth, or car dealership.

As the Depression intensified during the early 1930s, the percentage of new car sales dropped dramatically. Americans were hanging on to their old cars and driving as much as ever. In the *Middletown In Transition* study of 1935, the Lynds observed that "car ownership . . . was one of the most depression-proof elements of the city's life in the years following 1929." Their research indicated that while "people were riding in progressively older cars as the depression wore on, they manifestly continued to ride."[9] As a result, manufacturers of automotive products and services began to court the female consumer in advertising by recognizing her independence and sense of responsibility. That women could operate a car had not been an issue since the turn of the century. Instead, how women drove became, and would remain, a topic of debate between the sexes for decades to come. In a 1930 Texaco ad, the headline "What—another fender?" runs just beneath the illustration of a couple clearly having an argument, which would lead the reader to think the woman is being chastised by her husband for an auto accident. (Figure 7-7.) Instead, he was the guilty one, adding another dented fender to his list of driving transgressions, including also his speeding ticket and his dent in the radiator. A statistical footnote at the bottom of the ad acknowledges that "21% of the licensed drivers in the U.S.A. are women, yet they are involved in only 6% of all automobile accidents." Besides being

Figure 7-10. During World War II women found them-selves responsible for the care of "the car he left behind him," as a 1944 Pontiac ad acknowledged.

a safe driver, the ad copy noted, "the woman driver of today supplements care at the wheel with what is equally important—care in the servicing of her car."

Quaker State also approached women in ads by recognizing their self-confidence, responsibility, and independence with a car. (Figure 7-8.) A 1934 ad quoted from a letter wherein a woman complained, "I'm tired of hearing it said that women don't understand about cars. I know a half dozen girls who can coax as much out of a motor . . . and treat it as well . . . as any man who ever pressed a starter button."

Both these issues—women's understanding of cars and women's respon-sible care of cars—continued as significant advertising themes into the 1940s. When General Motors began displaying showroom price charts to explain "what makes up the prices of new cars delivered to customers," the advertising target was women. (Figure 7-9.) "Is buying the family automo-bile too involved a transaction for a woman, and therefore one better left to the menfolks?" asked a 1940 General Motors ad. Dangerously approaching condescension by referring to women's superior "shopping instinct," the ad copy finally acknowledged that with GM's "plainview wall chart" of pric-ing, women could more effectively exercise their own judgment.

Unlike during the Depression, when new car models were made but new car sales slumped, during World War II no new cars were manufactured except for military needs. For the duration of the war, that meant special care of the old car, and the automotive service sector stepped up its advertising efforts. For the first time, independence was thrust upon many women as their men went off to military service. They entered the workforce in record numbers and earned their own money, controlled their finances, and made decisions about most everything on their own. As a 1944 Pontiac ad noted, this independence also encompassed, maybe for the first time, driving and the care of a car—"the car he left behind him." (Figure 7-10.) Women in the millions took up the challenge and emerged at the end of the war with a new, or renewed, sense of freedom and self-confidence.

The emergence of the new generation of suburban homemakers of the postwar years presented a familiar target for car manufacturers. The issues that concerned women drivers in the twenties, thirties, and forties were still prevalent at midcentury. The opening copy in a 1952 Dodge ad summed up the selling points with a tour of the car's features as presented by a stereo-typical suburban housewife. She says, "I wanted a car that considered me, a woman . . . from every angle of comfort, convenience, ease-of-handling and safety." (Figure 7-11.) Even the slogan next to the Dodge logo reiterated a quality that women had demanded of cars a generation earlier: dependabili-ty.

The mobility and freedom the auto provided for women were not forgot-ten by advertisers in the 1950s. A 1956 ad by the J. Walter Thompson agency advised carmakers of the marketing potential of the American woman "stranded in suburbia." The ad copy noted that "while many harried wives drive Dad to the station, 11 million others stand and watch Dad go, taking

Figure 7-11. A new generation of suburban homemakers in the 1950s presented a familiar target for car manufacturers. Assurances of auto safety, comfort, styling, and reliability were frequently the focus of ads to women. Ad 1952.

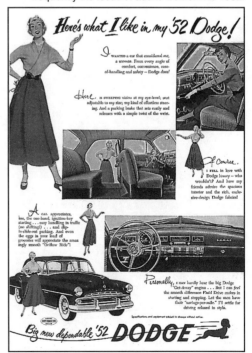

Figure 7-12. Since the 1960s, one way automakers advertised to the American woman was to focus on her contemporary life style. Chevy II ad 1967, Audi ad 1973.

with him their link with the outside world—the family car."[10] The recommendation was to promote in advertising the sale of a car for her, too.

By the 1960s and into the succeeding decades, ads promoting cars to women took two avenues. Those aimed at moms focused on child safety and reliability. (See Figure 4-24.) Those aimed at the contemporary, independent woman emphasized personal life style. (Figure 7-12.) The 1967 Chevy II was promoted to women as "the stylish economy car"; the fun, party girl stands on one side of the Chevy in her mod pantsuit, while the practical working girl stands at the other side. Economy was a key factor at the height of the oil crisis in 1973 when Audi introduced its Silver Fox model with an estimated twenty-three miles to the gallon. Still, the ad copy emphasized style with fashion verbiage including a banner that read "it's her size" and incorporated words like "sleek," "smart," and "trim."

Independent Thinking

The significance of the American woman's mobility, first with the bicycle and then with the automobile, has been mostly defined here in terms of her personal growth—discovering new horizons, establishing her self-confidence, proving her versatility beyond the Victorian concepts of housewife and mother. However, the real significance lay in where this freedom of mobility and independent thinking would eventually lead. Travel, even if only away from the farm or out of the city a short while, was an education. It brought with it new experiences and the exchange of different ideas with new acquaintances. Women began to discover they could think beyond the tenets that were provided for them by fathers, schoolteachers, ministers, husbands, and editors of women's periodicals. They began to realize that the early feminists were right in a great many respects, and none more so than the assertion of a woman's right to higher education.

1905
1913
1917

Figure 7-13. Early ads that depicted the college woman did so primarily as a novelty of setting, not as a social comment on women's higher education.

Prior to 1900, many scholars, professors, and physicians firmly believed the theories of educating women published by Edward Clarke in his 1873 study *Sex in Education; or a Fair Chance for the Girls.* Clarke and his supporters were convinced that the human body allocated energy resources set by gender. For men, it was the brain and heart that dominated, and for women, the reproductive system. It was thought, therefore, that to educate women with the same intensity as men would overstimulate their brains, upsetting the balance of energy resources and adversely affecting their reproductive organs. This idea was so commonplace that in 1893 the *Ladies'*

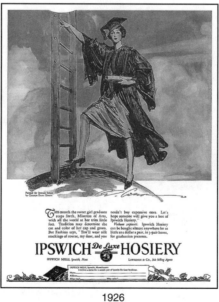

1925
1926
1927

Figure 7-14. Depictions of the female student in ads of the 1920s represented her as a graduate with the visual clichés of mortarboard, gown, and diploma.

Home Journal still took the position that "the frequent celibacy of intellectual women is a fact large enough to arrest the attention of the most superficial observer." The article recommended that a "clever" woman should keep her intelligence to herself or else "she must accept a book in place of a lover."[11]

Even as the stereotypes of gender were being challenged at the turn of the century, many proponents of women's education were cautious in their complete endorsement. Writing for *Popular Science* in 1902, David Jordan conceded that a college education "must depend on the character of the girl." The question for him was purpose: "The highest product of social evolution is the growth of the civilized home, the home that only a wise, cultivated and high-minded woman can make. To furnish such women is one of the worthiest functions of higher education."[12] In fact, Jordan was not far removed from Clarke in his estimation of women's learning capabilities in a university. "The 'motor' side of their minds and natures," he maintained, "is not strongly developed." Therefore, "women take up high education because they enjoy it; men because their careers depend on it."[13]

With this view so prevalent at the beginning of the twentieth century, marketers who depicted the college woman in ads did so primarily as a novelty. (Figure 7-13.) A 1905 Shredded Wheat ad showed a fashionably dressed young woman packing her books for "back to school." In the background are the requisite props of a school pennant and the pin-up of a male athlete. As for any commentary on the woman's education or aspirations, the ad copy simply declares that her brain "must have something to feed upon besides books." Other similar versions from the pre–World War I years included giggling sorority girls in an ad for Welch's Grape Juice from 1913 and a 1917 Betty Wales fashion ad featuring "just the dress for college." The portrayal of confidence and independence that going away to college would instill in women is noticeably absent in these early thematic ads—a marked distinction from ads of the same period showing women at the wheel of a car.

In 1918 the Commission on the Reorganization of Secondary Education set America on a new course of schooling. The commission had concluded that the typical college-prep curriculum of Latin, Greek, algebra, and philosophy not only deterred many young women (and men) from going to college but actually caused a large percentage of high school dropouts. The commission instead recommended gender-based vocational education. In *Failing at Fairness,* Myra Sadker wrote, "The adult world of work was highly sex-segregated, so vocational education courses separated students, sending girls into one sphere of study and boys into another"; even young women who were college bound "were required to take domestic science or home economics," she noted.[14]

Thirst, too, seeks quality

ORLON teaches new fall fashions to keep their figure in the wash!

ORLON® one of Du Pont's modern living fibers

Figure 7-15. College for women of the 1950s, as one historian wrote, had become "an interlude between high school and marriage." Most attended for a general education and a social life. Coca-Cola ad 1950, Du Pont ad 1953.

By the 1920s, women enrolled in college in unprecedented numbers. During this decade the percentage of degrees earned by women rose to almost 47 percent—a level that would not be achieved again until the mid-1970s.[15] Impressive numbers like these did not go unnoticed by marketers. The image of scholarship—the trite visual cliché of the gown and mortarboard—became commonplace in ads of the 1920s. (Figure 7-14.) More important, though, the idea of the educated woman had changed. She was not depicted preparing to attend school or in some frivolous pursuit at school, but rather was shown as a graduate—hence, the innumerable representations of cap, gown, and diploma used in ads during this time. Granted, it is not always clear in these depictions if the young woman has just finished high school or college. However, to the advertiser, the point was moot. For Elgin watches, the "girl graduate" illustrated in a 1925 ad is enjoying "the most wonderful time in her life"—especially since she got a new wristwatch as a congratulatory gift for her achievement. "The sweet girl graduate" of Ipswich's 1926 ad has "all the world at her trim little feet," while on the other hand, the confident "girl graduate" in Listerine's 1927 ad may find out her diploma will not guarantee success so long as she has dandruff.

The Depression impacted women's enrollment in college significantly. Between 1930 and 1950 the percentage of degrees earned by women declined to a forty-year low. As Mary Frank Fox wrote in *Women, A Feminist Perspective:* "Between the 1930s and 1960s, college women married earlier, bore more children, and turned their attention to homemaking in greater proportions than did the graduates of the 1920s. Studies indicate that during this period—and especially during the 1950s—few college women had clear vocational goals, and most attended for general education, prestige, and social life. Thus, college had come to occupy an interlude between high school and marriage (and motherhood) for young women."[16]

This idea of a general education and social pursuits of college women in the 1950s was ideal fodder for many advertisers. (Figure 7-15.) The college woman in a 1950 Coca-Cola ad is represented by a shadow on the dormitory

Figure 7-16. Ads of the 1960s used social issues and current event headlines to connect with college women. Ads 1967.

wall, while the props of her opera gloves and glasses, the tome of Shakespeare's works, a pin-up of the football team and a tearsheet of "architecture" reinforced the idea of a college woman's focus on a general study of liberal arts and a social life. Although in the 1953 Du Pont Orlon ad the female student seems to be given credit for using her brain by posing her over a molecule model and having her hold a chemistry book, the emphasis of the ad is her girlish flirtation with a male student. "One theory comes back: educate them as women," wrote Oliver Jensen in his 1952 book *The Revolt of American Women.*[17] Defining this sentiment, Lynn White, president of Hills College in Oakland, California, maintained that the college's programs for women in the fifties provided a "preparation for the whole process of living," including a curriculum of courses in decorative arts, textiles, and costume design, with heavy emphasis on nursery care, marriage, and family life.[18]

These attitudes would persist both in society and academia for another quarter of a century, even, surprisingly, during the great social upheavals of the 1960s. (Figure 7-16.) Advertisers who specifically wished to target young college women (or their parents) used current events from college campuses as a way to connect with this modern consumer group. Smith-Corona suggested to parents in 1967 that the vapid teenybopper would become a "studybopper" if she possessed an electric typewriter, or that she would "swing college" not by participating in a "sit-in" or "be-in," but rather with a studious "type-in."

By and large, marketers who depicted the female student in ads through the last decades of the century continued the traditions and formulas that had been devised in the 1920s. Manufacturers of gifts for the graduate—watches, pens, luggage—or for the graduation event itself—cameras, film—usually showed the happy women in the ubiquitous cap and gown without reference to her achievements or her future life in America with her education.

One significant leap forward for women's educational rights came in 1972 when Congress passed Title IX to the Education Amendments Act. For federally funded education programs, the key stipulation of the legislation was a prohibition against discrimination based on sex. Unfair requirements such as higher test scores for women applicants and practices such as limiting female enrollment with restrictive housing policies were eliminated with the new legislation. By the end of the decade, women were earning 24 percent of all professional degrees—up dramatically from 7 percent in 1970.[19]

This stride forward for women's equality in education during the 1970s was brief. The archconservatives of the Reagan-Bush administrations rolled back the clock on women once again. During the 1980s, programs such as the Women's Educational Equity Act were specifically undermined by severe budget cuts and hundreds of women's research grants were terminated or denied. "Encouraging the career potential of girls was seen as a threat to the family . . . the patriarchal family with a husband and father at its head," recalled Myra Sadker, former project manager for the National Institute of Education. Still, years later she optimistically wrote: "The Reagan-Bush administration may have cut off the flowers, but the plant had taken root. In huge cities and small towns in every part of America, parents and teachers continued to become aware of sexism in school. Through them the historic struggle for the full education of America's girls goes on."[20]

"A Perfect Stroke"

How many have you made? A perfect stroke means a "good drive." You can't drive successfully the enterprises of a life without vim, strength and enthusiasm. These come from foods that are rich in the vitalizing elements that make healthy tissue and clear brain. Such a food is

Shredded Whole Wheat

It contains all the body-building elements of the whole wheat in natural proportion and in digestible form. There are wheat foods and wheat foods—some "ground" and some "flaked"—but there's only one shredded whole wheat food. It is not a "pre-digested" food; it is a ready-to-digest food. "Pre-digested" foods soon put the stomach out of business.

"It's All in the Shreds."

Shredded Wheat is not "treated" or "flavored" with anything. It is the whole wheat and nothing but the wheat—the cleanest and purest cereal food made. It is made in two forms—BISCUIT and TRISCUIT. The BISCUIT is delicious for breakfast with hot or cold milk or cream, or for any other meal in combination with fruits or vegetables. TRISCUIT is the shredded whole wheat cracker which takes the place of white flour bread; delicious as a toast with butter or with cheese or preserves. "The Vital Question Cook Book" is sent free for the asking.

THE NATURAL FOOD COMPANY
Niagara Falls, N. Y.

1905

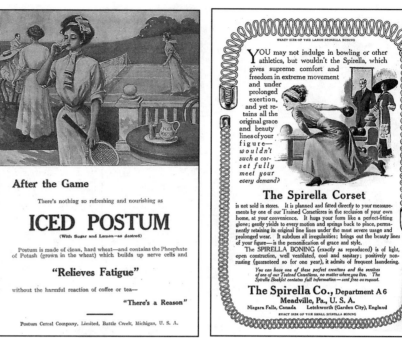

After the Game

There's nothing so refreshing and nourishing as

ICED POSTUM

(With Sugar and Lemon—as desired)

Postum is made of clean, hard wheat—and contains the Phosphate of Potash (grown in the wheat) which builds up nerve cells and

"Relieves Fatigue"

without the harmful reaction of coffee or tea—

"There's a Reason"

Postum Cereal Company, Limited, Battle Creek, Michigan, U. S. A.

1909

YOU may not indulge in bowling or other athletics, but wouldn't the Spirella, which gives supreme comfort and freedom in extreme movement and under prolonged exertion, and yet retains all the original grace and beauty lines of your figure—wouldn't such a corset fully meet your every demand?

The Spirella Corset

is not sold in stores. It is planned and fitted directly to your measurements by one of our Trained Corsetieres in the seclusion of your own home, at your convenience. It hugs your form like a perfect-fitting glove; gently yields to every motion and springs back to place, permanently retaining its original fine lines under the most severe usage and prolonged wear. It subdues all irregularities; brings out the beauty lines of your figure—is the personification of grace and style.

The SPIRELLA BONING (exactly as reproduced) is of light, open construction, well ventilated, cool and sanitary; positively non-rusting (guaranteed so for one year), it admits of frequent laundering.

You can have one of these perfect creations and the services of one of our Trained Corsetieres, no matter where you live. The Spirella Booklet contains full information—sent free on request.

The Spirella Co., Department A 6
Meadville, Pa., U. S. A.
Niagara Falls, Canada   Letchworth (Garden City), England

1911

Marketing Women Athletes and Their Sports

As the evolution of women's independence occurred through mobility with the automobile and through broader educational opportunities, women's sports also began to emerge as a contributing factor in the process. That women should exercise was not denied, even at the height of Victorianism. In 1849, *Godey's* published a series of articles on women's exercise including advice on walking and illustrated guides to isometrics. For women, the editorial in one concluded, "The general effect is to strengthen the body and counteract the early predisposition to a nervous temperament. With such constitution, no one can ever become an athlete, which, as we know, is converting mind into brute force. Nervous girls, then, should be strengthened; it will prevent them becoming invalids—it is certain they will remain clever."[21]

On many women's college campuses, "physical culture" moved from isometrics to the more gymnastic calisthenics in the 1870s, and by the 1880s, Vassar and Smith even experimented with women's baseball clubs. The social acceptability of women as athletes began to slowly emerge in the 1890s, coinciding with the popularity of the bicycle. In 1894, Vassar went so far as to offer women's tennis, bowling, and, with an appropriation of $12.50, golf.[22]

An excellent survey of women's sports at the turn of the century may be found in the comprehensive book *Athletics and Outdoor Sports for Women,* written in 1903 by Lucille Eaton Hill, athletic director at Wellesley College. Besides the expected lawn tennis, golf, and gymnastics, a surprising array of other sports activities were recommended for the college woman, including field hockey, rowing, basketball, hurdles, and even shot putting. Yet, despite Hill's enthusiasm for women's sports, her attitudes about women athletes were typical of the time. "Underneath the gayety of physical activity," she

AFTER THE GAME—
Golf, tennis or other physical recreation—
USE

LISTERINE

The Safe Antiseptic

—to provide a cooling, refreshing relief from perspiration—an excellent after-bath application

—to prevent the infection of broken blisters, scratches and small wounds

—to relieve irritations of the throat, impart a sense of cleanliness to the mouth.

USE
LISTERINE

1916

Figure 7-17. That women could demonstrate feats of athletic agility, strength, and speed was less surprising to most than the fact that they could do it all in the costumes modesty required them to wear.

Figure 7-18. Social changes of the 1920s allowed women's sports categories and competitions to proliferate. The depiction of a woman athlete would be widely used in ads as an eye-catching image through all the succeeding decades of the twentieth century.

wrote, "we must acknowledge that health of body and mind is the moving and governing principle."[23] This singular purpose was hardly different from that espoused by the *Godey's* editors a half century earlier. In Hill's estimation, the great danger—what she called the "abuse of men's athletics"—was competition. "Fiercely competitive athletics have their dangers for men, but they develop manly strength . . . for women, their dangers are greater, and the qualities they tend to develop are not womanly," her dean had said in a contemporary speech, a sentiment with which Hill concurred.[24] Although Hill recommended some of the most strenuous track and field activities for girls, including the high jump, broad jump, sprint, and long-distance run, she insisted that "grace of form be aimed at rather than speed and 'records.'"[25]

The surprise for many of us today would be not that women in Hill's time could run fast, jump high, and demonstrate all sorts of feats of strength and agility, but that they could do it in the costumes that modesty required them to wear. On campus the middy blouse, bloomers, and thick stockings provided some freedom of movement, but in public, most women athletes primarily wore looser-fitting variations of street clothes. (Figure 7-17.)

People objected more to women's involvement in public competitions than they did to women's sports. Women's intramural sports were common at the turn of the century, but were usually played in closed gymnasiums and only for women spectators. When the Olympics were revived in 1896 by Pierre de Coubertin and the athletes of the world were called to Athens, no women were invited to participate. Only reluctantly did the U.S. Amateur Athletic Union allow women to participate in the 1904 St. Louis Olympics, and then they were limited solely to archery. When the Stockholm committee agreed to allow women's swimming in the 1912 games, the AAU blocked American women's participation by refusing sponsorship of national championships.

Sports—whether schoolyard, back yard, or professional—were undeniably the bastion of men through World War I. Women's success in sports was regarded much as had been their success in other arenas such as education and professions—a novelty. "Are we wasting our women?" asked a headline in *Physical Culture* in 1920; "we must formulate some system or some scheme that will promote national physical training . . . for our young women," argued the editorial.[26] The notion of women's sports as a novelty was shattered by a rapid succession of events in the 1920s. American women entered Olympic aquatic competitions for the first time in 1920 and won all but one of the events. Two years later the National Amateur and Athletic Federation was founded with the commitment to both boys and girls competing by the same standards and regulations. The decade saw women set new records in sports: Gertrude Ederle swam the English Channel, beating all previous times by two hours; Glenna Collett became the first woman to break eighty for eighteen holes in golf; Hazel Wightman won four U.S. national championships in tennis; and Floretta McCutcheon defeated bowling champion Jimmy Smith.

The widely publicized athletic accomplishments of women in the 1920s gave advertisers exciting new themes and images for marketing. "The flapper was certainly not averse to sports," wrote athletics historian Allen Guttman, "nor were the men who courted her unaware of the erotic appeal of an athletic body."[27] Professional, Olympic, or recreational, women athletes no longer had to hide behind the screens of Victorian modesty to pursue sports goals and achievements. By the first quarter of the century, they had achieved a giant leap toward independence, and marketers exploited that idea in most every way. The image of the young female athlete was used to sell health and beauty products, breakfast cereals, soft drinks, travel, cigarettes, candy, ready-to-wear clothing, automobiles, and just about every other consumer product of the 1920s. In addition to the appeal of fashionable images of women tennis players and golfers, there was the youth and

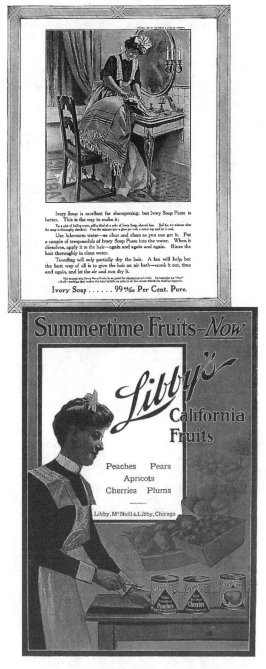

Figure 7-19. Maids and cooks were popular representations of the working woman in early-twentieth-century ads. Ivory ad 1908, Libby ad 1914.

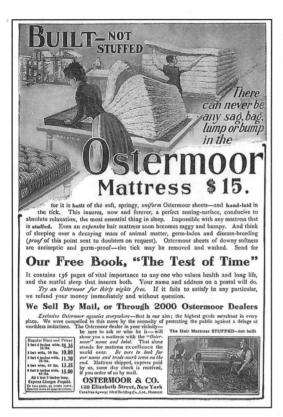

Figure 7-20. Because working conditions in factories were so infamously wretched, the female factory worker was seldom depicted in ads, and then only in idealized settings such as in this 1906 Ostermoor mattress ad.

Figure 7-21. The educated career woman shown in pre–World War I ads was usually represented by the nurse or teacher. Ad 1900.

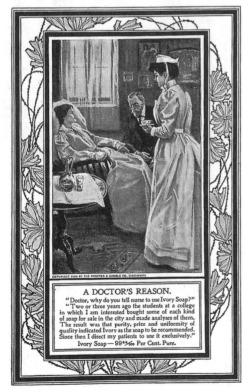

grace of ball players, and the sex sell of bared legs and arms or lithe swimmer's bodies clad in wet knits. Even if irrelevant to the product, the image of a vivacious woman athlete was eye-catching and remained so through the succeeding decades of the twentieth century. (Figure 7-18.)

True Independence through Employment

The foundations of women's independence at the start of the twentieth century—mobility, education, and sports—were a prelude for what really made women in America independent: employment. In 1900, less than 20 percent of the workforce of the United States was female, a total of about 5 million. Of that number more than 2 million were domestics in private households, more than a million were factory workers, and the rest were primarily retail sales associates, office clerks, nurses, and teachers.[28] (Figure 7-19.) Depictions of women occupied in these jobs as used in advertising were not celebrations of, or social comments on, the working woman. These images were used simply as a foil or the visual punctuation to promote a product or brand. For instance, uniformed maids and cooks were especially used to illustrate the effectiveness of household cooking and cleaning products, devices, or utensils; after all, they were supposedly the experts in their respective jobs.

Women factory workers were rarely shown in ads since sweatshop conditions were widely known and negatively publicized in pre–World War I years. Despite the clean, orderly factory shown in a 1906 ad for Ostermoor mattresses, the reality was probably quite grim. (Figure 7-20.) Writing for *Popular Science* in 1913, Malcolm Keir detailed many of the conditions and physical effects women suffered from working in factories. In most cases a female factory worker was not permitted to stop work even to "attend to her natural bodily needs." Breaks from repetitive motion routines were infrequent, and long hours of standing were common; the monotony of most factory work and the "nervous tension and strain" caused by piecework systems led to ailments ranging from "functional abnormalities" such as anemia to "chronic inflammatory disease in the pelvis."[29] Only with the labor movements of the 1920s and 1930s would many of these employer abuses be ameliorated.

Women with business or technical skills fared much better with working conditions than their factory-bound sisters. Such career choices as teaching and nursing were socially acceptable well before the turn of the twentieth century. For advertisers, these respectable professions provided visual scenarios that were complimentary to their product or brand positioning. (Figure 7-21.) In a 1900 Ivory Soap ad, for example, the illustration of a nurse in her crisp, clean uniform reinforced the extensively promoted "99 44/100 per cent" purity claim of the product. No ad copy comment was necessary on the profession of nursing since the melodrama and characters in the illustration were self-explanatory to the reader.

Figure 7-22. As more and more women were hired into offices at the turn of the century, clerical work was restructured to involve less responsibility, less status, and less pay than male clerks had received. Remington ad 1903, Oliver ad 1904.

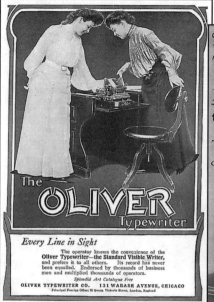

The first big boon for women's employment came in the late nineteenth century with what social historian Carol Hymowitz called "the feminization of office work."[30] In 1873, Phil Remington introduced the portable typewriter, which he promoted with demonstrations by female typists. At that time, office clerks were mostly men who handwrote business records and correspondence, maintained files, and kept the books. Businesses that bought the new typewriters also hired women as operators, especially since men found the process too tedious. (Figure 7-22.) As an increasing number of women were hired into offices, male clerks became accountants, office managers, and junior executives. The result, as Hymowitz noted, was that "clerical work was restructured, and its status declined" with less responsibility and lower pay for the new women employees.[31]

Another technological innovation that was to become the domain of women in the workplace was the telephone. (Figure 7-23.) As more offices installed the device, men withdrew from its interference behind the shield of female secretaries and receptionists. At the other end of the phone line, Bell central, women were employed in increasing numbers as switchboard operators. By 1902 almost 93 percent of Bell's forty thousand operators were women.[32] How this job was perceived by advertisers depended on the product and the sell message. In a 1912 Shredded Wheat ad, the job was shown

Figure 7-23. The switchboard also became the domain of working women in the years before the First World War. Shredded Wheat ad 1912, AT&T ad 1916.

to epitomize "the strain and stress of life" for working women, while in a 1916 American Telephone & Telegraph ad, a vignette in the illustration depicted an efficient battery of female switchboard operators as a significant component of the system's service.

The "pin money" operation was one other widely advertised source of income for women in the early decades of the twentieth century. (Figure 7-24.) Women who were unable to go into a workplace at regular hours could work between home chores and at their leisure selling goods and services on cash commission. The subscription departments of magazines especially benefited from this system, as did many retailers and distributors of products such as tea and coffee, flower seeds, sheet music, household linens, lingerie, and costume jewelry. Fuller Brush, Avon cosmetics, and Tupperware built giant operations through their networks of part-time female sales agents.

The period between the two world wars saw dramatic changes for women in the workplace, both on the legal and social fronts. World War I had introduced a great many women to their first employment away from home. After the national crisis had abated, many of those women chose to keep their jobs or, if fired to make way for a returning soldier, sought employment elsewhere. Although the 1920s saw the number of female college graduates triple, "three out of four of these educated young graduates entered the 'women's' professions: libraries, social work, teaching," noted historian Sheila Rowbotham.[33] During the Depression, the number of working wives increased from 11 percent to just over 15 percent despite the scarcity of jobs. One of the barriers women faced during this time was discrimination against the employment of married women. Between 1932 and 1937 the federal government forbade nepotism in civil service—a prohibition directed at wives—and twenty-six states specifically outlawed the employment of married women.[34] Only with reforms by the recovery acts under the New Deal in the late 1930s and the bombing of Pearl Harbor in 1941 did women begin to realize so many of their demands in the workplace.

For advertisers during the 1920s and 1930s, the use of images of working women changed little from pre–World War I formulas. (Figure 7-25.) Many of these ad layouts presented stereotyped models of working women that had become visual clichés. In a 1920 Kuppenheimer menswear ad, a secretary at work with her typewriter serves to aggrandize the businessman whose evident success can afford her services and whose towering placement in the composition denotes his importance. A 1922 "plain Jane" schoolteacher sits before a blackboard with the Maxwell House slogan written in chalk as she lectures the reader "on the first lesson to be learned about coffee." General Electric's happy factory worker of 1924 smiles at the viewer as she operates a sparkling-clean loom (with no indication of the deafening noise or air thickened with textile lint). In a 1937 ad for Listerine, the three most prevalent careers for women—in the estimation of their advertising department—were office worker, actress, and schoolteacher. Then, of course, there was

Figure 7-24. "Pin money" clubs and home sales parties allowed housewives to earn extra income throughout the twentieth century. World's Star ad 1916, *Good Housekeeping* ad 1936.

1920

1922

1924

1937

1938

1939

Figure 7-25. For advertisers of the 1920s and 1930s, images of working women had become visual clichés with few changes to the pre–World War I formulas.

Figure 7-26. Because of the publicity generated by Amelia Earhart's flights in the 1920s and 1930s, contemporary advertisers included female aviators in their line-up of images of working women. With the expansion of passenger airlines in the 1930s, a new type of working woman made her first appearances in ads: the stewardess. Fisher-Fleetwood ad 1928, Sal Hepatica ad 1938.

the switchboard operator, who, as represented in a 1938 ad, was happy to be one of the "170,000 women ... employed by the Bell System." Rounding out the stereotypes of working women depicted in ads was the nurse, whose duties, as featured in a 1939 FTD ad, included mundane delivery chores.

Not all advertisers, were content with the same tired images of working women. In 1928 Amelia Earhart became the first woman to fly across the Atlantic, albeit as a crew member responsible for keeping the logs. From the publicity of that adventure, she was hired as a vice president of Ludington Airways and helped found the Ninety-Nines, an organization of women pilots; four years later she became the first woman to solo across the Atlantic, greatly elevating her stature and fame. Almost instantly images of female aviators appeared in all sorts of ads. (Figure 7-26.) One of the first advertisers to capitalize on Earhart's popularity was General Motors, whose 1928 Fleetwood ad depicted a young woman aviator in flight fatigues. Although the copy made no connection between the product and the illustration, the reader recognized the image as being symbolic of a company poised on the cutting edge of the future. By the end of the 1930s, aviation had afforded women new career opportunities as pilots and as passenger plane stewardesses and as such provided fresh imagery for ads that depicted working women.

The national crisis of World War II and the ensuing labor shortage brought 6 million new women into the workforce. Because they were urgently needed for the war effort, the federal government endorsed at last the principle of equal pay for equal work. Bans on hiring married women or women more than thirty-five years old evaporated. Almost 75 percent of the new working women were older than thirty-five, and more than 60 percent were married. The percentage of women in the labor force during the war leapt from 25 percent to 36 percent. As Carol Hymowitz wrote of this women's labor force: "Former housewives, beauticians, waitresses, saleswomen and domestics dressed in overalls instead of skirts, tied up their hair in bandanas, and showed that they could do any job that needed to be done. They maneuvered giant overhead cranes, cleaned out blast furnaces, handled gunpowder, drove tanks off the production line, and used acetylene torches. They worked as stevedores, drill press operators . . . bus drivers, bellhops, lumberjacks, truck drivers, train conductors, gas station operators, barbers, policewomen, and lifeguards."[35] The working woman of World War II enjoyed an economic independence unparalleled in American history to that time.

Advertisers found a whole new assortment of working women images during the war years. (Figure 7-27.) Unlike in previous ads that used images of working women gratuitously, most of these depictions were sincerely in celebration of the working woman and her contribution to the nation's need.

Figure 7-27. As 6 million women entered the American workforce during World War II, advertisers celebrated their contributions in new versions of traditional ad formulas such as those depicting the secretary and telephone operator as well as new representations of factory workers and women in military uniform.

The secretary gets "no publicity, no medal . . . she's just in there slugging"; the switchboard operator is still smiling, except now she reminds customers to limit calls to five minutes; the "lady with a lamp" has graduated to be one of "7,250 women doctors"; and women join the field artillery as specially trained "Tractorettes." In the factory, Texaco salutes "Alice" for the plane she constructs; the Camels ad features the sacrifices of the "girl on the swing shift"; Chrysler recognizes the efforts of its twenty thousand women "employed in war-production"; and Scotch Tape notes that "only 56 out of 1900 war jobs are listed as 'unsuitable for women.'" The most powerful wartime images of working women in ads are those depicting women in uniform, risking the ultimate sacrifice on the frontlines of the conflict.

How could all this not forever change women's role in America's workforce? Ironically, at the beginning of the war, 95 percent of new women workers intended to quit their jobs when their men came home; by the end of the war, 80 percent had changed their minds and wanted to continue working. They had found the root of true independence with their own incomes and new feelings of self-worth. But within eighteen months of V-J Day, almost 2 million women had been fired from heavy industry.[36] In looking at the labor force participation rates for women in the half century preceding the war, the percentages of women to a total of all workers rose steadily from 17 percent in 1900 to a high of 36 percent in 1945. Two years later that progression of numbers dropped back to 27.4 percent. Almost ten years would pass before the percentage numbers of working women surpassed the 1945 high.[37]

The postwar turnaround in attitudes about working women in American society stemmed from several economic and social occurrences. Men returning from the war wanted their jobs back, even if it meant displacing women who had succeeded in those positions throughout the war years. These same

1953

1957

1969

Figure 7-28. The working women depicted in ads of the 1950s and 1960s were overwhelmingly presented as young, unmarried, and occupied with clerical-type or service work—presumably while waiting for Mr. Right to take them away from it all.

1972

1973

1979

men also wanted wives who would bear them children and provide the kind of home they had dreamed of while away in the service. Many employers had never liked the idea of working women and reinstituted restrictions on gender, age, and marital status. Sociologists, psychologists, educators, and journalists wrote volumes against the working woman. Magazines were filled with articles on the importance of women's roles as homemakers and mothers, and a new medium, television, presented America with dozens of model housewives in fictional programming. By the mid-1950s, "the new image of American woman, 'occupation housewife,' had hardened into a mystique, unquestioned and permitting no questions, shaping the very reality it distorted," wrote Betty Friedan in 1963, recalling her own experiences of a decade earlier.[38]

Although the housewife was the favorite image of advertisers, the working woman was not entirely forgotten during the 1950s. By decade's end, more than 32 percent of the labor force was comprised of women, and that number rose steadily to just under 37 percent by the end of the 1960s.[39] There was no shortage of secretaries, nurses, office clerks, teachers, stewardesses, and phone operators depicted in ads during these decades—overwhelmingly presented as young and presumably unmarried. (Figure 7-28.) Certainly, some of these women had to work for economic reasons, but most were viewed as merely filling space until their wedding day.

Even though working women of the post–World War II years enjoyed the economic independence and personal fulfillment provided by employment, they began to recognize and challenge the many inequalities to which they were subjected. Carol Hymowitz summed up the contradictions that "made the reemergence of feminism almost inevitable": "On the one hand women had legal rights and they could vote, but if politics meant power, then women remained disenfranchised. Women had educational opportunities, but they were not expected to use them. Perhaps the largest contradiction of

Figure 7-29. Advertisers of the 1970s capitalized on the constant publicity generated by high-profile feminists. Working women were depicted in scenarios and settings that previously had been exclusive to men.

What if your investment manager could add something unique to your portfolio?

Like maybe 150 years of experience.

For more than 150 years, PNC Bank has been helping individuals create and build wealth. We start by gaining a thorough understanding of you and your financial needs. We draw upon our highly regarded investment research — the same research used by over 250 other investment firms around the world — to identify opportunities for you. Then we apply our blended investment style and disciplined risk management process to help you to meet your objectives. Find out the difference our experience can make. Call PNC Private Bank at 1-800-449-7262.

PNC PRIVATE BANK

Investments • Trusts • Banking Services

PNC Private Bank is a service mark of PNC Bank Corp. Banking and trust services are provided as follows: Pennsylvania and New Jersey, PNC Bank, National Association; in Massachusetts and Connecticut, PNC Bank, New England; in Delaware, PNC Bank, Delaware; in Ohio and northern Kentucky, PNC Bank, Ohio, National Association; in western Kentucky, PNC Bank, Kentucky, Inc.; in Indiana, PNC Bank, Indiana, Inc.; in Florida, PNC Bank FSB. Members FDIC. Brokerage services are offered through PNC Brokerage Corp, a registered broker-dealer and member SIPC. PNC Brokerage Corp is a subsidiary of PNC Bank, National Association, which is not a broker-dealer.

Figure 7-30. By the close of the 1990s, the working woman had become such an integral part of the social and economic matrices of America that advertisers took her for granted and seldom depicted her on the job. Images of working women often were vague, with little reference to the status or nature of their actual work. Ad 1997.

all was the fact that 40% of American women held full-time jobs, yet they were defined as wives and mothers."[40]

In 1966 a group of activists formed the National Organization for Women to address these issues in a public forum and to lobby Congress. With well-publicized activities such as the picketing of the 1968 Miss America Pageant and the 1970 nationwide women's strike commemorating the fiftieth anniversary of the Nineteenth Amendment, coupled with innumerable talk-show appearances by feminist leaders, the needs and demands of the modern American woman were kept before the nation's consciousness.

As they had in the 1920s, advertisers jumped on board with the current social trends and began to represent the working woman of the 1970s in atypical ways. (Figure 7-29.) A 1972 ad from AT&T showed a young woman telephone installer perched high upon a telephone pole; a real-life employee had served as the model, and "she won't be the last," promised the ad copy. The following year, a Tampax ad showed two women in a broadcasting soundroom surrounded by hi-tech equipment under their control. A 1979 FDS ad put a woman in the executive boardroom making a presentation to the "boy's club."

During the 1980s, a counter movement to the new feminism, spawned by the chill of social conservatism under the Reagan-Bush administrations, found a substantial base of support from women who had felt left behind in their kitchens while their sisters marched forward in search of economic independence. Women's historian Annegret Ogden wrote that these women, "as mere wives and mothers," discovered by the 1970s that "they no longer stood on a pedestal, but were denigrated as gullible consumers of American products."[41] Yet, marketers were far from ready to count the homemaker out of the advertising picture.

Indeed, advertisers of the 1980s and 1990s still took their messages where the readers were. The percentage of women who worked may have crossed the 50 percent mark in 1982,[42] but marketing research proved they continued to cook, clean, and care for spouses and children. By the end of the 1980s, the management of *Good Housekeeping* had asserted that "the country was returning to their magazine's view of the world," and that American women "had had enough of the blatant careerism of the 1980s."[43] Thus, advertising lineage continued to expand in home and fashion magazines while publications such as *Ms.* and *Working Woman* struggled to capture ad dollars from marketers. When Gloria Steinem told the head of Estee Lauder, Leonard Lauder, that he should be advertising in *Ms.* because 60 percent of the women who used his products were salaried, he responded by saying that did not matter because he was selling a "kept woman mentality," and even if the majority of women did work today, "they would like to be kept women."[44]

In the last two decades of the twentieth century, depictions of the working woman in advertising seemed to be less significant to marketers than they had been during the great women's movements of the 1920s and 1970s. In fact, as the 1990s closed, images of working women became somewhat scarce in magazine advertising, except for in ready-to-wear ads that might have promoted "dress for success" or "menswear" business attire. Those ads that might possibly be representing the working woman did so ambiguously. (Figure 7-30.) Is the woman shown in the 1997 PNC bank ad the "investment manager" referred to in the copy or the target customer? It seemed that the working woman of the 1990s did not need to be bolstered by advertising as she was during World War I, celebrated as she was in the 1920s, glorified as she was during World War II, nor applauded as she was in the 1970s. The working woman had become such an integral part of American social and economic matrices that advertisers—and society—took her work and her independence for granted.

Conclusion: Marketing to the Independent Woman

The social and economic status of the nineteenth-century woman in America was hardly more than that of chattel. Her destiny was absolutely controlled by the male authorities in her life: her father, teachers, doctors, ministers, and ultimately her husband. As the Victorian era concluded, the first fissures in this formidable tradition began to appear with the aid of an unlikely source, the bicycle. Women of a wide socioeconomic sphere began to experience and acknowledge degrees of personal independence they had never known before, simply through recreational bicycling. From housewives who escaped the confines of the kitchen and nursery to single women who evaded parental supervision, women all across America found themselves in circumstances requiring their own decisiveness and control. Even forty years of organized efforts by feminist groups on social, legislative, and judicial fronts had not been able to make this kind of impact on the progress of women's independence.

Marketers selectively recognized the emergence of women's increased freedom and independence largely to sell more bicycles and related goods or services. Following the cycling craze, automobile manufacturers brought the message of women's mobility and freedom into their advertising, inspiring these women to influence their fathers and husbands in purchasing cars. Still, prior to the 1920s, most marketers were confident that even with this new sense of independence, the great masses of women consumers had not radically altered their priorities of housewifery and motherhood.

This confidence that marketers had about women consumers was further bolstered by the American educational system. Where the classroom might have inspired women's independent thinking and actions, instead, decade after decade, women were inculcated with ideas of domesticity. Except for brief segments of the 1920s and 1970s, higher education for women through the 1980s was regarded by many as an interim of social life and general study between high school and marriage. Most mass marketers continued to be certain that even as the number of women college graduates increased, these women would still seek marriage and a family, and would join the ranks of their sister consumers.

Sports, too, provided women with a particular sense of self and independence. During the first quarter of the twentieth century, society's view of women athletes changed dramatically. Women's sports events of the 1920s began to be widely publicized, and the resulting reports of the skill, speed, and endurance records of female athletes further broadened the possibilities for women's self-confidence and independence.

For marketers, though, the social issues of the female athlete were inconsequential for the most part. Manufacturers and retailers who had products to sell specifically to women athletes skewed their ad messages toward that purpose. Other marketers used the image of the woman athlete as a novelty. Such images were eye-catching and at the same time attached a feeling of modernity to the advertiser's brand or product. Eventually, women athletes with name recognition were as assiduously courted by advertisers as were Hollywood stars and other celebrities.

Yet, the impact on the social evolution of the American woman's independence brought about by her mobility, improved education, and proven athletic capabilities was negligible compared with that of her employment. Beginning with the feminization of office work in the 1870s, due in part to the marketing methods of typewriter manufacturers, an increasing number of women joined the workforce. During the national crises of the two world wars, massive numbers of women were mobilized to work outside the home. Women proved to themselves and to the nation that with skill and effectiveness they could master jobs that had previously been the exclusive domain of men. Most significantly of all, though, with their own income, women could be economically independent of the men in their lives.

For marketers, the working woman posed a dual challenge. On the one hand, she was a changeling whose nontraditional role was constantly evolving and, therefore, not always predictable. On the other hand, she became an opportunity to target with goods and services tailored to her life style.

Certainly, the American woman's independence was not achieved solely through the factors of her mobility, education, and employment. The many other influences of society and family, politics and religion, geography and economics of the twentieth century must be examined thoroughly to fully understand the social evolution of the American woman. However, for marketers, even momentous events such as the passages of the Nineteenth Amendment or the Equal Rights Amendment were too subtle to alter mass marketing strategies. To them, change—even inevitable change—would occur gradually. A cursory glimpse of the empirical evidence of a century of ads contained in this survey reveals how slowly American women achieved their independence.

—Chapter 8

TEACH
THEM
YOUNG

Gender role socialization of girls • Representations of the "Little Homemaker" and marketing to future consumers • Images of the "Little Mother" and social conformity • Lessons of beauty and social parables in advertising

Following the social upheavals of American society in the 1960s and 1970s, words and phrases such as "gender bias," "misogyny," "sexism," and "sex-role socialization" increasingly moved from research studies and feminists' rhetoric into the vocabularies of average American women. Many feminists had vigorously denounced the social attitudes and conditions that predestined women to live their lives in the limited confines of traditional female roles. Their activism lead to important civil rights legislation and a revitalized women's movement. However, they were surprised to discover that a great many women vehemently disagreed with their calls for social changes. In a 1971 survey on women's rights published by *Good Housekeeping,* the percentages of respondents who were against any changes in the role of women were astonishing. Some women readers actually voted against "equal pay for equal work" and against "equal hiring and promotion policies." It would hardly be surprising, then, that women would affirm their belief in the concept of sex-role socialization with 28 percent voting to preserve "child-rearing practices that make girls feel inferior and qualified only for domestic work."[1] (Figure 8-1.) In a similar poll for *Life* that same year, three in ten women believed there should be "separate behavior standards for boys and girls."[2] Even in the late 1990s, parental sexism persisted, as writer Anne Marie Kerwin confessed in a *Good Housekeeping* article. "Although I grew up in the age of feminism, I haven't completely accepted the compatibility of beauty and strength," she admitted after watching her daughter play-act the role of a princess who dispensed karate kicks to evildoers.[3] Such persistent sexism by women was a testament to what researchers had been gradually documenting

Figure 8-1. Advertisers not only reflected society's attitudes about sex-role socialization, but also helped perpetuate the segregation of the sexes with images of children performing gender-appropriate behavior. Ad 1958.

Figure 8-2. One of the most widely used images of girls learning the roles that would define them as women in American society was that of the little cook.

throughout the last quarter of the century. "Cultural assumptions about what is 'natural' for a boy or for a girl may be so deeply ingrained that parents may treat their children differentially without even being aware of it," concluded researcher Lenore Weitzman in 1984.[4]

For advertisers, the sex-role socialization of little girls throughout the twentieth century was a social certainty beyond questioning. Manufacturers of products for the home and family knew unequivocally that on the whole, girls were being taught first and foremost to be wives and mothers. Society's expectations and methods of preparing girls for their adult roles had been inherited from rigid standards, which had evolved and coalesced in the preceding century. Innumerable articles had appeared in women's publications of the nineteenth century urging mothers to train their daughters well in the domestic arts. Typical was an 1895 editorial in the *Ladies' Home Journal* in which the writer complained about "the wife's ignorance of the duties that belong to her" and blamed parents for not compelling girls to learn those

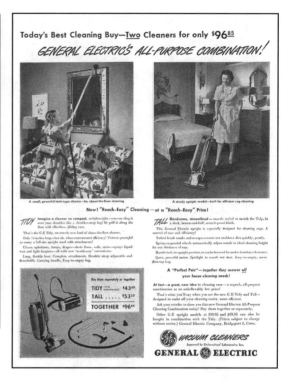

Figure 8-3. Ads that depicted girls helping with housework served to remind mothers that their daughters should be thoroughly taught domestic sciences early in childhood. Western Electric ad 1913, General Electric ad 1948.

duties early. Denouncing the time that girls wasted on trivialities such as music lessons, the editor avowed, "If we could split half of our pianos into kindling wood . . . and set our young girls to the practical task of learning how to sew and cook, and wash and iron . . . it would be a great benison to society in general, and to their own souls in particular."[5]

More than merely reflecting a social tradition, the representation of gender socialization in advertising was necessary for the continued success of a vast number of industries, including the manufacture of products and services for cooking, cleaning, sewing, child-rearing, fashion, or home decorating. Makers of these products unabashedly reinforced social sexism through their ads as a deliberate strategy to ensure future generations of predictable consumers. Girls viewing such ads were instructed in what they should do and expect in preparation for adulthood, and parents received confirmation of the goals they set for their daughters. As one 1923 house ad for the George Batten agency declared:

> Who is going to tell her?
> Mother and Father and playmates and teachers and books and nature will carry her far along the toilsome road to ladyship.
> But she must also be homemaker and stewardess of the family budget. In that sphere she will be guided largely by advertising. Good food, good clothing, good furnishings, good values for her household and children—these she will learn from advertising.[6]

To teach her to want a better home and to make a better home for her children than even her mother made—that truly is shaping public opinion. That is the work of advertising.

The "Little Homemaker"

Probably one of the most widely used images of girls learning the crafts that would define them as women in American society was that of the little cook.

Figure 8-4. Beginning in 1918, the U.S. educational system inaugurated gender-segregated vocational training with an emphasis on homemaking and motherhood for girls that would last well into the 1970s. Ad 1959.

Figure 8-5. Ads presenting girls helping with labor-intensive but unskilled household chores hinted to mothers that under the guise of training their daughters for their future role as homemakers, they also could benefit from help with housework. Top ad 1929, bottom ad 1938.

(Figure 8-2.) Manufacturers of food products, cooking utensils, and kitchen appliances had a vested interest in having girls learn to cook early in life. Future brand loyalty was at stake. Before the impact of television, most advertisers could expect girls to at least scan their mothers' magazines in which they would see representations of themselves as cooks—either in practice or as disciples of their mothers. Depictions of these girls confidently wielding kitchen utensils or proudly exhibiting their freshly baked, roasted, fried, or stewed achievements served a dual social purpose as well. First, girls seeing these ads would be inspired to urge their mothers to begin teaching them the fundamentals of cooking; second, these images of girls busily at work cooking reminded mothers that there was no time like the present to prepare their daughters for their future roles as housewives.

An equally popular image in advertising was that of "mother's little helper." As with the depictions of girls cooking, daughters frequently were shown either helping their moms with household chores or in training as future housewives. By the time the great age of consumerism had kicked into high gear during the 1920s, three changes in the American household had begun to affect the degree to which many girls participated in housework. First was technology. The electric machines that helped ease the burdens of housework had begun to make an impact in the home well before the First World War. Chores that had been labor intensive and required the strength of an adult woman could now be assigned to girls. (Figure 8-3.) Second was improved methods and education for birth control, which had resulted in smaller families and fewer daughters to help with the housework. Third was the ever increasing percentage of women entering the workforce, women who consequently had less time for homemaking. By the time of the Lynds' Middletown study in 1925, all three of these changes were significant enough for the researchers to note that with regard to housekeeping, many women admitted they were not as particular as their mothers had been.[7]

On the other hand, advertisers did not fear that girls were no longer being trained by their mothers in domesticity. They knew that most women, even those who worked full time, invested some time and effort in preparing their daughters for their futures in homemaking. Additionally, after 1918 the well-publicized changes in the U.S. public education system began to emphasize "domestic sciences" for girls. Gender-segregated vocational training, sanctioned by state and federal agencies, would inculcate girls with myopic ideas of homemaking and motherhood well into the 1970s. (Figure 8-4.) Within just a few years of this change in the educational system, the Lynds noted a significant difference from a generation earlier: " . . . nor do so many daughters learn cooking and sewing at their mothers' side; more than a few of the mothers interviewed said unhappily that their daughters, fresh from domestic science in school, ridicule the mother's inherited rule-of-thumb practices as 'old fashioned.' "[8]

The important issue for American marketers was that girls were still being taught above all else to be homemakers and mothers; whether the schools or home training perpetuated this sex-role socialization was immaterial to them, so long as future generations of consumers were forever on the horizon. To bolster the interests of these future homemakers, manufacturers unceasingly used the image of girls learning or doing their part in household

Figure 8-6. The tedious daily chore of washing dishes taught girls the necessity of housework despite its drudgery. Ivory ad 1913, Beeman's ad 1933.

The advantages of using Ivory Soap for washing dishes are threefold:

1st. Dish-washing with Ivory Soap does not make the hands red, rough and sore. On the contrary, they remain white, smooth and soft.

2nd. After washing with Ivory Soap, the dishes are clean in the best sense of the word; that is, the soap itself is of such high quality, so clean if you please, that no plate, no cup, not one piece could be cleaner.

3rd. Because of Ivory's freedom from alkali and all strong chemicals, the delicate tints on fine china are not injured, a consideration appreciated especially by those who have pieces with gold decorations.

IVORY SOAP .... 99 44/100 % PURE

fun!

Bring on your dishes! Daughter is ready for anything. Happy, healthy, helpful—that's the way young folks are when their digestion is good.

It's sad that mothers don't always know what's wrong. Don't realize that just a bit of indigestion is a handicap. Lots of girls chew Beeman's regularly just to be sure that they won't be troubled. They know it helps. And they love the Beeman's flavor.

Chew
BEEMAN'S PEPSIN GUM

ESPECIALLY MADE TO AID DIGESTION

chores. Bon Ami ads frequently featured little girls ecstatically cleaning, polishing, and scrubbing. (Figures 8-5 and 3-42.) The copy in one 1929 ad opened with a salutation to "Little Miss Housekeeper" who had just "Bon Ami'd" a candlestick all by herself and was insisting that her mother let her polish the other one as well. A decade later, Bon Ami continued the theme by showing a little girl sprawled over the edge of a bathtub smiling happily as she scoured away. "Bon Ami is so easy to use that even children can get the bathtub spotlessly clean," hinted the copy to busy mothers.

With the wide range of daily chores confronting the housewife, most every major maker of appliances and household consumables ran ads that included depictions of little girls industriously using their products. Tasks that did not require a high level of skill or involve danger, such as dishwashing, were routinely delegated to daughters. (Figure 8-6.) A 1913 Ivory Soap ad presents an interesting perspective in that the illustrator was female. In the rendering by Alice Beach Winter, the mother and daughter subjects are not rapturously engaged in a bonding moment while washing dishes, but rather look sullen as they tend to this daily tedium. Twenty years later an ad for Beeman's gum suggested that girls would have "fun" washing the dishes if given chewing gum; "daughter is ready for anything," the copy exclaimed. But if the photograph with its mountain of dishes filling the background was intended to be humorous, more than likely most women and their daughters missed the joke and instead perceived the notion as depressing.

Even for that most hated of chores, laundry, ads for detergents and, later, washing machines often included depictions of girls developing their homemaking skills or helping mom. (Figure 8-7.) After all, manufacturers wanted girls to learn the brand names that, as these ads advised, would benefit them most as future housewives. In a 1931 Rinso ad the little girl is cognizant of the superior whiteness of a neighbor's laundry, which she has observed hanging on the line. Girls who read the copy in this cartoon-format ad learned two valuable lessons in life. Besides discovering that the neighbor's success with her laundry was attributable simply to a brand of detergent, she also learned yet another way in which someday she would be judged

Figure 8-7. Girls learned that a clean laundry hung out to dry on a clothesline was an exhibition of household skill for neighbors to judge. Left ad 1931, right ad 1950.

Figure 8-8. The use of technology in the home to ease the burdens of housework was an important lesson for mothers to teach their daughters. Thor ad 1949, Speed Queen ad 1965.

by her peer housewives. "It was a matter of pride with housewives to have the washing hung before breakfast," wrote Mark Sullivan in 1927, "and neighbors would vie with one another in seeing whose laundry appeared earliest on the line."[9] Even well after the automatic clothes dryer became a common household appliance, women continued to prefer the fresh-air smell of line-dried laundry by which their homemaking skills would be measured by observant neighbors.

Besides product branding, these ads also taught girls to develop expectations of a modern, efficient home of their own someday. For washing machine manufacturers, ads showed how new technology continually improved their products. (Figure 8-8.) In thumbing through the issues of their moms' *Ladies' Home Journal* or *McCall's,* girls would recognize the obsolescence of earlier models and anticipate the washer they hoped to have as a young housewife. In 1949, a Thor ad presented girls the future of machine washing without the need of a wringer or separate rinse tubs, or any heavy lifting of water-laden clothes—all arduous chores most girls had seen their mothers endure. Fifteen years later, those little girls—now grown-up moms—were told by an ad to go to a laundromat to test the "dependable service" of the latest Speed Queen models before buying a washer for home use. Depicted

Figure 8-9. With a vested interest in future generations of consumers, advertisers often showed mothers instructing their daughters in the domestic skills traditionally assigned to women by society. Left ad 1928, right ad 1955.

Figure 8-10. As future purchasing agents for their homes and families, girls were taught lessons in the economics of shopping both at home and by the vocational-oriented educational system. Kellogg's ad 1915, Brand Names ad 1956.

in the photos at mom's side, both at the coin laundry and later in the home laundry room, was the daughter, being taught the appropriate sex-role behavior for girls of the 1960s.

The manufacturing of sewing machines was another industry that had a considerable interest in the sex-role socialization of girls. (Figure 8-9.) Sewing, as opposed to the male-dominated business of tailoring, had been women's dominion for centuries. "It is hardly possible for a woman to be happy and content who cannot use her needle," insisted an 1879 editorial in the *Nation*; "her life is incomplete without it," avowed the writer.[10] Fifty years later a 1928 Singer sewing machine offered "a word to mothers" about teaching their daughters to sew. "The interest stirred in that one hour of revelation will be a priceless possession through all her life," assured the copy. At least Singer and similar manufacturers hoped this to be true, and banked on future sales of their products with their investment in advertising.

In observing the changing household in Middletown and the training of young girls in domesticity, the Lynds noted in 1925 that "advertising and the multiplication of alternative standardized brands and methods are thrusting new illiteracies upon the home and its members more rapidly than the traditional 'liberal education' and the deeply grooved patterns under which 'vocational education' is conceived are shifting to meet them."[11] In other words, since the turn of the century, purchasing had become a much more important aspect of a woman's role than it had been in earlier decades. Instead of learning how to spin and weave, make and prepare cooking ingredients, cultivate vegetable gardens, and tend to livestock, girls had to be taught the economics of shopping. Christine Frederick recognized this great change in American society in her 1929 book *Selling Mrs. Consumer.* She noted that almost one-third of all new homes had been started by young women educated since World War I and that "these young women are educated as consumers to a degree never before reached in America."[12]

Figure 8-11. Advertisers of better quality or luxury products often encouraged mothers to instill a taste for refinement in their daughters. Ads 1926.

Being the purchasing agent for the home and family was an unquestioned role for twentieth-century women. For little girls, role-playing a shopper was an acceptable playtime simulation of mom. (Figure 8-10.) Even at the end of the century, toy companies manufactured play shopping carts, and some grocery stores provided small-scale versions of their carts so little girls could help mom with her shopping. For advertisers, the theme of the little girl imitating mom, whether as the little shopper, little cook, or little housekeeper was highly effective in capturing the attention of women.

Where the schools might have taught girls the basics of consumer economics, some manufacturers of better quality or luxury goods still relied on the mothers of higher socioeconomic classes to teach their daughters about taste and quality. (Figure 8-11.) "Her first lesson in recognizing good towels," was the header of a 1926 Cannon ad. The illustration depicts a young girl examining the label, committing the brand name to memory for the day when "she will be the administrator of a household." Quite beyond the significance of knowing about canned foods, cleaning products, or other such

1922

1930

1955

Figure 8-12. Toy versions of real products manufactured for the home imprinted girls with brand recognition and provided tools for gender-appropriate training.

Figure 8-13. Many toys were designed to allow girls to rehearse social activities that prepared them for sex-role standards. Fleischmann's ad 1920, American Can ad 1953.

household topics, mothers were encouraged by a 1926 ad from the Silversmith Guild to teach their daughters to appreciate sterling silver beginning with a toddler's first drinking cup. Such narratives were popular with marketers of upscale products such as fine furniture, clocks, and jewelry throughout the entire century.

Even with the direct overtures to girls and their mothers by advertisers of home appliances, cleaning and food products, silverware, and clocks, gender socialization was reinforced by one particular industry with a much more powerful yet subtle influence. Following the tenets of women's roles in an industrialized society, toy manufacturers produced all sorts of miniature versions of household implements and home furnishings for girls. (Figure 8-12.) "Small scale washing machines, carpet sweepers, stoves, and games directed girls toward housework imitative of their mothers, and working sewing machines helped 'little women' sew clothes for their dolls," noted historian Harvey Green.[13] More important to many manufacturers was the positioning of their brand name for the next generation of homemakers. Using the washing machine as an example, home economist Ida Bailey Allen advised attendees of a 1923 advertising conference: "Take the child as a little girl; win her confidence. Make possible for her doll's house a cardboard cut-out of your washing machine and a booklet of Washing Dolly's Clothes your way. She will buy your product later on."[14]

The toy sink offered in the Standard Plumbing Fixtures catalog from 1922 served precisely this purpose, since the company was clearly not in the toy-making business. Similarly, Bon Ami often depicted little girls cleaning their gender-appropriate toys, hoping to inspire girls to use the product today on a diminutive scale and then remember the brand tomorrow as an adult. "It's never too early to learn," suggested the bold-type header in a 1930 Bon

1900

1914

1918

1928

1959

1971

Figure 8-14. From Victorian times girls were encouraged to play with dolls as practice for motherhood. For advertisers, the image of a little girl playing mommy was a sentimental favorite irrespective of the product message.

Ami ad. The girl's toy set of Revere Ware cookware replicated in miniature the pieces used by her mom and was embossed with the same distinctive logo as the adult versions.

Besides those toys that simulated the tools for housework, toy tea sets and playroom furniture prepared girls for their social roles as hostesses. (Figure 8-13.) However, many girls did not regard the role-playing that these toys inspired as the most enjoyable playtime activities, social researchers have told us. In studies, more girls preferred boys' toys and games than "girl toys."[15] As Lenore Weitzman observed, though, the typical American girl "seeks the acceptance of parents and peers and wants to avoid their rejection"; such motives "predispose her . . . to shun inappropriate activities and

Figure 8-15. Since 1959 the Barbie doll has been both acclaimed and reviled for its influence on girls. To some the doll taught girls vacuous values centered on beauty, while for others Barbie showed girls the many possibilities ahead of them as adults. Ad 1969.

Barbie* is the number 1 doll. There is no number 2.

For good reasons.
Other dolls are fashion dolls or talking dolls or something dolls.
But BARBIE is more. She can be almost anything a little girl imagines her to be. A little girl plays with her and projects herself into the future—into the teen-ager she will become—just like BARBIE.*
By taking care of BARBIE'S clothes and combing her hair and playing with BARBIE'S friends and reading the BARBIE magazine, a little girl learns about her own hair and clothes. She also learns more about playing and getting along in the world.
For over ten years more little girls in 52 countries have played with BARBIE than any other doll.
For good reasons.

MATTEL

to choose responses that are congruent with sex-role standards."[16] The seemingly innocent tea parties that advertisers used simply as innocuous illustrations represented something much more significant in the socialization of girls. According to women's researcher Mary Pipher: "Many girls become good haters of those who do not conform to our culture's ideas about femininity. Like any recent converts to an ideology, girls are at risk of becoming the biggest enforcers and proselytizers for the culture. What's important is the message that not pleasing others is social suicide."[17] Consequently, in playing hostess, girls were able to practice the pretensions of etiquette as well as peer manipulation and control.

The "Little Mother"

Playing with dolls allowed girls to wield the double-edged sword of control and social conformity. (Figure 8-14.) Since the days of ancient Egypt and Mesopotamia, girls were expected and encouraged to play with dolls in preparation for their roles as mothers. Instructed one *Ladies' Home Journal* editorial in 1895: "Little girls should be encouraged in a fondness for dolls. In a very few it is undeveloped and requires to be stimulated. The mother instinct is usually strong; when it is weak it needs fostering."[18] Only late in the twentieth century did researchers examine the way doll play served as a device for sex-role socialization. Social researcher David Matza suggested that girls learn to become "socializing agents" when they play with dolls; "by 'training' their dolls to do the right thing, the girls themselves gain a vast amount of experience in articulating and sanctioning the cultural norms."[19] For writer Germaine Greer, playing with dolls makes girls "realize that it is advantageous to operate in the favored way." Sex-role socialization to Greer was more conditioning than socialization. "Generally it is the little girls who are given presents of pretty things and spoilt and flattered who capitulate to the doll-makers earliest," she concluded.[20]

For advertisers, none of this was significant to their marketing objectives; the end result was still that little girls continued to play with dolls. Besides the obvious product ads by doll manufacturers, depictions of girls playing mommy with their baby dolls were always sentimental favorites of advertisers, regardless of the product being promoted.

The exception to the baby doll rule was the success of Mattel's Barbie doll. (Figure 8-15.) Ironically, Barbie was a knock-off of the German Lilli doll, which was a three-dimensional pin-up for men sold in tobacco shops in the 1950s. In her book *Forever Barbie,* M. G. Lord wrote that in 1959, Mattel co-founder Ruth Handler "took Lilli, [who was] described as a 'hooker or an actress between performances,' and recast her as the wholesome all-American girl."[21] Barbie was not a baby doll to be cuddled and nurtured. Unlike the diapers and bibs of Betsy Wetsy or the little-sister wardrobe of Chatty Cathy, the fashions Barbie wore were grown-up styles. Barbie was to be appropriately sex-role dressed and accessorized as a contemporary, fashion-conscious woman.

By the 1970s, the Barbie doll had become for many feminists an icon of the misplaced values with which American society inculcated girls. The word "Barbie" became a pejorative. For instance, in objecting to the Miss America Pageant, Sherrye Henry wrote that she and other feminists had believed the beauty event symbolized what "men wanted women to be: passive, bland Barbie dolls whose value was judged by their faces and their measurements."[22] In 1997 Karen Lehrman hoped that the "feminist critique" had begun finally to change notions of beauty "beyond the Barbie standard."[23]

To Barbie devotees, such disparaging assessments were considered misplaced because, to them, Barbie represented more than just an idealized beauty. Barbie "was her own woman [who] could invent herself with a costume change: sing a solo in the spotlight one minute, pilot a starship the next," insisted Lord.[24] A 1998 *Advertising Age* editorial credited Barbie's longevity to the success of Mattel's marketing strategy to keep the doll "timeless" and yet "trendy." Said Gene del Vecchio in the article: "Through Barbie, girls can dream of the achievement, glamour, romance, adventure and nurturing opportunities that may someday be theirs. Such dreams touch upon many timeless needs, ranging from pride and success to belonging and love. Barbie, for example, has been a teacher, a fashion model, a girlfriend, an astronaut and a big sister. Mattel then introduces new Barbie dolls every year in order to keep up-to-date with the latest definitions of achievement, glamour, romance, adventure and nurturing."[25]

One significant sex-role lesson that girls learned from the Barbie doll and its many knock-offs was a keen awareness of fashion. With the proliferation of mass media, especially television, girls of the second half of the century developed a sophisticated sense of contemporary style and fashion—one based on an adult glamour of high heels, evening gowns, and cosmetics in which they did not yet indulge. In real life, a girl's wardrobe was closely regulated; parents, school dress codes, churches, advertisers, and peers influenced the development of a girl's sense of fashion—usually with a conforming, conservative edge. With her Barbie doll, though, a girl's fantasy, supported by Mattel's imaginative lines of doll's clothing, was open to unlimited fashion possibilities.

The "Little Beauty"

Mothers especially had always been targeted by the fashion industry with style and wardrobe directions for their children, particularly girls. In 1849, *Godey's* advised mothers that "in dressing children, the first thing to be looked to is securing their health and comfort; then display the taste you may possess."[26] For some mothers, the taste overrode both the health and the comfort of the girl, as corset ads demonstrated at the turn of the century. (Figure 8-16.) To the fashion-conscious mother of that time, it seemed her duty to prepare her daughter with every advantage for catching a husband, even if that meant constricting the girl in a corset for most of her childhood.

Figure 8-16. One of the rites of passage for girls at the turn of the century was learning to be constricted by a corset to prevent her waist from "spreading," as was cautioned in one ad. Ad 1901.

How a Girl Grows up in a
FERRIS Good Sense **WAIST**

She grows with all the grace of nature. She lives in easy, flexible comfort, unconscious that the contour of her body is being naturally developed. When she reaches the state of womanhood no rigid stays will be required to force her figure into pleasing outlines. Natural beauty—Ferris beauty—requires no artifice. Every mother should heed the lesson of the Ferris Waist.

Made in all shapes and sizes to suit every form—with long or short waist, high or low bust. Sold by all leading retailers. Illustrated catalogue free. Finest material and workmanship.

THE FERRIS BROS. COMPANY, 341 Broadway, New York.

Ad copy suggested to mothers that wearing a corset would help a girl develop "her beauty naturally, healthfully, permanently" and prevent "the waist from spreading."[27]

The direct influence of mothers on their daughters' sense of fashion and style worked two ways. First, mothers chose the clothing for their children—styles, colors, accessories. Second, mothers, and other adult women, were role models for their daughters. (Figure 8-17.) In researching learned gender-role behavior, Lenore Weitzman wrote that girls "imitate the people whom they perceive to be good examples of their sex role" and "may drop a particular parentally inspired behavior from their repertoire if they realize that it is not sex-appropriate."[28] Thus, imitating their mothers' sense of style may not be as much of a guiding factor for girls as the influence of other female role models. In a 1920 Fashion Publicity ad, a little girl strolls about in one of her mother's high heels; "some day I'm going to wear shoes like mother's," the girl tells her dog. From the other perspective, the little girl in a 1946 Carnation ad has taken her inspiration for femininity and fashion from the cover of a movie magazine rather than crediting guidance from her mother. The fine line of distinction between the two types of feminine influences on little girls was as immaterial to advertisers as was the sex-role socialization of dolls, cooking, or shopping. The images of little girls playing dress-up reflected expected norms of behavior and, as such, appealed to the broadest range of target customers.

Relative to fashion, and one of the most controversial aspects of the sex-role socialization of girls in America, is the concept of beauty. Wrote Mary Pipher: "In early adolescence girls learn how important appearance is in defining social acceptability. Attractiveness is both a necessary and a sufficient condition for girls' success. This is an old, old problem. Helen of Troy didn't launch a thousand ships because she was a hard worker. Juliet wasn't loved for her math ability."[29] Researchers such as Lenore Weitzman went

Figure 8-17. Girls learned appropriate sex-role behavior from their mothers as well as other adult women they observed. F. B. & C. shoes ad 1920, Carnation ad 1946.

Figure 8-18. In observing their mothers' beauty regimens, girls received explicit instructions on acceptable female behavior. Ad 1924.

even further back than adolescence to find the first influences of beauty on a girl's socialization. "Around age three or four, the child begins to make sex-role distinctions and express sex-role preferences," she noted.[30] In observing their mothers' beauty regimens girls received explicit instructions on acceptable female behavior. (Figure 8-18.) Even if the mother was not the type of beauty featured in women's magazines, she most likely maintained some methods of hair care, skin care, and, after World War I, makeup application. For beauty product companies, the pitch was more direct. "A mother's duty is to help her child keep that schoolgirl complexion," stated the header in a 1925 Palmolive Soap ad; and "many girls owe much of their hair's beauty to the healthful shampoos their mothers gave them from early childhood," suggested the copy in a 1922 Packer's Tar Soap ad.[31]

Beauty enhancement with cosmetics is another influential sex-role observation girls would have made about their mothers and other adult women. At the turn of the century the use of cosmetics for respectable women was confined to the application of facial powder, but by the 1920s a full range of makeup possibilities was available to women of all socioeconomic strata. In emulating their sex-role models, Christine Frederick noted, even girls "down to the earliest years of girlish adolescence" were freely using cosmetics by the end of the 1920s; "American women desire to be beautiful from the first years of their social consciousness," she maintained.[32]

Bridging the gap between playthings and actual consumer products were the packaged sets of toiletries and matched dresser sets created specifically for girls. (Figure 8-19.) Magazine ads, displays in toy departments, and television commercials all suggested to mothers and daughters that it was not too early to begin learning the proper steps for a correct beauty regimen. In 1955, Helene Pessl ads offered preteen girls "glamour" sets including powder compacts, nail polish, and fragrances, and in a 1970 ad for girl's cosmetics, the headline attempted to assure mothers that "Tinkerbell won't rush her," while depicting in the photo a sex-role message for girls disguised as playtime.

In the 1970s and especially the 1980s, feminists began to challenge the messages sent to girls about the importance of beauty, particularly following the first studies on eating disorders. Naomi Wolf lambasted popular mass media and Madison Avenue for perpetuating the "beauty myth" that "women must want to embody it and men must want to possess women who embody it."[33] To Karen Lehrman, the "beauty hierarchy" persisted because in American society "youth, beauty and thinness matter more than anything else."[34] In reviewing some of the newly launched periodicals that targeted girls in 1997, an *Adweek* editorial noted that "in today's teen magazines, the ties that bind young women seem to be a deep sense of embarrassment and shame." A supporting example was "the inevitable 'improve your body' features" that included photos of "'real' girls with fat thighs, bulging stomachs and flabby arms—although the heads of the models are always cropped, as if to protect the identity of the poor soul afflicted with such bodily embarrassments."[35]

Yet, it was not just society or the mass media that told girls that beauty and thinness were all-important. Girls themselves experienced the results of possessing, or artificially acquiring, beauty. They witnessed firsthand the popularity of pretty girls with their peers, teachers, and especially boys.

Figure 8-19. Toy cosmetic lines and packaged sets of toiletries helped girls prepare for the beauty regimens many of them would undergo daily throughout their adult lives. Little Lady ad 1955, Tinkerbell ad 1970.

Psychologist Mary Pipher discovered that "anorexic young women tend to be popular with the opposite sex. They epitomize our cultural definitions of feminine: thin, passive, weak and eager to please."[36]

Attempting to attract the opposite sex was a gender-typed behavior for girls that all parents anticipated, even if reluctantly. Advertisers especially had fun depicting the bumbling, preambulary courtship rituals of children. The expected scenario most often presented the pretty girl to whom the boys devoted their best efforts to impress. (Figure 8-20.) The subtext message in these ads was only too clear to parents and girls—that is, homely girls, chubby girls, poorly dressed or ill-groomed girls, or girls with dental braces, eyeglasses, or other anomalies could not be contenders for the attentions of boys. "The growing girl is encouraged to use her feminine charm, to be coy and alluring," wrote Germaine Greer, and she is expected to begin her dealings with boys "based upon her attractiveness as a sexual object."[37] In a 1926 Baby Ruth ad, the girl smiles captivatingly at the handsome boy who gives her a candy bar and takes her books to carry. In a 1927 Monarch ad the girl demonstrates her awe at the boy's physical prowess by tilting her head in deference to him and dropping her mouth open in amazement. In a 1944 Carnation ad the girl dangles her bookstrap as a privilege for one of the boys in her trailing entourage to take and carry for her. Hundreds of ads like these emphasized to girls the social importance of beauty in successfully achieving their ultimate gender role of wife and mother.

When at last the young lady was old enough to be asked out on her first date, certain protocols were expected and required—at least in respectable social circles. However, judging from the Lynds' Middletown research of 1925 and 1935, the polite romance stories of popular fiction, as well as the idealized visuals of ads, were far from reality. The Lynds' found that girls had long since abandoned their corsets and, with them, their Victorian social mores. By 1925 the social behavior of girls and boys had changed so dramatically that, according to the Lynds, "the more sophisticated social life of today has brought with it another 'problem' much discussed by Middletown parents, the apparently increasing relaxation of some of the traditional prohibitions upon the approaches of boys and girls to each other's persons."[38]

Although the Lynds were speaking more of teenagers, especially those of high school age, advertisers frequently used depictions of the preteen girl and boy engaged in courtship rituals. (Figure 8-21.) Such images were safely devoid of sexual overtones and were intended to be amusing to parents despite the rapid changes of post–World War I social mores. These ads served as empirical proof for parents that they were on the right track and teaching the next generation properly. In a 1937 Hires Root Beer ad and a 1940 Listerine ad, parents could be reassured that boys were still being taught to be "gentlemen" and, as such, were unquestionably expected to be in command of social situations involving girls. The copy in the Listerine ad specifically addressed the mother on her duties of preparing her son for

1926

1927

1944

Figure 8-20. Preambulary courtship rituals of girls and boys were favorite scenarios for advertisers.

socially acceptable courtship rituals. Besides paying attention to his personal grooming, the copy advised, her son "must bow and perform a hundred other little gallantries which ... are the keys which unlock a woman's heart." After all, the mother is forewarned, soon her son will discover that "little girls ... are now strangely changed ... mysterious, delicate, and beautiful things to be attended, cared for, and protected."

The great challenge for advertisers was in presenting depictions of teenagers actually out on a date where they were free of parental scrutiny. (Figure 8-22.) During the 1920s, images of the flapper, such as those done for *Life* and *McClure's* by illustrator John Held, many times depicted a young woman engaged in heavy petting in her boyfriend's car. Confronted

Figure 8-21. Ads with themes that depicted social dramas between girls and boys provided guides to parents for accepted sex-role behavior of their offspring. Hires ad 1937, Listerine ad 1940.

Figure 8-22. Depictions in ads of adolescent girls and boys on dates were usually swathed in idealized innocence and formality. National Dairy ad 1946, Bell Telephone ad 1960.

with such evidence in the mass media, parents were especially wary of a boy who called for their daughter in a car. For marketers, using these kinds of scenarios in ads could be safely achieved with a polite presentation of dress and decorum or the presence of adult supervision. A suit jacket and tie on the boy and a respectable party dress for the girl in ad illustrations set a tone of anachronistic propriety that posed no threat to parents who might worry about their daughter's virtue (or entrapment of their son). Instead, the happy teenage couples merely ate ice cream cones in the moonlight, went to drive-ins for soft drinks, or attended a well-chaperoned prom or home party.

Advertisers dared depict teenagers touching in ways that might suggest intimacy only if the action took place in a public forum. (Figure 8-23.) The nose-to-nose bite on a Halloween apple or the compromising placement of a hand or leg upon the Twister game mat was acceptable only when adult supervision was present or implied. The appearance of promoting lax morals or promiscuity could become a public relations nightmare for any advertiser. Although sexually charged embraces and kisses have been mainstay images in ads throughout the century, and countless couples have been depicted in ads showing innumerable variations of passion (with ringless fingers in evidence), the participants have always been adults. For an advertiser to seem to promote promiscuity for school-age teenagers could be business suicide. In 1995, for instance, Calvin Klein became the target of a Justice Department investigation because of a series of fashion ads that had female and male models who appeared to be under eighteen years of age provocatively posed to reveal glimpses of their briefly clad crotches. Although all models proved to be over eighteen years old, the public hysteria forced Klein to immediately withdraw the ad campaign.[39]

Still, from the beginning to the end of the twentieth century, advertisers captured the attention of parents with depictions of girls and boys performing their prescribed social rituals with the opposite sex. (Figure 8-24.) The

Figure 8-23. Advertisers depicted physical contact between school-aged teenagers only with strict limitations such as having adult supervision present or implied in the illustrations. Coke ad 1944, Monsanto ad 1967.

visual messages of these ads were understood instantly by readers and accepted as truthful representations of American society as it should and must be. Ads depicting the many varieties of children's gender-appropriate behavior not only reflected but confirmed the importance of parents' sex-role socialization of their offspring. As researcher Jessie Bernard wrote in 1975: "There is probably no aspect of child rearing that is more insisted upon than the inculcating of culturally-approved gender identity. And most infants are pliable enough to accept it. Having, then, been dealt with as a girl, the child develops appropriate feminine feelings, thoughts, and behaviors so that by the time she is two-and-a-half years old . . . she is fixed in her responses."[40]

Conclusion: Advertising and Gender Socialization

Images of children at play have been used in advertising since well before the dawn of the twentieth century. For marketers, the theme served foremost as an attention-grabber in targeting women consumers. The effect was fail-proof, even if the product or service being advertised was unrelated to the child's play scenario.

On a secondary front, marketers would use imagery of children to instruct parents. Ads by makers of household cleaning products or home appliances would demonstrate to mothers that the products were so easy to use that even a child could manage. Such ads also hinted to mothers that perhaps their daughters might be able to take on the less arduous chores, such as dishwashing or vacuuming, to ease the burden of housekeeping tasks.

Before the daughter could assist in housework, she first had to be trained. The care and operation of household appliances or cleaning implements, and the proper methods of using soaps, cleansers, and detergents, were important lessons for girls in preparation for their future roles as housewives. For

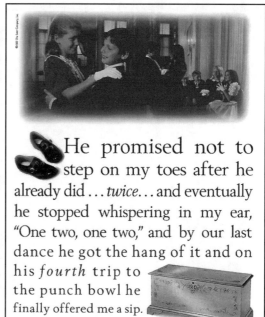

Figure 8-24. Throughout the twentieth century, advertisers depicted girls and boys performing their expected roles in social rituals with the opposite sex. Children viewing such ads received messages of accepted gender-appropriate behavior, and parents were reassured of the proper sex-role training of their offspring. Auto-Grand Piano ad 1906, Lane ad 1993.

advertisers, the lessons of domesticity that girls learned from their mothers could develop brand loyalty and provide for a future market of consumers. Teach them young, these ads reminded mothers, to your benefit and theirs.

In addition to directing mothers to prepare their daughters for their adult roles as homemakers and wives, the children themselves also received important social messages from these ads. Representations of the "Little Cook," the "Little Homemaker," and the "Little Shopper" reinforced society's expectations for girls. By the same token, these kinds of ads generated expectations from the child and, marketers hoped, might inspire her to request her first lesson in cooking, sewing, or housekeeping. Other expectations that a girl learned from ads were standards of social behavior. Ads showed her that she was supposed to play the "Little Mother" with her baby dolls and have tea parties with other little girls; she was supposed to be concerned with her beauty and wardrobe, since that was the proven way to attract boys. All of these kinds of information contained in these ads were designed to lead both mothers and daughters to brand awareness, product loyalty, and, ultimately, mass-market consumption.

Across the length and breadth of the twentieth century, marketers effectively exploited images of children in advertising. Whether as a visual gimmick merely to capture attention or as a social lesson to both children and parents, these representations were integral to the success of the marketing strategies of many manufacturers, distributors, and retailers. If girls were taught well, and taught young, a future filled with brand-loyal consumers was possible.

—Chapter 9

BAD HABITS, VICES, AND TABOOS

Stereotyping the American woman • Marketing and the social stigmas of chewing gum and phone gossip • Advertising products that undermine social mores: billiards, playing cards, tobacco and alcohol • The advent and evolution of sex-sell in advertising

In the preceding chapter we examined what sociologists, scholars, and researchers came to label as the sex-role socialization of girls in America. On all fronts—from parents, schools, churches, and peers—girls were taught how females were expected to behave in preparation for womanhood. For advertisers from one end of the twentieth century to the other, these modes of social behavior and traditions were particularly significant in their continual predictability. The long-term marketing strategies of manufacturers, distributors, and retailers hinged on these social continuums. The wedding would always be an excellent social tradition to depict in ads to sell diamond rings and sterling flatware, images of a sick child used in cold remedy ads would remind Dr. Moms to stock up on medications for the inevitable flu season, and representations of the Happy Homemaker in ads by food and

Figure 9-1. Stereotyping the American woman was a deliberate marketing strategy for most manufacturers. Shown here is the typical work-week of the ideal female consumer. Ad 1954.

appliance makers would instruct, advise, and persuade women of the joy of cooking. However, as Ronald Berman cautioned in *Advertising and Social Change,* "One man's or woman's role model is another's stereotype."[1] For most advertisers, stereotyping the female was a deliberate marketing strategy. (Figure 9-1.) In their estimation, such ads instructed a woman how to behave and represented what her role in society was supposed to be. These stereotyping ads told the housewife that not only was she supposed to cook, clean, and care for her husband and children, but she was supposed to do it all happily with the aid of General Foods, General Mills, General Electric, General Motors, and a host of other general marketers.

These ads simply reflected society's view of itself in general, and women in particular, advertisers might argue—if not in reality then at least as things ought to be. Germaine Greer indirectly supported this notion by writing that "women are contoured by their conditioning to abandon autonomy and seek guidance," whether from an ad or psychoanalysis; "the feminine stereotype," she warned, "is nothing more than a blueprint for the approved woman and as such it presents an artificial unattainable ideal."[2] This unattainable ideal was the brass ring that advertisers held out to American women in millions of pages of magazines and millions of radio and TV spots broadcasting to homes coast to coast.

Representations of the stereotyped American woman also were important to advertisers in another consumer arena. Marketing strategies for products that instigated what were regarded as bad habits, or promoted vices, or violated social taboos required a different approach from those selling soap, food products, or home appliances. Images and themes of the ideal woman were used to break down social barriers and to create a market for products and services that might have been beyond the acceptability of mainstream society. If, as these ads seemed to demonstrate, the ideal woman indulged in the benefits, pleasures, and advantages of these controversial products, then so could, and should, all normal women.

Marketing and the Social Stigma of Bad Habits

For Thomas Adams, brothers Frank and Henry Fleer, and William Wrigley, the controversial product was chewing gum, and the social stigma was the perception of a vulgar habit. (Figure 9-2.) As most every child was taught from an early age, talking while chewing food was repugnant. Gum chewing simulated this breach of good manners. Even more than a century after the launch of the great advertising campaigns by gum manufacturers, the stigma of gum chewing persists still. When Hollywood wants to cheapen the look of a female character in a movie she often is given a wad of gum to chomp on, and children who are to be viewed as ill-mannered will crack and pop bubblegum. Despite a century-long campaign, chewing gum manufacturers succeeded in generating phenomenal sales but never in dispelling the social stigma of vulgarity. "Gum chewing is another of those pleasures that is never proper," avowed a Miss Manners' guide,[3] and in the 1997 edition of *The New Etiquette,* Marjabelle Young Stewart wrote, "Chewing gum is crass; that is the bottom line."[4]

The practice of chewing various substances had an ancient heritage long before the manufacture of chewing gum became an American industry. For

Figure 9-2. Thomas Adams created the first commercially produced chewing gum in the 1870s. He used advertising extensively to introduce this unfamiliar product to a consumer market. Top ad 1918, bottom ad 1920.

YOUR teeth are on display when you smile. They should be gleaming, sparkling white behind your lips. Men and women who value clean, white teeth now chew delicious Dentyne—the gum that makes teeth white and beautiful.

· KEEPS THE TEETH WHITE ·

AFTER A STRENUOUS DAY

Figure 9-3. To overcome the stigma of gum chewing as a vulgar habit, manufacturers advertised the health benefits of using their products. Dentyne ad 1927, Wrigley's ad 1934.

centuries, Eskimos had chewed whale blubber; various native Americans had likewise chewed tobacco, coca leaves, and the tree resin chicle; and European children had chewed paraffin wax. In the 1870s, inventor Thomas Adams met former Mexican general Santa Anna, of the Alamo fame, from whom he received a sample of chicle. Adams later imported a large quantity of the tree resin with the intention of creating a less expensive alternative to rubber. Instead, after observing his son and Santa Anna delighting in chewing the substance, he decided to market chicle as a better alternative to paraffin wax. He added flavorings and contracted jobbers to place the product in drugstores all along the East Coast. To Adams's creation the Fleer brothers added a candy coating in 1910 to produce Chiclets, and in 1928 they created a processed variety called Double Bubble Gum.

It was William Wrigley, however, who specifically launched a broad marketing strategy to undermine social mores about chewing gum. His flavored gums began with Spearmint in 1892, followed by Juicy Fruit a year later. Although he advertised aggressively in magazines and newspapers, his favorite marketing device was the free sample. "Everybody likes something for nothing," he would often remind his sales teams as he armed them with boxes of samples to give out to the public to "get them hooked."[5] Wrigley's most famous marketing ploy was the campaign of 1916 in which he mailed cards bearing samples of gum to more than seven million households. At a staggering cost of a quarter of a million dollars, these cards contained four sticks of gum, one sample each of Doublemint and Spearmint and two of Juicy Fruit. By the time of the mailing Wrigley could claim in the accompanying copy that "probably 80% of the gum consumed in the world is made of these three brands."[6]

Satisfied with his results in America, Wrigley expanded globally to face his most formidable challenge, English social decorum. In 1921 *Printers' Ink* noted that Wrigley had emphasized "the educational effect of his advertising in overcoming the British idea that gum chewing was a 'vulgar American habit.'"[7] Part of the success Wrigley and other gum manufacturers had in overcoming the public's view of gum chewing as vulgar came from revising the marketing message. Whereas early ads had focused on brand positioning, with dancing logos and nursery rhyme themes, ads of the late 1920s and 1930s returned to the old patent medicine method of preaching health and beauty benefits. (Figure 9-3.) In a 1927 ad, Dentyne promised to keep teeth "gleaming, sparkling white behind your lips," while a few years later a Wrigley's ad suggested that the exercise from gum chewing was "lubricating the delicate little muscles of the face—thus helping to relax tight, unbecoming lines which come around the eyes and mouth." Similar chewing gum ads promised to "tone up saggy muscles of your face and neck," or to enhance "circulation which is the very basis of a good complexion," or even to "prevent 'seasickness.'"[8]

To make these ad messages relevant to society at large, the women depicted in chewing gum ads were traditionally presented: the pretty girl, the mother and child, the movie actress, the woman of fashion. Any of these stereotyped images could have been equally applicable in ads for products from soaps to breakfast cereals. As such, they were familiar to the consumer and acceptable as representative of women in mainstream society.

One image that became a favorite female stereotype in advertising was that of the woman talking on the phone. (Figure 9-4.) Prior to World War I, the Bell Telephone Company largely concentrated its marketing efforts toward offering telecommunications systems for businesses. In the succeeding years, Bell ads began to target the housewife, who, in the isolation of her domestic domain, they hoped would become an avid subscriber. These efforts paid off with an ever increasing rate of home phone subscriptions through the teens and twenties. In a 1927 study of thirty-seven U.S. consumer markets produced by *Literary Digest,* the "proportion of telephone homes" was 49 percent nationwide with households having incomes of forty dollars a week or less, and up to 95 percent with households having incomes of two hundred dollars a week or more.[9] The counts cited in the *Literary Digest* survey, and also in the 1925 Middletown study, would have been much higher were it not "due in part to lack of plant facilities."[10] Indeed, the American housewife eagerly accepted the benefits of telephone service. The Lynds noted that "around the telephone have grown up such time-savers for the housewife as the general delivery system for everything from groceries to a spool of thread."[11] Yet, it was the housewife's connection with friends and family outside the home that was especially promoted by phone companies. Catchphrases such as "reach out and touch someone" successfully ran in their ads for decades.

Since Bell Telephone manufactured and rented the telephones as well as providing the service, the company began to promote the installation of home extensions. (Figure 9-5.) Ads of the 1950s suggested that teenage girls should get a phone for their own room—in a decorator color—and housewives were advised that a kitchen extension "saves time and steps every day, lets you take and make calls when you're busiest."

With such continued success in selling phone service and unit rentals, it must have dismayed telephone officials to see their advertising campaigns satirized in other unrelated ads. (Figure 9-6.) These negative depictions, probably much more than the comparable images in AT&T ads, created and perpetuated the stereotype of a woman's bad habit of endlessly socializing and gossiping on the phone.

Advertising Products and Images of Vice

Bad habits could be tolerated in most social circles, but breaking social taboos and indulging in vices could have significant consequences ranging from social ostracism to imprisonment. Christian dogma had for centuries

Figure 9-4. The telephone company specifically targeted the homebound American woman following World War I. Long-running ad campaigns such as the "reach out and touch someone" theme were primarily aimed at housewives. Bell Telephone ads 1928 and 1959.

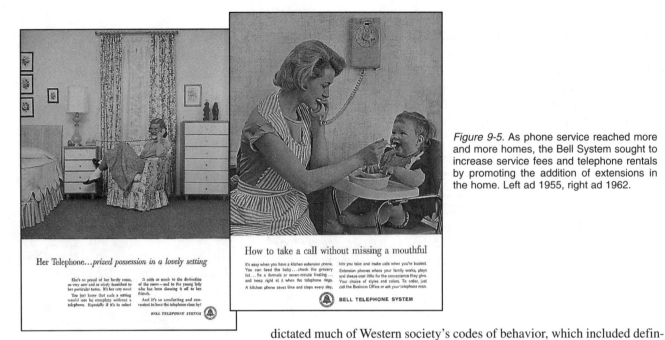

Figure 9-5. As phone service reached more and more homes, the Bell System sought to increase service fees and telephone rentals by promoting the addition of extensions in the home. Left ad 1955, right ad 1962.

dictated much of Western society's codes of behavior, which included defining vices and establishing taboos. Some church doctrines, especially those of nineteenth- and twentieth-century Protestant sects, promulgated their guides to a proper Christian life in ordinances of doctrine or declarations of faith. A glance through the comprehensive *Profiles in Belief* by Arthur Clark Piepkorn reveals that dozens of different sects with memberships totaling in the tens of millions shared common ground when defining vices. Many of these religious groups forbade consuming tobacco and intoxicating beverages, wearing immodest attire and makeup, dancing, playing cards, attending theaters and movies, wearing jewelry (including wedding rings), and a

Figure 9-6. The stereotype of a woman's bad habit of gossiping on the telephone was common imagery used in ads for products that were unrelated to phone service. Keystone ad 1924, Bigelow ad 1969.

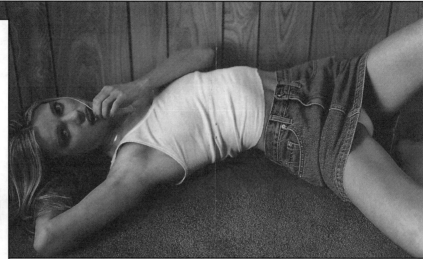

Figure 9-7. Some advertisers flouted social convention and risked negative publicity with sexually charged ad presentations. Springmaid ad 1949, Calvin Klein ad 1995 (detail of an insert).

vast array of other behaviors.[12] Such prohibitions defined the social structure of all those who became members of these sects. Religious dogma was to be observed every day in all aspects of home life as stringently as on Sunday morning with the church congregation.

Manufacturers of products whose use ran counter to religious doctrine had to make a choice not if to advertise their products, but how, so as to offend as few people as possible and thereby avoid negative publicity. Jewelry makers, cosmetic manufacturers, movie theaters, tobacco companies, and breweries, to name a few, all had to face the challenge of reaching their target customers and expanding their market share in the face of resistance or even hostility from some segments of society. "It is essential to appeal to the ones who might buy your product," wrote advertising researcher Eric Clark; "alienate only those who do not matter."[13]

Sometimes, however, those who do not matter as customers can very much matter in the court of public opinion. The risk of negative publicity is an ever present concern for advertisers. Some, such as Elliot White Springs, president of Springmaid Fabrics in the 1940s and 1950s, and Calvin Klein in the 1980s and 1990s, seemed to have deliberately courted danger with their sexually charged ad presentations. (Figure 9-7.) Ironically, for one Springmaid ad in 1949 the company received more than ten thousand letters requesting reprints, and *Liberty* increased the circulation of its next issue containing a Springmaid ad by 180,000 additional copies.[14] On the other hand, a 1995 series of fashion ads and TV spots by Calvin Klein so outraged religious and conservative organizations that the controversy made the evening TV newscasts and Klein discontinued the campaign. An *Advertising Age* editorial noted that Klein "doesn't care about the people who care about these ads. By pulling the ads now, he's saved a quarter of his ad budget and gets all this free publicity. Calvin Klein knew precisely what he was doing."[15] For most marketers, though, the decision to run a certain image or theme in an ad is always carefully weighed against the possible public backlash.

One such ad theme that many might have regarded as controversial was that of dancing. Throughout the twentieth century, a number of evangelical Christian sects have forbidden dancing even between married couples. Lutheran newsletters of the 1920s declared modern dancing a "training school for fornication," and Methodists refused to grant membership to dancing instructors until they repented of "teaching lasciviousness and adultery and of ruining homes and youth."[16] Such moral attitudes and dictates were so commonly understood in American culture that even as late as 1984 the prohibition on religious grounds was used as a credible premise for the movie *Footloose,* in which a community ordinance is passed to outlaw dancing of any kind.

Nevertheless, dancing was commonly depicted in ads all through the century, even in those unrelated to music products. (Figure 9-8.) Whether selling shoes, cigarettes, floor wax, or deodorant, these ads carried the risk of inviting angry letters and phone calls from those to whom the images might seem offensive. This group of offended consumers might well extend

1903

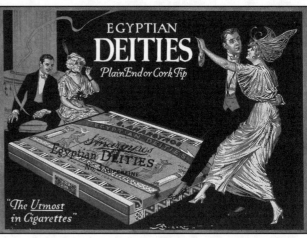

1914

1929

1948   1967

Figure 9-8. Images of dancing were common in advertising all through the century despite bans against such social activities by religious and conservative groups.

beyond dogmatic religious sects into mainstream society. For instance, in the 1903 ad for Sorosis Shoes, the scenario of an upper-class ball suggested to some readers that even for a woman of a high social caliber, dancing might compromise her modesty, since her whirling about the dance floor would exhibit the motion of her hips pressed against those of a man and reveal ankles beneath dress hems. The scandalous tango was used in a 1914 ad for Egyptian Deities cigarettes to ally the product with an avant-garde social set. Old Gold cigarettes doubly risked the public's ire in 1929 by showing a flapper kicking up the Charleston in the basement with a black, "kinky-haired old furnaceman." A generation later, the jitterbug was the shocking dance of the day with its rapid twirls and flips that often lifted a girl's skirt high enough to expose underthings; nevertheless, the makers of Old English Wax thought a modest representation of the vigorous dance in a 1948 ad would aptly serve to emphasize the claim of floor protection. Similarly, the aerobic workout of dances from the 1960s may have confused and dismayed many parents, but depictions of the twist, the jerk, or the watusi perfectly suited the point of Arrid deodorant ads from 1967. Despite the seemingly abrupt challenges to social mores that dance fads foisted upon succeeding generations, a *Ladies' Home Journal* editorial offered a perspective for incensed social conservatives that was as applicable at the end of the century as when written in 1916: "The wave of wrath over the 'Turkey Trot' is just receding, though 'modern dances' are still in disrepute. Those who first appeared on dance floors to the stirring strains of 'Too Much Mustard' were depraved beings, and conservatives sighed for the beautiful and discarded waltz, forgetting naturally enough that the waltz, when new, was not considered beautiful—neither it nor the polka, the scottische nor the gavotee, which were 'modern' and therefore 'scandalous' dances of 1860!"[17]

Although linking their products with images of vices such as dancing was risky in advertising, some manufacturers faced an even greater challenge—the dilemma of knowing that their products were used illicitly just as often as not. For instance, billiard tables had been a common fixture of saloons, nightclubs, and gambling halls since the early nineteenth century; they also were popular games-room fixtures in the homes of the wealthy and upper-middle classes. Yet images of the smoke-filled milieu of corner bars with their besotted denizens were especially prevalent in the public's mind when billiard was the topic. (Figure 9-9.) Is the woman in an 1899 Jenkinson tobacco ad a lady of quality in the games room of a private home, or is she a demimonde in a tavern who entices men to foolish wagers with her revealing décolletage and winsome smile? The question was immaterial to the tobacconist who was targeting men in the ad, since both types of women suited the scenario of a man's pursuit of pleasure. To the manufacturers of pool tables, though, such images tarnished an otherwise respectable family pastime. Counter measures were taken in product advertising to present billiards as a game for the whole family. (Figure 9-10.) In fact, copy messages alluded to those other iniquitous sites where sons, and in later decades, daughters, might seek the game. "Mothers—keep your boys at home," declared the headline of a 1900 Brunswick-Balke-Collender ad. "Provide them with the amusement they want," continued the copy, with a thinly veiled warning that boys will otherwise find pool games in the wrong places with the wrong people. A generation later, the company went one step further

Figure 9-9. Rightly or wrongly, some products were inextricably associated with social vices in the minds of most Americans. For example, a great many people thought billiards was a form of gambling primarily played in saloons and pool halls. Ad 1899.

Figure 9-10. In an attempt to mitigate the stigma associated with billiards, manufacturers of pool tables advertised the game as wholesome home entertainment. Top ad 1900, bottom ad 1926.

in a 1926 ad featuring an editorial by a juvenile court judge who recommended the billiard table as a way to offset "the revolt of modern youth." Wrote the judge: "It could very easily be provided in thousands of homes where now it is unknown, and where youth, yearning for the healthful, absorbing, wholesome amusement that the game affords, is left to the lure of the streets." Unfortunately for most American households, not only was the cost of a billiard table prohibitive, but they lacked the functional space to place one. So the "lure of the streets"—at least down to the local pool hall—was not diminished, thus fixing in the American psyche a social stigma forever associated with the game of billiards.

Card games suffered much the same reputation as did billiards. Having been introduced to the West from Arab countries during the Crusades, card games became instantly popular for wagering. With a long history so integrally linked to the vice of gambling, to millions of religious Americans card playing of any kind ranked as a sin comparable to drinking intoxicating beverages and smoking cigarettes. In examining the leisure time of Middletown residents, the Lynds noted that "In 1924 the sectional state conference of the numerically most powerful religious denomination in Middletown renewed its traditional prohibition upon card playing, and in some of the more religious working class families the ban is still maintained not only upon cards but upon checkers and other games as well."[18] To mitigate the product's bad image, many ads for playing cards presented images of attractive, respectable women enjoying harmless games of whist, cribbage, or bridge. (Figure 9-11.) Advertisers took great care to avoid representations of women who might be thought of as saloon gals whose experience with cards was more likely to include wagering on stud poker. In addition, the ad copy complemented the safe images with phrases such as "clean, wholesome, spirited amusement" and "cards are fun for one . . . fun for all." Although religious folk might not have been convinced to become product consumers by the imagery or the copy, neither would they be threatened by such benign representations.

Marketing and Social Taboos

The degrees that differentiate a bad habit from a tolerated vice or a societal taboo can be distinct in controlled social groups such as religious sects, but often overlap and become gray when applied to a society at large. For instance, all socioeconomic classes might have indulged in the perceived bad habit of gum chewing despite admonitions from etiquette guides, but playing billiards—perceived as a gambling vice—was enjoyed largely by upper classes who could afford the expensive equipment and by lower classes who frequented pool halls. Throughout the twentieth century, these perceptions remained fairly constant. Ironically, though, when it came to smoking and women, the three social distinctions merged into one process of social evolution: from a nineteenth-century taboo to an early-twentieth-century vice, and concluding at the end of the century as a reviled bad habit.

Although some advertising historians have stated that the first time a woman smoker appeared in a cigarette ad was in a billboard poster for Chesterfield in 1926, they probably meant the depiction of a "typical" American woman smoker.[19] In actuality, women had frequently appeared in cigarette and tobacco ads from as early as the 1860s. However, as Victor Margolin wrote, "Mythical ladies of pleasure could smoke a Murad, but not the girl next door."[20] (Figure 9-12.) This was a significant distinction. The types of women who were shown actually smoking were exotic foreigners or women on the fringe of society such as demimondes or actresses. Even when Marshall's used the representation of a lady of fashion puffing out the

Figure 9-11. Playing card manufacturers also had to contend with a social stigma attached to their product. Ads often presented the stereotypes of respectable middle-class women enjoying presumably harmless bridge games.

1904

1922

1959

Figure 9-12. Although images of women smokers had appeared in advertising even in the nineteenth century, the targeting of women as a significant consumer group did not occur until after World War I.

company logo in a cloud of smoke as its trademark in the 1890s, the aura of Victorian feminine style was impugned by the cigarette she held. As for the representations of respectable ladies shown in so many early tobacco ads, their presence served solely as accompaniments to the men who were usually puffing away on a cigarette. The women themselves were never seen smoking.

Just because smoking was a social taboo for women prior to World War I did not mean they all completely eschewed cigarettes. There was a market for women smokers even in the nineteenth century despite the entrenched taboo. During the 1880s the Kimball Tobacco Company produced a perfumed brand packed in a drawstring satin bag for carrying in a lady's purse, and some tobacco companies tentatively approached women with ads, such as the 1894 version shown in Figure 9-12, which specifically addressed "ladies" in its headline. In his exhaustive study of tobacco advertising, Gerard Petrone wrote that "The cigarette had, by the turn of the century, found a place in the affections of proper American womanhood, exploding the myth that no one but those with peroxided pasts and skirts that showed ankles smoked. In many households of social prominence, the feminine contingent joined their husbands or brothers in taking cigarettes after dinner— and the presence of guests was not allowed to interfere with this tradition."[21]

In spite of this assertion, most Americans were shocked to see a woman smoking even well into the 1920s. Petrone conceded that for the overwhelming majority of Americans, "between the lips of a woman, a cigarette

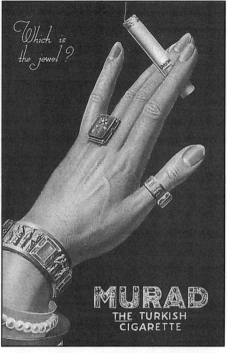

Figure 9-13. Prior to the 1920s, some tobacco ads featured women with cigarettes but never actually smoking. Milo ad 1918, Murad ad 1919.

was regarded as a badge of the stage adventuress, or certainly one inclined to 'the Bohemian persuasion.'"[22] Public displays of lighting up by daring women resulted in newspaper headlines or even jail right up to the First World War.[23] For advertisers the women's market was left untouched as a target for the most part. Religious doctrines, fierce antismoking forces, community ordinances, and arbiters of social decorum vehemently opposed smoking by minors and women. Even in 1918, when Milo Violets were introduced as a scented, gold-tipped cigarette "for the woman of discernment," the women illustrated in the ads were shown reaching for the package but not actually smoking.[24] Similarly, with the 1919 Murad ad showing a well-manicured woman's hand holding a lit cigarette, the presumption was that it belonged to one of the exotic houris tobacco companies had depicted in ads for decades. (Figure 9-13.)

The decision to specifically market cigarettes to all women is a classic tale in the annals of advertising. As the story goes, one day in 1926 Albert Lasker, marketing genius at Lord & Thomas agency, was lunching with his wife, after which she lit up a cigarette. The restaurant manager promptly informed Mrs. Lasker that women were not permitted to smoke in the dining room. Lasker was outraged and set out to find a way of undermining this social taboo. Since he had the American Tobacco Company account, he decided to position Lucky Strike as the brand for women, with the blessing of the company's owner, George W. Hill. (Figure 9-14.) In 1927 Lasker collected endorsements from female celebrities and film stars that were used in

Figure 9-14. In 1927 the American Tobacco Company teamed up with marketing genius Albert Lasker to position Lucky Strike as the brand of cigarettes for women. Campaigns included endorsements from women celebrity smokers. Ad 1927.

Figure 9-15. By the late 1920s, all tobacco companies began to target women with advertising. The results were so effective that record numbers of women took up smoking. Marlboro ad 1927, Camels ad 1928.

a national advertising blitz. By 1929 Lucky Strike sales tripled, and the following year sales of Luckies surpassed Camels, the market leader.[25] The endorsement campaign was quickly followed by ads with the theme "reach for a Lucky instead of a sweet" in 1929 and the "do you inhale" promotion of 1932. Putting aside the leap in profits for the American Tobacco Company and Lasker's substantial commissions, the impact on American women was devastating as they responded to these and similar ads by other cigarette makers, and took up smoking in record numbers. (Figure 9-15.) In 1959 advertising historian Julian Lewis Watkins said of the "reach for a Lucky instead of a sweet" theme: "Many in marketing today believe that campaign created more women smokers than any other promotional effort."[26]

Fashion was another device used for targeting women as potential smokers. Whether scenting cigarettes with floral fragrances, as with the Milo Violets of the late teens, or using the image of fashionable women, as in Marlboro ads of the twenties, thirties, and forties, marketing efforts integrally connected smoking to a sophisticated life style. (Figure 9-16.) Decades before the appearance of the Marlboro cowboy, Philip Morris promoted the brand as a woman's cigarette. "Its image was elegant, if not downright prissy," commented Leslie Savan of the brand's advertising.[27] Nor was Philip Morris alone in this regard. Even with the success the American Tobacco Company had with the various Lucky Strike ad campaigns, fashion also was a part of its early marketing strategy. Juliann Silvulka noted that company owner George W. Hill "was concerned that women were resisting the green packaging because it clashed with their clothes. . . . To solve the problem, he hired . . . a public relations [expert], who promoted the color green as fashionable in fashion shows so that the dark green Luckies packages would complement women's ensembles."[28]

Tobacco marketers never seemed to run out of advertising gimmicks with which to target women customers generation after generation. (Figure 9-17.) To appear more patriotic during World War II, Lucky Strike changed its

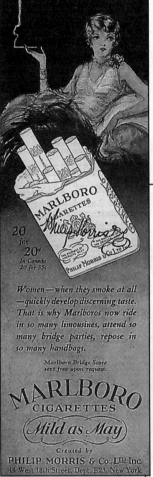

Figure 9-16. Philip Morris positioned Marlboro cigarettes as a woman's brand until the appearance of the Marlboro cowboy in 1954. Left ad 1927, right ad 1945.

green package design to white with a red logo circle in 1942; at about the same time, its radio slogan "Lucky Strike means fine tobacco" moved into print with the memorable acronym "L.S./M.F.T." Lorillard modified the old "reach for a Luckies instead of a sweet" theme to become "for a treat instead of a treatment" for use in Old Gold ads in the 1950s. In the 1960s, Tareyton ads included depictions of women sporting black eyes as a visual testimonial that these loyal smokers "would rather fight than switch." From the late 1960s through the end of the century, Virginia Slim ads created dozens of then-and-now scenarios of women smokers with the caption, "You've come a long way, baby." Women of the 1970s were included in the Benson & Hedges 100's "cigarette break" campaign, which presented comical situations where the extra-long cigarette got bent while being smoked. In ads for Camel Lights in the 1990s, icon Joe Camel was replaced with subliminal representations of a dromedary such as a smoky silhouette emanating from a woman's mouth or in the puddle of condensation from a chilled cocktail held by a woman.[29]

Although the taboo against women smoking dissolved into a tolerated social vice in the late 1920s, the antismoking forces persisted. Between the 1890s and the First World War, well-organized groups sponsored by the YMCA, the Women's Christian Temperance Union, and other similar religious-based organizations had repeatedly emphasized health issues in their campaigns against tobacco. To counter these clouds of concern, cigarette advertisers began to employ old patent medicine tactics by invoking vague references to physicians or using images of health-care professionals. (Figure 9-18.) For example, a 1930 Lucky Strike ad declared that "20,679 physicians say Luckies are less irritating." However, such unsubstantiated endorsements, and advertised claims such as "toasting removes dangerous irritants that cause throat irritation and coughing," were quickly challenged by the Federal Trade Commission. A ruling in 1930 forced tobacco advertisers to stop featuring endorsements by anyone who had not actually used the product, to indicate when testimonials had been bought, and to cease claims that smoking controlled a person's weight.[30] Still, tobacco advertisers continued to maneuver around such rulings any way they could to hook female smokers even before they were old enough to vote.

The first serious blow to the tobacco industry occurred in 1964 when the U.S. Surgeon General's report linked smoking to lung disease. The following year, warning labels were required on all cigarette packages. Tobacco commercials were banned from television in 1971, and warning labels were required in print advertising. Excise taxes continued to rise on tobacco products, and antismoking forces succeeded in procuring restrictive legislation ranging from bans on smoking in public buildings to restrictions on

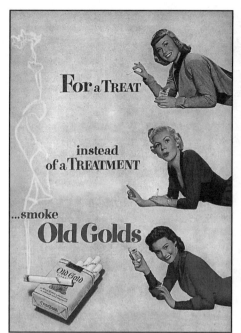

1951

1969

1974

Figure 9-17. Tobacco companies seemed to have an endless supply of advertising slogans and gimmicks with which to target women consumers.

promotional giveaways, outdoor signage, brand sponsorships, and advertising in magazines with a heavy youth readership. Numerous state health services departments used tobacco tax revenues to aggressively wage antismoking campaigns. (Figure 9-19.) In 1997 California even managed to outlaw smoking in bars.

Still, profits were considerable for tobacco companies despite diminishing sales in many quarters and the ever tightening noose of state and federal regulations. A sizeable chunk of those profits was poured into advertising to sway public opinion. As an *Adweek* editorial noted in 1997, "$5 billion buys a lot of societal influence."[31] In 1998, one public relations campaign alone cost the tobacco industry $40 million and succeeded in convincing a Republican Congress to kill the McCain antismoking legislation. Much to the alarm of many advocacy groups, that powerful influence was directed with great success at the young. In spite of the decades of warnings and eight years of the Clinton administration's antismoking activism, the number of young women smokers continued to increase through the 1990s. Even cigar makers began to court women by featuring images of fashion beauties and female celebrities in ads. Advertising critic Mark Dolliver wrote: "Among young folks the prospect of dying is too remote to discourage indulgence in pleasures of the moment. If anything, the risks enhance the glamour of tobacco for those who wish to show the world how tough they are."[32] Thus, in answer to the old debate of whether or not advertising reflected society or influenced society, proponents of the latter could point to the history of the tobacco industry in America to support their case. The taboo against women smoking dissolved into a tolerated vice during the second quarter of the century and into a bad, albeit deadly, habit during the last quarter.

Figure 9-18. Antismoking organizations vociferously argued the health issues against smoking. To counter these charges, tobacco companies employed vague endorsements by physicians or used images of health-care workers in ads. Lucky Strike ad 1930 (detail), Camel ad 1932 (detail).

Paralleling the social evolution of women's smoking was that of women's drinking. At the beginning of the twentieth century, the taboo against women's consumption of intoxicating beverages was far more stringent than it was for tobacco. The social campaigns against "demon rum" extended well back into the eighteenth century and came to fruition in the nineteenth century with the creation of numerous temperance societies sponsored by churches, Christian organizations, and women's clubs; their chief objective was legislation against all forms of intoxicating drink throughout the land. Some historians have viewed "the moralism of Prohibition," as it emerged during the early years of the twentieth century, as "the last-ditch stand of the rural state of mind" in America.[33] Despite the clamoring of these groups, though, it was wartime patriotism that finally tipped the scales toward a national prohibition in 1919. Temperance groups beat the drum of God, America, and the sober, steady doughboy going over the top. Beer was German and liquor was the kaiser's greatest ally, they chorused. Finally, Congress reacted in a flush of idealism to restrict the production of alcoholic beverages, ostensibly to preserve grain reserves, and a de facto prohibition was put in place six months before the prohibition statutes of the Eighteenth Amendment went into effect.

Advertising for breweries, distilleries, wineries, and retail liquor establishments was carefully administered before 1920. Most magazines refused to advertise alcohol products, although newspapers were less discriminating. As with early tobacco advertising, the target market for spirits was the American man. The appearance of women in beer or liquor ads was rare and represented either allegories, logo maidens, or bohemian women of questionable reputation. (Figure 9-20.)

The one great irony of Prohibition was that it significantly contributed to the increase in women's drinking. The law prohibited the manufacture and

Figure 9-19. By the end of the century, anti-smoking campaigns became more aggressive, resulting in restrictive state and federal legislation against smoking. Ad 1997.

1896

1899

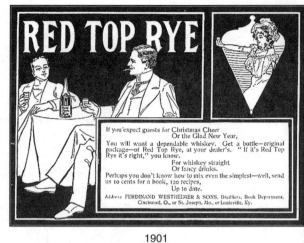

1901

Figure 9-20. As with early tobacco advertising, women who were depicted in ads for intoxicating beverages were either allegories, logo maidens, or women of questionable repute.

sale of alcohol, but it did not prohibit the consumption or possession for consumption of alcohol. To many that meant the nullification of laws that had set the drinking age at twenty-one. Without such regulations, young women barely of high school age were admitted to the thousands of illegal speakeasies that had sprung up across the country almost overnight. There they were served coffee cups filled with bootleg whiskey or the newest varieties of cocktails made from recipes brought in by sophisticates from Europe. In addition, a popular fad for the flapper was to carry a flask concealed in the rolled garter of her stocking or in her handbag whenever she went out on a date or to the Friday night football games. Wrote historian Edmund Stillman: "What prohibition did accomplish was to make drinking initially a furtive affair, then a defiant practice. And it spread the habit of drinking, along with contemporary marks of equality of the sexes, to the ladies."[34]

In 1933 Prohibition was repealed by the passage of the Twenty-first Amendment. In the throes of the Depression, the nation received a psychological boost with the lifting of the ban, despite the outcries from the WCTU and the antisaloon forces. "The women of the city seem in general never to have approved of drinking and repeal," noted the Lynds in their *Middletown in Transition* study.[35] In fact, for a while most of these groups anticipated the return to prohibition after the American people reflected upon the evils unleashed upon the land by booze.

Though the stigma of women's drinking persisted long after the repeal of Prohibition, the societal view—except in religious circles where the taboo remained in place—had evolved into that of a tolerable vice. Advertisers of alcoholic beverages moved rapidly to capitalize on this more relaxed attitude and within weeks of the repeal produced their first ads ever that specifically targeted women. (Figure 9-21.) In 1934, Dixie Belle Gin presented the formality of an elegant socialite enjoying a martini, while Pabst celebrated a more casual "Blue Ribbon girl" in its art and copy. Sometime during the late

1930s, the liquor industry began to take a separate marketing direction from the beer manufacturers. The latter continued to specifically target women in advertising throughout the remainder of the century, but liquor manufacturers put a moratorium on marketing to women. (Figure 9-22.) In 1956, Bacardi Imports broke with the tradition and began advertising to women again. A *Printers' Ink* writer noted at the time that "the liquor industry has always had an unwritten law that its advertising would not feature women nor would copy be directed to women." When Bacardi president H. B. Estrada was asked about the change, he commented: "Rum in this country is

Figure 9-21. Following the repeal of Prohibition in 1933, women were specifically targeted for the first time by advertising for beer and liquor manufacturers. Ads 1934.

Figure 9-22. Liquor companies practiced a self-imposed moratorium on advertising to women from the late 1930s through the 1950s, but beer makers continued to target the female segment of the market. Schlitz ad 1954, Budweiser ad 1957.

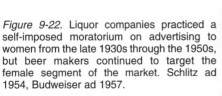

Figure 9-23. By the end of the 1950s, liquor companies renewed advertising efforts to directly target women. Gilbey's ad 1961, Smirnoff ad 1975.

an ingredient for cocktails—Bacardi and daiquiri cocktails which appeal primarily to women. We were faced with a potential market and we were not appealing to the consumers.... Wherever we find it feasible in our advertising plans we are going to use techniques to appeal to women. If we keep good taste within our advertising techniques using women, there's no reason why the American people should be aware of the difference."[36] With the success of Bacardi's new marketing venture, the gloves came off for the competitors and women were once again the focal point of many liquor ads. (Figure 9-23.)

Tasteful or otherwise, the successful advertising did not spell across-the-board social acceptance. Fear of the same kind of restrictive legislation imposed upon tobacco advertising kept liquor ads "voluntarily" off television, despite the outcry against unfair advantages enjoyed by the beer industry, which poured billions of dollars into TV spots. By the end of the 1990s, the social stigma attached to alcohol consumption, including beer and wine, remained significant. Child advocacy and conservative family groups raised the pitch of their protests as beer commercials replaced brewsky bimbos with talking frogs and chameleons. As *Adweek* editor Debra Goldman concluded: "As brewers are dragged into the brouhaha over alcohol advertising on TV, they are also finding themselves in the paradoxical position of claiming their marketing isn't all that influential, while their opponents insist it succeeds all too well. Beer marketers, like the tobacco industry, could swear that they don't target underage consumers. They could even be telling the truth, and it still won't matter."[37]

Such social changes as those inaugurated by the tobacco and liquor industries were nothing compared to those set in motion by the sexual revolutions of the 1920s and 1960s. Puritanism had reigned supreme over all strata of American society as the twentieth century dawned. Victorian notions of sex as something to be tolerated by women for the purpose of procreation were as prevalent in the years before World War I as they had been generations earlier when Queen Victoria was a teenage bride. Ignorance of the subject was pervasive, even among the well-educated.

The first chips off the block of America's sexual puritanism came in the early teens at the hands of feminist reformers such as Emma Goldman, whose public forum lectures launched the birth control movement, and Margaret Sanger, who made headlines by going to jail for dispensing an "obscene" material: the newly developed diaphragm. Concurrent with the activism of these and other women's leaders was the influence of the research work done on women's sexuality by Sigmund Freud and the British sexologist Havelock Ellis. Both men had asserted that women were sexual beings and had a capacity for enjoying sex. Historian Dorothy Brown wrote that Freud's and Ellis's combined efforts of sex research, and the resulting publicity about their conclusions, did more than anything to "free men and women from the stranglehold of Victorian convention and conditioning."[38] As the 1920s began to roar, women stepped into a new realm of independence that could not have been imagined by their mothers and grandmothers. Not only could they now vote, with the passage of the Nineteenth Amendment in 1920, but they also were told they could enjoy sex as well as be free of unwanted pregnancies. "The new sex mores, combined with contraceptive progress, laid open the possibility of a more satisfied, self-sufficient, and worldly wise womanhood," wrote Mary Ryan.[39]

The epitome of the modern, free woman of this era was the flapper. She unabashedly wore makeup, bobbed her hair, donned skimpy one-piece swimsuits to acquire a suntan, shortened her skirt above the knees, and cast off her corset to be free to gyrate to the cacophony of jazz. She also experimented with sex. Her relaxed morals became the benchmark for a decade of young women who pushed the limitations of their new-found independence. Lamented one 1928 editorial in *Physical Culture:* "Life has become a swift business. The auto, the films, the stupendous modern output of books and magazines and papers, the radio—each has popped in upon the American home and helped create an ever-widening horizon. Where Grandmother could slowly steer each girl along the path of propriety, today a girl has so many ideas and emotions and reactions flung in front of her that by sixteen she knows many things Grandmother was still wondering about at sixty."[40]

The era that was described, even as it occurred, as "a dangerous age, a flaming youth age, a companionate-marriage age, and a whoopee age"[41] did not spring into existence all at once. In a backlash to Victorianism the Edwardians had begun to ease social and sexual mores, and a decade later the awesome consequences of World War I had inspired many Americans to adopt wholeheartedly the credo "carpe diem."

In reflecting these social changes in their ads, marketers had preceded the exhibitionism of the flapper by more than a dozen years with risqué images and scenarios that flouted convention and seemed to promote an easing of deference between the sexes. In 1905 an Oldsmobile ad depicted a young couple out for a drive in the country—alone and, presumably, far from a chaperone. (Figure 9-24.) The two are clearly not interested in the bucolic landscape; the young man lets the woman drive, leaving his hands free to caress her arm and embrace her shoulders—a shocking display out in the

Figure 9-24. The automobile is often credited as one of the earliest influences on the easing of Victorian deferences between the sexes. Ad 1905.

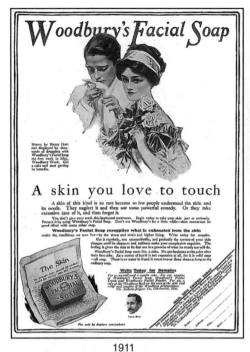

1911

1916

Figure 9-25. Images of carnal caresses and kisses between the sexes first appeared in American advertising just before World War I.

1916

open, even if the reader presumes the two are married. This sex-sell of the automobile by Oldsmobile and most other carmakers was a highly successful marketing strategy generation after generation. In examining changes in courtship patterns from the 1890s to the 1920s, the Lynds specifically credited the automobile as being a contributing factor in the easing of how boys and girls approached each other, as well as how parents viewed these changes. "In an auto . . . a party may go to a city halfway across the state in an afternoon or evening," wrote the Lynds, "and unchaperoned automobile parties as late as midnight, while subject to criticism, are not exceptional."[42]

These relaxed approaches quickly became less suggestive and more explicit as themes and visual subjects in ads of the teens. (Figure 9-25.) The shocking header in Woodbury ads, "a skin you love to touch," was introduced in 1911 with the illustration of a young man chastely kissing the hand of his sweetheart as she demurely looks away. A few years later, other versions showed passionate embraces with masculine hands caressing bare feminine arms, shoulders, and necks. Similarly, during this era the first carnal kisses appeared in advertising, such as the clandestine kiss of a young man and woman behind father's back in a 1916 promotion for Egyptian Deities cigarettes.

As the social climate of the 1920s evolved, the flapper did present somewhat of a dilemma for advertisers. Manufacturers may have helped loosen the knot of social mores with sex-sell depictions of caresses, embraces, and kisses in their ads, but they were cautious not to cross the line from passion to indecency. Magazines such as *True Story* and movies such as those starring sex symbols Theda Bara and Rudolph Valentino held no such compunction. Likewise, "Held's Hellions," created by illustrator John Held, often featured the flapper wrestling with a "sheik" in his roadster or engaged in a passionate kiss at a petting party. These and similar depictions of sexual activities increasingly populated the articles in mass-circulation publications such as *Cosmopolitan, Life,* and *McClure's.*

By comparison to scenes of passionate romance in movies and magazines, the once shocking illustrations of caresses and kisses used in ads seemed tame and passé. Indeed, this limited method of showing male/female contact became the threshold that advertisers would not cross until the 1970s. For fifty years following World War I, the sex-sell of caresses and kisses depicted in ads did not venture far afield from the groundwork laid by the Woodbury soap ads. (Figure 9-26.) In 1936, Listerine dared to show a man leaning over a woman in bed. Both of the models are clearly dressed, and the ad header hastens to declare that the man's intention is merely "to kiss her good night." Even that is immediately disclaimed with the opening sentence in the body copy: "MARRIED eight years." In a subtle attempt to up its own ante, Woodbury ads of the 1940s featured bare skin and ringless fingers in ads depicting caressing couples, but the sexual tension was presented to the reader through the couple's restraint and anticipation rather than by demonstrative physical actions. Even by the late 1950s, the sex-sell of caresses and kisses had remained a formula in ads and required contrivances to even moderately titillate. A Veto deodorant ad from 1957 slightly pushed the boundary with the scenario of a literal roll in the hay, punctuated with an extra button undone on the woman's sweater and her ringless left hand in clear evidence.

The self-imposed limitations of these ads reflected society's continued taboo against anything to do with sex. The Depression had been a douse of ice water over the exuberance of the 1920s, and that included the flapper's sexual independence. In revisiting Middletown in the mid-1930s, the Lynds found that "sex is one of the things Middletown has long been taught to

Figure 9-26. For fifty years following the First World War, depictions in ads of physical contact between the sexes was limited to carefully staged variations of caresses and kisses.

1936

1945

1957

Figure 9-27. The sexual revolution of the 1960s inspired advertisers to move beyond illustrations of mere caresses and kisses. Ads depicting nude couples engaged in sensual activities were accepted in mainstream periodicals by the start of the 1970s. Vivitar ad 1970, Sony ad 1971.

fear"; as a result, "its institutions . . . operate to keep the subject out of sight and out of mind as much as possible." Case studies showed that many Middletown parents refused to discuss the topic with their children, nor did parents allow the schools to broach the subject. Even the libraries had removed any books on sex from the shelves.[43] This puritanical conservatism would remain in place until the turbulent changes of the 1960s helped inaugurate the second great sexual revolution.

As the 1950s merged into the 1960s, the ever increasing level of explicit sexual content in books, magazines, movies, and pop music had a profound influence on changing Americans' attitudes—and more significantly, behaviors—about sex. As researcher Jessie Bernard wrote of the increase in premarital sex during the 1960s: "The young people themselves were talking a great deal about the pros and cons of intercourse outside of marriage, the nature of sexual relationships, of marriage, of virginity, and a host of other interpersonal relationships. The talk apparently had its effect."[44] This effect was confirmed by a 1974 *Redbook* survey of one hundred thousand women that showed that 90 percent of women under the age of twenty-five had had premarital sex.[45]

Widely available contraception also was a significant contribution to this second revolution. Condoms were easily accessible for a dime from dispensers in the men's rooms of many gas stations and bars. For women, the birth control pill replaced the mess and inconvenience of the diaphragm.

Even so, a generational schizophrenia about sex emerged in American society of the 1960s. Many later researchers were to look back and claim that the dialogue on sex was not where it should have been—that is, with the parents.[46] Just as the Lynds had revealed of parents in the 1930s, parents of the 1960s were equally unwilling to discuss sex with their children, nor would they allow schools to teach sex education, especially before high school. Even by the end of the decade, hysteria about sex education was at a fevered pitch nationwide, as *Life* reported in 1969: "A young woman who taught it gets obscene phone calls. A Lutheran minister who supports its faces rebellion in his church. Former bridge partners who disagree over it now snub each other on the street. Some 20 state legislatures have considered bills to control the curriculum or abolish it. Angry parents are banding together in POSSE (Parents Opposed to Sex and Sensitivity Education), SOS (Sanity on Sex), and MOMS (Mothers Organized for Moral Stability)."[47]

So closed was the subject of sex to children that M. G. Lord noted that in the sixties, she and her peers had to resort to the Barbie doll "to unravel the mystery of gender differences." As Lord recalled, "Barbie with her torpedo orbs, and Ken with his mysterious genital bulge, were the extent of our exposure to the secrets of adulthood."[48]

The sexual revolution of the 1960s would provide the catalyst to finally push advertisers beyond the threshold of depicting sexual contact merely as caresses and kisses. Ads that began to feature more explicit sexual content served two purposes: to educate the mass market about the use of a product for or during sexual encounters, and brand positioning for products that sought to establish an image connected with sensuality.

The manufacturers of music sound systems were among the first advertisers to move sexual content to the next level. (Figure 9-27.) Although the

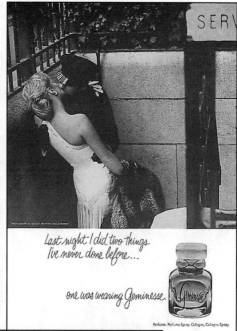

Figure 9-28. The old repertoires depicting caresses and kisses in ads to project sexual moods evolved to include more explicit variations by the 1970s.

1971   1977

use of music for setting a romantic mood had been a cliché of movies and television programs for decades, by depicting nude couples in ads such as Vivitar's "sensuous sound" and Sony's "great indoors," music was mass marketed as a part of the sexual experience.

By the 1970s even the repertoires of caresses and kisses depicted in ads expanded to reflect this new visual freedom in sex-sell marketing. (Figure 9-28.) Whereas in earlier decades Woodbury ads had created sexual tension primarily by the propinquity of the man and woman rather than with depictions of overtly passionate actions, advertisers now began to present a myriad of more sexually explicit scenarios. A White Shoulders fragrance ad from 1971 places a man atop a woman with his face upon her breast; her décolleté bodice barely remains in place on the visible side, implying the man has nuzzled the fabric down on the other to expose more than just her white shoulders to his kisses. Cri d'amour suffused the color photo of a nude man and woman in its 1975 ad to resemble an old master's painting, but the eroticism prevails nonetheless. In a 1977 ad Geminesse also presented a new approach to the scenario of caresses and kisses—adultery. The wealthy and, presumably, married woman is accompanying her handsome, young chauffeur down the stairwell to the servant's entrance and apparently on to his bedroom.

As for the boundaries of depicting the sex act itself, those too became blurred during the succeeding decades of the 1980s and 1990s. (Figure 9-29.) Intimations of oral sex and oral gratification were especially popular in ads by liquor manufacturers. In the 1984 Cointreau ad the woman kisses the end of the man's erect thumb, which extends upward from the neck of the bottle. Meanwhile at the other extreme, Gucci's raw version showing a man stripped to his briefs in the backseat of a car with a woman leaning her face into his lap brought criticism even from the editors of *Advertising Age.*[49]

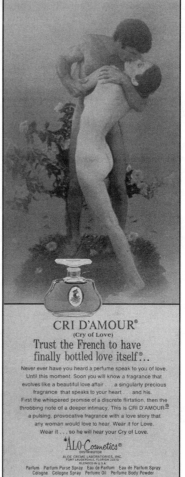

1975

Figure 9-29. Graphic representations implying oral sex reached extreme proportions by the 1980s and 1990s. Cointreau ad (detail) 1984, Gucci ad 1998.

Then, finally, there was the presentation of premarital sex. (Figure 9-30.) In staging the intimate scene of a sleeping couple in the 1997 Ralph Lauren Home Collection ad, the art director intentionally positioned the left hands of the man and woman so that the absence of wedding rings was evident. The discarded clothes on the floor and glimpses of the nude bodies entangled in the bed linens leave no doubt as to what had occurred the night before.

What was gained by these challenges to the taboo of sex? Researchers who have examined the use and effectiveness of sexual content in advertising tell us that "using sex in advertising is a very risky business." Wrote Thomas Whipple in *Advertising and Popular Culture:* "Its success or failure will depend upon the type of the product, the consumer's gender and personal bias towards sex, the sex of the model or presenter, the image of the sponsoring company, and the numerous 'sexy' treatments which are possible to portray in an advertisement."[50] For researcher Eric Clark, it means advertisers can count on angry letters and negative reactions from "older people and feminists," while on the other hand, for a younger, targeted audience—male or female—brand recall would be "significantly increased as the level of nudity of the model in the advertisement increased."[51] "Sex doesn't sell," wrote James Twitchell, "but it does capture attention."[52] So far as the marketers were concerned, when that attention connects a life style, a mood, or an image to a product, the target customer will respond and the sales will come. For three decades, Calvin Klein has masterfully used depictions in advertising that have been interpreted variously as sexual foreplay (Escape ads), group sex (Obsession ads), straight sex (Eternity ads), homosexuality (Obsession ads), pedophilia (CK Jeans ads), and masturbation (CK underwear ads), all while battling opposing social forces. Brand recognition—and sales—have been stupendous for him.

In answering the question "Shock values: do they sell?" a 1995 *Women's Wear Daily* editorial concluded about sex in advertising: "The worst thing is

not to have anybody comment. When you know a brand you're more likely to buy it. You'll always turn some people off, but those people you turn off may never have bought the product anyhow."[53]

Figure 9-30. Depending upon the reader's perspective, a 1997 Ralph Lauren Home Collection ad either depicted a one-night stand or a co-habitating couple; wedding rings are clearly absent. (Detail of ad.)

Conclusion: Reflecting and Overturning Social Values with Advertising

The argument is an old one: does advertising reflect and support the values of society or does advertising undermine and change society?

For a great many marketers, the answer was not so black and white. In the case of manufacturers and distributors of products such as chewing gum, cigarettes, and alcoholic beverages, monumental marketing and public relations battles had to be fought to overturn entrenched social stigmas that deterred the sale of their goods. In some instances state and federal laws, including a constitutional amendment, had to be changed before market share could be achieved. For any marketer of these kinds of products to successfully convert a social taboo into accepted behavior, even if still regarded as a vice or bad habit, was a stellar accomplishment. By the end of the twentieth century, the fact that so many women ordinarily chewed gum, smoked, and drank may have been anathema to social critics, but to mass marketers, such results were a tribute to the efficacy of their advertising strategies. Here, then, is where the lines blend from black and white to gray; for many mass marketers, advertising contributed first to the undermining of social values in order for them to introduce products or expand market share, and then reflected the new society it helped create in order to sustain mass consumption.

Yet, certain social values were more resistant to change than others and most marketers steered clear of subjects that might create controversy, especially themes involving politics, religion, and, most of all, sex. Of course, advertising was used to sell the product of politics (political candidates and election results) and religion (church attendance and religious events), but sex was another issue entirely, both as a product and an ad theme. Until the last quarter of the century, the sex-sell of advertising ironically had always lagged behind the reality of social change. American puritanism became diluted more from the impacts of Hollywood and television, science and technology, and politics and jurisprudence than from the influences of sex-sell advertising. The tame and tentative repertoires and formulas for sex-sell ads that had been ventured by marketers in the teens and twenties did not change much during the following fifty or sixty years, even though society's attitude toward sex continued a steady transition away from Victorianism. This is not to say that the whole of American society shed its nineteenth-century inhibitions about sex. Indeed, throughout the twentieth century marketers knew only too well that a huge segment of the population was reactionary to the subject of sex in any form—in school health classes, in public library books, in movies or television programming, and in mass media. For the overwhelming majority of marketers, to lose any market share, let alone the possibility of such a large block of consumers, was not worth the price of being avant-garde or sexually provocative in their advertising. To preserve or enhance business, it was a safe bet for marketers to appear benign, even trite, in their advertising to those consumers with more contemporary, tolerant views toward sex in order to appear socially correct to those who were not tolerant of the subject. The former group might be indifferent to an innocuous ad, but the latter group could become rabid at the slightest hint of sexual content in ads.

Still, some advertisers were willing to chance the sex-sell approach, especially those that marketed brand images of modern style, such as fashion and fragrances, or contemporary life style, such as distillers or travel services. Any public relations backlash would most likely come from groups and individuals outside the target customer base. Conservative groups, for instance, might have decried the use of sexy youths in provocative advertising for Calvin Klein jeans, but retailers responded by moving the racks of CK merchandise to center aisles and happily ringing up the sales as young people clamored for the brand label. Even at the end of the century, the subject of sex as a theme in advertising could be a significant gamble for a marketer, even when the product itself was for sexual safety and health. For example, despite months of reports in 1998 and 1999 on President Clinton's adulterous affair in the White House, with all the lurid details of breast fondling and oral sex being broadcast on TV newscasts, condom manufacturers struggled to get even generic ads accepted by mainstream magazines and network television.

Hence, in the changing panorama of twentieth-century American culture, advertising simultaneously reflected and helped alter social values. Certainly, most marketers had a much greater vested interest in preserving the status quo of the social order, especially those manufacturers and retailers that targeted traditional homemakers, wives, and mothers. Nevertheless, some marketers had no choice but to undertake the dismantling of social taboos if their businesses were to survive and thrive; to overcome the odds they enlisted the persuasion, cajoling, nudging, berating, and enticing of advertising. The efforts of these peddlers of vice and bad habits helped create and expand huge industries and fueled the progress of an enormous American mass market, and in their own limited way, ultimately influenced the evolution of American society toward the twenty-first century.

─Chapter 10

TURNING
THE TABLES
ON MEN

Popular culture and the use of the beautiful woman in marketing
• The Arrow Man • The ideal attentive male • Images of father
• Marketing male heroes and idols • The sexual objectification of
the American male • Advertising and masculine sexuality: men's
swimwear, underwear and fragrances • Representations of the
emasculated male

Even the most cursory glance at the ads illustrated throughout this book, shows that the pretty woman has been a prevalent and potent visual device in advertising all through the twentieth century. The preceding chapter outlined several ad themes using the female image—the purpose of each theme being to reach a target customer to promote the benefits of a product or service, or to enhance a brand image. The beauty and health industries used pretty models to establish standards of feminine beauty and as guides to perpetually redefine those standards in order to market products with a planned obsolescence. The world of fashion has always been a realm of contrived aesthetics and has required the image of a beautiful woman to elevate its craft to an art. Women in business were sent the message in ads that beauty and style should be used as a competitive advantage for corporate success. The Happy Homemaker was rarely shown as anything but attractive, irrespective of the demanding household chore in which she may be engaged.

Whereas feminists have blamed "men's institutions and institutional power" for perpetuating American women's preoccupation with beauty,[1] a great many women subscribe to a different perspective. Writer Norman Mailer has often been quoted in his assessment that: "Women dress for other women; women do their hair for other women. It's competitive as hell. Among every hundred women, there will be a few who set the trends. The rest will follow like slaves, and all complain that men are getting superficial. We men go for beauty because we have no option. All the women pointed us toward it. It's not easy for a man to say, I'd like to get out of this rat race and settle with one woman who has virtues."[2]

Whether the prodigious number of pretty women used as images in advertising stems from the influence of sexist men in a male-dominated ad industry, society's gender-role socialization of girls, a manufacturer's vested interest in selling beauty-related products and services, or any combination of these, the formula worked. Decade after decade the pretty woman depicted in ads showed other women how they should or could look—and behave, whether stirring a pot in the kitchen, scouring a bathtub, nurturing the kids, or going out on the town in the newest cocktail dress.

1910

1920

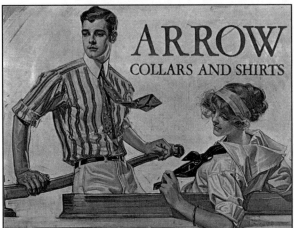

1912

Figure 10-1. In the first decades of the century, the Arrow Man as depicted by illustrator J. C. Leyendecker represented the epitome of ideal masculine beauty for millions of American women.

Marketing "Male Pulchritude"

It wasn't all as one-sided as it may first appear. In 1929, Christine Frederick wondered why "advertising to women does not exploit male pulchritude."[3] In actuality, many advertisers already had learned the lesson decades earlier and were not hesitant to play that card frequently. One shining example from the early years of advertising was the Arrow Man. (Figure 10-1.) Created by the illustrator J. C. (Joseph Christian) Leyendecker in 1905, the handsome, square-jawed men used in ads for Cluett, Peabody, and Company, makers of Arrow detachable shirt collars, would set the standard for masculine looks and demeanor for almost forty years. As biographer Michael Shau noted in his 1974 monograph on Leyendecker, women especially responded to the Cluett, Peabody ads, judging from the volume of mail sent to the company's corporate offices. "In one month in the early 1920s," Shau noted, "the Arrow Man received 17,000 fan letters, gifts, marriage proposals, and notes threatening suicide—a deluge surpassing even Rudolf [*sic*] Valentino's mail at the star's apex."[4] Ironically, the model for the Arrow Man was the young artist's lover, with whom he was to eventually share fifty years together.

For most women, masculine beauty extended beyond the superficial ideals of "tall, dark, and handsome." There were the many trappings of masculinity that could transcend the physiological: the beauty of character, action, purpose, and the masculine roles valued in American society. To a great extent, these defining characteristics became idealized in their own right based on the qualities of manliness espoused in contemporary literature, movies, and mass media and preached by society's leaders.

1925   1958   1981

Figure 10-2. The theme of attracting and holding a man's attention was used as a promise or a warning by advertisers.

Certainly, men often found themselves confounded and perplexed as to how they might live up to these idealized standards. Women were seldom willing to spell out the priorities and perceived shortcomings of their man's masculinity any more than they might openly object to his physical anomalies. Yet they did complain about their disappointments—major and minor—with the men in their lives across backyard fences to neighbors, in sewing circles, over lunch with friends, and in letters to the editors of periodicals.

For manufacturers and service industries, many of women's complaints about men became marketing opportunities. One special complaint, that of neglect, served well as a theme in advertising. That women suffered inattentiveness from the men in their lives—fathers, brothers, teachers, beaus, and husbands—was an age-old argument. In 1895 the inimitable Edward Bok wrote an editorial in his *Ladies' Home Journal* denouncing men who ignored their wives by hiding behind the newspaper at the breakfast table. "It is little to ask of them that in this matter, at least, they show that sense of respect to their wives which is their due," he chided.[5] The following year, a contributing editor advised men in the *Ladies' Home Journal* that the occasional "dumb, voiceless present" was not enough to make up for their lack of attention day in and day out to a woman and her needs. "A man never seems to be able to get it into his head that in order to obtain the supremest pleasure from an act of thoughtfulness to his wife, he must be, if necessary, wholly unselfish and give it to her in her line, and the way she wants it, and the way you know she wants it—if you would only stop to think."[6]

Advertisers knew too well this particular plight of many American women and responded by creating one of the fantasies women especially dreamed of—a man's complete attention and adulation. (Figure 10-2.) The images in advertising of men adoring women were promises to female consumers. If you buy this brand of soap, toothpaste, or soft drink, the ads

Figure 10-3. Women readily connected with the warm, personal approach used by TV spokesmen even if they were not stereotypically masculine or good looking. Ad 1953.

implied, your man—or the man of your dreams—will adore you. "When you neglect to care for your skin, you are running the risk of being neglected yourself," warned the copy in a 1925 Pompeian Night Cream ad. A 1958 ad for Pepsi promised a lifetime of sharing, but only if you stay "slim, trim and lovely," which its low-calorie soft drink could help you do. In 1981 Gillette modified a famous line from a Bogart/Bacall film to read, "If you want to get someone's attention, just whistle," only in this case it was smoothly shaved legs that did the job.

The men depicted in these ad scenarios were not always on a par with the handsome beings seen in ads such as those for Arrow shirts. After all, women well understood that handsome is as handsome does, so good looks were not a prerequisite for them to appreciate personal qualities such as attentiveness. Certainly this worked to the advantage of TV spokesmen such as Arthur Godfrey, Art Linkletter, Ed Sullivan, Phil Silvers, or advertising's many other hawkers with less than matinee idol features. (Figure 10-3.) Their success, both in print and on TV, was due to the appearance of sincere attentiveness to women. A 1957 *Printers' Ink* editorial noted, for example, that Arthur Godfrey is such a successful spokesman because he is "a man who gives a listener or viewer a personal warmth and friendliness."[7] In addition, use of the pronoun "you" in ad copy and TV scripts emphasized a personal touch with which viewers could connect.

Of course, the opposite scenario worked just as effectively for some advertisers. Instead of presenting the dream of most every woman—the devoted, attentive man—ads sometimes depicted the heartbreak of neglect, or even the worst case, abandonment. The use of such scare tactics, known in the biz as "negative appeal," has been an effective method of advertising since the nineteenth century. (Figure 10-4.) Wrote Roland Marchand of these ad narratives: "Scare copy posited a universe in which the fate of each consumer lay in the hands of external disinterested forces and unsympathetic, judgmental observers, a world of normative expectations applied with unmerciful severity. By contrast, the advertiser was solicitous and caring, a friend in need."[8] The wrong lipstick could cause your man to kiss you only "hastily, gingerly"; underwear that "neither looks nor smells attractive" could be "what's wrong with marriage"; your "loneliness and discontent" might be because your breath is "off-color"; or "morning mouth" may scare off your man first thing each day. The subhead of a 1942 Listerine ad summed it up with the warning to all women, "suspect yourself." Once the scare drama was in place, to the rescue with simple solutions came ads from Tangee Lipstick, Lux Detergent, Listerine Antiseptic, Chlorodent Toothpaste, and an indeterminable number of other consumer products with guaranteed answers and favorable results.

Marketing the Paternal Image

Another image of men that readily captured women's attention was that of the father figure. In early ads, representations of the father being presented his newborn popularly depicted him as remote, hesitant, or clumsy. (Figure 10-5.) For example, in a 1916 Malt-Nutrine ad the father is reluctant to even enter the room where a cheerful nurse coos at the newborn. In a 1922 Kuppenheimer ad the beaming papa strikes a pose of pride and confidence—

1934

1938

1942

1953

Figure 10-4. Negative appeal ads subjected women to all manner of scare tactics, including the threat of neglect by their men, unless the advertiser's words of advice were heeded.

feet apart, shoulders back, and hands on hips—as he grins down at his achievement. An Aetna ad from 1931 makes light of a young, new father who nervously holds his firstborn with "pride giving way to panic." These and countless similar versions in ads delighted women who would have found such images irresistible.

Contrary to social mores and accepted standards of American masculinity, for much of this century many fathers enjoyed child nurturing. As Nancy Friday observed, though, even at the end of the twentieth century, "mass public opinion/sentiment is against them."[9] She argued that the stigma against dads in the nursery was very much the fault of women themselves. Even well-educated career women did not want their men in the nursery, preferring instead to cling to the "exaggerated vision" of fathers as the family's providers and protectors. Friday proposed that "The argument isn't whether men have or don't have nurturing qualifications . . . that has been proven. The issue is that we can afford to abandon the traditional womanly-looking mothers/women to the competitive workplace far more easily than we can part with our fantasy of Big Daddy. . . . How interesting that the look of a man with a papoose is more upsetting than that of the corporate female captain."[10] Most sociologists and researchers, though, place the blame for perpetuating the stigma against the nurturing father with men. In *Boys Will Be Boys*, Myriam Miedzian wrote: "In the traditional family being a good father means primarily being a good provider. . . . Since traditional fathers are not expected to nurture their children in the sense of directly caring for their physical and emotional needs, there is no need to develop the same degree of empathy, sensitivity, and caring in little boys as in little girls."[11] Psychiatrist Harvey Kaye went so far as to suggest in *Male Survival* that perpetuating such stigmas could not be helped since the "psychosexual predisposition" of the male exists "in utero, or at least prior to the introduction of any form of social conditioning."[12]

Thus, in American society the nursery and the care of an infant have largely been regarded as the domain of the mother. She bore him and it is

It's a Boy
—and your wife's doing splendidly

1916

Kuppenheimer
GOOD CLOTHES

1922

His FUTURE
—will you handle it as awkwardly?

ÆTNA-IZE

1931

Figure 10-5. The father image used in early ads often represented men as remote, hesitant, or clumsy.

she who will mostly feed, clean, and nurture him in his early years. Yet, when advertisers occasionally did choose to depict the father nurturing an infant, most readers probably perceived this to be a temporary situation. (Figure 10-6.) The mother somehow must be out of the picture only briefly, and dad's nurturing would cease upon her return. In a perfect world as represented in advertising there are no male primary care givers; all children have the ideal, gender-appropriate set of original parents. (The exception would be ads for insurance or funeral businesses, which might depict a distressed single parent in the crisis of a lost spouse.)

For advertisers who chose to depict a father nurturing older children, the traditional narratives were overwhelmingly prevalent. (Figure 10-7.) Ads usually depict the father and son bonding in masculine rituals such as fishing, hunting, sports, and horseplay. On the other hand, the father and daughter bonding is most often represented in a domestic scene or, as with the British Sterling ad, in a presentation of daddy's little princess.

Only in research of the last quarter of the century have alternatives to these stereotyped roles been suggested by child-care experts. In behavioral studies researchers have documented the gender-role socialization of fathers to sons and fathers to daughters as being vastly different beginning in the earliest phases of childhood. It is the boy who is most likely to be treated

"Colic, nothing! She has insomnia!"

Rexall
DRUGS

Figure 10-6. Since most women preferred to think of the nursery as their exclusive domain, representations of the nurturing father were rarely used in ads. Ad 1947.

Figure 10-7. Images of fathers with older children in ads overwhelming represented traditional themes. Fathers and sons bonded in masculine pursuits, whereas daughters were depicted in domestic roles or as daddy's little princess.

roughly and tossed about, while little girls are spoken to softly and handled with greater care.[13] However, researchers such as Myriam Miedzian have determined that: "Men who feel very secure in their traditional masculine traits are more able and willing to confront the enormous social pressure against men's becoming primary caregivers. They no longer have to pretend. They can be full human beings."[14] Miedzian concluded that "for the sons of nurturant fathers, achieving a masculine identity is easier, not harder."[15] Meanwhile, most American men remained reluctant to modify the gender-role socialization they had learned as boys. The societal messages all around them demanded otherwise. "There is an apparent need for a definition and reaffirmation of both masculinity and femininity in our culture," wrote

Harvey Kaye in 1974. To this purpose he published a "masculinity index" that did not include any aspect of the nurturing father.[16]

It was this non-nurturing father figure that was represented most in the images and narratives of ads, even at the end of the century. In a 1988 study of male parent images in advertising, Rita Hubbard reviewed more than twelve hundred ads from *Parents, Parenting,* and *Children* magazines over a consecutive six months. "Only 27 ads showed children with fathers," she wrote, "most of them presenting fathers engaged in behaviors considered traditionally male, such as showing a boy how to use or install equipment." Only five ads showed a father nurturing a child: one bathing a child, one preparing to cook for a child, two feeding an infant, and one cuddling an infant. In her conclusion, Hubbard noted: "Viewers construct gender meanings from advertising's abstract representations of acceptable gender displays and ritual actions. With regard to advertising's representation of male parenting, the major question to be resolved is whether advertising is representing the present repertoires of daily life or is perpetuating regressive forms of social relations."[17] Indeed, this has been the recent debate among psychologists, psychiatrists, sociologists, child-care professionals, researchers, and even everyday dads and moms. But whether the role of a non-nurturing father was a repertoire of daily life or a regressive form of social relations, both signposts meant the same thing to advertisers. That is, the female consumer of the 1990s would respond to images of fathers in traditional roles as effectively as had her great-grandmother.

There was one aspect of traditional fatherhood that advertisers had abandoned by the middle of the century: corporal punishment. In American

1928

Figure 10-8. Societal views of the father figure as administrator of corporal punishment were so commonplace that the theme was used as an everyday subject in advertising.

1939

1941

society, the attitude of "spare the rod and spoil the child" had been so prevalent that it was seldom seriously questioned. Only in the 1870s did the first chapters of the Societies for the Prevention of Cruelty to Children begin their campaigns for social change. To SPCC members, spanking a child versus savagely beating a child was a distinction without a difference since the result was the same in either instance—a brutalized child. As data began to be collected by SPCC chapters and social welfare organizations, child abuse became recognized as a "gendered phenomenon" linked to the man's role of patriarchal disciplinarian. According to Linda Gordon, "Because men spend, on the whole, so much less time with children than do women, what is remarkable is not that women are violent toward children but that men are responsible for nearly half the child abuse."[18] That abused children often grew up to become child abusers became widely publicized, and advertisers began to avoid any hint of the socially sensitive subject.

From today's perspective, it seems astounding that severe corporal punishment was so commonplace in the first half of the century—not only in the home but in public institutions such as schools, community boy's clubs, and religious organizations—that advertisers were at ease to use it as a theme of everyday life. (Figure 10-8.) Representations of the father figure as administrator of corporal punishment were menacing enough without having to resort to depictions of actual violence. A 1928 Ivory ad illustrated an irate father who had "thundered into the bathroom breathing fire and looking daggers—going to spank" merely because the child was taking too long to bathe. A 1939 Castoria ad presented a minidrama in multiple frames depicting an angry father waving a hairbrush with which he was about to paddle his son—again—because the child refused to take a foul-tasting laxative. So commonly accepted was corporal punishment in these early years that advertisers even depicted the act as a humorous domestic scene. In 1941, a Texaco ad featured a little boy shoving a book into the seat of his pants as his father storms out of the house rolling up his sleeves and brandishing a leather strap because of a baseball through the window. In most of these types of ads, it is the father who inflicts the punishment. The mother either is depicted as helpless to protect her child or represents a buffer to the violence.

Among the many social changes that swept America during the late 1950s and into the 1960s was a reexamination of corporal punishment for children. States began to pass laws prohibiting corporal punishment in schools; national organizations such as the Kiwanis clubs advocated alternative discipline measures; editorials in mass-circulation forums ranging from *Redbook* to Ann Landers's columns colored corporal punishment as child abuse.[19] Advertisers recognized the change in the social wind and modified images of the patriarchal disciplinarian into more benign depictions. (Figure 10-9.) The Norman Rockwellesque tableau in a 1963 ad from Kellogg's

Figure 10-9. By the second half of the century, images of the father-punisher in advertising were more benign and suggestions of violent corporal punishment were scrupulously avoided. Ad 1963.

was typical of the new images of the father-punisher. It is still he who must administer discipline, although the punishment may now fit the crime in the mind of the reader who may imagine curbed TV or playtime privileges instead of physical abuse. For advertisers, the subject of the violent father-punisher had moved onto the social taboo list.

Marketing Male Heroes

Images of male heroes were among those that remained at the top of the list for advertisers. Foremost among these, especially to women in the teens and the forties, was that of the soldier. Although the age-old cliché is that women cannot resist a man in a uniform, it mostly has been in times of war that images of soldiers were widely used in advertising. Under the guise of patriotism—sometimes genuine, sometimes pretentious—advertisers used representations of America's heroic soldier boys. Ad makers knew that such images touched everyone who viewed them, especially all the women who waited by the home fires.

Certainly such depictions were not new in history. War is one of the "three Ws," along with women and work, that define men, wrote Warren Farrell.[20] The commercial appeal of representations of the soldier is evidenced by the innumerable depictions of warriors and battles on artifacts from most all ancient civilizations. Representations of these heroes have decorated everything from utilitarian kitchen crockery to the walls of temples and palaces. In the nineteenth and twentieth centuries, the particular importance of the images of contemporary soldiers, according to George Mosse, is that they "provide a climax to a concept of modern masculinity." This masculinity embodies "quiet strength and self-control" with "moral fitness" and a "spirit of adventure."[21] All of these qualities especially culminated in the image of the soldier of the First World War. Wrote Mosse of the doughboy: "Although the warrior image of masculinity had existed ever since the

Figure 10-10. During World War I images of the heroic doughboy were used in all types of ads targeting women, whether the message was relevant to the war or not. Ads 1917–18.

French Revolution and the Napoleonic Wars, the Great War further accentuated certain aspects of masculinity that of themselves did not have to be warlike but—like willpower, hardness, or perseverance—were qualities that peacetime society prized as well."[22]

America entered World War I almost three years after hostilities had opened in Europe. In the nineteen months (April 1917 through November 1918) that the United States was at war with Germany, the mass media blanketed the nation with photographs, illustrations, news reports, editorials, movie dramas, and newsreels about the war. The tragedy was brought into every American home in unprecedented graphic detail.

Advertisers had the advantage of enjoying the halo effect of the doughboy without having to contend with the realities of the death and destruction of warfare. (Figure 10-10.) Some advertisers merely inserted illustrations of soldiers into ads with no specific link or reference to the war, as in the Gorham silverware ad. Fisk Tires included a soldier flirting with two young women in a car, but the military connection was made only in the sidebar copy about War Savings Stamps and with the WSS pavilion shown in the background. Most marketers, though, chose a direct approach by depicting soldiers and war narratives in ads. The intent was most certainly to target consumers who either had a family member in the war or at least knew someone who was in the service, which would have included most of the American population in 1918. The Iver Johnson Arms and Cycle Works suggested in an ad that the "thoughtful soldier" would present his wife with a revolver for her protection while he was away. A Hinds skin cream ad recommended that "soldier boys should have it in your kits" for relief of sunburn and windburn, and Ivory Soap and Kodak ads showed how little things from home could make a difference to the boys holed up in camps far away. Such ads were swathed in patriotic appeal that invited a double consumption—home use and sending a bit of home "over there."

One striking, full-color ad that did strive to remind consumers of the soldier's sacrifice was produced only a month before Armistice by Bauer and Black, makers of surgical dressings. (Figure 10-11.) The dramatic visual allegory of soldiers killed in battle and who now "lie in Flanders fields" was startling among the other innocuous pages of the November 1918 issue of the *Ladies' Home Journal.* The accompanying poem, "We Shall Not Sleep," was written by a Canadian officer who had been killed in the second battle of Ypres and was buried in Flanders fields. For those consumers who might have complained about the shortages and rationing caused by the war, this ad would have had a profound impact on their consciences, while at the same time elevating the company's brand name to the league of true patriotism. "Is it conceivable," asked the closing paragraph of copy, "that we shall break faith with those who die for us?" In other words, the inconvenience of some empty store shelves can and must be endured—for them, our heroes.

In the years following the Great War, historians had already begun to refer to it as the war to end all wars. They were proven wrong all too soon. In September 1939, Germany invaded Poland and the first shots of World War

Figure 10-11. Depictions of the fallen hero were used to convey public service messages about America's wartime needs and conditions. Sponsoring advertisers received a halo benefit that served branding and goodwill marketing initiatives. Ad 1918.

Figure 10-12. Due to the lengthy duration of the Second World War, images of soldiers used in advertising not only connected the product to the patriotic cause but reminded civilian consumers of the need for self-sacrifice. Ad 1943.

II rang out. During the following two years America became a de facto participant in the war through such policies as lend-lease and embargoes against the Axis powers. Some American men even joined Canadian and British military units. Daily reports on the war filled the mass media, which in 1940 included radio and even some early television broadcasts. Pictures of soldiers were everywhere—except in consumer advertising. Many Americans opposed entry into the war and that made depictions of soldiers too politically controversial for business. Officially, America was neutral, and displays of patriotism were limited to the symbolic eagle, Statue of Liberty, or flag.

All that abruptly changed in December 1941 when Japan attacked the U.S. fleet in Pearl Harbor, and America was thrust into World War II as an active participant. Unlike the brief, though terrible, nineteen months the U.S. fought in the First World War, this global calamity would last three and a half years for Americans.

Advertisers responded almost instantly. The January and February 1942 issues of magazines were filled with ads depicting soldiers. Over the lengthy duration of the war, a number of themes emerged that advertisers adapted to fit their respective marketing messages. Manufacturers of consumer products that were typically used by soldiers, such as tobacco and foodstuffs, especially included images of the soldier in ads. (Figure 10-12.) This marketing approach achieved two objectives. First, the hero became an anonymous but significant endorser of the product or brand; second, consumers were reminded that their home sacrifices were inconsequential by comparison to those of the frontline soldier.

During the war years the soldier hero stood out from crowds of civilian men by virtue of his uniform. The battle ribbons on the khaki shirtfront or the white naval blouse were evidence of dutiful manhood for all women to acknowledge. These beautiful young men were their knights in shining armor brimming with masculinity and romance. (Figure 10-13.)

Advertisers did not always represent the soldier in uniform as a hero, though. The military was a great social leveler, with rich and poor, educated and illiterate, urban and rural, men and boys all standing shoulder to shoulder with a common objective. Having passed the scrutiny of recruiters and endured training, the soldier had won the right to wear a uniform. His dignity of manhood was confirmed by the particular styles, colors, and insignia of his costume, and was displayed for all to see. On the other hand, the institution of the military required services of its members beyond the battlefield. As a comic relief to the mayhem of combat, advertisers sometimes depicted scenarios such as K. P. (kitchen police) and other less romanticized duties of a uniformed soldier. (Figure 10-14.)

Nor was every uniform depicted in ads meant to be an adulation of the warrior and his respective manhood. Early in the war, advertisers sometimes represented the enemy in uniform, as a bogeyman or even a caricature of ignominy. (Figure 10-15.) In those instances the soldier in uniform, mindlessly goose-stepping or bowing in subservience to an imperial monarch, is the antithesis of the ideal American hero, and the uniform of the enemy becomes a theatrical costume representing villainy, akin to the black hat of

Figure 10-13. Depictions of the hand-some soldier in uniform bespoke knights in shining armor brimming with a warrior's masculinity and romance to the female audience. Ads 1944.

western novels and movies. "Them versus us" is reinforced in these visual narratives, and the branded logo is featured as one of the good guys.

The most significant part of the romance of the idealized warrior emanated from the rigors of his purpose—to defend his nation. The offer to sacrifice one's life is awe-inspiring in and of itself, but the flip side of that, to take another's life, is regarded by many soldiers as the more terrifying.[23] Both are heroic sacrifices that advertisers presented to American consumers in numerous depictions of battle scenes. (Figure 10-16.) As readers viewed such ads they would feel, perhaps, anxiety for the safety of a loved one who was a soldier, but also humility for the warrior's courage, and pride that he would do this on their behalf.

Figure 10-14. Depictions of the less heroic aspects of military service provided comic relief to the barrage of images of war's mayhem featured daily in news reports. Ads 1943.

Figure 10-15. Not all depictions of warriors in uniform were imbued with heroism. To the American audience, images of enemy soldiers represented the antithesis of the ideal American hero. Ads 1942.

The emotionalism attached to the soldier and the job he had to do was also used as a theme in ads to motivate civilians to do their part. Copywriter Nelson Metcalf became infuriated at hearing civilians gripe about train service during World War II, so he decided to "write an ad that would make everybody feel ashamed to complain."[24] (Figure 10-17.) "The Kid in Upper 4," created for the New Haven Railroad in 1942, not only achieved Metcalf's objective but really brought it all home to the heart for many Americans. The copy opens with "It is 3:42 a.m. on a troop train," and continues with a narrative of a teenage soldier's mixed feelings and thoughts on all he is leaving behind: "The taste of hamburgers and pop ... the feel of driving a roadster over a six-lane highway ... a dog named Shucks, or Spot, or Barnacle Bill. The pretty girl who writes so often ... that gray-haired man, so proud and awkward at the station ... the mother who knit the socks he'll

Figure 10-16. Graphic depictions of dramatic battle scenes were used in ads to remind consumers of the soldier's purpose and sacrifice to the nation. Pepperell ad 1942, Grapefruit Juice ad 1943.

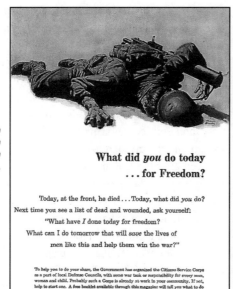

Figure 10-17. Poignant images of the soldier's sacrifices helped motivate the public to do its part and to stay the course. New Haven Railroad ad 1942, Magazine Publishers ad 1943.

wear soon. Tonight he's thinking them over. There's a lump in his throat. And maybe—a tear fills his eye. It doesn't matter, Kid. Nobody will see . . . it's too dark." Civilians were then reminded that if they had to stand on a train so a soldier could sit, or wait in a diner so a soldier could eat, it was "the least we can do to pay a mighty debt of gratitude."

At the other end of the motivational scale were public service ads. One exceptional example was produced by the Magazine Publishers group in 1943. The image is of a GI who has just been killed in action—the ultimate sacrifice. "Today, at the front, he died," begins the copy. As a witness to this tragedy the reader becomes personally involved in the message of the ad. "What did you do today . . . for freedom?" the ad header asks readers, reminding them to do their part to help win the war.

Advertisers also used views of the front to mark the progress of America's war efforts. In 1944 and 1945, Coca-Cola ran a series of ads that illustrated

Figure 10-18. As the war progressed toward its conclusion, marketers such as Coca-Cola bolstered home front morale with ads that depicted lighter moments in the lives of American GIs far from home. Ads 1944–45.

GIs in places that a short while earlier had been occupied by, or imminently threatened by, the enemy. These kinds of ads provided renewed hope for the war-weary nation. (Figure 10-18.)

As the ordeal of the war inched its way to a conclusion in 1944 and 1945, advertisers confidently used the scenario that so many Americans dreamed of—the homecoming. (Figure 10-19.) The nation stood on the threshold of a return to normalcy, and advertisers began to position their brands, products, and services as a part of that way of life for which the soldier had fought and the civilian had endured deprivations.

Even after the last uniform disappeared from the pages of postwar advertising, the standards of American manhood would continue to be exemplified by the warrior. Historians have described the need of many American presidents to prove their "manhood" by endorsing war: Lyndon Johnson's fear that "his manhood might be inadequate" contributed to the escalation of the Vietnam War; Ronald Reagan's intervention policy for Nicaragua was described as "machismo"; and George Bush's "wimp factor" was a motivating force in going to war with Iraq.[25] However, the disappointment of the outcome of the Korean conflict, capped by the national discontent with the Vietnam War, altered the way many Americans thought about government leaders and the methods and process of war. A distrust of official authority developed that was inconceivable during the two world wars. Despite this significant social change, the citizenry still continued to respect and admire the soldier and the qualities they had come to associate with his character.

For post–World War II advertisers the man in a uniform may have had sex appeal to women, he may have exemplified masculinity and all the idealized virtues associated with manliness, but he also represented war. The national crises of the two world wars were not manifested during the Korea, Vietnam, Granada, Persian Gulf, or Kosovo engagements. Since World War II, images

Figure 10-19. As the war drew to an end, advertisers provided renewed hope with representations of homecomings. Ads 1944–45.

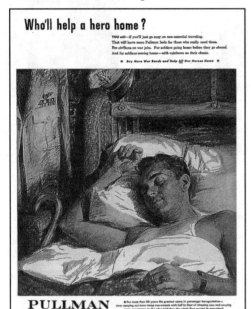

Charlie Chaplin, 1928

Fred MacMurray 1937

Ronald Reagan 1947

John Wayne 1953

Rock Hudson 1967

Orson Welles 1972

of soldiers have had no consumer marketing value; products and brand labels could not bask in the reflected glory of the warrior in advertising.

On the other hand, the halo effect of Hollywood's leading men has never diminished for advertisers. As is discussed in the next chapter, interest in movie stars reached a crescendo with the American public well before the First World War and continued to resonate with audiences throughout succeeding decades. The masses had an insatiable appetite for images and information about their favorite film stars. Observed an editor for *Vogue* in 1986: "We have always been obsessed with the lives of the stars. We read fan magazines, gossip columns, and unauthorized biographies, measuring the facts and fancies we find there against the ones we seek on screen."[26] For

Figure 10-20. Advertisers created a symbiotic relationship with Hollywood. Film celebrities endorsed commercial products, and movie studios received publicity for their stars.

advertisers, this keen interest in the lives and personalities of movie stars translated into a method of automatically capturing an audience with ads that featured these celebrities. (Figure 10-20.)

The importance of Hollywood's massive influence on society's view of men was twofold. First, men were intentionally objectified into sex symbols for the first time in American social history; second, ideas of masculinity began to be reinterpreted. The catalyst for both of these influences came with the appearance of Rudolph Valentino in the 1921 epic *The Four Horsemen of the Apocalypse*. Frederick Allen Lewis wrote shortly after the actor's early death that Valentino "had quickened the pulses of innumerable motion-picture addicts; with his sideburns and his passionate air, 'the sheik' had set the standard for masculine sex appeal."[27] This new standard was what later historians would define as androgyny. "Though Valentino was a predatory male," suggested George Mosse, "his dancer's body and languid posture signaled not a truly masculine but a more androgynous beauty that combined masculine brutality with an almost feminine tenderness."[28] This beautification and softening of the edges of the image of the American male had a powerful impact on women's ideas of masculinity and paved the way for the success of stars such as Douglas Fairbanks Jr., Tyrone Power, Alan Ladd, and William Holden. Into the 1950s and 1960s, noted Margo Jefferson, this line forked yet again and created "beautiful hunks" such as Rock Hudson and Burt Lancaster, "who were permitted flashes of thought or feeling so long as action dominated." Concurrent with this later Hollywood type of leading man emerged the "misfits" such as James Dean, Marlon Brando, and Montgomery Clift, with their "kinetic beauty that couldn't be separated from what they thought or felt."[29]

Figure 10-21. Early images of the nude male were presented in the form of product demonstrations.

1901

1917

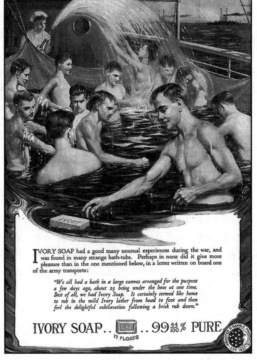

1919

1922

Figure 10-22. Following the women's sexual revolution of the 1920s, depictions of the nude male bather in ads were infused with eroticism to deliberately target women.

1934

1943

1996

This is not to say that the "man's man" stars such as Clark Gable, John Wayne, Gary Cooper, and Humphrey Bogart did not have great sex appeal, for they certainly did. Even decades after their deaths their images conjured up these ideals of no-nonsense masculinity and were magnets still for capturing the attention of women in advertising.

The Male Body as a Sex Object in Advertising

As many marketers had anticipated, the use of images of men in advertising could in and of itself attract the attention of women. For example, not all of J. C. Leyendecker's illustrations of the Arrow Man included a scenario that represented manly pursuits; most were, in fact, simply silhouetted portraits of the clean-cut, square-jawed, all-American male. The success of using depictions of attractive men in advertising to achieve a high level of response from women was recognized from the earliest part of the century. Surprisingly, early marketing efforts even daringly expanded this concept to include the use of titillating glimpses of the nude male body in consumer product ads.

Probably one of the first "safe" depictions of the unclad male was that of the bather, which made its first appearances in ads at the end of the

1917

1935

1938

Figure 10-23. The eroticism of the male figure clad in revealing swimwear provided an eye-catching image when advertising to women.

nineteenth century. The question for many, though, is whether the images were meant to be simply illustrative of product use or if they were intended to be provocative. Certainly no early marketing records seem to exist that document a deliberate strategy to target women with sexually enticing views of the nude male. In fact, the concept would have been alien to early ad men since, until about the time of the First World War, normal women were not thought to be sexual beings. The results of research into women's sexuality

1959

1969

1977

Figure 10-24. Since women purchased more than 70 percent of all men's underwear, manufacturers specifically targeted them in advertising.

Figure 10-25. Early ads for men's underwear were merely product presentations with any suggestions of eroticism airbrushed away. Mentor ad 1907, Chalmers ad 1917.

by Sigmund Freud and Havelock Ellis were still not widely known outside the scientific community. In addition, early depictions of the male bather were either functional, as with the demonstration photo used in the Melchers' Shower Yoke ad from 1901, or were aesthetic—subjective classical uses by illustrators. (Figure 10-21.) Still, it is hard to image, when examining, for example, the numerous depictions of men bathing in early Ivory Soap ads, that some discussions about the effect of the nude male on the female consumer had not occurred in the Procter & Gamble boardroom.

From the 1920s on, the use of the nude male bather in ads was most certainly intentional, complete with voyeuristic overtones. (Figure 10-22.) Even if marketers had never heard of Freud or Ellis, the success of love-story movies, romance novels, and confession magazines such as *True Story* had proven that women sexually fantasized about men. The question was how to take that next step beyond just showing the handsome Arrow Man face; that is, how to show some skin in a sexually suggestive way. Certainly for an ad to depict Martex or Cannon towels in use did not require a demonstration by a nude male, and the eroticism in the J-Dream ad of the nude male writhing in ecstasy to the pulse of a shower system and the stroke of his hand all over his body was a far cry from the demure demonstration of Melchers' Shower Yoke ninety-five years earlier.

Another opportunity for advertisers to display male flesh to women consumers was with the swimsuit. (Figure 10-23.) Men's swimwear in the early twentieth century consisted of a one-piece suit with a tank top and knee-length shorts. Still, that allowed a lot of skin to be openly revealed at beaches and riverside parks. When Carl Jantzen invented the process for a lightweight, stretchable knit fabric in 1915, skintight swimwear immediately replaced the voluminous poplin and serge pieces for both men and women. (See chapter 6.) Through the 1920s and into the 1930s men's swimsuits

Figure 10-26. Even the later—and briefer—versions of the union suit were advertised in a prosaic manner. Ad 1915.

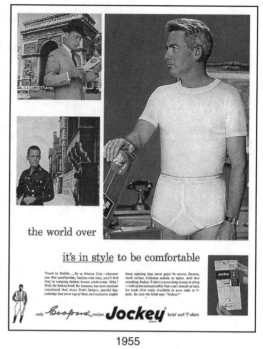

1939   1944   1955

Figure 10-27. Derived from European designs of men's swimwear, the brief was introduced in America in the 1930s. In the tradition of earlier ads for men's underwear, depictions of the brief were largely neutered.

became ever briefer and more revealing. The neck and arm openings of tanks became wider and the shorts continued to inch up the thigh until, in the early 1930s, the topless brief was introduced from France. Variations on men's swimwear designs remained fairly fixed in rise and lengths until the 1960s. Then, influenced by the brevity of men's Olympic swimwear, the bikini style began to appear on American beaches.

Unlike images of nude bathers—at least prior to the 1970s—men in swimwear could be shown interacting with women. This added a dimension of sexual fantasy that advertisers would exploit repeatedly. The muscular lifeguard in the 1917 Hinds ad is not only allowed to bring his semidressed body next to the young woman, but he actually has an excuse for holding her as he teaches her to swim. The bronzed young man in the background of a 1935 Spud cigarette ad complements the scantily clad woman in the foreground with a baroque sexual tension. In ads for men's swimwear, depictions of youthful jocks with exceptional builds and uninhibited exhibitionism established for women what their fantasy men should look like. Ironically, in a true turning of the tables, men's advocacy groups such as OASIS (Organized Against Sexism and Institutionalized Stereotypes)

Figure 10-28. Other methods of advertising men's underwear without any sexual connotations included using cartoon characters or insetting the product as a still life. (Details of ads.) Hanes ad 1957, Jockey ad 1959.

Figure 10-29. By the late 1950s, styles of men's underwear were specifically designed to be a sexy fashion accessory. Yet ads were still as innocuous as earlier product presentations. Ad 1959.

began to complain about these objectifying ads in the 1980s and 1990s. "Like women," complained OASIS, "men must endure impossible comparison in ads to the ideal body.'"[30]

One particular type of men's image that evolved from product mannequin to sex object was the underwear model. In the nineteenth and early twentieth centuries men's underwear ads specifically targeted women as consumers. (Figure 10-24.) After all, it was the housewife who purchased such basic commodities for her family. Even at the end of the century, marketing research indicated that as much as 78 percent of men's underwear was bought by women.[31]

In the beginning the product was the union suit—so called not because it was made by union labor but because the bottom drawers were united with knit tops in one piece. Ads depicting these garments were little more than pedestrian product presentations. (Figure 10-25.) No sexual mystique was present in the images of the male models used to demonstrate the practical fit and function of the union suit. In fact, any hints of the genital bulge in photographs were most often airbrushed away and then touched up with painted seams that denied any contours of the male anatomy.

For summer months, the union suit was made into a short-sleeved, knee-length version or separate undershirt and drawers, both made of lighter-weight fabrics than winter long johns. Ads for the more revealing "step-ins" were just as prosaic as for the longer styles. In the 1915 version shown in Figure 10-26 the models are presented in an environment where men who are strolling about outdoors in their underwear provoke no notice from their peers. In case there might be any doubt about this scene, the copy tells readers that these are "red-blooded, right-living men who find clean fun in keen sport, from tramping to camping." Nevertheless, these "droopy-drawers"—as later ads would refer to the garments—were also depicted without any evident anatomical detail of the wearer or hints of sexuality.

The design of men's underwear was revolutionized in 1935. Inspired by the new, snug-fitting brief styles of men's swimwear, which had been popular in Europe the year before, the Wisconsin firm of Cooper & Sons launched the Jockey brief. The style was a huge success, and other makers soon introduced their own versions. (Figure 10-27.) Still, ad men could not seem to comfortably find a way to promote the product. Locker-room scenes of men discussing their underwear were a contrived stretch. For women who might be drawn to these relatively sexless ads, at least the pedantic list of product benefits might register with them, even if the potential sexuality did not. In fact, the potential sexuality of men's underwear,

Figure 10-30. To broaden the base of consumers, men's underwear ads featured professional athletes wearing fashion styles to reach men who were reluctant to give up their white cotton briefs. Ad 1977.

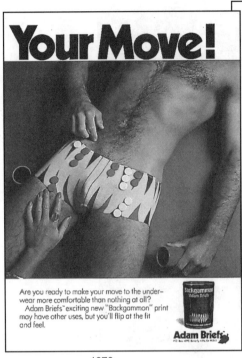

1976

1985

1996

Figure 10-31. Influenced by the sexual revolution and the emergence of the new feminism of the 1960s and 1970s, images in men's underwear ads became increasingly erotic.

either as a marketing device or an end-user benefit, would lie dormant till the end of the 1950s largely due to concerted efforts by advertisers to eliminate any vestige of eroticism in photographs and illustrations. Pictures of men in their underwear for ads were simply not supposed to be sexy. Mostly the models were statically posed, resembling more the plaster mannequins in department stores than real men, and photos were flatly lit to minimize any details of the male anatomy. When those attempts failed, opaque photographer's paints and the airbrush were employed. Other sexless variations of men's underwear ads included cartoon caricatures of men or simplistic product still lifes. (Figure 10-28.)

In 1959, Jockey International made the bold marketing leap that took men's underwear "from being simply a glorified pants-liner to an object of intrinsic aesthetic interest subject to innovation and change."[32] The company introduced the bikini-cut Skants in six colors. (Figure 10-29.) Although the ad illustrations were still innocuous, the text unmistakably sold the new style as erotic. The nylon fabric "molds to your body . . . with minimum coverage," said the copy. Men's underwear had entered the realm of fashion. As Daniel Harris noted in

Figure 10-32. By the end of the 1990s, ads for men's underwear included a male model minus the product entirely. Ad 1997.

1972

NORTH BEACH LEATHER

1984

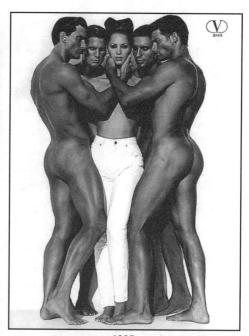

1995

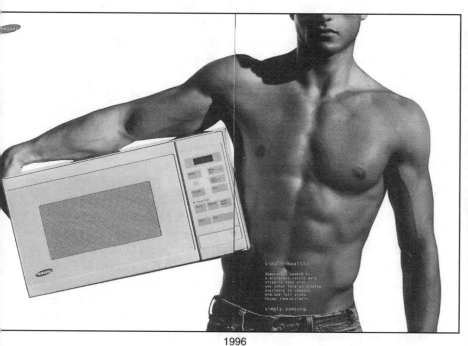

simply healthy.

1996

VERSACE
HOME SIGNATURE

1997

Figure 10-33. Beefcake magazines for women helped open the door to the sexual objectification of men in ads.

his 1993 examination of men's "lingerie": "This upgrading of underwear from a necessity to a luxury, from a hygienic requirement to a stylish accessory, has resulted in an extravagant period of research and development. Manufacturers have taken this recalcitrantly uninteresting and monotonous staple and made it a playground of market forces, a wild experiment in the ingenuity of the free enterprise system, which has at last conquered the final frontier of fashion, the plain white brief."[33]

This final frontier was not conquered immediately, despite all the promotional efforts of Jockey, Hanes, Fruit of the Loom, and Munsingwear.

DEP DRY STYLING SYSTEM/REMINGTON MIST-AIR HOT COMB™

The bare essentials for Christmas gift giving. The Dep for Men Dry Styling System — shampoo, conditioner, styling gel, hair control spray and brush. All the things a guy needs to keep his hair looking soft, clean and natural. And the Mist-Air Hot Comb™ from Remington — directs a fine spray of water onto his hair for better and easier styling. Controls waves, curls, cowlicks and adds more body to a man's hair than he knew he had. Two great gifts. Two great ways to say, "Merry Christmas."

Figure 10-34. Depictions of nude males in ads targeting men were designed to link a masculine sexuality to the product. Remington ad 1972, Studio 54 ad 1982.

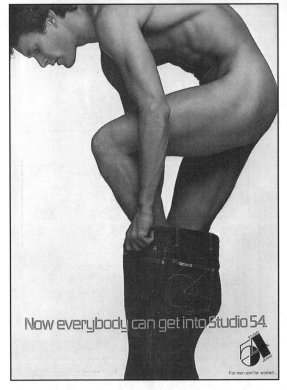

Now everybody can get into Studio 54.

For men and for women.

Instead, the initial response to the new, erotic styles of men's underwear stemmed from two converging social currents: the sexual revolution of the 1960s and the simultaneous emergence of an open homosexual subculture. As a market segment the gay community had never been researched by the marketing departments of ready-to-wear manufacturers, let alone specifically targeted by the industry. Yet, subsequent analysis of sales results proved the significance of this segment of consumers both in repeat purchases and in eagerness for innovative designs of men's underwear. "While in most instances large corporations have commercialized the gay subculture by exploiting it for their own financial gain," wrote Daniel Harris, "men's lingerie provides a peculiar example of reverse commercialization because it is the subculture that has actually helped commercialize an aspect of the dominant culture."[34]

By the 1970s, underwear manufacturers gladly accepted the dividends of successful sales to the gay community, but marketers knew this was only a sliver of the male consumer pie. Heterosexual men seemed reluctant to surrender their basic cotton y-fronts for the underwear styles now being produced in a myriad of colors, textures, prints, and fabrics. Taking their cue from cigarette and breakfast cereal makers, men's underwear manufacturers brought in the big-gun endorsers: jocks. (Figure 10-30.) If it was okay for these idols of millions of men across America to pose in the Tropez brief or patterned Skants, then, manufacturers hoped, the average American male would follow suit. In broadening the base of core customers, not only did men's underwear makers advertise in *Esquire* and *GQ,* but the ad shown in Figure 10-30 was featured in women's magazines such as *Redbook.*[35] Many of the women viewing the ad would not have known the difference between the Cincinnati Reds and the Cincinnati Bengals, but they did recognize that of the eight professional athletes shown in the ad, not one was wearing the basic white brief.

From the mid-1970s through the 1990s styles of men's underwear were mostly variations on earlier themes. Fashion designers stitched their logos on exterior waistbands and tabs and marketed these as new and original styles. Color palettes changed and novelty prints and patterns followed seasons and key gift-giving holidays.

Most significant was the way men's underwear began to be depicted in ads. (Figure 10-31.) The method of lining crotches to disguise the shapes of the genitals was discarded. Photographers intentionally used chiaroscuro lighting to delineate and accent details of the genitals of the models.

Figure 10-35. With the proliferation of nude males used in advertising during the 1980s and 1990s to target both women and men, the product message could sometimes be confusing. Keora ad 1984, Versace ad 1997.

Eroticism moved dangerously close to what some perceived as pornography.[36] Static poses gave way to suggestions of sex games, such as in the "Backgammon" Adam Briefs ad in 1976 or later versions that simulated male striptease revues. By the 1990s, the public was virtually impervious to the shock of seeing anatomically detailed photos of men in revealing underwear—much to the chagrin of social conservative groups. Such images abounded in most mainstream periodicals and in television spots, as well as on mammoth billboards and oversized posters in department stores. Nevertheless, a significant number of women still enjoyed the eroticism of the extraordinary male specimens used in men's underwear ads. Wrote one *Playgirl* editor of these ads: "Images of scantily clad females have been a media mainstay for years, and for us gals, it's hard to believe that those genius copywriters have taken this long to figure out that what's good for the goose is also gravy for the gander. We women are very susceptible—and appreciative—of the fine, semi-dressed, masculine form."[37]

Just when readers thought all that was permissible for advertising men's underwear had been said and done, Body Body Wear eliminated the product entirely and presented a full-page photo of a nude male in profile. Not even a still-life shot of the garment or its packaging was inset. (Figure 10-32.)

Figure 10-36. Most men's fragrance products were purchased by women. Ad 1940.

The evolution of the images of men used in underwear ads from static mannequins to erotic life-style representations was the result of two key changes in the American social landscape. The sexual revolution of the 1960s coupled with the emergence of a new generation of feminists paved the way for a sexual objectification of men in a way that mirrored the methods with which women had been exploited in literature, movies, and especially advertising. One result was the launch of beefcake periodicals for women in the early 1970s and male stripper revues in the 1980s. The genie was out of the bottle, and women consumers responded enthusiastically to the "sexploitation" of men. A *Newsweek* editor noted in 1973 that *Playgirl* was "a pastiche of the sleaziest features of Cosmopolitan and Playboy," which, nevertheless, "promptly sold out 600,000 copies" of its debut issue.[38]

When Temple University researchers asked if men were "ready to see themselves as sex objects," the conclusion was predictable: "Men like ads that show women as sex objects and ads that show men as 'jocks,' but they become nervous about those that feature men as sex objects."[39] Though men were unhappy to see this turning of the tables, marketers recognized the effectiveness of their new license in advertising for targeting women. Marketing researchers discovered that women more so than men could "tolerate an advertisement that produced a high level of sexual arousal and still recall the product."[40] The image of the nude or nearly nude hunk as a prop in ads for women's products increasingly became standard fare. (Figure 10-33.) Business writer Jennifer Foote noted in 1988 that "after decades of selling products by depicting women as anxious half-wits and sultry fantasy objects, advertisers have switched bimbos . . . now it's *his* torso, stripped and moist, promoting everything from Calvin Klein underwear to Kodak film."[41]

This is not to say that the nude male did not serve as an image for simultaneously targeting women as well as heterosexual males. (Figure 10-34.) The standards for depicting masculinity or male sexuality and beauty rose to levels not imagined in the days of the Arrow Man. For example, Burt Reynolds's famous nude pose in a 1972 *Cosmopolitan* centerfold was copied

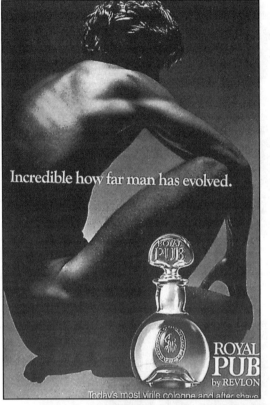

Incredible how far man has evolved.

ROYAL
PUB
by REVLON

Today's most virile cologne and after shave.

Zino, The Fragrance of Desire.

Robinsons-May   Hecht's   Foley's
Kaufmann's   Filene's   Famous Barr   Meier & Frank

Figure 10-37. The use of the nude male in men's fragrance ads was primarily aimed at women consumers. Royal Pub ad 1973, Zino ad 1993.

1902

1939

1943

Figure 10-38. Images that represented the incompetence of men in women's domestic arenas were popular narratives in ads throughout the century.

1962

right down to the bearskin rug by Remington for an ad for a men's hair-styling system. Reynolds's sexual confidence and masculinity were linked to the product, which in 1972 was still thought of as feminine by many men. Similarly, for the basic commodity of jeans the erotic imagery of nude or seminude males in ads told men how sexy they could look snugly fastened into tight denim. Women readers viewing the same ads received a message about the kind of sexually confident man who branded his behind with designer denim labels.

Sometimes the target of these ads was not clear at first glance. For instance, with fragrance ads, the nude male was used in marketing both men's and women's products. (Figure 10-35.) The 1984 Keora ad may have been created to evoke thoughts of Nijinsky's infamous love scene with a woman's scarf in the ballet "Afternoon of a Faun," but first the reader had to decipher the photograph and recognize the elements of the nude male and woman's robe. Similarly, in the 1997 ad for Gianni Versace Fragrances Jeans Collection, only the inset of the product gives the reader a clue about which gender was intended to be the consumer, and even then there could be doubt. The fragrance industry presumed that all consumers were savvy enough to know that "parfum" was for women and "eau de toilette" was for men.

As with men's underwear manufacturers, the men's fragrance industry recognized that the largest segment of its customer base was women. The problem was to get men to use the product so women (or men themselves) would purchase more, but fragrance makers had been unsuccessful in developing scents men enjoyed wearing. Estee Lauder struggled with this challenge in

Figure 10-39. The sexually emasculated male became a recurring theme in advertising during the 1970s and 1980s. Saks Fifth Avenue ad 1973, I. Magnin ad 1984.

the early 1960s, noting that most men's fragrance products "were either sickeningly sweet or smelled strongly of chemicals." Yet, she also knew the history of marketing men's fragrance products, most of which were bought by women. (Figure 10-36.) "That's because their women know what's best for them," she said in her autobiography.[42]

Marketing researchers in the 1980s concluded in studies of sex and advertising that "men and women rated advertisements carrying models of the opposite sex higher than those portraying a model of the same sex."[43] How then were heterosexual men supposed to be captivated by seeing the sculpted bodies of twenty-year-old male athletes in fragrance ads? (Figure 10-37.) Did male readers thumbing through the June 1973 issue of *Esquire* even pause at the Royal Pub ad, or did they think that the sleeping nude male in a 1993 Zino ad represented their "desire," or desirability, as the header might have implied? The residual effect of placing such ads in men's magazines was to reinforce brand recognition and create a sexual image associated with the product. Once men were given a fragrance as a Christmas or Valentine's Day gift, they might actually use the product, and women consumers would therefore be encouraged to purchase more for the men in their lives.

Marketing and the Theme of the Emasculated Male

One final means of turning the tables on men in ads involves representations of the emasculated man. In *Gender Advertisements,* Erving Goffman examined the many nuances and social connotations used by advertisers in depicting men and women. One popular method of showing men "in the domains of the traditional authority and competence of females—the kitchen, the nursery, and the living room when it is being cleaned" was to "present the

The way a woman wants to feel.

Daisy Plus from Gillette

Figure 10-40. Depictions of the androgynous male in ads of the late 1980s and 1990s represented the discarding of stereotyped masculinity in American society. Gillette ad 1989.

man as ludicrous or childlike, unrealistically so, as if perhaps in making him candidly unreal the competency image of real males could be preserved."[44] (Figure 10-38.) Often dressed in frilly or patterned aprons, men would be shown struggling with the simplest of domestic tasks. Women no doubt delighted in these images, although men were also a target of such ads. Men of 1902 reading the copy of the Pearline ad probably had never thought of laundry soap, much less the possibility of "washing made easier" by a particular brand. Maytag recognized that during World War II huge numbers of women were required to join the labor force, which meant that men who were not in service had to help more in the home. Good cooking made so simple that even men could achieve it was a favorite theme in ads for food products. To the woman the ad message was that food preparation could be "so simple even he could do it," while to the man the ad copy offered guidance for those little emergency situations.

The sexual implications of the emasculated male began to appear in ads about the same time as the introduction of the beefcake women's magazines. These publications often featured photo essays of women's fantasies where the male partner was subordinated, controlled, and manipulated in erotic scenarios. Stepping through this newly opened door, advertisers began to expand into new realms with fantasy emasculation versions of their own. (Figure 10-39.) The male model in the 1973 Saks Fifth Avenue ad seems about to have an anxiety attack at being trod upon by a woman. He is not worshiping at her feet so much as being emasculated by the woman's display of contempt. "Ferragamo knows the art of strewing men at your feet," explained the copy; this woman has evidently treated other men similarly. A decade later, the emasculated man became featured as a boy-toy in ads such as the 1984 I. Magnin version. The elegant, older woman stands between the thighs of her enervated lover, towering over him and facing away, implying emotional detachment. Such images were far more than mere sexual fantasies for women readers, they were statements of female assertiveness and power. In the narratives of these ads the source of the woman's power over men may have been her money or her beauty and sensuality, but the man was nevertheless under her domination.

By the last years of the century, the emasculated male began to be supplanted by the androgynous male. (Figure 10-40.) Male models used in advertising of this period, said George Mosse, "were not transexuals—they had undergone no sex change—but [were] men who seemed to have discarded most vestiges of the manly stereotype."[45] The 1989 Gillette ad depicts a man curled up in a fetal position, arranged in the composition of the photograph on a subordinate picture plane to that of the woman. However, the modern woman reader viewing this ad feels that he is a secure, participating partner in the relationship, rather than the dominated boy-toy of the 1980s or emasculated househusband of earlier decades. Such glimpses of romantic partnership reflected the changing ideals of American masculinity as well as the changing expectations of women as the twentieth century closed.

Conclusion: The Objectification of Men in Advertising

In the late nineteenth century, when the process of advertising was beginning to get organized into structured agencies and service bureaus, the focus was primarily on media planning and placement. Sophisticated methods of market research on consumers' purchasing habits, customer's demographics, product branding and segmentation, and competitive analysis were still decades away. Yet, the antecedents of twentieth-century advertising and marketing professionals had a keen instinct from the start about targeting customers. The cliché "a picture is worth a thousand words" served early advertisers especially well in creating ads that would appeal to women consumers. These advertisers merely had to exercise experiential common sense to generate a lengthy list of objects that could be used as effective, eye-catching visuals for women, objects as diverse as children, flowers, food, fashions, baby animals, and attractive men.

In using images of men in ads targeting women, early marketers thought more in terms of masculine themes rather than the specific object of the male: the attentive beau, the devoted husband, the doting father, and the noble warrior. Narratives used in ads reinforced women's expectations of the American male and reflected society's views of stereotyped masculine roles. Throughout the entire twentieth century, as the standards of masculinity became redefined, marketers adjusted their advertising scenarios and images of men to best attract women readers.

At what point the deliberate use of the male figure as a sex object in advertising first occurred is not clear. Certainly, by World War I popular culture had already eased much of the social constraints of Victorianism. Research on women's sexuality by Sigmund Freud and Havelock Ellis had been published a generation earlier, and the impact of their studies was beginning to emerge in mass media—magazines, movies, literature, and advertising. Even before the First World War marketers had already witnessed women's responses to the sexuality of the Arrow Shirt Man in advertising and to the sex appeal of Hollywood's leading men on the screen. By the 1920s, the objectification of the American male as a sex object, without the social narratives of husband and father roles, was undeniably in play by advertisers. Home economist Christine Frederick endorsed the practice in her 1929 book *Selling Mrs. Consumer.*[46] The eroticism of the male figure began to be featured in ads where its use might be logical, such as depictions of nude male bathers in ads for soaps or towels, and in representations of the athletic body in ads for men's swimwear. By the 1950s, men's underwear manufacturers introduced new designs of their products that were created specifically to have sex appeal. Since about three-quarters of all men's underwear was purchased by women, that meant rethinking the product-oriented formats of men's underwear ads to more directly convey to women the message of men's sexuality. Coinciding with the new styles of men's underwear was a second sexual revolution and a second rise of feminism in American society in the 1960s. Deriving from these two social changes was the launch of the beefcake magazine for women in the 1970s, which in turn paved paths for advertisers to objectify the male figure into a sexual prop. From ads for fashions and fragrances to those for china and microwave ovens, the eroticism of the unclad male was exploited to capture the attention of women consumers. All through the last quarter of the twentieth century, new sexual scenarios appeared in ads that represented men as subjugated lovers and even as boy-toys.

Whether masculine or feminine, "love objects and beauty objects get noticed," remarked an ad agency executive in the 1980s.[47] Over the years advertisers may have exploited images of women in almost every conceivable manner, but the image of the American male has also served marketers well. Although tentatively approached in the early years of advertising, depictions of the handsome face, the father figure, the warrior, and eventually the male sex object proved highly effective for marketers in targeting their primary customer, the American woman. The evolution may have progressed slowly, but by the close of the century the tables had been fully turned on men.

Chapter 11

FEMALE ICONS, LOGOS, AND SPOKESWOMEN

The advent of the trademark • Contemporary female icons and obsolescence • The historical female figure as a brand icon • Representations of little girls as icons • Fantasy females as logos • Spokeswomen and testimonials

By the third quarter of the nineteenth century, the second great industrial revolution was well under way with ever improving advances in manufacturing technology. With mass production and mass distribution emerged a mass consumer market. Competition expanded from regional pockets of industries to a national scale, and manufacturers sought better ways to secure market share. As was discussed in chapters 1 and 2, the evolution of marketing strategies eventually included advertising in all its many forms. For companies introducing products that consumers had never used or thought they needed before, such as bar soap, chewing gum, or deodorant, the purpose was product education. For manufacturers with products already known and accepted by consumers, the advertising focus was product differentiation through branding. One early device used for branding was the trademark.

In October 1870 Congress passed the first in a series of trademark protection acts. The first of 121 businesses at the time that registered their

Figure 11-1. The primary problem with using images of contemporary women as trademark icons was obsolescence. Fashions, hairstyles, and ideas of feminine beauty changed constantly. (Details of ads.)

| 1902 | 1919 | 1929 |

trademarks with the Patent Office was the Averill Chemical Paint Company, which in its application described the design as bearing an eagle perched upon a rock, "holding in his mouth a paint-pot or canister, with a brush, and a ribbon or streamer, on which are the words Economical, Durable, Beautiful."[1] The patriotic allegory of the Averill trademark was typical of the grandiose designs of post-Civil War branding attempts. More important, though, was that Averill and the other companies that registered their trademarks that year understood that a trademark was a promise to customers. With the subjective word "beautiful" aside, Averill's trademark assured customers that the company's paints were "durable," which meant less frequent painting, and therefore "economical." By marking their products with trademarks, manufacturers made themselves accountable for quality and the conditions under which the products were made.

Subsequent statutes passed in 1876, 1881, 1882, and 1905 affirmed the significance of the trademark to an individual business and confirmed the legality of "goodwill" that had legal precedents stretching back to Elizabethan English law. American companies finally had legal recourse to protect themselves against infringement, including the destruction of infringing labels and packaging plus the recovery for damages for infringement. Before the passage of the Pure Food and Drugs Act in 1906, these laws were as significant to consumers as they were to manufacturers. For example, before Smith Brothers began packing its cough drops in paper boxes bearing its trademark, consumers had been easily deceived by imitators that used such company names as Smith & Bros. or Schmitt Brothers to sell inferior versions. Similarly, by 1915 Nabisco had won thirteen lawsuits and quashed 882 other attempts to imitate its registered trademarks, and Coca-Cola spent ten years in litigation to force Espo Cola to forgo copying Coca-Cola's bottle, label, and script trademark.[2]

With the strengthening of the trademark laws in 1905, more than ten thousand new marks were registered within a year. In the rush for a branding image, some manufacturers made poor choices. Case in point was the Brown Shoe Company, which purchased the rights to the comic strip character Buster Brown. Soon after the first ads appeared featuring the pumpkin-headed cartoon boy and his dog, Tige, customers started referring to the company as the "Buster Brown Shoe Company." Much to the chagrin of the owners, nothing could be done to stem the public's response to the branding campaign. Another example of a trademark that failed was the chameleon first used by paint manufacturer Sherwin-Williams. The allusion was not only too sophisticated for the public, but most people thought the creature was a snake. Once the reptile was replaced by the "Covers the Earth" emblem, sales improved considerably.

Contemporary Female Icons and Obsolescence

One of the most difficult images to adapt to a trademark was that of a girl or woman. (Figure 11-1.) The image of the ideal contemporary woman would quickly become obsolete due to changes in hairstyles, fashions, and even ideas of beauty. In figure 1-3 the Sozodont Girl remained unchanged in ads for nearly two decades. Presumably the toothy grin that revealed her "pearls in the mouth" particularly enhanced her stellar beauty to the

Figure 11-2. Some companies capitalized on the old-fashioned image of their icons. Against the mod images of women in ads of the 1960s, the pre-World War I look of the Vermont Maid reminded consumers of old home-style recipes. Ad 1967.

Victorian consumer, but by the time of the flapper her image would have frightened small children. Other contemporary women such as the Lowney's Cocoa Girl, Kelly Springfield's Lotta Miles, or Ethyl Gasoline's Ethyl were fashionable beauties of their day. Their contribution to a branding strategy was short-lived since their clothing and hairstyles were locked in time. To prevent their products from being associated with an out-of-date image, manufacturers had to redesign labels or packaging to keep current, and point-of-sale promotional materials had to be frequently replaced.

To some manufacturers, though, the female icon representing their company was intentionally kept unchanged. This trademark consistency bespoke a product longevity that in itself was a significant brand equity. In a 1967 Vermont Maid Syrup ad, the logo icon is enlarged to fill most of the full-page layout. (Figure 11-2.) Among the many magazine pages of the time featuring models with bouffant hairstyles, frosted lipstick, miniskirts, and mod jewelry, the Vermont Maid appeared old-fashioned with her pre–World War I visage. It was precisely the statement the manufacturer wanted to make, connecting the product with the homemade cooking of bygone days at a time when artificial flavorings and cheap ingredients were common in processed foods.

Changing the female logo or icon for a more current look could in itself be a promotional opportunity. One of the success stories with this approach was Kellogg's Sweetheart of the Corn maiden. In 1906, William K. Kellogg acquired the rights to a process for making corn flakes that had been invented by his brother, John Harvey Kellogg. The following year, W. K. began mass production of the boxed cereal and launched the first ads for Kellogg's Corn Flakes, which featured a robust farm maiden christened "Sweetheart of the Corn." (Figures 1-7 and 11-3.) In addition it was W. K.'s initials rather his brother's that were exclusively scripted before the family surname in ads and on packaging. An ardent advocate of advertising, W. K. even wrote most of his own copy and spent as much on sales promotion as he paid in dividends to stockholders.[3] For years, the smiling corn maid was highly visible everywhere, from billboards in Manhattan to point-of-sale displays in hundreds of rural grocery stores across the country. Almost half a century later company officials decided to capitalize on the product's brand equity with an extensive advertising campaign to present an updated version of the Kellogg's Sweetheart. Ads included an inset of the original model for comparison. The gingham checked garments of the two lasses were about all they had in common, though. The 1950s version was a svelte blonde who wore lipstick and nail polish, although to tone down her contemporary glamour she also sported a frilly sunbonnet. Further, the ad copy credited W. K. as having created the "secret recipe" for corn flakes with no mention of his brother, John Harvey. Despite crediting the wrong brother with the product's invention, the ads succeeded in conveying their dual message to consumers: Kellogg's Corn Flakes had been a nutritional favorite in Grandpa's boyhood days of 1906 and they still are now in 1953.

1946

1954

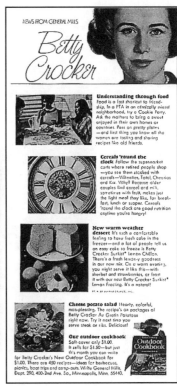

1969

"Today, as then," the ad copy affirmed about the new Sweetheart, "she symbolizes the goodness in the heart of the corn."

Of all the contemporary female icons that underwent periodic updating, few are in a league with Betty Crocker. (Figure 11-4.) She was originally created in 1921 as a fictional columnist to answer cooking questions in Gold Medal flour ads, and was named after an emeritus director of the company,[4] but her visual representation did not debut until 1936. Her image as the ideal homemaker became so successfully marketed that in addition to questions about baking, General Mills began receiving proposals of marriage for Betty. This in itself became the inspiration for an ad in 1945 headlined "to the man who wanted to marry Betty Crocker." The copy was in the form of a polite rejection letter in which the company acknowledged that other such letters had been sent to Betty. With careful wording, the copy did not admit the fictional nature of the high-profile icon, but did conclude that she was too busy baking to marry anyone.[5] Besides never marrying, neither was Betty Crocker to change her look for almost thirty years. Although she received a new portrait in the mid-1950s, she was still represented as a matron with streaks of gray in the hair and discernable age lines around the eyes and mouth. However, with the youth culture of the 1960s, the gray hair was eliminated and she was given younger skin in a third version painted in 1965. Then, in rapid succession—1968, 1972, 1980, and 1986—she was updated with new hairstyles and current makeup trends, and seemed to become ever younger. Her new look for the 1980s was designed to make her appear "as comfortable in the board room as she is in the dining room," wrote Juliann Sivulka.[6] Finally, in celebration of her seventy-fifth anniversary in 1996, she was given a completely new look in her eighth portrait. The promotional and public relations efforts in announcing this revised image

1996

Figure 11-4. Between 1936 and 1996 the likeness of Betty Crocker was revised eight times. Her seventy-fifth anniversary portrait received so much promotional hype that the new look was even noted in mainstream news reports.

were enormous and even netted human-interest sound bites on network television newscasts. Full-page ads in women's magazines heralded the transition to the new image. As the ad copy noted, the photos of seventy-five women had been blended to create the new look—women who were not "'models' so much as role models." The oversized script type that opened and closed the body copy emphasized that "she looks a little . . . like you."

In the marketing strategies of many manufacturers, realistic images of women helped to maintain more of a real-life connection with the public. Specific individuals sometimes served as distinctive models for artwork or were photographed to become logos or trademark icons. For example, the Jell-O girl and Sun-Maid raisin girl were actual people used in print materials for years, and character actresses convincingly portrayed Madge the manicurist, Josephine the plumber, and Rosie the waitress in TV commercials of the 1960s and 1970s. For some manufacturers, the trademark or icon was the depiction of a contemporary person, such as Betty Wales's portrait used in many of her dress ads or little Angela Meadors's portrait used in Meadors' candy ads. (Figure 11-5.)

Certainly, one of the most enduring and famous portraits of an actual woman used as an icon in the early days of advertising was that of Lydia Pinkham. (Figure 5-31.) In the 1870s, Pinkham, a Quaker housewife, cooked up mixtures of herbs, roots, and alcohol as a health tonic for her friends and relatives. Her two sons persuaded her to bottle the "vegetable compound" for sale, which they began promoting in brochures. By the 1880s the brothers had expanded their advertising into women's magazines such as *Godey's* and began to include a woodblock illustration of their mother. Beneath the benevolent gaze of Lydia the ad copy promised cures for just about everything, including "bloating, headaches, nervous prostration, general debility, sleeplessness, depression . . . ovarian troubles, inflammation and ulceration, falling and displacements, also spinal weakness and is particularly adapted to the change of life."[7] In addition, women were invited to write for answers to their most intimate health and physical problems. Mountains of letters and orders poured into the little Lynn, Massachusetts, post office. Some of these responses eventually were included as testimonials in ads. Although Lydia Pinkham died in 1883, her prim Victorian image remained the product's icon in newspaper and magazine ads, billboards, and trolley cards for decades.

Branding the Historical Figure

Besides the use of portraits of actual people, another way to avoid the problem of having to keep a female icon looking contemporary was to choose or create a historical figure. (Figure 11-6.) Virginia Dare Wine took the name of the first child born in America of English parents in 1587. Spring Cotton Mills also used an anachronistic depiction of a colonial-era woman for its Springmaid trademark, as did Armstrong Cork Company for its Quaker-Felt Rugs. Similarly, Diamond Crystal Salt Company adopted the image of a nineteenth-century Shaker matron for its packaging to make the link to the religious sect's famous

Figure 11-5. Portraits of actual living people often served as trademark icons. (Details of ads.) Betty Wales ad 1920, Meadors' ad 1948.

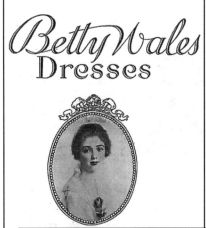

1928

Figure 11-6. Icons represented by real or invented historical figures eliminated the need for updating clothing and hairstyles. (Details of ads.)

1926

1947

1951

honesty, purity, and sensibility, as well as to create a contrived connection to salt shakers. In addition to eliminating the need to keep an icon image contemporary, such historically costumed figures used in trademarks also suggested product longevity and established quality to consumers. Was Virginia Dare Wine made by her descendants, consumers might wonder. Did Springmaid or Quaker-Felt use the same high-quality production standards of their colonial antecedents? Was Diamond Crystal salt the trusted brand actually used by the Shakers?

Of all the historical images used in advertising, the most prolific has been that of La Belle Chocolatière, which has appeared in the packaging and advertising designs for Baker's Chocolate since 1825. (Figure 11-7.) The figure of a chocolate shop waitress wearing a white cap and apron and carrying a tray of cups was derived from a pastel rendering in the Dresden Museum believed to have been made in 1742 by the Viennese court painter Jeanne-Etienne Liotard.[8] As the romantic legend behind the drawing goes, one day a young Austrian prince stopped at one of Vienna's chocolate cafes to try the new beverage. His server was the beautiful Anna Baltauf, the daughter of an impoverished knight, and it was love at first sight for the prince. When they were at last married the prince presented his bride with the portrait of her in the chocolate server's costume she was wearing when he first saw her. This historical figure has served Baker's well for the better part of two centuries. The company's famous trademark icon was also variously adapted for contemporary interpretations in later ads where the tray of cups was replaced by a plate of brownies, a giant chocolate bar, or other related props.

The Sun-Maid raisin girl looks the part of a historical figure but actually originated from a marketing gimmick. (Figure 11-8.) In 1912 a West Coast grower's cooperative founded the California Associated Raisin Company, and in 1915 it adopted the name Sun-Maid for its raisins. That same year, the company set up an exhibit at the Panama-Pacific Exposition held in San Francisco. Several young women were employed to wear red sunbonnets and white peasant's blouses to distribute free samples to visitors. One teenage girl, Lorraine Collett, even made daily airplane flights over the fairgrounds and sprinkled raisins on the crowds below. One day Lorraine was

Figure 11-7. Copied from an eighteenth-century Viennese drawing, La Belle Chocolatière has been the icon for Baker's Chocolate since 1825. Left ad 1889, right ad 1951.

asked to pose in her costume with a basket of grapes for a new package design, and the image of the Sun-Maid raisin girl was launched. Over the decades, the likeness of the trademark maiden changed, but the historical costume, basket of grapes, and stylized sun in the background remained constant elements.

One of the female trademarks that made the transition from historical figure to contemporary icon was that of Aunt Jemima, whose name and image were first marketed in 1890. (Figure 11-9.) Milling company entrepreneurs Christopher Rutt and Charles Underwood had developed a packaged pancake mix, which at first was sold generically in paper sacks with no trade name. One evening while attending a vaudeville theater, Rutt saw a blackface comedy routine that featured a character dressed as a Southern cook with an apron and red bandanna headcover who danced to a tune called "Aunt Jemima." Rutt thought the image perfect for his pancake mix and appropriated both the likeness and the name as his trademark. Later the product was acquired by the J. T. Davis Milling Company, which had the resources to better promote the label. Davis hit on the idea of bringing his newly acquired logo to life with a representative to tour the country doing cooking demonstrations.

The first live Aunt Jemima was Nancy Green, a personable woman who was also an excellent cook. Her debut was at the 1893 Columbian

Figure 11-8. The Sun-Maid icon originated from a promotional photo taken of a young woman in a Victorian-style sunbonnet who distributed free raisin samples at the 1915 Panama-Pacific Exposition. Left ad 1917, right ad 1935.

1910

1921

1936

1945

1955

Exposition in Chicago, where she fried stacks of flapjacks and distributed them free to the visitors. Her smiling image was also lithographed onto souvenir lapel pins with the slogan "I'se in town, honey!" In the six months she conducted her demonstrations at the fair, more than fifty thousand merchant's orders for the packaged mix were generated.[9] After the Chicago expo, Green continued her cooking demonstrations across the country. These personal appearances, coupled with extensive advertising, made the image of Aunt Jemima so famous that for decades dolls representing her and her fictitious family, Uncle Mose and the twins, Diana and Wade, were popular boxtop premiums. Among the series of ads that especially proved effective were those created by the J. Walter Thompson agency in the 1920s featuring episodes from Aunt Jemima's life. During the Depression sales volume

Figure 11-9. The icon for Aunt Jemima evolved from a stereotype of an antebellum Southern cook to a contemporary African-American woman in the 1990s.

1913

1915

1962

Figure 11-10. Stereotypes of the noble Indian maiden in her buckskin garments and feathered headdress were popular icons for processed agricultural products. (Details of ads.)

began to suffer, so the Quaker Oats Company, which had purchased the Aunt Jemima brand in 1926, decided to revive the living logo. Anna Robinson, a convivial, three-hundred-fifty-pound housewife from Chicago, was hired to represent the legendary icon until her death in 1951. The Quaker company continued an aggressive marketing of the brand, creating product-line extensions in the 1950s with frozen waffles and in the 1960s with frozen corn sticks, cinnamon twists, and pancake syrup. By the 1980s, the historical figure of the antebellum plantation cook had been replaced with a slimmer, more contemporary-looking black model who had discarded the gingham headcover and now wore pearl earrings.

Ethnic stereotypes used as advertising icons were not limited solely to blacks. Depictions of Native Americans appeared in ads throughout the entire twentieth century, even during early years when certain tribes were still in open conflict with various federal and state authorities. The trademark figure of the female Native American was especially popular for products derived from agriculture. (Figure 11-10.) Stereotypes of the noble Indian maiden in her buckskin garments and feathered headdress were used by Puritan Foods for its Red Wing grape-juice label, Corn Products Refining Company for its Mazola brand of cooking oil, and Land O' Lakes for dairy products, to name a few. In writing of the image of the Native American as used by advertisers, historian William O'Barr noted that "although their recent cultures may have been fierce and unfriendly, their ancient civilizations are mysterious and worthy of attention."[10] Such ads, then, would achieve a measure of success in the pages of magazines crowded with trademarks that struggled for distinction and visibility.

Icons of Little Girls

One particular way for a trademark to gain a commanding distinction was to incorporate the image of an animal or child. Any student of advertising can easily rattle off dozens of animal icons, which have occupied their share of ad space linage and TV airtime. Among these have been dogs (RCA phonographs, Mack Trucks, Greyhound Buslines, Hushpuppies shoes), cats (Catspaw shoe heels, Eveready batteries, Nine Lives cat food), rabbits (Kix cereal, Energizer batteries, Playboy), plus a host of lions, tigers, and bears—and even a brontosaurus. Even more eye-catching to women consumers were depictions of children, which for the purpose of this chapter means icons of little girls. (Figure 11-11.) As was discussed in chapters 4 and 8, images of little girls were used to market everything from food and household products to medications and automobiles. The frills, laces, ribbons, buttons, and bows with which the little girl could be attired expanded her versatility as a distinct logo. She could be a costumed character such as the little Bab-O girl, or she could be a contemporary image such as the pre-World War I National Oats girl and the modern Wendy of the fast-food chain.

Some depictions of little girls were used only briefly while others endured across the century. In the first category is the Jell-O girl. She represented a product that itself almost did not survive its inception. The original product was created by a cough syrup manufacturer in 1897 and was given the name Jell-O by the owner's wife. Two years later sales were still far below expectations, and the brand was sold to Genesee Pure Food Company. Soon afterward the new owner, O. F. Woodward, called in the Dauchy Advertising Agency to create a promotional campaign for Jell-O. Since no trademark for the brand was being used at the time, the agency suggested featuring a child to convey the idea that Jell-O was easy to make and that children would love the healthful dessert. Unable to find a suitable child image, the art director, Franklin King, one day happened to notice his four-year-old daughter playing with building blocks on the sunporch. He snapped some candid shots of her with his camera and presented the photos to his colleagues. Everyone was delighted with the charming images, and Elizabeth King became the Jell-O girl in ad campaigns from 1904 till World War I. After 1908 head shots of Elizabeth from earlier photo sessions were incorporated into artists' renderings to keep the icon looking the same preschool age, and these photos were used in ads for several years afterward. (Figure 11-12.)

Another little girl icon that was a delight to consumers for only a few years was Betsy Bell. (Figure 11-13.) Illustrator Peter Hawley was commissioned to create Betsy in 1958. Better known as an

Figure 11-11. Depictions of little girls were used to market everything from food and household products to pharmaceuticals and automobiles. (Details of ads.)

1916

1932

1937

1950

1960

1999

Figure 11-12. The daughter of an advertising executive served as the model for the Jell-O Girl from 1904 till World War I. Left ad 1906, right ad 1913.

illustrator of sexy women and men in skintight Jantzen swimwear, Hawley delighted everyone with his scenarios of the toddler playing with her phone. For five years the Bell Telephone System used depictions of Hawley's Betsy Bell to promote long distance service.

The image of one little girl (and her brother) had a prolific run as an icon for more than half a century. She was one of the "roly-polies"—pudgy, cherubic children created by illustrator Grace Drayton. With slight variations from the characters Drayton created for her comic strip *Dimples,* the "Campbell Kids" made their advertising debut in 1904. Apparently the kids never had names, and sometimes additional roly-polies were featured in ads. Often, though, the little girl appeared solo in her own cartoon dramas. (Figure 11-14.) In the days before women could vote, she was even daringly shown as a political activist at a convention in a 1915 ad and with a ballot in a 1916 version. Mostly, however, she and the other roly-polies were presented in innocuous vignettes as a support for the product. Other illustrators followed Drayton's prototypes through 1959 when the Campbell Kids made their last regular appearances in ads. In that same year they were also featured as one of the "100 greatest advertisements" in Julian Watkins's book by the same name. "Certainly no book of great advertisements would be complete without an example of this truly outstanding series beloved by young and old alike," wrote Watkins of the roly-polies.[11] Why then, one might wonder, would a

1958

1962

1963

Figure 11-13. Illustrator Peter Hawley created scenarios for his Betsy Bell between 1958 and 1963 for the Bell Telephone Company.

Figure 11-14. The Campbell Kids made their advertising debut in 1904 and were widely promoted in ads through the 1950s. After 1960 the Kids continued to be used in marketing but less frequently than in earlier years. (Details of ads.)

company abandon such highly recognizable icons after investing millions of dollars over half a century to build brand equity into the images? Unfortunately, by the end of the 1990s no one in the marketing or public relations offices of Campbell's could remember.[12] One suggestion from an advertising scholar is that the soup maker's marketing strategy shifted to target "physically active inner directed women" instead of the "all-American apron-clad Mom."[13] That meant replacing the "m'm, m'm good" home-and-hearth themes—and images of the Kids—with the "soup is good food" direction. However, the roly-polies made a few appearances in ads of the 1960s and were used in marketing devices such as premiums or even the occasional soup can label.

One manufacturer that capitalized on the brand equity of its little-girl icon decade after decade was the Morton Salt Company. (Figure 11-15.) Incorporated in 1910, the company had developed a free-running granulated salt, which it packaged in a cylindrical container with a patented pour spout. Shortly afterward, the N. W. Ayer agency was contracted to create a series of ads to place in women's magazines. As he reviewed the campaign proposal, Sterling Morton's eye was caught by an alternate layout that featured a little

1918

1946

1957

1968

Figure 11-15. The Morton Salt Girl was introduced in 1914 and was revised five times between 1921 and 1968. The classic styling of the hair and costume of the last version has endured more than three decades.

girl in a rain shower holding an oversized umbrella in one arm and a container of salt under the other, with salt spilling out of the opened spout. "Here was the whole story in a picture," he was to later say; "the message that the salt would run in damp weather was made beautifully evident."[14] The development of the accompanying slogan evolved from "flows freely" to "runs freely," and finally to a modification of the proverb "It never rains but it pours" to become "When It Rains It Pours." The finalized versions of the Morton Salt Girl and slogan were rolled out in 1914. As with most icons contemporary to their time, such as Betty Crocker, the Morton Salt Girl underwent revisions to update her look in 1921, 1933, 1941, 1956, and last in 1968. Her final makeover became an opportunity for special marketing and promotions such as the "sentimental offer" of four versions of the icon imprinted on a set of mugs. For the remaining three decades of the century, her cropped hairstyle and short-waisted dress were so classic that further updates were not needed.

Imaginary Female Characters and Caricatures

In addition to historical and allegorical female figures, manufacturers could avoid the issue of updating hairstyles and wardrobes of their icon by using the image of a character from mythology. For the owners of the White Rock Mineral Springs Company of Waukesha, Wisconsin, that decision came in 1893 at the Chicago Columbian Exposition. In the fine arts pavilion the

Figure 11-16. The icon for White Rock Mineral Springs Company was taken from a painting of the nymph Psyche by German artist Paul Thumann. Ad 1895.

White Rock proprietors came upon a painting by the German artist Paul Thumann that depicted the nymph Psyche gazing at her reflection in a woodland pool. (Figure 11-16.) The imagery seemed perfect for the White Rock product—natural spring water—as well as a way to elevate the status of the label to that of classical fine art. Perhaps the company management was unaware that the story of Psyche and Cupid, the son of Venus, had for centuries been a favorite way for artists to depict the subject of teenage premarital sex, or perhaps the mystique of a mythological creature with wings precluded any sexual consideration at all. Nevertheless, White Rock officials immediately secured the rights to use the image in marketing and redesigned bottle labels to include their new icon that same year. Unfortunately for the White Rock company, the Thumann painting was in the public domain and was often reproduced for library portfolios, calendars, and premiums without violating trademark infringement regulations.

Ironically, White Rock was not content to leave its classical icon unchanged for very long. In the 1920s Psyche was repainted to resemble a Hollywood starlet complete with makeup, marcelled fingerwaves in her hair, and more pronounced breasts with pointy nipples. Additional tinkering changed the Hollywood version somewhat over the next two decades until 1944, when she was completely overhauled. (Figure 11-17.) Historian Frank Rowsome described her at this stage as "three inches taller, twenty-eight pounds lighter, and [measuring] 35-25-35."[15] Although her diaphanous garment remained topless and slit up the side, her hair was now swept back into

Figure 11-17. Although icons represented by mythical creatures could remain impervious to changing tastes, White Rock nevertheless chose to periodically update the look of its Psyche.

1937

1946

1950

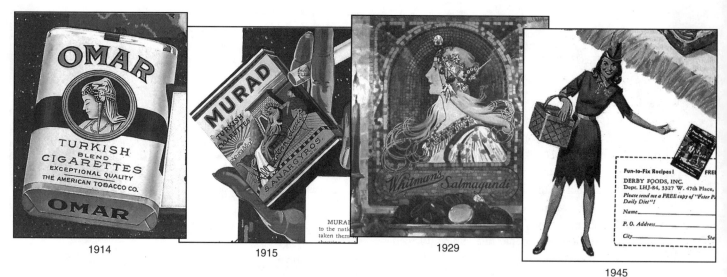

Figure 11-18. Exotic women and fantasy females used as logo icons did not require contemporary updating. (Details of ads.)

a French twist and her facial features were more fine-boned. The most dramatic change was that of her pose, which was altered to bring her knees together, arching her back and lifting her shoulders. This new image of Psyche was then used in a number of unusual scenarios in ads of the 1940s and 1950s, which required contrived angles and poses to conceal her nudity. In later versions she was given an asymmetrically tied bodice to cover her breasts.

Other types of female images that worked well for trademarks and did not require updating were imaginary or exotic women from distant lands. (Figure 11-18.) During the Turkish tobacco craze of the pre-World War I years, the strangely costumed houris were frequently featured as trademark icons on cigarette packages and in ads. So too was the queenly figure of Whitman's Chocolates used for decades in ads and packaging designs. Most people thought the art nouveau painting, created by the famous illustrator Alphonse Mucha, was that of an exotic noblewoman called Salmagundi,

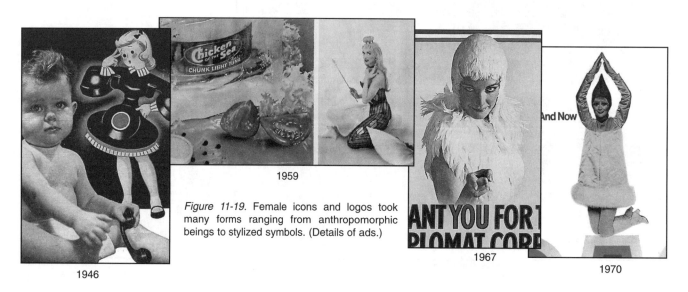

Figure 11-19. Female icons and logos took many forms ranging from anthropomorphic beings to stylized symbols. (Details of ads.)

when in reality the name on the label was derived from a French word for "assortment." One of the most unusual icons of an imaginary female was that used for Peter Pan Peanut Butter. Rather than the prepubescent boy of James Barrie's book, Derby Foods instead chose the incongruous image of an adult woman attired in a crenellated dress, feathered cap, and high heels.

Fantasy female creatures and symbols could escape the need for wardrobe or hairstyle revisions. (Figure 11-19.) Ads for Chicken of the Sea tuna have for decades directed the consumer to "look for the mermaid on the label." Similarly, the costumed personification of animals or inanimate objects could create memorable icons for products where brand parity made marketing difficult. For example, White Owl cigars were not significantly different from those made by the competition in quality or price, yet the sexy, befeathered woman version of the avian icon created a distinct differentiation. "When advertising works at all," wrote Leslie Savan of image marketing, "it's because the public more or less believes that something serious is going on between a product and its image, as if the latter reveals intrinsic qualities of the former."[16] For instance, for a tuna processor, the mermaid was a memorable (and somewhat authoritative) icon for the company's image, and for a cigar maker, a buxom sex symbol created a contemporary, sensuous image for a commonplace product.

Fantasyland provided the greatest versatility for establishing or defining the image of an icon and, hence of the product. For instance, a fantasy creature could be removed from the confines of the terrestrial world. Like the dream sequence used in books and movies anything was possible since the laws of physics and reality did not apply. Cartoon characters especially functioned well in this realm. (Figure 11-20.) That cows and pigs could walk upright, wear clothing, and speak in ads and TV commercials was not so astounding for most consumers given the ancient precedence of fable and folklore. To make the images and personalities of the animal icons compelling was the main challenge for the ad agency professionals. The somewhat primitive simplicity of Brooksie the cow and her farmyard pals of the 1930s was soon eclipsed by the sophisticated and well-rendered versions of Elsie, Elmer, and their offspring, Beulah and Beauregard, in the forties, fifties and sixties. As children's television programming expanded during the 1950s, advertisers began to animate established print cartoon characters such as Kellogg's Snap, Crackle, and Pop, or created new ones that worked well with the medium such as Tony the Tiger, Sugar Bear, Toucan Sam, Captain Crunch, and a host of others. The TV spots became minicartoons and established brand positioning with their preteen target customers. By the end of the 1990s, computer animation gave these minicartoons added dimension and provided special effects that enhanced the icons' personalities and expanded the range of story situations.

The puppet also served as a differentiating product icon especially suitable for television. In the 1950s, simple puppet shows featuring the popular

Figure 11-20. Female cartoon characters were the most versatile icons, since they could defy logic and the laws of physics yet still compellingly represent a product. Brookfield ad 1934, Borden ad 1946.

Kukla, Fran, and Ollie and the lethargic Howdy Doody were not much different from the puppet shows of ancient times. Still, they featured highly recognizable characters and effectively reached the children's market for their sponsors. With the expressive sophistication of Jim Hensen's Muppets in the 1960s and 1970s the quality standard rose appreciably on depicting advertising icons in a marionette form. Muppet diva Miss Piggy was a commanding performer to virtually all market segments. Likewise, model animation evolved from the limited range of motion exhibited by

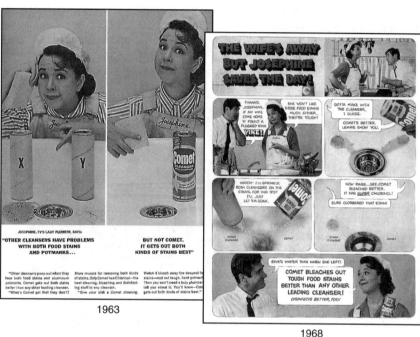

1963

1968

1977

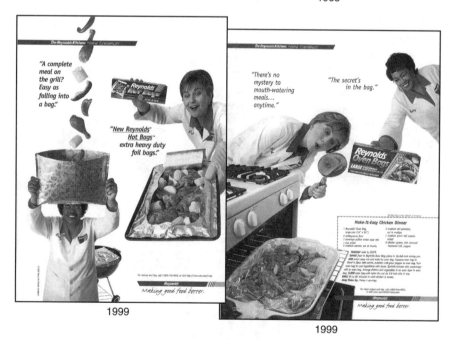

1999

1999

1979

Figure 11-21. Fictional spokeswomen characters became famous icons of branded products in television advertising of the 1960s and continued to be a popular marketing method throughout the remaining decades of the century.

1934

1941

1923

Figure 11-22. Advertisers enlisted spokeswomen from America's "branded" families to boost the taste level and credibility of ad messages.

Alka-Seltzer's character icon Speedy in the 1950s to the theatrical performances by Swiss Miss in the 1970s, and eventually to the extravaganzas done by the likes of the California Raisins in the 1980s and Ronald McDonald and friends in the 1990s.

Spokeswomen and Testimonials

Television especially presented a unique opportunity for spokeswomen icons. Whereas print may have afforded advertisers the chance to imprint a mass market with the image of an icon, the design, illustration, or photograph was two-dimensional and often subject to interpretation. Take, for example, the public's misunderstanding of the Sherwin-Williams chameleon mentioned earlier. Even though a television screen itself was as flat as a printed page, the motion of a living person across its pixels presented a three-dimensional reality to the viewer. Voice, music, and sound effects added still another dimension, and by the mid-1960s color added one more. Then, just as the pages of magazines had become crowded with ads, each seeking its own distinction, so too did television; and just as icons helped differentiate branded products in print, so too did characters created as television icons.

In the early 1950s, the successful salesmanship of TV and film stars such as Dinah Shore, Eve Arden, Rosemary Clooney, and Lucille Ball, to name but a few, laid the groundwork for the creation of female television icons. Wrote an editor for *Printers' Ink* in 1954: "Personality on TV is fast and sure. There's a flash of recognition when the listener sees the face. Housewives, working by themselves, like to hear a familiar voice during the day when the personality comes on and in a friendly, unaffected way talks about the product and its use. Mrs. Stay-at-home gets to feel that she knows the speaker."[17] Beyond the use of established stars, television exposure created stars, including advertising stars. Branded products that were featured by program sponsors in the early days of television became inextricably linked to the names and images of certain women: Betty Furness for Westinghouse, Kathi Norris for General Electric, Anita Colby for Pepsi-Cola, Zella Lane for Ivory Snow, Jean Sullivan for Maxwell House, and dozens of others. As one ad agency casting director in the 1950s insisted, "Credibility demands a woman on household products and other merchandise sold to and used largely by women."[18]

After the quiz show scandals of 1959, television programming was revamped across the board to a magazine format. That is, instead of one sponsor for an entire program or segment, slots of airtime were sold to any advertiser. Building on the long success of the icon image, advertisers blended TV spot buying with the spokesperson notoriety to create a whole new roster of fictional spokeswomen icons. (Figure 11-21.) These living caricatures presented thirty- or sixty-second sitcoms around the benefits of a product or the image of a brand. For Comet Cleanser, Josephine, "the lady plumber," was made more feminine with eyeshadow, liner, and lipstick and at the same time was presented as a clown with baggy overalls and workman's cap with the brim flipped up. In the 1970s comedienne Nancy Walker went from being Rock Hudson's housekeeper on *McMillan and Wife* to being Valerie Harper's mother on *Rhoda,* and then Rosie, the Bounty paper towel icon. So successful was the combination of television and print in creating spokeswomen icons that the formula continued to be used throughout the rest of the century. In the 1990s Reynolds Metals produced a long-running series of television and print ads featuring "Pat and Betty." Even though both women were in fact certified home economists from the Reynolds test kitchens, their combination of soft-sell humor and hard-sell benefits would have been familiar territory for Josephine and Rosie years earlier.

The successful link of a brand to a spokeswoman or icon also hinged on credibility. White Rock's Psyche knew about natural spring water, Borden's Elsie knew about milk, Betty Crocker knew about baking ingredients, Comet's Josephine knew about sink stains, and Bounty's Rosie knew about cleanups. They were users of the products they sold, even if only in farfetched fiction. The ad or TV commercial that featured such characters was, in effect, a testimonial on which this person or personality staked her reputation.

Figure 11-23. Commanding fees in the thousands of dollars, many of Europe's crowned and coroneted heads were often featured in American ads. Hoff's ad 1898, Pond's ad 1937.

Testimonials were certainly not new to advertising of the twentieth century, nor were they always credible. Most lacking in credibility were patent medicine ads, which often included fake testimonials avowing miraculous results from use of the products. (See Figure 5-31.) Even after the Federal Trade Commission was created in 1914, advertisers continued to stretch the truth, or invent their own versions of the truth, with inaccurate or fabricated testimonials—especially when they could be linked to celebrities.

Throughout history the masses have been fascinated by those who have achieved glory through fate or feat. According to professor Richard Ohmann, in the socioeconomic class structures of twentieth-century America, those deserving of celebration could be measured in four categories: "the leading standard of success, followed by social contribution, achievement in field, and monetary standard."[19] With seemingly no more sinew, tissue, or brains than a host of their fellow human beings, selected people starred in movies, married Vanderbilts and Du Ponts, triumphed in sports arenas and on battlefields, or achieved fortune and celebrity in any one of a hundred other ways. People wanted to read about their favorite celebrities, to see them, to be associated with them.

Advertisers provided one of the avenues for the masses to connect with popular celebrities. Ads featured the likenesses of famous and important people, and sometimes included anecdotal information about their superlative lives. Personal appearances sponsored by manufacturers and distributors brought celebrities up close to their adoring public. Most important, the shampoos, coffees, cigarettes, and soaps used (supposedly) by celebrities

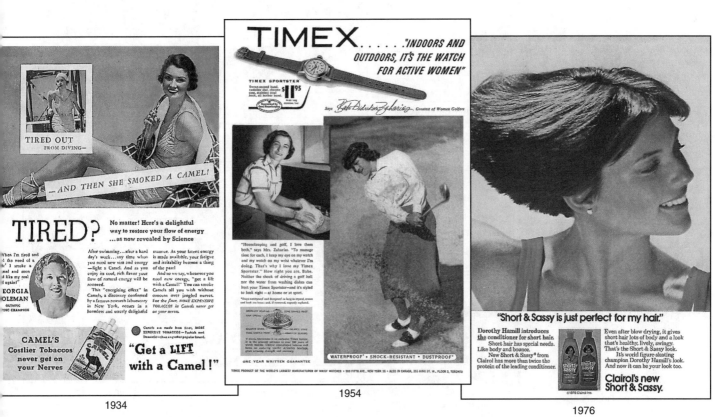

1934

1954

1976

Figure 11-24. Female champion athletes and Olympians became popular advertising spokeswomen from the late 1920s forward.

Marion Davies 1917

Helen Chadwick 1919

Gloria Swanson 1925

Mae West 1934

Shirley Temple 1936

Norma Shearer and
Joan Crawford 1939

Judy Garland 1941

Carole Lombard 1941

Ginger Rogers 1942

Marlene Dietrich 1942

Rita Hayworth 1943

Lana Turner 1945

Figure 11-25. Advertising provided Hollywood studios and stars with publicity and mass exposure.

Maureen O'Hara 1950

Marilyn Monroe 1951

Jane Wyman 1952

Elizabeth Taylor 1957

could be purchased by ordinary folk, which could provide a vicariously shared experience for the consumer. In the 1920s, legendary adman Stanley Resor recognized the marketing significance of what he called "the spirit of emulation." He explained, "We want to copy those whom we deem superior in taste or knowledge or experience."[20]

None could be more superior in taste, knowledge, or experience than America's "branded" families. Between the World Wars a surge of socially prominent women, including First Ladies Grace Coolidge and Eleanor Roosevelt, lent their images and names to product marketing. (Figure 11-22.) Why would these socialites and notables subject themselves to possible peer criticism by endorsing mattresses, cameras, cigarettes, and beauty creams? Three particular reasons are evident.

First is precedence. Society's real crème de la crème—the titled nobility of Europe, including England's Queen Victoria and the future Queen Alexandra—had been presented in testimonial ads even in the nineteenth century. Once that door was opened, ad agencies ardently scoured the social circles of Europe for aristocrats willing to license themselves for advertising. In numerous pages of American magazines, crowned and coroneted heads posed in regal splendor beneath product headlines or next to brand logos. (Figure 11-23.) In a 1925 survey of consumers about the endorsers featured in Pond's Cold Cream ads, three of the four top draws were titled Europeans: Princess Marie de Bourbon, Queen Marie of Romania and the Duchesse de Richelieu.[21]

The second reason is ego. America's socially prominent women were featured in ways that likened them to royalty. Ad agencies spared no expense in procuring the finest painters and photographers to create portraits of these grand dames that would be worthy of the most elegant Park Avenue, Mainline, or Beacon Hill salon. In addition, ego could lead to competition. Just as a photo in the society pages of the Sunday papers would be welcomed by most of these women, so too was the well-executed ad in a national magazine. If Mrs. Astor posed for a Pond's ad and received such glamorous notoriety, then so could Mrs. Belmont, Mrs. Morgan, and Mrs. Drexel. Wrote

Debbie Reynolds 1963

Audrey Hepburn 1972

COUNTESS ISSERLYN MAKEUP.
IT WAS CREATED FOR THE WOMEN
EVERY OTHER WOMAN WANTED TO LOOK LIKE.

There was something electric about the great stars then.
The way they looked, dressed, walked and even talked was alluring and exciting.
And the makeup they wore was part of their magic. For it illuminated their complexions
and made everything about them look radiant. That makeup was Countess Isserlyn.
Countess Isserlyn makeup is as radiant as it ever was. It's the classic of all makeups today.
And the women who wear it are often like the stars. The envy of every woman.
COUNTESS ISSERLYN MAKEUP BY ALEXANDRA DE MARKOFF
Available in liquid or creme

Figure 11-26. Even deceased celebrities continued to have popular appeal and were represented in ads decades after their deaths. Ad 1977.

Roland Marchand of this high-society phenomenon: "The 'society' of the wealthy, moreover, was an organized society. As revealed in advertisements, it had distinct boundaries and standards of admission. People who were 'in society' could be confidently labeled as such."[22]

Third, but certainly not least, is the huge fees paid by agencies. Although many socialites donated their fees to charity, for those who kept the cash, the subject would not have been open to discussion in polite circles any more than would have been the worth or income level of their husbands.

It was the huge fees above all else that made possible the capture of such a wide range of celebrity spokeswomen in the advertising net. As the walls against women athletes began to crumble in the 1920s, Olympians and professional champions received front-page headlines and news stories that made them commodities to advertisers. (Figure 11-24.) The relationship between advertisers and athletes—female and male—became symbiotic. The advertisers enjoyed the halo effect of the athlete's glory, while the athlete, in addition to big endorsement fees, received publicity which made her even more marketable.

Of all the female icons, logos, and spokeswomen used in advertising, none can rival the prolific number and exposure of Hollywood's stars. (Figure 11-25.) Public interest in movie stars had reached a frenetic level even before World War I. Specialized periodicals such as *Photoplay, Screenland, Movie Thriller,* and *Motion Picture* detailed the biographies and daily activities of the various studios' living properties. In their Middletown study the Lynds noted that the public library's most current issue of *Motion Picture* was already in a "coverless, thumbmarked condition" barely two weeks after arriving.[23]

In its own way, advertising contributed to this pool of public information about the stars, even if largely fictionalized. The consumer received glimpses of the star's "favorite" brand of shampoo, soft drink, makeup, or automobile. Many times the ads revealed tidbits of the star's personal life in the copy, and provided photos that advertisers expected to be pinned up in fans' homes.

Advertising's relationship with Hollywood was so profound that in the 1920s the J. W. Thompson agency even kept a representative in residence there. The agency would sign up starlets while they were still unknowns for key accounts such as Lux Soap. Clara Bow, Janet Gaynor, and Joan Crawford were a few of those who went on to stardom and then appeared in ads for JWT.[24] Frederick Lewis Allen recorded in 1931 that "one queen of the films was said to have journeyed from California all the way to New York to spend a single exhausting day being photographed for testimonial purposes in dozens of costumes and using dozens of commercial articles,

1935

1967

1976

Figure 11-27. The most prevalent form of testimonials in advertising was that of advice, warnings, and confessions from "savvy neighbors." These formats created the feeling of a personal relationship for the reader.

many of which she had presumably never laid eyes on before—and all because the appearance of these testimonials would help advertise her newest picture."[25]

The mystique of Hollywood and its stars never diminished. The cult of celebrity adoration extended even to a sort of worship of the dead. Countess Isserlyn cosmetics featured one of the great beauties of all time in its 1977 ads—Vivien Leigh as Scarlett O'Hara. (Figure 11-26.) No explanation or disclaimer was required since Leigh's face was still as famous as it had been forty years earlier. The trend of resurrecting images of deceased stars to use in ads and even in computer-enhanced television spots continued throughout the 1980s and 1990s: James Dean endorsed khakis for the Gap, Marilyn Monroe touted Diet Coke, uniformed John Wayne commandeered Coors beer from an army sergeant, and Fred Astaire danced with a Dirt Devil vacuum cleaner. The glory of some celebrities, especially those of Hollywood, is eternal. So too is their "sellebrity," as James Twitchell called the exploitation.[26]

A spokeswoman did not necessarily have to be from the upper crust of society or the celestial sphere of Hollywood to be compelling. Indeed, the most prevalent form of testimonial came from what Richard Ohmann labeled the "savvy neighbor" who could effectively "urge, exhort, even needle the reader."[27] (Figure 11-27.) This good neighbor is more experienced than are we, the readers of her ad. She has had an epiphany of some sort and claims the right, as any good neighbor might, to advise us of her findings. A homey syntax would invite the reader to participate in the ad, to hear the neighbor's confession or tale of redemption. "Suddenly, my easy life slid

Figure 11-28. Anita Bryant became so inextricably linked with an antigay group in the 1970s that she was dropped by the Florida Citrus Commission as its spokeswoman. Ad 1969.

away from me . . . " began the 1935 letter of Mrs. Middleton to Chipso; "I must admit . . . " opened Mrs. Santoro's admission to Cold Power in 1967; "Your age is just a number . . ." insisted Mrs. Davison in a 1976 Ivory Liquid ad. The sell copy of such ads was friendly—no preaching, no condescending spouting of science and technology. The good neighbor testimonial ad became a personal relationship with the reader.

However, an advertiser can be faced with an expensive dilemma when negative circumstances tarnish its spokesperson. Anita Bryant, runner-up to Miss America in 1959, was featured for years as its spokeswoman for the Florida Citrus Commission. (Figure 11-28.) During the mid-1970s she became affiliated with religious groups in a campaign against the gay community. The orange growers and retailers who sponsored Bryant as their product spokeswoman found themselves being accused of homophobia, bigotry, and intolerance—guilt by association. Making no distinction between Florida, California, or foreign citrus growers, the industry as a whole was targeted with a national boycott. Despite millions of dollars in print and TV ads to build the credibility of its spokeswoman, the Florida Citrus Commission terminated its $100,000 contract with Bryant.[28] Even so, until she retired from the controversial limelight the citrus industry continued to be stigmatized, since the public still connected Bryant with the orange juice she had touted for years.

Unlike Bryant, who created months of negative publicity, for some advertising spokespersons all it took was one incident. Reports of substance abuse caused a parting of the ways between Bruce Willis and Seagram's; Diet Pepsi fled from Mike Tyson following charges of spousal abuse; Campbell's Soups sidelined football star Reggie White after his anti-gay remarks in a speech before the Wisconsin legislature; and Hertz lost no time in severing ties with O. J. Simpson upon his arrest for a double murder.

Conclusion: Delivering the Message and Imprinting the Image

As the second industrial revolution steadily gained momentum following the Civil War, manufacturers of consumer products began to carve out their respective niches in the rapidly expanding mass market. Improvements in production technology and more efficient channels of distribution helped spawn fierce competition in every arena of manufacturing. To protect their businesses and ensure growth in market share, manufacturers explored new methods of marketing, including a focus on brand enhancement. Part of the product branding strategy for most marketers was the creation of a trademark, a symbol that stood for the company's reputation and that made certain guarantees and assurances to consumers.

Many marketers delivered such messages to the public with the image of an attractive woman, an idealized personification of the company she represented. Depictions of contemporary women that were used in trademark logos and promotional materials signified to the consumer a freshness and modernity for the image of the product, brand, or manufacturer. Such representations, though, were doomed to obsolescence as standards of beauty and fashion changed. For instance, to maintain a contemporary look for Kelly Springfield Tires or Ethyl Gasoline, the flapper icons (Lotta Miles and

Ethyl) of the 1920s needed makeovers virtually every season. Other marketers avoided the obsolescence issue by choosing historical figures, fantasy creatures, allegories, cartoon characters, or exotic foreigners as their logo icons. Elsie the cow, the Sun-Maid raisin girl, and the Chicken of the Sea mermaid did not need new costumes or hairstyles despite marketing tenures that extended over decades. Still other marketers continued to build equity in their icons by periodically updated their images. The representation of Aunt Jemima, for example, evolved from the caricature of an antebellum plantation cook in 1900 to that of a modern African-American homemaker in 1999. Even without any supporting verbiage, icons could effectively deliver the marketer's message of product, brand, or company image.

Icons also served a second function, to capture the consumer's attention. Children icons were especially effective as eye-catching images. From the realism of the Jell-O girl and Morton Salt girl to the caricatures of Betsy Bell and the Campbell Kids, depictions of children were visual magnets for women. Similarly, familiar icons such as Betty Crocker inspired trust and confidence in a product because they represented a believable sincerity that crossed generations of consumers. Some marketers even created living icons by inventing TV personalities such as Josephine the plumber and Madge the manicurist whose fictional expertise validated the quality of the product they represented. Whether it was Betty Crocker's warm smile or Betsy Bell's precocious antics, icons provided marketers with a competitive advantage in imprinting the image of their product or brand with the consumer.

As a derivation of the icon, the spokeswoman also became a significant component of many marketing strategies. Famous socialites, athletes, actresses, and other celebrities not only served to capture the attention of women consumers in ads and promotional materials, they also established or reinforced an image for the product or brand. Unlike with children icons, though, the high-profile real-life spokeswomen were sometimes risks for marketers. The particular marketing value of celebrities was the reflected glory of their fame to the sponsoring product or brand. Their endorsement was a testimonial that target customers found logical and credible. By the same token, controversial personal behavior by a spokeswoman could reflect negatively on the product with which she was so publicly associated. Even so, the salesmanship of a credible spokewoman was so effective that marketers continued to take their chances.

Whichever course manufacturers chose in their marketing strategies—a trademark logo, an icon, or a spokeswoman—they banked on two key results from their efforts and investment. First was an effective delivery of their message to the consumer, whether it was about their product, service, brand, or company image; second was the imprinting of the image of their logo, icon, or spokeswoman on the consumer so that the message and the image were instantly recognized and accepted by the public. Given the longevity of so many trademarks, this aspect of marketing has proven to be successful for more than a dozen decades.

NOTES

Preface

1. Curtis Publishing Company ad: *Ladies' Home Journal,* August 1915, inside back cover.
2. Bridget Biggane, ed., "Magazine Ad Review," *Retail Ad World,* September 1998, 43.
3. Christine Frederick, *Selling Mrs. Consumer* (New York: Business Bourse, 1929), 12.
4. Gilbert Burck, "You Can Only Estimate the Power of a Woman," *Fortune,* August 1956, 95.
5. Ibid.
6. Helen Woodward, *The Lady Persuaders* (New York: Ivan Obolenky, 1960), 1–2.
7. Richard Ohmann, *Selling Culture* (London: Verso, 1996), 25.
8. Ibid., 29.
9. Hearst ad: *Superbrands* (*Adweek* supplement), October 20, 1997, 17.
10. Ann Marie Kerwin, "Recast Seven Sisters Still Seek Points of Difference," *Advertising Age,* April 6, 1998, 10.
11. Magazine Publishers of America ad: *Adweek,* October 20, 1997, 43.
12. Rance Crain, "'Reader's Digest' Isn't about Selling Stuff to Its Readers," *Advertising Age,* October 12, 1998, 30.
13. Mary Tolan, "Holidays Are Here and So Is Ad Puzzle," *Advertising Age,* November 16, 1998, 36.
14. Judann Pollack and Alice Cuneo, "Energy Bars Examine Strategy as Entries Hike Competition," *Advertising Age,* September 2, 1998, 3.
15. Debra Goldman, "No-Man's Land," *Adweek,* November 16, 1998, 62.
16. Report on ABC's *Good Morning America,* November 30, 1998.
17. Roland Marchand, *Advertising the American Dream* (Berkeley: University of California Press, 1985), xvii.
18. Ohmann, *Selling Culture,* 25.

Chapter 1

1. Crisco ads: *Ladies' Home Journal,* March 1913, 49; October 1916, 50.
2. Franco American ads: *Cosmopolitan,* September 1891, 11; February 1894, 69.
3. Susan Strasser, *Satisfaction Guaranteed* (Washington, D.C.: Smithsonian Institution Press, 1989), 255.
4. Colgate ad: *Literary Digest,* October 27, 1906, 621; Jell-O ad: *Literary Digest,* July 20, 1907, 108; Ralston Purina ad: *Literary Digest,* September 14, 1907, 388; Coca-Cola ad: *Literary Digest,* July 13, 1907, 74.
5. Anna Reese Richardson, "Just as Good," *Ladies' World Magazine,* November 1913, 12.
6. John Schlachter, "This Is the Way Some National Advertisers Fight Substitution," *Printers' Ink,* March 17, 1921, 182.
7. W. M. Steuart, *Retail Distribution, Part 1, Fifteenth Census of the United States* (Washington, D.C.: U.S. Department of Commerce, 1933), 47.
8. Schlachter, "This Is the Way Some National Advertisers Fight Substitution," 182.
9. Ibid., 177.
10. Tamar Nordenberg, "Recalls: FDA, Industry Cooperate to Protect Consumer," *FDA Home Page,* www.fda.gov/fdac/features/895_recalls.html, October 1995, 3–4.
11. Ivan Preston, *The Tangled Web They Weave* (Madison: University of Wisconsin Press, 1994), 168; Ira Teinowitz, "FTC Faces Test of Ad Power," *Advertising Age,* March 30, 1998, 26.

12. John Irving Romer, ed., "President Coolidge Pays Advertising Its Highest Tribute," *Printers' Ink,* November 4, 1926, 196.
13. J. Walter Thompson ad: *Fortune,* May 1931, 103.
14. W. M. Steurat, *Abstract of the Fifteenth Census of the United States* (Washington, D.C.: U.S. Department of Commerce, 1933), 82.
15. W. M. Steurat, *Abstract of the Fourteenth Census of the United States* (Washington, D.C.: U.S. Department of Commerce, 1923), 481.
16. Christine Frederick, "Teach Women What Advertising Does," *Printers' Ink,* June 10, 1920, 178.
17. Jane Traulsen, ed., "Direct Media," *DM News,* October 13, 1997, 9; "Name Finder's Lists," *DM News,* 38; "Brylane," *DM News,* October 27, 1997, 26; "Focus U.S.A.," *DM News,* October 27, 1997, 32; "List Services," *DM News,* November 3, 1997, 29.
18. Magazine Publishers of America ad: *Adweek,* October 20, 1997, 43.
19. Frank Rowsome, *They Laughed When I Sat Down* (New York: Bonanza Books, 1959), 23.
20. Gloria Steinem, *Moving beyond Words* (New York: Simon & Schuster, 1994), 155–57.
21. Anne Marie Kerwin, "Magazines," *Advertising Age,* Special Section, October 27, 1997, s10.
22. *Philadelphia Record* ad: *Printers' Ink,* December 16, 1920, 109.
23. *Saturday Evening Post* ad: *Printers' Ink,* September 23, 1955, 112.
24. *Saturday Evening Post* ad: *Printers' Ink,* September 28, 1956, 78.
25. Henry Luce, ed., "Angry Battler for Her Sex," *Life,* November 1, 1963, 84–88.
26. Magazine Publishers of America ad: *Adweek,* October 20, 1997, 43.
27. Hearst ad: *Superbrands* (*Adweek* supplement), October 20, 1997, 17. (*Cosmopolitan, Good Housekeeping, Harper's Bazaar, Marie Claire, Redbook, Town & Country, Victoria*)
28. Magazine Publishers of America ad: *Advertising Age,* October 20, 1997, 35.
29. Ann Marie Kerwin, "Recast Seven Sisters Still Seek Points of Difference," *Advertising Age,* April 6, 1998, 10.

Chapter 2

1. William Weilbacher, *Advertising* (New York: Macmillan Publishing, 1979), 328.
2. Alvin Harlow, *Old Post Bags* (New York: Appleton, 1928), 332–33.
3. Karen and James Claus, *The Sign User's Guide* (Cincinnati: S. T. Publications, 1988), 3.
4. David Jenkins, *Rock City Barns, A Passing Era* (Chattanooga, Tenn.: Free Spirit Press, 1996), 9.
5. Nathan Danziger, "Profit Making Displays," *Printers' Ink,* October 18, 1934, 72.
6. Sara Schneider, *Vital Mummies* (New Haven, Conn.: Yale University Press, 1995), 8.
7. John Irving Romer, ed., "Radio and Tomorrow's Advertisers," *Printers' Ink,* April 13, 1922, 170.
8. Robert Campbell, *The Golden Years of Broadcasting* (New York: Rutledge Books, 1976), 24.
9. John Irving Romer, ed., "Radio as an Advertising Medium," *Printers' Ink,* April 27, 1922, 201.
10. Bernard Grimes, "To Improve Radio," *Printers' Ink,* May 23, 1935, 24.
11. Yolanda Mero-Irion, "What the Women Like and Dislike about Radio," *Printers' Ink,* March 21, 1935, 67–70.
12. Harold Clark, "Women and Radio Programs," *Printers' Ink,* September 12, 1935, 66.
13. Recamier ad: *Cosmopolitan,* June 1891, 19; Pear's ad: *Delineator,* July 1897, back cover.
14. Mero-Irion, "What the Women Like and Dislike about Radio," 67.
15. Roy Durstine, "Radio Advertising's Future in the United States," *Printers' Ink,* January 24, 1935, 43.
16. Francis Wheen, *Television* (London: Century, 1985), 33–38.
17. Ibid., 35.
18. Campbell, *The Golden Years of Broadcasting,* 58.
19. Robert Goldsborough, "The Postwar Era: 1945–1950," *Advertising Age,* July 31, 1995, 25.

20. Wayne Cox, *Sixteenth Annual Report of the Federal Communications Commission,* Washington, D.C., 1951, 117–18.
21. Henry Luce, ed., "Television, It Is a Commercial Reality but Not Yet an Art," *Life,* December 1, 1947, 118.
22. Max Wilk, *Golden Age of Television* (New York: Delacorte Press, 1976).
23. Susan Faludi, *Backlash* (New York: Crown, 1991), 53.
24. Betty Friedan, *The Feminine Mystique* (New York: W. W. Norton, 1963), 72.
25. Eldridge Peterson, ed., "Top 162 TV Markets—With Number of TV Sets," *Printers' Ink,* October 23, 1953, 192–93.
26. Wheen, *Television,* 185–86.
27. Chuck Ross, "ABC Withholds Ad Info on Controversial Shows," *Advertising Age,* September 29, 1997, 58; " 'Nothing Sacred' Keeps Faith Despite Boycott Push," *Advertising Age,* October 20, 1997, 16.
28. Howard Brunsman, *1960 Census of Population* (Washington, D.C.: U.S. Department of Commerce, 1964), 213; Vincent Barabba, *1970 Census of Population,* 1971, 679; Barbara Bryant, *1990 Census of Population,* 1992, 120.
29. Laura Rich, "A Brand New Game," *Adweek,* September 22, 1997, 56.
30. Todd Wallack, "Net Music Customers Lose Cards; Amex, Discover React to Hacker Attack," *San Francisco Chronicle,* January 19, 2000, www.sfgate.com/cgi-bin/article.cgi?file=chronicle/article/ 2000/01/19/ bu9822.dtl.
31. Thrive Online ad: *Adweek,* August 18, 1997, 21; Home Arts Network ad: *Adweek,* November 17, 1997, 39.
32. Beth Snyder, "New Networks, Site Upgrades Target Women," *Advertising Age,* September 15, 1997, 52.

Chapter 3

1. Evan Jones, *American Food* (New York: E. P. Dutton, 1975), 28.
2. John Mariani, *The Dictionary of American Food and Drink* (New York: Hearst Books, 1994), xvii.
3. Ruth Cowan, *More Work for Mother* (New York: Basic Books, 1983), 62.
4. Daniel Cohen, *The Last Hundred Years, Household Technology* (New York: M. Evans, 1982), 20.
5. Christine Frederick, *The New Housekeeping* (Garden City, N.Y.: Doubleday, Page, 1913), 79.
6. Mark Sullivan, *Our Times* (New York: Charles Scribner's Sons, 1927), 428.
7. Robert and Helen Lynd, *Middletown, A Study in Contemporary American Culture* (New York: Harcourt, Brace, 1929), 98.
8. P. Ranganath Nayak and John Ketteringhan, *Breakthroughs* (New York: Rawson Associates, 1986), 186.
9. Ibid., 197.
10. Lynd and Lynd, *Middletown, A Study in Contemporary American Culture,* 172.
11. Cowan, *More Work for Mother,* 132–33.
12. Susan Strasser, *Never Done* (New York: Pantheon Books, 1982), 265.
13. Leon Truesdell, *Sixteenth Census of the United States, 1940: Housing,* vol. II (Washington, D.C.: Bureau of the Census, 1943), 84, 92.
14. Louise Michele Newman, ed., *Men's Ideas/Women's Realities* (New York: Pergamon Press, 1985), 181.
15. Strasser, *Never Done,* 105.
16. Whirldry ad: *Better Homes and Gardens,* June 1927, 33.
17. Sullivan, *Our Times,* 428.
18. Ibid., 430.
19. Clara Zillessen, "My Favorite Coworker—Electricity," *Ladies' Home Journal,* February 1927, 141.
20. KitchenAid ads: *McCall's,* July 1959, 150; May 1960, 14; July 1960, 28.
21. Bissell ad: *Munsey,* April 1902, 210.
22. Electrolux ad: *Better Homes and Gardens,* December 1955, 27; Kingston ad: *Good Housekeeping,*

October 1955, 258; Rexair ad: *Woman's Home Companion,* December 1955, 95; Singer ad: *Woman's Home Companion,* December 1956, 70.

23. Franz Premier ads: *Saturday Evening Post,* October 31, 1914, 32; September 1, 1917, 33.

24. Ronald Kline, "Agents of Modernity: Home Economics and Rural Electrification," in *Rethinking Home Economics,* ed. Sara Stage (Ithaca, N.Y.: Cornell University Press, 1997), 250.

25. Hoover ad: *American,* October 1924, 80.

26. Victor Margolin, Ira Brichta, and Vivian Brichta, *The Promise and the Product* (New York: Macmillan, 1979), 81.

27. Glenna Matthews, *Just a Housewife* (New York: Oxford University Press, 1987), 101.

28. Harvey Green, *The Light of the Home* (New York: Pantheon Books, 1983), 82.

29. Christine Frederick, "What You Should Know about the Can You Buy," *Ladies' Home Journal,* October 1916, 54.

30. Green, *The Light of the Home,* 61.

31. Strasser, *Satisfaction Guaranteed,* 34–35.

32. Dorothy Marsh, "Visits to the Grocer," *Good Housekeeping,* April 1939, 130.

33. Strasser, *Never Done,* 275.

34. Carol Hymowitz and Michael Weissman, *A History of Women in America* (New York: Bantam, 1978), 327.

35. Betty Friedan, *The Feminine Mystique* (New York: Dell, 1983), 211.

36. Rowsome, *They Laughed When I Sat Down,* 26.

37. Mary Seehafer Sears, "Doin' the Wash," *Country Living,* November 1991, 201.

38. Cohen, *The Last Hundred Years, Household Technology,* 91.

39. Ivory ads: *Literary Digest,* January 20, 1906, 99; February 3, 1906, 173; February 17, 1906, 255; March 17, 1906, 415; March 31, 1906, 493; November 24, 1906, 769.

40. George Hay Brown, *1970 Census of Housing: Housing Characteristics for States, Cities, and Counties* (Washington, D.C.: U.S. Department of Commerce, 1972), 1/230.

41. Truesdell, *Sixteenth Census of the United States, 1940: Housing,* 78.

42. Demetria Taylor, "Let the Cleanser Do the Cleaning," *Good Housekeeping,* January 1936, 82.

43. Newman, *Men's Ideas/Women's Realities,* 187.

44. Friedan, *The Feminine Mystique,* 210.

Chapter 4

1. Friedan, *The Feminine Mystique,* ix.

2. Faludi, *Backlash,* 454.

3. Karen Lehrman, *The Lipstick Proviso* (New York: Anchor Books, 1997), 62.

4. Lynd and Lynd, *Middletown, A Study in Contemporary American Culture,* 116.

5. Robert Stein, ed., "Right Now," *McCall's,* April 1976, 87.

6. Oliver Jensen, *The Revolt of American Women* (New York: Harcourt, Brace, 1952), 5.

7. Marchand, *Advertising the American Dream,* 207.

8. Ibid., 344.

9. Lillian Eichler, *The Customs of Mankind* (New York: Doubleday, 1924), 29, 228–32.

10. DeBeers ad: *Rolling Stone,* December 8, 1983, 54.

11. George Napheys, *The Physical Life of Woman* (Philadelphia: George MacLean, 1870), 69.

12. Margery Lawrence, "I Don't Want to Be a Mother," *Cosmopolitan,* January 1929, 41.

13. Cosmopolitan ad: *Good Housekeeping,* January 1929, 7.

14. Lynd and Lynd, *Middletown, A Study in Contemporary American Culture,* 131.

15. Annegret Ogden, *The Great American Housewife* (Westport, Conn.: Greenwood Press, 1986), 174.

16. Maxine Margolis, *Mothers and Such* (Berkeley: University of California Press, 1984), 89.

17. Carol Moog, *Are They Selling Her Lips?* (New York: William Morrow, 1990), 167.

18. Nestlé ad: *Ladies' Home Journal,* January 1895, 24.

19. Napheys, *The Physical Life of Woman,* 245.

20. Mellin's ad: *Ladies' Home Journal,* November 1893, 35.

21. Allenbury and Eskay ads: *Ladies' Home Journal,* March 1906, 28; Nestlé ad: *Ladies' Home Journal,* July 1909, 32.

22. Green, *The Light of the Home,* 41.

23. Lynd and Lynd, *Middletown, A Study in Contemporary American Culture,* 454.

24. Napheys, *The Physical Life of Woman,* 240–43.

25. Ivory ad: *Ladies' Home Journal,* October 1892, 24.

26. Moog, *Are They Selling Her Lips?* 180.

27. Robert and Helen Lynd, *Middletown in Transition* (New York: Harcourt, Brace, 1937), 397.

28. Laurence Johnson, *Over the Counter and on the Shelf* (New York: Bonanza Books, 1961), 117.

29. Tylenol ad: *Redbook,* November 1977, 42; Bayer ad, 29.

30. Frederick, *Selling Mrs. Consumer,* 197.

31. Lynd and Lynd, *Middletown, A Study in Contemporary American Culture,* 456–57.

32. Lynd and Lynd, *Middletown in Transition,* 401.

33. Association of American Soap and Glycerine Producers ad: *Ladies' Home Journal,* October 1928, 233.

34. Wilson Sports Equipment ad: *Ladies' Home Journal,* August 1943, 70.

35. W. Livingston Larned, "Some Possibilities of the Child Appeal," *Printers' Ink,* September 25, 1924, 72.

Chapter 5

1. Robert Howard Russell, "How Charles Dana Gibson Started," *Ladies' Home Journal,* October 1902, 8.

2. Maitland Edey, ed., *This Fabulous Century,* vol. 1 (New York: Time-Life Books, 1969), 181.

3. Robert Lazich, ed., *Market Share Reporter* (Detroit: Gale, 1998), 141.

4. Charles Panati, *Panati's Extraordinary Origins of Everyday Things* (New York: Perennial Library, 1987), 225.

5. Mary Roberts Rinehart, "The Chaotic Decade: The 1920s," in *The Journal of the Century,* ed. Bryan Holme (New York: Viking Penguin, 1976), 148.

6. Ralph K. Andrist, ed., *The American Heritage History of the 1920s and 1930s* (New York: American Heritage, 1987), 122.

7. Mary Ryan, *Womanhood in America* (New York: Franklin Watts, 1983), 227.

8. Sullivan, *Our Times,* 381.

9. Carol Hymowitz and Michaele Weissman, *A History of Women in America* (New York: Bantam Books, 1978), 292.

10. Maggie Angeloglou, *A History of Make-up* (London: Macmillan, 1965), 121.

11. Hymowitz and Weissman, *A History of Women in America,* 292.

12. Angeloglou, *A History of Make-up,* 128.

13. Frederick, *Selling Mrs. Consumer,* 195.

14. Faludi, *Backlash,* 202.

15. Nancy Friday, *The Power of Beauty* (New York: Harper Collins, 1996), 530.

16. Naomi Wolf, *The Beauty Myth* (New York: Anchor Books, 1991), 65.

17. Hall's ad: *Outlook,* February 1898, xxiii.

18. Eichler, *The Customs of Mankind,* 552.

19. Imperial ad: *Cosmopolitan,* September 1891, 32.

20. Susan Brownmiller, *Femininity* (New York: Linden Press, 1984), 56–57.

21. Bernice Kanner, "Do You Lie about Your Age?" *More,* Spring 1997, 38.

22. Panati, *Panati's Extraordinary Origins of Everyday Things,* 233.

23. Jack Neff, "Revlon Extends ColorStay to Shampoo," *Advertising Age,* October 19, 1998, 4.

24. Betty Friedan, *The Fountain of Age* (New York: Simon and Schuster, 1993), 55–62.

25. Paul Nystrom, *Economics of Fashion* (New York: Ronald Press, 1928), 75.

26. Clara Zillessen, "My Favorite Coworker—Electricity," *Ladies' Home Journal,* February 1927, 141.

27. Napheys, *The Physical Life of Woman,* 285.

28. Ivory ad: *Outlook,* October 3, 1896, 631; Pear's ads: *Cosmopolitan,* February 1891, 1; August 1893, 1; June 1894, 1.

29. Frederick, *Selling Mrs. Consumer,* 195.

30. Panati, *Panati's Extraordinary Origins of Everyday Things,* 227–28.

31. L'Oreal ad: *In Style,* July 1997, 89.

32. Chantal Tode, "Oil of Olay Hits Maturity," *Women's Wear Daily,* May 8, 1998, 10.

33. Pat Sloane, "With Aging Boomers in Mind, P&G, Den-Mat Plan Launches," *Advertising Age,* April 13, 1998, 38.

34. Rembrandt ad: *Vogue,* May 1998, 94–95.

35. Pond's ad: *Good Housekeeping,* July 1929, 111.

36. Brownmiller, *Femininity,* 136.

37. Joanne Chen, "Still Think You Can Get a Safe Tan?" *Glamour,* July 1997, 58.

38. Hawaiian Tropic ad: *Mirabella,* May/June 1997, 73.

39. Melanie Ward, "The Art of the Indoor Tan," *Harper's Bazaar,* June 1997, 144.

40. Gale Hansen, "How To Fake the Darkest Tan," *Harper's Bazaar,* June 1997, 50.

41. Brownmiller, *Femininity,* 148.

42. Christine Fellingham, "Painless Hair Remover?" *Glamour,* July 1997, 144.

43. Spa Thira ad: *Vogue,* June 1997, 149.

44. Napheys, *The Physical Life of Woman,* 27–30.

45. Johnson, *Over the Counter and on the Shelf,* 115–16.

46. Carol Tavris, *The Mismeasure of Woman* (New York: Simon and Schuster, 1992), 131–43.

47. Statement on the product packaging for Dimensyn, 1998.

48. Fleischmann's ad: *Ladies' Home Journal,* September 1934, 49.

49. Panati, *Panati's Extraordinary Origins of Everyday Things,* 208–13.

50. Lynd and Lynd, *Middletown, A Study in Contemporary American Culture,* 435–57; *Middletown in Transition,* 391.

51. Marchand, *Advertising the American Dream,* 344.

52. Listerine ads: *American,* October 1924, 137; *Ladies' Home Journal,* June 1929, 74; *Woman's Home Companion,* June 1930, 49; *Pictorial Review,* December 1937, 1; *McCall's,* November 1947, 3; *Good Housekeeping,* February 1948, 3; Lavoris ad: *American,* February 1930, 113.

53. Charles Goodrum and Helen Dalrymple, *Advertising in America, The First 200 Years* (New York: Harry N. Abrams, 1990), 151.

54. Marchand, *Advertising the American Dream,* 344–46.

55. Lysol ad: *Good Housekeeping,* November 1933, 142.

56. Kotex ads: *Redbook,* April 1926, 173; *Ladies' Home Journal,* August 1926, 101; July 1927, 82; September 1927, 82.

57. Modess ad: *Woman's Home Companion,* June 1938, 69.

58. Lehrman, *The Lipstick Proviso,* 84–87.

59. Susan McQuillan, "Lose 10 Lbs. by Summer," *McCall's,* May 1998, 72–76; Elizabeth Somer, "Lose 5 Pounds—This Week," *Redbook,* June 1998, 50–52; Janis Jibrin, "Drop 10 Pounds by Summer," *Family Circle,* April 21, 1998, 50–53; Kathy Smith, "Think Your Way Thin," *Woman's Day,* April 1, 1998, 62–67; Michelle Stacey, "All You Can Eat," *Elle,* March 1998, 318–20; Phyllis Posnick, "The Fat of the Land," *Vogue,* March 1998, 488–91; Janet Bailey, "The Diet of the Century," *Ladies' Home Journal,* April 1998, 166–87; Nancy Miller, "Cosmo Diet," *Cosmopolitan,* April 1998, 112; Mary Ann Marshall, "The Very Scary New Diet Drugs," *Mademoiselle,* April 1998, 103–4; Michele Meyer, "Do Diets Work?" *Marie Claire,* May 1998, 162–66.

60. Timothy Walsh, "A Question of Treatment," *Vogue*, September 1997, 674.

61. Elizabeth Berg, "In Praise of the Imperfect Body," *Good Housekeeping*, July 1997, 58.

62. Delia Hammock, "The I-Just-Need-To-Lose-10-Pounds Diet," *Good Housekeeping*, May 1996, 116–18.

63. Lucky Strike ad: *Golden Book*, January 1930, back cover; Old Golds ad: *Life*, March 13, 1950, 71.

64. Edwin Morris, *Fragrance* (New York: Charles Scribner's Sons, 1984), 204.

65. Yardley ads: *American*, November 1942, 77; *Good Housekeeping*, March 1947, 161; *McCall's*, May 1949, 136; *Ladies' Home Journal*, April 1954, 145.

66. Frederick, *Selling Mrs. Consumer*, 189.

67. Estee Lauder, *Estee, A Success Story* (New York: Random House, 1985), 133.

68. Faludi, *Backlash*, 205–8.

69. Brownmiller, *Femininity*, 152.

70. James Servin, "Mirror, Mirror, Are We Happy Yet?" *Harper's Bazaar*, September 1997, 300.

71. Jennifer M. Preuss and Meredith Asplundh, "First Look," *Harper's Bazaar*, September 1997, 261–82.

Chapter 6

1. Jenny June Croly, ed., "The Fashions," *Godey's Lady's Book*, December 1888, 501.

2. *Vogue* ad: *Cosmopolitan*, "Advertising Department," February 1893, 19.

3. *Vogue* ad: *Life*, December 28, 1898, 557.

4. Nystrom, *Economics of Fashion*, 282.

5. Anna Westermann, "Can America Originate Its Own Fashions?" *Ladies' Home Journal*, September 1909, 11, 81.

6. Nystrom, *Economics of Fashion*, 181.

7. Georgina Howell, *In Vogue* (New York: Schocken Books, 1976), 1.

8. Anne Hollander, *Seeing through Clothes* (New York: Viking Press, 1978), 339.

9. Nystrom, *Economics of Fashion*, 394.

10. Jane Mulvagh, *Vogue History of 20th Century Fashions* (New York: Viking Press, 1988), 54.

11. Bruce Bliven, "Flapper Jane," *New Republic*, September 9, 1925, 67.

12. Mulvagh, *Vogue History of 20th Century Fashions*, 52.

13. Nystrom, *Economics of Fashion*, 223.

14. Mulvagh, *Vogue History of 20th Century Fashions*, 89.

15. Howell, *In Vogue*, 62.

16. Gilles Lipovetsky, *The Empire of Fashion*, trans. Catherine Porter (Princeton, N.J.: Princeton University Press, 1994), 80.

17. Ibid., 60.

18. Hollander, *Seeing through Clothes*, 342.

19. Mulvagh, *Vogue History of 20th Century Fashions*, 123.

20. Wilhela Cushman, "New York Fall Collections," *Ladies' Home Journal*, November 1940, 21.

21. Marian Corey, "The Spring Suit Story," *McCall's*, February 1946, 151; "Fall Fashions," August 1948, 127.

22. Mulvagh, *Vogue History of 20th Century Fashions*, 182.

23. Lee Hall, *Common Threads* (New York: Bulfinch Press, 1992), 175.

24. Mulvagh, *Vogue History of 20th Century Fashions*, 241.

25. Ibid.

26. Peter Peterson, *1970 Census of Housing*, vol. 1, part 1 (Washington, D.C.: U.S. Department of Commerce, 1972), 290.

27. Howell, *In Vogue*, 305.

28. Grace Mirabella, ed., "Fashion Now," *Vogue*, September 1973, 251.

29. Grace Mirabella, ed., "Fashion Now," *Vogue*, September 1975, 221.

30. Hollander, *Seeing through Clothes*, 345.

31. Prudence Glynn, *In Fashion* (Oxford: Oxford University Press, 1978), 204/8.

32. Mulvagh, *Vogue History of 20th Century Fashions,* 347.

33. Caroline Milbank, *New York Fashion* (New York: Harry N. Abrams, 1989), 264.

34. Grace Mirabella, ed., "A Different Slant on Fall," *Vogue,* September 1987, 681.

35. Grace Mirabella, ed., "The Forward Edge," *Vogue,* September 1988, 200.

36. Anna Wintour, ed., "Global Fashion," *Vogue,* September 1990, 513.

37. Suzy Menkes, "The Couture Controversy," *Vogue,* October 1991, 267.

38. Anna Wintour, ed., "Letter From the Editor," *Vogue,* September 1992, 30.

39. William Norwich, "New York Style Stories," *Vogue,* September 1994, 599.

40. Grace Coddington, "Mixed Messages," *Vogue,* September 1997, 584.

41. Anna Wintour, ed., "Letter from the Editor," *Vogue,* September 1992, 30.

42. Robert Lazich, ed., *Market Share Reporter* (Detroit, Mich: Gale, 1998), 117–18.

43. Napheys, *The Physical Life of Woman,* 280–81.

44. Susan Kaiser, *The Social Psychology of Clothing* (New York: Macmillan, 1990), 80–113; Green, *The Light of the Home,* 121–22, 130.

45. *Ladies' Home Journal,* September 1895, 27.

46. Bliven, "Flapper Jane," 65.

47. P. N. Practical Front Corset ad: *Ladies' Home Journal,* February 1925, 134.

48. Rene Hafley, "Is the Flapper's Boyish Form a Menace?" *Physical Culture,* October 1925, 33.

49. Howell, *In Vogue,* 260.

50. Elizabeth Ewing, *Dress and Undress* (New York: Drama, 1978), 173.

51. Wade Nichols, ed., "Women's Rights: How GH Readers Feel about Liberation and Equality," *Good Housekeeping,* March 1971, 34.

52. Elaine Benson and John Esten, *Unmentionables* (New York: Simon & Schuster, 1996), 51.

53. Panati, *Panati's Extraordinary Origins of Everyday Things,* 321–22.

54. Andrist, *The American Heritage History of the 1920s and 1930s,* 63.

55. Martin Landey, "Where's the Idea in These Ads?" *Advertising Age,* December 15, 1997, 26.

56. Tom Peters, "Brands Still Rule Supreme," *Advertising Age,* January 26, 1998, 26.

57. William Packer, *Fashion Drawing in Vogue* (New York: Thames and Hudson, 1989), 16.

58. Ibid., 14.

59. Herwig Zahm, ed., *The Art of Creating Fashion* (Pocking, Germany: Mondi Group, 1991), 4.

60. Page counts of advertising-free editorial pages in *Vogue,* May 8, 1902, issue, and the "American Number," February 1, 1950.

Chapter 7

1. Faludi, *Backlash,* 48–49.

2. Columbia ad: *Cosmopolitan,* November 1891, 57.

3. Sullivan, *Our Times,* 494.

4. Peerless Motor Car ad: *Country Life in America,* November 1903, 52.

5. Ford ad: *Ladies' Home Journal,* January 1924, 48.

6. Frederick, *Selling Mrs. Consumer,* 6.

7. Julius Klein, "Two Women at the Counter," *Ladies' Home Journal,* March 1929, 35.

8. Marchand, *Advertising the American Dream,* 138.

9. Lynd and Lynd, *Middletown in Transition,* 267.

10. J. Walter Thompson ad: *Printers' Ink,* November 9, 1956, 33.

11. Amelia E. Barr, "Why Do Not Literary Women Marry?" *Ladies' Home Journal,* November 1893, 10.

12. David S. Jordan, "The Higher Education of Women," in *Men's Ideas/Women's Realities,* ed. Louise Michele Newman (New York: Pergamon Press, 1985), 96.

13. Ibid., 98–102.
14. Myra and David Sadker, *Failing at Fairness* (New York: Charles Scribner's Sons, 1994), 32.
15. Mary Frank Fox, "Women and Higher Education: Sex Differentials in the Status of Students and Scholars," in *Women, A Feminist Perspective,* ed. Jo Freeman (Palo Alto, Cal.: Mayfield, 1984), 241.
16. Ibid., 240.
17. Jensen, *The Revolt of American Women,* 114.
18. Ibid.
19. Fox, "Women and Higher Education: Sex Differentials in the Status of Students and Scholars," 342.
20. Sadker, *Failing at Fairness,* 41.
21. Louis Antoine Godey, ed., "Health and Beauty," *Godey's Lady's Book,* February 1849, 145.
22. Jensen, *The Revolt of American Women,* 129.
23. Lucille Eaton Hill, *Athletics and Outdoor Sports for Women* (New York: Macmillan, 1903), 5.
24. Ibid., 6.
25. Ibid., 179–80.
26. Hugo Masters, "Are We Wasting Our Women?," *Physical Culture,* November 1920, 50–59.
27. Allen Guttman, *Women's Sports: A History* (New York: Columbia University Press, 1991), 136.
28. Hymowitz and Weissman, *A History of Women in America,* 234; Jensen, *The Revolt of American Women,* 84.
29. Malcolm Keir, "Women in Industry," in *Men's Ideas/Women's Realities,* ed. Louise Michele Newman (New York: Pergamon Press, 1985), 292.
30. Hymowitz and Weissman, *A History of Women in America,* 303.
31. Ibid., 304.
32. Ibid., 303.
33. Sheila Rowbotham, *A Century of Women* (New York: Viking Press, 1997), 156.
34. Hymowitz and Weissman, *A History of Women in America,* 306.
35. Ibid., 312.
36. Ibid., 314.
37. Francine Blau, "The Working Woman," in *Women, A Feminist Perspective,* ed. Jo Freeman (Palo Alto, Cal.: Mayfield, 1984), 302.
38. Friedan, *The Feminine Mystique,* 50.
39. Blau, "The Working Woman," 302.
40. Hymowitz and Weissman, *A History of Women in America,* 341–42.
41. Ogden, *The Great American Housewife,* 190.
42. Blau, "The Working Woman," 302.
43. Joseph Turow, *Breaking Up America* (Chicago: University of Chicago Press, 1997), 68.
44. Gloria Steinem, *Moving beyond Words,* 149–50.

Chapter 8

1. Wade Nichols, ed., "Women's Rights: How GH Readers Feel about Liberation and Equality," *Good Housekeeping,* March 1971, 34.
2. Ralph Graves, ed., "Change, Yes—Upheaval, No," *Life,* January 8, 1971, 27.
3. Anne Marie Kerwin, "Lessons I Learned from My Kids," *Good Housekeeping,* June 1997, 88.
4. Lenore Weitzman, "Sex-role Socialization: A Focus on Women," *Women, A Feminist Perspective,* ed. Jo Freeman (Palo Alto, Cal.: Mayfield, 1984), 161.
5. Charles Parkhurst, "Compulsion in Child Training," *Ladies' Home Journal,* September 1895, 13.
6. George Batten Advertising Agency ad: *Printers' Ink,* March 29, 1923, 51–52.
7. Lynd and Lynd, *Middletown, A Study in Contemporary American Culture,* 171.
8. Ibid., 133.

9. Sullivan, *Our Times,* 426.
10. Edna Kenton, "Whatever Is New for Women Is Wrong," *Ladies' Home Journal,* October 1916, 12.
11. Lynd and Lynd, *Middletown, A Study in Contemporary American Culture,* 176.
12. Frederick, *Selling Mrs. Consumer,* 275.
13. Green, *The Light of the Home,* 49.
14. Ida Bailey Allen, "Helpfulness—the Big Idea in Advertising to Women," *Printers' Ink,* June 14, 1923, 140.
15. Weitzman, "Sex-Role Socialization," 173.
16. Ibid., 172.
17. Mary Pipher, *Reviving Ophelia* (New York: Grosset-Putnam Books, 1994), 68.
18. Elizabeth Robinson Scovil, "Playthings for Children," *Ladies' Home Journal,* January 1895, 24.
19. Weitzman, "Sex-Role Socialization," 173.
20. Germaine Greer, *The Female Eunuch* (New York: McGraw-Hill Books, 1971), 71.
21. M. G. Lord, *Forever Barbie* (New York: William Morris, 1994), 7–8.
22. Sherrye Henry, *The Deep Divide* (New York: Macmillan, 1994), 44–45.
23. Lehrman, *The Lipstick Proviso,* 67.
24. Lord, *Forever Barbie,* 9.
25. Gene del Vecchio, "Keeping It Timeless, Trendy," *Advertising Age,* March 23, 1998, 24.
26. Louis Antoine Godey, ed., "Description of the Fashion Plate, Children's Costumes," *Godey's Lady's Book,* May 1849, 370.
27. Ferris girl's corset ad: *Ladies' Home Journal,* October 1900, 37.
28. Weitzman, "Sex-Role Socialization," 169.
29. Pipher, *Reviving Ophelia,* 40.
30. Weitzman, "Sex-Role Socialization," 163.
31. Packer's Tar Soap ad: *Ladies' Home Journal,* June 1922, 182; Palmolive Soap ad: *Ladies' Home Journal,* May 1925, 54.
32. Frederick, *Selling Mrs. Consumer,* 195.
33. Wolfe, *The Beauty Myth,* 12.
34. Lehrman, *The Lipstick Proviso,* 66.
35. Debra Goldman, "Girl Crazy," *Adweek,* November 17, 1997, 50.
36. Pipher, *Reviving Ophelia,* 175.
37. Greer, *The Female Eunuch,* 78.
38. Lynd and Lynd, *Middletown, A Study in Contemporary American Culture,* 137.
39. Lisa Lockwood, "Calvin Klein Withdraws Controversial Ad Campaign," *Women's Wear Daily,* August 29, 1995, 2; "Justice Dept.: Those Calvin Ads Violated No Child Porn Laws," *Women's Wear Daily,* November 16, 1995, 18.
40. Jessie Bernard, *Women, Wives, Mothers: Values and Options* (Chicago: Aldine, 1975), 47.

Chapter 9

1. Ronald Berman, *Advertising and Social Change* (Beverly Hills, Cal: Sage, 1981), 56.
2. Greer, *The Female Eunuch,* 82, 86–87.
3. Judith Martin, *Miss Manners' Guide to Excruciatingly Correct Behavior* (New York: Warner Books, 1982), 25.
4. Marjabelle Young Stewart, *The New Etiquette* (New York: St. Martin's Griffin, 1997), 73.
5. Panati, *Panati's Extraordinary Origins of Everyday Things,* 417.
6. Strasser, *Satisfaction Guaranteed,* 142.
7. G. A. Nichols, "How Wrigley Is Teaching the English to Chew Gum," *Printers' Ink,* December 8, 1921, 49.

8. Wrigley ads: *Ladies' Home Journal*, September 1931, 116; May 1934, 121; *Good Housekeeping*, June 1934, 227.

9. R. O. Eastman, *Zanesville and 36 Other American Communities* (New York: Literary Digest, 1927), 135.

10. Lynd and Lynd, *Middletown, A Study in Contemporary American Culture*, 173.

11. Ibid.

12. Arthur Clark Piepkorn, *Profiles in Belief*, vols. 2, 3, 4 (New York: Harper and Row, 1979), 13, 22–26, 30–34, 39–49, 109, 149, 619–20.

13. Eric Clark, *The Want Makers* (New York: Viking Press, 1989), 113.

14. Goodrum and Dalrymple, *Advertising in America, The First 200 Years*, 79.

15. James Brady, "Fueling, Feeling the Heat," *Advertising Age*, September 4, 1995, 34.

16. Dorothy Brown, *Setting a Course, American Women in the 1920s* (Boston: Twayne, 1987), 183.

17. Edna Kenton, "Whatever Is New for Women Is Wrong," *Ladies' Home Journal*, October 1916, 96.

18. Lynd and Lynd, *Middletown, A Study in Contemporary American Culture*, 281.

19. Julian Lewis Watkins, *The 100 Greatest Advertisements* (New York: Dover, 1959), 77; Woodrow Wirsig, ed., "The Great Ads of All Time," *Printers' Ink*, June 14, 1963, 15.

20. Margolin, Brichta, and Brichta, *The Promise and the Product*, 72.

21. Gerard Petrone, *The Great Seduction* (Atglen, Penn.: Schiffer, 1996), 212.

22. Ibid., 192.

23. Ibid., 214–16.

24. Ibid., 223.

25. Julian and Juliann Silvulka, *Soap, Sex, and Cigarettes* (Belmont, Cal: Wadsworth, 1998), 166; Petrone, *The Great Seduction*, 260; Goodrum and Dalrymple, *Advertising in America, The First 200 Years*, 197.

26. Watkins, *The 100 Greatest Advertisements*, 79.

27. Leslie Savan, *The Sponsored Life* (Philadelphia: Temple University Press 1994), 7.

28. Silvulka, *Soap, Sex, and Cigarettes*, 167.

29. Lucky Strike ad: *Ladies' Home Journal*, October 1948, 227; Benson & Hedges ad: *Family Circle*, May 1974, 155; Camels ad: *Details*, April 1997, 72.

30. Petrone, *The Great Seduction*, 262; Silvulka, *Soap, Sex, and Cigarettes*, 169.

31. Debra Goldman, "Smoke Screen," *Adweek*, April 28, 1997, 58.

32. Mark Dolliver, "What's New," *Adweek*, April 14, 1997, 38.

33. Andrist, *The American Heritage History of the 1920s and 1930s*, 28.

34. Ibid., 84.

35. Lynd and Lynd, *Middletown in Transition*, 278–80.

36. Roberta Gerry, "How to Persuade a Lady," *Printers' Ink*, August 31, 1956, 23.

37. Goldman, "Smoke Screen," 58.

38. Brown, *Setting a Course, American Women in the 1920s*, 37.

39. Ryan, *Womanhood in America*, 234.

40. Edward Underwood, "Eighteen—the Most Dangerous Age for Girls," *Physical Culture*, December 1928, 119.

41. Ibid., 44.

42. Lynd and Lynd, *Middletown, A Study in Contemporary American Culture*, 137–38.

43. Lynd and Lynd, *Middletown in Transition*, 169–70.

44. Jessie Bernard, *Women, Wives, Mothers: Values and Options* (Chicago: Aldine, 1975), 82.

45. Robert Levin, "The Redbook Report on Premarital and Extramarital Sex," *Redbook*, October 1975, 38.

46. Bernard, *Women, Wives, Mothers*, 86.

47. Ralph Graves, ed., "Facing the 'Facts of Life,'" *Life*, September 19, 1969, 35–38.

48. Lord, *Forever Barbie*, 13.

49. Rance Crain, "Ads We Can Do Without," *Advertising Age*, February 9, 1998, 46.

50. Thomas Whipple, "The Existence and Effectiveness of Sexual Content in Advertising," *Advertising and Popular Culture, Studies in Variety and Versatility*, ed. Sammy Dana (Bowling Green, Ohio: Bowling

Green State University Popular Press, 1992), 138.

51. Clark, *The Want Makers,* 114–15.
52. James Twitchell, *Adcult USA* (New York: Columbia University Press, 1996), 157.
53. Janet Ozzard, "Shock Values: Do They Sell?" *Women's Wear Daily,* August 25, 1995, 12.

Chapter 10

1. Wolf, *The Beauty Myth*, 13.
2. Friday, *The Power of Beauty,* 370–71.
3. Frederick, *Selling Mrs. Consumer,* 350.
4. Michael Shau, *J. C. Leyendecker* (New York: Watson-Guptill Publications, 1974), 30.
5. Edward Bok, "The Newspaper at Breakfast," *Ladies' Home Journal,* January 1895, 2.
6. Lillian Bell, "From a Girl's Standpoint," *Ladies' Home Journal,* October 1896, 13.
7. Carroll Swan, ed., "Star Performers Will Do More Selling on TV No Matter What Critics Say," *Printer's Ink,* December 10, 1957, 39.
8. Marchand, *Advertising the American Dream,* 14.
9. Friday, *The Power of Beauty,* 55.
10. Ibid., 60.
11. Myriam Miedzian, *Boys Will Be Boys* (New York: Doubleday, 1991), 88–89.
12. Harvey Kaye, *Male Survival, Masculinity without Myth* (New York: Grosset and Dunlop, 1974), 36.
13. Weitzman, "Sex-Role Socialization," 161; Miedzian, *Boys Will Be Boys,* 83.
14. Miedzian, *Boys Will Be Boys,* 92-93.
15. Ibid., 91.
16. Kaye, *Male Survival, Masculinity without Myth,* 45–47.
17. Rita Hubbard, "Male Parent Images in Advertising," in *Advertising and Popular Culture, Studies in Variety and Versatility,* ed. Sammy Dana (Bowling Green, Ohio: Bowling Green State University Popular Press, 1992), 144–45.
18. Linda Gordon, "Family Violence, Feminism, and Social Control," in *Gender and American History since 1890,* ed. Barbara Melosh (London, Routledge, 1993), 289.
19. LeRoy Ashley, *Endangered Children* (New York: Twayne, 1997), 154.
20. Warren Farrell, *The Myth of Male Power* (New York: Simon & Schuster, 1993), 123.
21. George Mosse, *The Image of Man* (New York: Oxford University Press, 1996), 106–9.
22. Ibid., 115.
23. Farrell, *The Myth of Male Power,* 147.
24. Nelson Metcalf, "The Story behind 'The Kid in Upper 4,'" *The 100 Greatest Advertisements,* ed. Julian Watkins (New York: Dover, 1959) 149.
25. Miedzian, *Boys Will Be Boys,* 20–21.
26. Margo Jefferson, "American Manhood: Made in Hollywood," *Vogue,* January 1986, 267.
27. Frederick Allen Lewis, *Only Yesterday* (New York: Harper and Brothers, 1931), 212.
28. Mosse, *The Image of Man,* 146.
29. Jefferson, "American Manhood," 220.
30. Sammy Dana, ed., "Changing Male Image in Advertising: An Investigation," in *Advertising and Popular Culture, Studies in Variety and Versatility,* (Bowling Green, Ohio: Bowling Green State University Popular Press, 1992), 147.
31. Interview with Nicholas Graham, president of Joe Boxer Inc., featured in "Unmentionables," Weller/Grossman Productions, *A&E TV,* January 17, 1999.
32. Daniel Harris, "The Current Crisis in Men's Lingerie: Notes on the Belated Commercialization of a Non-Commercial Product," *Salmagundi,* Fall 1993, 131.
33. Ibid., 131–32.

34. Daniel Harris, *The Rise and Fall of Gay Culture* (New York: Hyperion, 1997), 161.
35. Jockey ad: *Redbook,* November 1977, 214.
36. Karyn Monget, "Warnaco's Wachner Stands by Calvin—But Not by That Ad," *Women's Wear Daily,* November 3, 1995, 14.
37. Judy Cole, ed., "The Naked Truth in Advertising," *Playgirl,* May 1997, 32.
38. Osborn Elliot, ed., "The Beefcake Mags," *Newsweek,* May 28, 1973, 113.
39. Dana, "Changing Male Image in Advertising," 158.
40. Clark, *The Want Makers,* 115.
41. Jennifer Foote, "The Ad World's New Bimbos," *Newsweek,* January 25, 1988, 44.
42. Lauder, *Estee, A Success Story,* 124–27.
43. Clark, *The Want Makers,* 115.
44. Erving Goffman, *Gender Advertisements* (Cambridge, Mass.: Harvard University Press, 1979), 36.
45. Mosse, *The Image of Man,* 186–87.
46. Frederick, *Selling Mrs. Consumer,* 350.
47. Barbara Lippert, "Advertising's New Hunks: A Post Feminist 'Tat for a Tit,'" *Adweek's Marketing Week,* October 26, 1987, 60.

Chapter 11

1. Margolin, Brichta, and Brichta, *The Promise and the Product,* 32.
2. Strasser, *Satisfaction Guaranteed,* 49–50.
3. Goodrum and Dalrymple, *Advertising in America, The First 200 Years,* 62.
4. Ibid., 40.
5. Betty Crocker ad: *McCall's,* July 1945, 63.
6. Sivulka and Sivulka, *Soap, Sex, and Cigarettes,* 373.
7. Lydia E. Pinkham's Vegetable Compound ad: *Godey's Lady's Book,* April 1888, x.
8. Johnson, *Over the Counter and on the Shelf,* 61.
9. Strasser, *Satisfaction Guaranteed,* 183.
10. William O'Barr, *Culture and the Ad* (Boulder, Colo.: Westview Press, 1994), 53.
11. Watkins, *The 100 Greatest Advertisements,* 5.
12. Correspondence from Campbell Soup Company, May 8, 1998; Sloane Lucas, "Campbell Serves Up Kids' Advertising Duties to BBDO," *Adweek,* May 25, 1998, 2.
13. William Meyers, *The Image Makers* (New York: Times Books, 1984), 140.
14. Molly Wade McGrath, *Top Sellers, U.S.A.* (New York: William Morrow, 1983), 111.
15. Rowsome, *They Laughed When I Sat Down,* 104. (Robert Beckerer, president of the White Rock Collectors Association, suggests the weight loss was twenty-two pounds.)
16. Savan, *The Sponsored Life,* 8.
17. Genevieve Smith, "Are the Gals Taking Over Radio-TV Commercials?" *Printers' Ink,* July 2, 1954, 19.
18. Ibid., 20.
19. Ohmann, *Selling Culture,* 240.
20. Stanley Resor, "Stanley Resor on Testimonial Advertising," *Printers' Ink,* April 11, 1929, 148.
21. Marchand, *Advertising the American Dream,* 196.
22. Ibid., 194.
23. Lynd and Lynd, *Middletown, A Study in Contemporary American Culture,* 242.
24. Stephen Fox, *The Mirror Makers* (Urbana, Ill.: University of Illinois Press, 1997), 89.
25. Allen, *Only Yesterday,* 172.
26. Twitchell, *Adcult USA,* 132.
27. Ohmann, *Selling Culture,* 191.
28. Cliff Jahr, "Anita Bryant's Startling Reversal," *Ladies' Home Journal,* December 1980, 60–63.

Acknowledgments

The author thanks the following companies for permission to use their ads in this publication. Every effort was made to contact all copyright holders. In the event of an omission, please notify the author through The Ohio State University Press.

Aetna, Inc.; Alberto-Culver, Inc.; Allied Domecq Spirits & Wines; Bayer Corporation; Blue Cross Blue Shield Corporation; Body Bodywear; Borden, Inc.; Bristol-Myers Squibb Company; Brunswick Corporation; California Department of Health Services; Case Corporation; CBS Television Network; Celanese AG; Chattem, Inc.; Coca-Cola Company; Commemorative Brands, Inc.; Cosmair, Inc.; Culligan Inernational Company; DaimlerChrysler Corporation; Donna Karan International; Eastman Kodak Company; Eiseman Company; Exxon Mobil Corporation; Farm Journal; Faultless Starch/Bon Ami Company; Federated Department Stores; Forstmann Company; Fortune Brands, Inc.; General Mills, Inc.; Gianni Versace S.P.A.; Gillette Company; Greater Atlantic & Pacific Tea Company; H. J. Heinz Company; Halston Newco LLC; Hoffman Fabrics; Interstate Brands Company; Jockey International, Inc.; Johnson & Johnson; Jordache, Inc.; Kayser-Roth Corporation; Kimberly-Clark Corporation; Kiplinger's Personal Finance; Koret of Califonia; Lane Furniture; Leslie Fay Company; Liz Claiborne, Inc.; Magazine Publishers of America; Maidenform; Maytag Corporation; Mirro Company; National Broadcasting Company, Inc.; Nestlé USA; Newell Rubbermaid; North Beach Leather; Ocean Spray Cranberries, Inc.; Pabst Brewing Company; Piggly Wiggly Stores; Pillsbury Company; PNC Advisors; Primedia Magazines; Procter & Gamble; Reckitt Benckiser, Inc.; Remington Products Company; Renaissance Cosmetics; Revlon; Reynolds Metals Company; Samsung; Sanofi-Synthelabo, Inc.; See Rock City, Inc.; Seventeen Magazine; Simplicity Pattern Company, Inc.; Smith Corona Corporation; Sony Electronics, Inc.; Spiegel; Stage Stores, Inc.; State Farm Insurance; State of Florida Department of Citrus; Steven Sandler Design; Texaco; United Distillers & Vintners; Warnaco, Inc.; Warner-Lambert Company; Westpoint Stevens, Inc.; White Rock Products Corporation; Whitman's Candies, Inc.; Wilkes Group; Williamson-Dickie Manufacturing

INDEX